AF770011

Introduction to Health Psychology

Introduction to Health Psychology

Edited by
Tim Byrne

Larsen & Keller
www.larsen-keller.com

Introduction to Health Psychology
Edited by Tim Byrne
ISBN: 978-1-63549-717-5 (Hardback)

© 2018 Larsen & Keller

Larsen & Keller
Published by Larsen and Keller Education,
5 Penn Plaza,
19th Floor,
New York, NY 10001, USA

Cataloging-in-Publication Data

Introduction to health psychology / edited by Tim Byrne.
p. cm.
Includes bibliographical references and index.
ISBN 978-1-63549-717-5
1. Clinical health psychology. 2. Medicine and psychology.
I. Byrne, Tim.
R726.7 .I58 2018
616.89--dc23

This book contains information obtained from authentic and highly regarded sources. All chapters are published with permission under the Creative Commons Attribution Share Alike License or equivalent. A wide variety of references are listed. Permissions and sources are indicated; for detailed attributions, please refer to the permissions page. Reasonable efforts have been made to publish reliable data and information, but the authors, editors and publisher cannot assume any responsibility for the vailidity of all materials or the consequences of their use.

Trademark Notice: All trademarks used herein are the property of their respective owners. The use of any trademark in this text does not vest in the author or publisher any trademark ownership rights in such trademarks, nor does the use of such trademarks imply any affiliation with or endorsement of this book by such owners.

The publisher's policy is to use permanent paper from mills that operate a sustainable forestry policy. Furthermore, the publisher ensures that the text paper and cover boards used have met acceptable environmental accreditation standards.

Printed and bound in China.

For more information regarding Larsen and Keller Education and its products, please visit the publisher's website www.larsen-keller.com

Table of Contents

Preface

The subject of health psychology deals with the study of human behavior and psychological processes concerned with healthcare. The main focus of this field is developing an understanding of health and prevention of diseases. Health psychology is primarily divided into four branches – community health psychology, clinical health psychology, critical health psychology and public health psychology. This textbook, with its detailed analyses and data, will prove immensely beneficial to professionals and students involved in this area at various levels. Through it, we attempt to further enlighten the readers about the new concepts in this field.

Given below is the chapter wise description of the book:

Chapter 1- Many consider the absence of physical disease to be the primary condition of good health. However, health is considered to be a state of mental, social and physical well-being. The matter is studied under health psychology, which analyses psychological, cultural, and behavioral factors that affect the well-being of an entity. This chapter will provide an integrated understanding of health psychology.

Chapter 2- Various factors such as habitat, food habits, physical activity, alcohol dependence, etc. can impact health both positively and negatively. An individual's socio-economic status and income can point to their quality of life, which plays an important part in health as well as access to health care. The section strategically encompasses and incorporates the major factors that affect health, providing a complete understanding of the subject matter.

Chapter 3- Through health communication, many health-related events can be propagated among the public. It is a method to improve health literacy and health choice. The central motive of this practice is the idea that prevention is a better measure in fighting diseases than curing diseases. Health communication has been shown to be more effective than support or control groups. The section also delves into the concepts of fear appeal, health education, health literacy etc. This chapter has been carefully written to provide an easy understanding of the varied facets of health communication.

Chapter 4- Health issues related to employment and the working place falls under occupational health. As a person spends a significant amount of her/his time at his work place, it can have a great impact on their health. Even many researchers believe job satisfaction to be a factor in a person's well-being. It can have three aspects, social, physical and psychological. This chapter discusses in detail the theories and concepts related to occupational health.

Chapter 5- A health care system is an organization that provides people with health care facilities. Although health care systems' structure varies from nation to nation, every country usually shares common elements such as public health measures and primary health care. All the diverse aspects of health statistics and health care systems have been carefully analyzed in this section.

At the end, I would like to thank all those who dedicated their time and efforts for the successful completion of this book. I also wish to convey my gratitude towards my friends and family who supported me at every step.

Editor

1

Understanding Health Psychology

Many consider the absence of physical disease to be the primary condition of good health. However, health is considered to be a state of mental, social and physical well-being. The matter is studied under health psychology, which analyses psychological, cultural, and behavioral factors that affect the well-being of an entity. This chapter will provide an integrated understanding of health psychology.

Health

Health is a term that has been hard to define. Is it the absence of illness- an infection or a chronic condition?

If a person is confined to living in a certain space without any mental stimulation or hope would such a person be considered healthy?

People living in a war zone under daily threat would they be considered healthy?

People persecuted for their religious beliefs and insulted on a daily basis – are they healthy?

The poor who have to face many humiliations, as well deal with frustration (unable to meet their basic necessities as well as goals) would they be considered healthy?

Thus people compromised in ways other than the physical may also be in acute distress. The word health derives from anglo saxon words meaning 'whole' 'hale' 'holy'. In traditional systems of medicine health is conceptualized as a state of balance or harmony with nature (Marks, Murray, Evans, Willig, Woodall & Sykes, 2005). Both Ayurveda and the traditional Greek system emphasize balance of physiological elements as well as behavior.

Health is the level of functional and metabolic efficiency of a living organism. In humans it is the ability of individuals or communities to adapt and self-manage when facing physical, mental or social changes. The World Health Organization (WHO) defined health in its broader sense in its 1948 constitution as "a state of complete physical, mental, and social well-being and not merely the absence of disease or infirmity." This definition has been subject to controversy, in particular as lacking operational value, the ambiguity in developing cohesive health strategies, and because of the problem created by use of the word "complete". Other definitions have been proposed, among which a recent definition that correlates health and personal satisfaction. Classification systems such as the WHO Family of International Classifications, including the International Classification of Functioning, Disability and Health (ICF) and the International Classification of Diseases (ICD), are commonly used to define and measure the components of health.

History

The definition of health has evolved over time. In keeping with the biomedical perspective, early definitions of health focused on the theme of the body's ability to function; health was seen as a state of normal function that could be disrupted from time to time by disease. An example of such a definition of health is: "a state characterized by anatomic, physiologic, and psychological integrity; ability to perform personally valued family, work, and community roles; ability to deal with physical, biologic, psychological, and social stress". Then, in 1948, in a radical departure from previous definitions, the World Health Organization (WHO) proposed a definition that aimed higher, linking health to well-being, in terms of "physical, mental, and social well-being, and not merely the absence of disease and infirmity". Although this definition was welcomed by some as being innovative, it was also criticized as being vague, excessively broad, and was not construed as measurable. For a long time it was set aside as an impractical ideal and most discussions of health returned to the practicality of the biomedical model.

Just as there was a shift from viewing disease as a state to thinking of it as a process, the same shift happened in definitions of health. Again, the WHO played a leading role when it fostered the development of the health promotion movement in the 1980s. This brought in a new conception of health, not as a state, but in dynamic terms of resiliency, in other words, as "a resource for living". The 1984 WHO revised definition of health defined it as "the extent to which an individual or group is able to realize aspirations and satisfy needs, and to change or cope with the environment. Health is a resource for everyday life, not the objective of living; it is a positive concept, emphasizing social and personal resources, as well as physical capacities". Thus, health referred to the ability to maintain homeostasis and recover from insults. Mental, intellectual, emotional, and social health referred to a person's ability to handle stress, to acquire skills, to maintain relationships, all of which form resources for resiliency and independent living.

Since the late 1970s, the federal Healthy People Initiative has been a visible component of the United States' approach to improving population health. In each decade, a new version of Healthy People is issued, featuring updated goals and identifying topic areas and quantifiable objectives for health improvement during the succeeding ten years, with assessment at that point of progress or lack thereof. Progress has been limited for many objectives, leading to concerns about the effectiveness of Healthy People in shaping outcomes in the context of a decentralized and uncoordinated US health system. Healthy People 2020 gives more prominence to health promotion and preventive approaches, and adds a substantive focus on the importance of addressing societal determinants of health. A new expanded digital interface facilitates use and dissemination rather than bulky printed books as produced in the past. The impact of these changes to Healthy People will be determined in the coming years.

Systematic activities to prevent or cure health problems and promote good health in humans are undertaken by health care providers. Applications with regard to animal health are covered by the veterinary sciences. The term "healthy" is also widely used in the context of many types of non-living organizations and their impacts for the benefit of humans, such as in the sense of healthy communities, healthy cities or healthy environments. In addition to health care interventions and a person's surroundings, a number of other factors are known to influence the health status of individuals, including their background, lifestyle, and economic, social conditions, and spirituality; these are referred to as "determinants of health." Studies have shown that high levels of stress can affect human health.

Determinants

Generally, the context in which an individual lives is of great importance for both his health status and quality of their life. It is increasingly recognized that health is maintained and improved not only through the advancement and application of health science, but also through the efforts and intelligent lifestyle choices of the individual and society. According to the World Health Organization, the main determinants of health include the social and economic environment, the physical environment, and the person's individual characteristics and behaviors.

More specifically, key factors that have been found to influence whether people are healthy or unhealthy include the following:

• Income and social status	• Personal health practices and coping skills
• Social support networks	• Healthy child development
• Education and literacy	• Biology and genetics
• Employment/working conditions	• Health care services
• Social environments	• Gender
• Physical environments	• Culture

Donald Henderson as part of the CDC's smallpox eradication team in 1966.

An increasing number of studies and reports from different organizations and contexts examine the linkages between health and different factors, including lifestyles, environments, health care organization, and health policy – such as the 1974 Lalonde report from Canada; the Alameda County Study in California; and the series of World Health Reports of the World Health Organization, which focuses on global health issues including access to health care and improving public health outcomes, especially in developing countries.

The concept of the "*health field,*" as distinct from medical care, emerged from the Lalonde report from Canada. The report identified three interdependent fields as key determinants of an individual's health. These are:

- Lifestyle: the aggregation of personal decisions (i.e., over which the individual has control) that can be said to contribute to, or cause, illness or death;
- Environmental: all matters related to health external to the human body and over which the individual has little or no control;
- Biomedical: all aspects of health, physical and mental, developed within the human body as influenced by genetic make-up.

The maintenance and promotion of health is achieved through different combination of physical, mental, and social well-being, together sometimes referred to as the *"health triangle."* The WHO's 1986 *Ottawa Charter for Health Promotion* further stated that health is not just a state, but also "a resource for everyday life, not the objective of living. Health is a positive concept emphasizing social and personal resources, as well as physical capacities."

Focusing more on lifestyle issues and their relationships with functional health, data from the Alameda County Study suggested that people can improve their health via exercise, enough sleep, maintaining a healthy body weight, limiting alcohol use, and avoiding smoking. Health and illness can co-exist, as even people with multiple chronic diseases or terminal illnesses can consider themselves healthy.

The environment is often cited as an important factor influencing the health status of individuals. This includes characteristics of the natural environment, the built environment, and the social environment. Factors such as clean water and air, adequate housing, and safe communities and roads all have been found to contribute to good health, especially to the health of infants and children. Some studies have shown that a lack of neighborhood recreational spaces including natural environment leads to lower levels of personal satisfaction and higher levels of obesity, linked to lower overall health and well being. This suggests that the positive health benefits of natural space in urban neighborhoods should be taken into account in public policy and land use.

Genetics, or inherited traits from parents, also play a role in determining the health status of individuals and populations. This can encompass both the predisposition to certain diseases and health conditions, as well as the habits and behaviors individuals develop through the lifestyle of their families. For example, genetics may play a role in the manner in which people cope with stress, either mental, emotional or physical. For example, obesity is a very large problem in the United States that contributes to bad mental health and causes stress in a lot of people's lives. (One difficulty is the issue raised by the debate over the relative strengths of genetics and other factors; interactions between genetics and environment may be of particular importance.)

Potential Issues

There are a lot of types of health issues common with many people across the globe. Disease is one of the most common. According to GlobalIssues.org, approximately 36 million people die each year from non-communicable (not contagious) disease including cardiovascular disease cancer, diabetes, and chronic lung disease (Shah, 2014).

As for communicable diseases, both viral and bacterial, AIDS/HIV, tuberculosis, and malaria are the most common also causing millions of deaths every year (2014).

Another health issue that causes death or contributes to other health problems is malnutrition majorly among children. One of the groups malnutrition affects most is young children. Approximately 7.5 million children under the age of 5 die from malnutrition, and it is usually brought on by not having the money to find or make food (2014).

Bodily injuries are also a common health issue worldwide. These injuries, including broken bones, fractures, and burns can reduce a person's quality of life or can cause fatalities including infections that resulted from the injury or the severity injury in general (Moffett, 2013).

Some contributing factors to poor health are lifestyle choices. These include smoking cigarettes, and also can include a poor diet, whether it is overeating or an overly constrictive diet. Inactivity can also contribute to health issues and also a lack of sleep, excessive alcohol consumption, and neglect of oral hygiene (2013). There are also genetic disorders that are inherited by the person and can vary in how much they affect the person and when they surface (2013).

The one health issue that is the most unfortunate because the majority of these health issues are preventable is that approximately 1 billion people lack access to health care systems (Shah, 2014). It is easy to say that the most common and harmful health issue is that a lot of people do not have access to quality remedies.

Mental

The World Health Organization describes mental health as "a state of well-being in which the individual realizes his or her own abilities, can cope with the normal stresses of life, can work productively and fruitfully, and is able to make a contribution to his or her community". Mental Health is not just the absence of mental illness.

Mental illness is described as 'the spectrum of cognitive, emotional, and behavioral conditions that interfere with social and emotional well-being and the lives and productivity of people. Having a mental illness can seriously impair, temporarily or permanently, the mental functioning of a person. Other terms include: 'mental health problem', 'illness', 'disorder', 'dysfunction'.

Roughly a quarter of all adults 18 and over in the US suffer from a diagnosable mental illness. Mental illnesses are the leading cause of disability in the US and Canada. Examples include, schizophrenia, ADHD, major depressive disorder, bipolar disorder, anxiety disorder, post-traumatic stress disorder and autism.

Many teens suffer from mental health issues in response to the pressures of society and social problems they encounter. Some of the key mental health issues seen in teens are: depression, eating disorders, and drug abuse. There are many ways to prevent these health issues from occurring such as communicating well with a teen suffering from mental health issues. Mental health can be treated and be attentive to teens' behavior.

Maintaining

Achieving and maintaining health is an ongoing process, shaped by both the evolution of health care knowledge and practices as well as personal strategies and organized interventions for staying healthy.

Diet

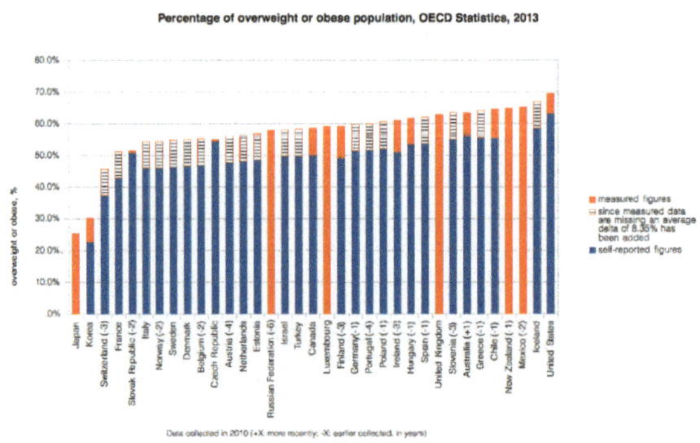

Percentage of overweight or obese population in 2010

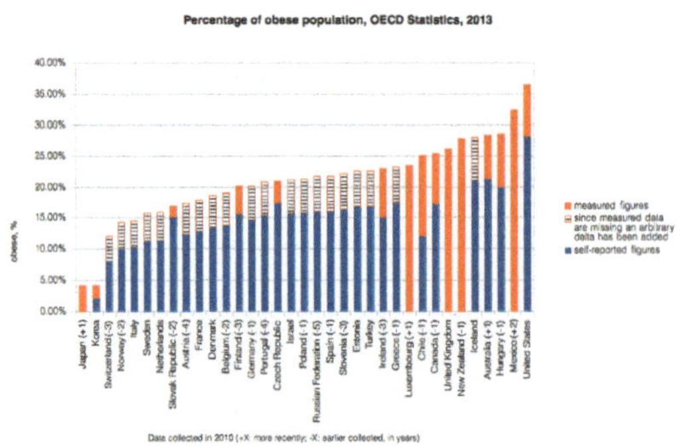

Percentage of obese population in 2010

An important way to maintain your personal health is to have a healthy diet. A healthy diet includes a variety of plant-based and animal-based foods that provide nutrients to your body. Such nutrients give you energy and keep your body running. Nutrients help build and strengthen bones, muscles, and tendons and also regulate body processes (i.e. blood pressure). The food guide pyramid is a pyramid-shaped guide of healthy foods divided into sections. Each section shows the recommended intake for each food group (i.e. Protein, Fat, Carbohydrates, and Sugars). Making healthy food choices is important because it can lower your risk of heart disease, developing some types of cancer, and it will contribute to maintaining a healthy weight.

The Mediterranean diet is commonly associated with health-promoting effects due to the fact that it contains some bioactive compounds like phenolic compounds, isoprenoids and alkaloids.

Exercise

Physical exercise enhances or maintains physical fitness and overall health and wellness. It strengthens muscles and improves the cardiovascular system.

Sleep

Sleep is an essential component to maintaining health. In children, sleep is also vital for growth and development. Ongoing sleep deprivation has been linked to an increased risk for some chronic health problems. In addition, sleep deprivation has been shown to correlate with both increased susceptibility to illness and slower recovery times from illness. In one study, people with chronic insufficient sleep, set as six hours of sleep a night or less, were found to be four times more likely to catch a cold compared to those who reported sleeping for seven hours or more a night. Due to the role of sleep in regulating metabolism, insufficient sleep may also play a role in weight gain or, conversely, in impeding weight loss. Additionally, in 2007, the International Agency for Research on Cancer, which is the cancer research agency for the World Health Organization, declared that "shiftwork that involves circadian disruption is probably carcinogenic to humans," speaking to the dangers of long-term nighttime work due to its intrusion on sleep. In 2015, the National Sleep Foundation released updated recommendations for sleep duration requirements based on age and concluded that "Individuals who habitually sleep outside the normal range may be exhibiting signs or symptoms of serious health problems or, if done volitionally, may be compromising their health and well-being."

Age and condition	Sleep Needs
Newborns (0–3 months)	14 to 17 hours
Infants (4–11 months)	12 to 15 hours
Toddlers (1–2 years)	11 to 14 hours
Preschoolers (3–5 years)	10 to 13 hours
School-age children (6–13 years)	9 to 11 hours
Teenagers (14–17 years)	8 to 10 hours
Adults (18–64 years)	7 to 9 hours
Older Adults (65 years and over)	7 to 8 hours

Role of Science

The Dutch Public Health Service provides medical care for the natives of the Dutch East Indies, May 1946

Health science is the branch of science focused on health. There are two main approaches to health science: the study and research of the body and health-related issues to understand how humans (and animals) function, and the application of that knowledge to improve health and to prevent and cure diseases and other physical and mental impairments. The science builds on many sub-fields, including biology, biochemistry, physics, epidemiology, pharmacology, medical sociology. Applied health sciences endeavor to better understand and improve human health through applications in areas such as health education, biomedical engineering, biotechnology and public health.

Organized interventions to improve health based on the principles and procedures developed through the health sciences are provided by practitioners trained in medicine, nursing, nutrition, pharmacy, social work, psychology, occupational therapy, physical therapy and other health care professions. Clinical practitioners focus mainly on the health of individuals, while public health practitioners consider the overall health of communities and populations. Workplace wellness programs are increasingly adopted by companies for their value in improving the health and well-being of their employees, as are school health services in order to improve the health and well-being of children.

Role of Public Health

Postage stamp, New Zealand, 1933. Public health has been promoted – and depicted – in a wide variety of ways.

Public health has been described as "the science and art of preventing disease, prolonging life and promoting health through the organized efforts and informed choices of society, organizations, public and private, communities and individuals." It is concerned with threats to the overall health of a community based on population health analysis. The population in question can be as small as a handful of people or as large as all the inhabitants of several continents (for instance, in the case of a pandemic). Public health has many sub-fields, but typically includes the interdisciplinary categories of epidemiology, biostatistics and health services. Environmental health, community health, behavioral health, and occupational health are also important areas of public health.

The focus of public health interventions is to prevent and manage diseases, injuries and other health conditions through surveillance of cases and the promotion of healthy behavior, communities, and (in aspects relevant to human health) environments. Its aim is to prevent health problems from happening or re-occurring by implementing educational programs, developing policies, administering services and conducting research. In many cases, treating a disease or controlling a pathogen can be vital to preventing it in others, such as during an outbreak. Vaccination programs and distribution of condoms to prevent the spread of communicable diseases are examples of common preventive public health measures, as are educational campaigns to promote vaccination and the use of condoms (including overcoming resistance to such).

Public health also takes various actions to limit the health disparities between different areas of the country and, in some cases, the continent or world. One issue is the access of individuals and communities to health care in terms of financial, geographical or socio-cultural constraints to accessing and using services. Applications of the public health system include the areas of maternal and child health, health services administration, emergency response, and prevention and control of infectious and chronic diseases.

The great positive impact of public health programs is widely acknowledged. Due in part to the policies and actions developed through public health, the 20th century registered a decrease in the mortality rates for infants and children and a continual increase in life expectancy in most parts of the world. For example, it is estimated that life expectancy has increased for Americans by thirty years since 1900, and worldwide by six years since 1990.

Self-care Strategies

A lady washing her hands c. 1655

Personal health depends partially on the active, passive, and assisted cues people observe and adopt about their own health. These include personal actions for preventing or minimizing the effects of a disease, usually a chronic condition, through integrative care. They also include personal hygiene practices to prevent infection and illness, such as bathing and washing hands with soap; brushing and flossing teeth; storing, preparing and handling food safely; and many others. The information gleaned from personal observations of daily living – such as about sleep patterns, exercise behavior, nutritional intake and environmental features – may be used to inform personal decisions and actions (*e.g.*, "I feel tired in the morning so I am going to try sleeping on a different pillow"), as well as clinical decisions and treatment plans (*e.g.*, a patient who notices his or her shoes are tighter than usual may be having exacerbation of left-sided heart failure, and may require diuretic medication to reduce fluid overload).

Personal health also depends partially on the social structure of a person's life. The maintenance of strong social relationships, volunteering, and other social activities have been linked to positive mental health and also increased longevity. One American study among seniors over age 70, found that frequent volunteering was associated with reduced risk of dying compared with older persons who did not volunteer, regardless of physical health status. Another study from Singapore reported that volunteering retirees had significantly better cognitive performance scores, fewer depressive symptoms, and better mental well-being and life satisfaction than non-volunteering retirees.

Prolonged psychological stress may negatively impact health, and has been cited as a factor in cognitive impairment with aging, depressive illness, and expression of disease. Stress management is the application of methods to either reduce stress or increase tolerance to stress. Relaxation techniques are physical methods used to relieve stress. Psychological methods include cognitive therapy, meditation, and positive thinking, which work by reducing response to stress. Improving relevant skills, such as problem solving and time management skills, reduces uncertainty and builds confidence, which also reduces the reaction to stress-causing situations where those skills are applicable.

Occupational

In addition to safety risks, many jobs also present risks of disease, illness and other long-term health problems. Among the most common occupational diseases are various forms of pneumoconiosis, including silicosis and coal worker's pneumoconiosis (black lung disease). Asthma is another respiratory illness that many workers are vulnerable to. Workers may also be vulnerable to skin diseases, including eczema, dermatitis, urticaria, sunburn, and skin cancer. Other occupational diseases of concern include carpal tunnel syndrome and lead poisoning.

As the number of service sector jobs has risen in developed countries, more and more jobs have become sedentary, presenting a different array of health problems than those associated with manufacturing and the primary sector. Contemporary problems, such as the growing rate of obesity and issues relating to stress and overwork in many countries, have further complicated the interaction between work and health.

Many governments view occupational health as a social challenge and have formed public organizations to ensure the health and safety of workers. Examples of these include the British Health and Safety Executive and in the United States, the National Institute for Occupational Safety and Health, which conducts research on occupational health and safety, and the Occupational Safety and Health Administration, which handles regulation and policy relating to worker safety and health.

Health Psychology

Health psychology is the study of psychological and behavioral processes in health, illness, and healthcare. It is concerned with understanding how psychological, behavioral, and cultural factors contribute to physical health and illness. Psychological factors can affect health directly. For example, chronically occurring environmental stressors affecting the hypothalamic–pituitary–adrenal axis, cumulatively, can harm health. Behavioral factors can also affect a person's health. For example, certain behaviors can, over time, harm (smoking, excessive alcohol consumption) or enhance health (exercise, diet low in saturated fat). Health psychologists take a biopsychosocial approach. In other words, health psychologists understand health to be the product not only of biological processes (e.g., a virus, tumor, etc.) but also of psychological (e.g., thoughts and beliefs), behavioral (e.g., habits), and social processes (e.g., socioeconomic status and ethnicity).

By understanding psychological factors that influence health, and constructively applying that knowledge, health psychologists can improve health by working directly with individual patients or indirectly in large-scale public health programs. In addition, health psychologists can help train other healthcare professionals (e.g., physicians and nurses) to take advantage of the knowledge the discipline has generated, when treating patients. Health psychologists work in a variety of settings: alongside other medical professionals in hospitals and clinics, in public health departments working on large-scale behavior change and health promotion programs, and in universities and medical schools where they teach and conduct research.

Although its early beginnings can be traced to the field of clinical psychology, four different divisions within health psychology and one related field, occupational health psychology (OHP), have developed over time. The four divisions include clinical health psychology, public health psychology, community health psychology, and critical health psychology. Professional organizations for the field of health psychology include Division 38 of the American Psychological Association (APA), the Division of Health Psychology of the British Psychological Society (BPS), and the European Health Psychology Society. Advanced credentialing in the US as a clinical health psychologist is provided through the American Board of Professional Psychology.

Overview

Recent advances in psychological, medical, and physiological research have led to a new way of thinking about health and illness. This conceptualization, which has been labeled the biopsychosocial model, views health and illness as the product of a combination of factors including biological characteristics (e.g., genetic predisposition), behavioral factors (e.g., lifestyle, stress, health beliefs), and social conditions (e.g., cultural influences, family relationships, social support).

Psychologists who strive to understand how biological, behavioral, and social factors influence health and illness are called health psychologists. Health psychologists use their knowledge of psychology and health to promote general well-being and understand physical illness. They are specially trained to help people deal with the psychological and emotional aspects of health and illness. Health psychologists work with many different health care professionals (e.g., physicians, dentists, nurses, physician's assistants, dietitians, social workers, pharmacists, physical and occupational therapists, and chaplains) to conduct research and provide clinical assessments and treatment services. Many health psychologists focus on prevention research and interventions designed to promote healthier lifestyles and try to find ways to encourage people to improve their health. For example, they may help people to lose weight or stop smoking. Health psychologists also use their skills to try to improve the healthcare system. For example, they may advise doctors about better ways to communicate with their patients. Health psychologists work in many different settings including the UK's National Health Service (NHS), private practice, universities, communities, schools and organizations. While many health psychologists provide clinical services as part of their duties, others function in non-clinical roles, primarily involving teaching and research. Leading journals include *Health Psychology*, the *Journal of Health Psychology*, the *British Journal of Health Psychology*, and *Applied Psychology: Health and Well-Being*. Health psychologists can work with people on a one-to-one basis, in groups, as a family, or at a larger population level.

Clinical health psychology (ClHP)

> ClHP is the application of scientific knowledge, derived from the field of health psychology, to clinical questions that may arise across the spectrum of health care. ClHP is one of many specialty practice areas for clinical psychologists. It is also a major contributor to the prevention-focused field of behavioral health and the treatment-oriented field of behavioral medicine. Clinical practice includes education, the techniques of behavior change, and psy-

chotherapy. In some countries, a clinical health psychologist, with additional training, can become a medical psychologist and, thereby, obtain prescription privileges.

Public health psychology (PHP)

PHP is population oriented. A major aim of PHP is to investigate potential causal links between psychosocial factors and health at the population level. Public health psychologists present research results to educators, policy makers, and health care providers in order to promote better public health. PHP is allied to other public health disciplines including epidemiology, nutrition, genetics and biostatistics. Some PHP interventions are targeted toward at-risk population groups (e.g., undereducated, single pregnant women who smoke) and not the population as a whole (e.g., all pregnant women).

Community health psychology (CoHP)

CoHP investigates community factors that contribute to the health and well-being of individuals who live in communities. CoHP also develops community-level interventions that are designed to combat disease and promote physical and mental health. The community often serves as the level of analysis, and is frequently sought as a partner in health-related interventions.

Critical health psychology (CrHP)

CrHP is concerned with the distribution of power and the impact of power differentials on health experience and behavior, health care systems, and health policy. CrHP prioritizes social justice and the universal right to health for people of all races, genders, ages, and socioeconomic positions. A major concern is health inequalities. The critical health psychologist is an agent of change, not simply an analyst or cataloger. A leading organization in this area is the International Society of Critical Health Psychology.

Health psychology, like other areas of applied psychology, is both a theoretical and applied field. Health psychologists employ diverse research methods. These methods include controlled randomized experiments, quasi-experiments, longitudinal studies, time-series designs, cross-sectional studies, case-control studies, qualitative research as well as action research. Health psychologists study a broad range of variables including cardiovascular disease, (cardiac psychology), smoking habits, the relation of religious beliefs to health, alcohol use, social support, living conditions, emotional state, social class, and more. Some health psychologists treat individuals with sleep problems, headaches, alcohol problems, etc. Other health psychologists work to empower community members by helping community members gain control over their health and improve quality of life of entire communities.

Origins and Development

Psychological factors in health had been studied since the early 20th century by disciplines such as psychosomatic medicine and later behavioral medicine, but these were primarily branches of medicine, not psychology. Health psychology began to emerge as a distinct discipline of psychology in the United States in the 1970s. In the mid-20th century there was a growing understanding in medicine of the effect of behavior on health. For example, the Alameda County

Study, which began in the 1960s, showed that people who ate regular meals (e.g., breakfast), maintained a healthy weight, received adequate sleep, did not smoke, drank little alcohol, and exercised regularly were in better health and lived longer. In addition, psychologists and other scientists were discovering relationships between psychological processes and physiological ones. These discoveries include a better understanding of the impact of psychosocial stress on the cardiovascular and immune systems, and the early finding that the functioning of the immune system could be altered by learning.

Psychologists have been working in medical settings for many years (in the UK sometimes the field was termed medical psychology). Medical psychology, however, was a relatively small field, primarily aimed at helping patients adjust to illness. In 1969, William Schofield prepared a report for the APA entitled *The Role of Psychology in the Delivery of Health Services*. While there were exceptions, he found that the psychological research of the time frequently regarded mental health and physical health as separate, and devoted very little attention to psychology's impact upon physical health. One of the few psychologists working in this area at the time, Schofield proposed new forms of education and training for future psychologists. The APA, responding to his proposal, in 1973 established a task force to consider how psychologists could (a) help people to manage their health-related behaviors, (b) help patients manage their physical health problems, and (c) train healthcare staff to work more effectively with patients.

Led by Joseph Matarazzo, in 1977, APA added a division devoted to health psychology. At the first divisional conference, Matarazzo delivered a speech that played an important role in defining health psychology. He defined the new field in this way, "Health psychology is the aggregate of the specific educational, scientific and professional contributions of the discipline of psychology to the promotion and maintenance of health, the prevention and treatment of illness, the identification of diagnostic and etiologic correlates of health, illness and related dysfunction, and the analysis and improvement of the healthcare system and health policy formation." In the 1980s, similar organizations were established elsewhere. In 1986, the BPS established a Division of Health Psychology. The European Health Psychology Society was also established in 1986. Similar organizations were established in other countries, including Australia and Japan. Universities began to develop doctoral level training programs in health psychology. In the US, post-doctoral level health psychology training programs were established for individuals who completed a doctoral degree in clinical psychology.

A number of relevant trends coincided with the emergence of health psychology, including:

- Epidemiological evidence linking behavior and health.
- The addition of behavioral science to medical school curricula, with courses often taught by psychologists.
- The training of health professionals in communication skills, with the aim of improving patient satisfaction and adherence to medical treatment.
- Increasing numbers of interventions based on psychological theory (e.g., behavior modification).
- An increased understanding of the interaction between psychological and physiological

factors leading to the emergence of psychophysiology and psychoneuroimmunology (PNI).

- The health domain having become a target of research by social psychologists interested in testing theoretical models linking beliefs, attitudes, and behavior.
- The emergence of AIDS/HIV, and the increase in funding for behavioral research the epidemic provoked.

In the UK, the BPS's reconsideration of the role of the Medical Section prompted the emergence of health psychology as a distinct field. Marie Johnston and John Weinman argued in a letter to the *BPS Bulletin* that there was a great need for a Health Psychology Section. In December 1986 the section was established at the BPS London Conference, with Marie Johnston as chair. At the Annual BPS Conference in 1993 a review of "Current Trends in Health Psychology" was organized, and a definition of health psychology as "the study of psychological and behavioural processes in health, illness and healthcare" was proposed. The Health Psychology Section became a Special Group in 1993 and was awarded divisional status within the UK in 1997. The awarding of divisional status meant that the individual training needs and professional practice of health psychologists were recognized, and members were able to obtain chartered status with the BPS. The BPS went on to regulate training and practice in health psychology until the regulation of professional standards and qualifications was taken over by statutory registration with the Health Professions Council in 2010.

Understanding Behavioral and Contextual Factors

Health psychologists conduct research to identify behaviors and experiences that promote health, give rise to illness, and influence the effectiveness of health care. They also recommend ways to improve health care policy. Health psychologists have worked on developing ways to reduce smoking and improve daily nutrition in order to promote health and prevent illness. They have also studied the association between illness and individual characteristics. For example, health psychology has found a relation between the personality characteristics of thrill seeking, impulsiveness, hostility/anger, emotional instability, and depression, on one hand, and high-risk driving, on the other.

Health psychology is also concerned with contextual factors, including economic, cultural, community, social, and lifestyle factors that influence health. The biopsychosocial model can help in understanding the relation between contextual factors and biology in affecting health. Physical addiction impedes smoking cessation. Some research suggests that seductive advertising also contributes to psychological dependency on tobacco, although other research has found no relationship between media exposure and smoking in youth. OHP research indicates that people in jobs that combine little decision latitude with a high psychological workload are at increased risk for cardiovascular disease. Other OHP research reveals a relation between unemployment and elevations in blood pressure. Epidemiologic research documents a relation between social class and cardiovascular disease.

Health psychologists also aim to change health behaviors for the dual purpose of helping people stay healthy and helping patients adhere to disease treatment regimens. Health psychologists employ cognitive behavior therapy and applied behavior analysis for that purpose.

Preventing Illness

Health psychologists promote health through behavioral change, as mentioned above; however, they attempt to prevent illness in other ways as well. Health psychologists try to help people to lead a healthy life by developing and running programmes which can help people to make changes in their lives such as stopping smoking, reducing the amount of alcohol they consume, eating more healthily, and exercising regularly. Campaigns informed by health psychology have targeted tobacco use. Those least able to afford tobacco products consume them most. Tobacco provides individuals with a way of controlling aversive emotional states accompanying daily experiences of stress that characterize the lives of deprived and vulnerable individuals. Practitioners emphasize education and effective communication as a part of illness prevention because many people do not recognize, or minimize, the risk of illness present in their lives. Moreover, many individuals are often unable to apply their knowledge of health practices owing to everyday pressures and stresses. A common example of population-based attempts to motivate the smoking public to reduce its dependence on cigarettes is anti-smoking campaigns.

Health psychologists help to promote health and well-being by preventing illness. Some illnesses can be more effectively treated if caught early. Health psychologists have worked to understand why some people do not seek early screenings or immunizations, and have used that knowledge to develop ways to encourage people to have early health checks for illnesses such as cancer and heart disease. Health psychologists are also finding ways to help people to avoid risky behaviors (e.g., engaging in unprotected sex) and encourage health-enhancing behaviors (e.g., regular tooth brushing or hand washing).

Health psychologists also aim at educating health professionals, including physicians and nurses, in communicating effectively with patients in ways that overcome barriers to understanding, remembering, and implementing effective strategies for reducing exposures to risk factors and making health-enhancing behavior changes.

There is also evidence from OHP that stress-reduction interventions at the workplace can be effective. For example, Kompier and his colleagues have shown that a number of interventions aimed at reducing stress in bus drivers has had beneficial effects for employees and bus companies.

The Effects of Disease

Health psychologists investigate how disease affects individuals' psychological well-being. An individual who becomes seriously ill or injured faces many different practical stressors. These stressors include problems meeting medical and other bills, problems obtaining proper care when home from the hospital, obstacles to caring for dependents, the experience of having one's sense of self-reliance compromised, gaining a new, unwanted identity as that of a sick person, and so on. These stressors can lead to depression, reduced self-esteem, etc.

Health psychology also concerns itself with bettering the lives of individuals with terminal illness. When there is little hope of recovery, health psychologist therapists can improve the quality of life of the patient by helping the patient recover at least some of his or her psychological well-being. Health psychologists are also concerned with providing therapeutic services for the bereaved.

Critical Analysis of Health Policy

Critical health psychologists explore how health policy can influence inequities, inequalities and social injustice. These avenues of research expand the scope of health psychology beyond the level of individual health to an examination of the social and economic determinants of health both within and between regions and nations. The individualism of mainstream health psychology has been critiqued and deconstructed by critical health psychologists using qualitative methods that zero in on the health experience.

Conducting Research

Like psychologists in the other main psychology disciplines, health psychologists have advanced knowledge of research methods. Health psychologists apply this knowledge to conduct research on a variety of questions. For example, health psychologists carry out research to answer questions such as:

- What influences healthy eating?
- How is stress linked to heart disease?
- What are the emotional effects of genetic testing?
- How can we change people's health behavior to improve their health?

Teaching and Communication

Health psychologists can also be responsible for training other health professionals on how to deliver interventions to help promote healthy eating, stopping smoking, weight loss, etc. Health psychologists also train other health professionals in communication skills such as how to break bad news or support behavior change for the purpose of improving adherence to treatment.

Applications

Improving Doctor–patient Communication

Health psychologists aid the process of communication between physicians and patients during medical consultations. There are many problems in this process, with patients showing a considerable lack of understanding of many medical terms, particularly anatomical terms (e.g., intestines). One area of research on this topic involves "doctor-centered" or "patient-centered" consultations. Doctor-centered consultations are generally directive, with the patient answering questions and playing less of a role in decision-making. Although this style is preferred by elderly people and others, many people dislike the sense of hierarchy or ignorance that it inspires. They prefer patient-centered consultations, which focus on the patient's needs, involve the doctor listening to the patient completely before making a decision, and involving the patient in the process of choosing treatment and finding a diagnosis.

Improving Adherence to Medical Advice

Health psychologists engage in research and practice aimed at getting people to follow medical advice and adhere to their treatment regimens. Patients often forget to take their pills or consciously opt not to take their prescribed medications because of side effects. Failing to take prescribed medication is costly and wastes millions of usable medicines that could otherwise help other people. Estimated adherence rates are difficult to measure; there is, however, evidence that adherence could be improved by tailoring treatment programs to individuals' daily lives. Additionally, traditional cognitive-behavioural therapies have been adapted for people suffering from chronic illnesses and comorbid psychological distress to include modules that encourage, support and reinforce adherence to medical advice as part of the larger treatment approach.

Ways of Measuring Adherence

Health psychologists have identified a number of ways of measuring patients' adherence to medical regimens:

- Counting the number of pills in the medicine bottle
- Using self-reports
- Using "Trackcap" bottles, which track the number of times the bottle is opened.

Managing pain

Health psychology attempts to find treatments to reduce or eliminate pain, as well as understand pain anomalies such as episodic analgesia, causalgia, neuralgia, and phantom limb pain. Although the task of measuring and describing pain has been problematic, the development of the McGill Pain Questionnaire has helped make progress in this area. Treatments for pain involve patient-administered analgesia, acupuncture (found to be effective in reducing pain for osteoarthritis of the knee), biofeedback, and cognitive behavior therapy.

Health Psychologist Roles

Below are some examples of the types of positions held by health psychologists within applied settings such as the UK's NHS and private practice.

- Consultant health psychologist: A consultant health psychologist will take a lead for health psychology within public health, including managing tobacco control and smoking cessation services and providing professional leadership in the management of health trainers.
- Principal health psychologist: A principal health psychologist could, for example lead the health psychology service within one of the UK's leading heart and lung hospitals, providing a clinical service to patients and advising all members of the multidisciplinary team.
- Health psychologist: An example of a health psychologist's role would be to provide health psychology input to a center for weight management. Psychological assessment of treatment, development and delivery of a tailored weight management program, and advising on approaches to improve adherence to health advice and medical treatment.
- Research psychologist: Research health psychologists carry out health psychology research, for example, exploring the psychological impact of receiving a diagnosis of dementia, or evaluating ways of providing psychological support for people with burn injuries. Research

can also be in the area of health promotion, for example investigating the determinants of healthy eating or physical activity or understanding why people misuse substances.

- Health psychologist in training/assistant health psychologist: As an assistant/in training, a health psychologist will gain experience assessing patients, delivering psychological interventions to change health behaviors, and conducting research, whilst being supervised by a qualified health psychologist.

Training

In the UK, health psychologists are registered by the Health Professions Council (HPC) and have trained to a level to be eligible for full membership of the Division of Health Psychology within the BPS. Registered health psychologists who are chartered with the BPS will have undertaken a minimum of six years of training and will have specialized in health psychology for a minimum of three years. Health psychologists in training must have completed BPS stage 1 training and be registered with the BPS Stage 2 training route or with a BPS-accredited university doctoral health psychology program. Once qualified, health psychologists can work in a range of settings, for example the NHS, universities, schools, private healthcare, and research and charitable organizations. A health psychologist in training might be working within applied settings while working towards registration and chartered status. A health psychologist will have demonstrated competencies in all of the following areas:

- Professional skills (including implementing ethical and legal standards, communication, and teamwork),
- Research skills (including designing, conducting, and analyzing psychological research in numerous areas),
- Consultancy skills (including planning and evaluation),
- Teaching and training skills (including knowledge of designing, delivering, and evaluating large and small scale training program),
- Intervention skills (including delivery and evaluation of behavior change interventions).
- All qualified health psychologists must also engage in and record their continuing professional development (CPD) for psychology each year throughout their career.

There are two dominant models in the health psychology discourse that explain illness and health

- The Biomedical Model - proposes biological problems as causes of illness and emphasizes illness and its causes over health and its causes. Mind –body dualism is implied and they are considered separate systems that don't influence each other. The allopathic system is aligned with the biomedical model.
- The Biopsychosocial Model acknowledges the role of social and psychological factors and their interaction with biological factors in influencing health or illness. This model emphasizes health as well as illness and is more aligned with the health promotion approach. The interactive relationship of the mind and body is espoused by this model (Taylor, 1995).

"Health Psychology is an interdisciplinary field concerned with the application of psychological knowledge and techniques to health, illness and healthcare."(Marks et al, 2005).

Health psychology is concerned primarily with physical rather than mental health. However the interface between mental and physical health is a part of health psychology.The orientation of contemporary psychology is very American and European and therefore may not be applicable universally when discussing health in other cultures.The dominant perspective in psychology is an individualistic perspective where the individual is perceived as an active agent and is the figure whereas society and culture are the ground. Thus the individual is exerting an influence on the environment.

The collectivist perspective which is prevalent in more traditional societies emphasizes the role of culture and society within whose parameters the individual functions.

Given the focus on individualism in contemporary psychology the onus of responsibility for illness tends to rest on the individual. This maybe exaggerated and it is necessary to look at illness and health with a wider lens, thus considering the contextual factors.

Health Psychology uses the contributions of the discipline of psychology for the promotion and maintenance of health, and prevention and treatment of illness.

When considering the origin of the field some of the early works published in the area is a book by William James in 1922 'On Vital Reserves: The Energies of Men; The Gospel of Relaxation'. In this book he discusses how people were sent abroad to rest their nerves because of overwork but in fact because of the feeling of hurry and breathlessness and tension. G Stanley Hall had a chapter "Diseases of the Body and Mind" in his book Adolescence where he mentions the lack of preventive medicine(Hall 1904). As early as 1911 the American Psychological Association (APA) instituted a committee to see how psychology could be taught to medical students (Rodin & Stone, 1987).

Psychologists and psychiatrists have traditionally focused on psychopathology and behavioral disturbances whereas health psychology focuses on physical health. There was some work from the fifties onward on preparing patients for surgical procedures, the effect of personality or mental states on physical health, the effects of pain, health attitudes and decision making and reproductive health behavior until the seventies. The Health Belief Model was developed in this period by Hochbaum and Rosenstock (1958, 1966) which was a major theoretical influence in health psychology (Rodin & Stone, 1987). A separate Division of Health Psychology (Division 38) in the APA was formed in 1978 (Rodin & Stone, 1987).

The Scope of Health Psychology(Marks et al, 2008)

Although health psychology developed relatively recently as a formal sub discipline, there are four sub areas into which it could be categorized on the basis of scale or unit of analyses. Clinical Health Psychology is focused on the individual whereas public and community health psychology focus on larger groups and critical health psychology focuses on macro structural factors.

Clinical Health Psychology

Seeks to understand health outcomes and the quality of life from a psychological perspective. An example of the work in this area would be understanding the impact of stress on blood pressure or developing an intervention for smoking cessation and running randomized controlled trials. It is the most well established of the four approaches and the most rigorous in terms of methodology.

Public Health Psychology

Is concerned with the general population especially vulnerable groups and health policy and how it gets translated and its impact on health outcomes – evaluates its impact. It is multidisciplinary and draws from epidemiology as well as psychology. The typical methods are large scale surveys.

Community Health Psychology

The focus is on social change and the research methods are participative research and action research. The link between the community and individuals is emphasized and the aim is to improve or develop the community.

Critical Health Psychology

Is concerned with larger influences such as power, economics and social institutions on health and health care. It aims to analyze the assumptions and discourse in the field of health of researchers and health professionals and policy makers.

Terms used in Public Health

To introduce some terms used in the field of health psychology – we discuss the terms mortality, morbidity and epidemiology.

Mortality refers to the number of deaths due to particular causes or general causes in a particular population in a time period

Mortality – an example would be maternal mortality rate (MMR) – number of mothers who die in child birth (the convention is to take the number of maternal deaths per 100,000 women of reproductive age in that time period)

MMR in India is 212 for 2007-2009 (Sample Registration System, 2011)

Infant mortality rate – number of deaths before the age of 1 per 1000 live births.

Infant Mortality Rate for India is 50.3 for 2009 (SRS, 2011).

Morbidity refers to the number of cases of disease at a given point in time in a particular population

Morbidity – the morbidity rate refers to the prevalence of a certain disease – for example prevalence of diarrhea among children below 6 in India is 15.4% (Census of India, 2001).

Epidemiology

The study of the frequency, distribution and causes of disease in a particular population

An example of an epidemiological study would be 'Incidence of Thalasemia in the Sindhi community or the incidence of HIV among Intravenous Drug Users – these would be examples of descriptive studies

When trying to understand the causes or determinants of a particular disease in a certain population – this would be an example of an analytical study - for example trying to understand the determinants of diabetes among Gujratis.

Leading Causes of Death in the United States in 1900 and 1990 (National Center for Health Statistics, 1992)

1900	1990
Influenza & Pneumonia	Diseases of the Heart
Tuberculosis	Malignant Neoplasms (cancer)
Gastroenteritis	Unintentional Injuries
Diseases of the Heart	Cerebrovascular Stroke
Vascular Lesions of the cns	Chronic Obstructive Pulmonary Disease
Chronic Nephritis	Pneumonia and Influenza
All accidents	
Cancer	
Certain diseases of early infancy	
Diptheria	

(Adapted from Taylor, 1995 pp 8)

Notice the change in the leading causes of death from 1900 to 1990 What causes these causes?

Top 3 leading causes of death are all viral and bacterial in 1900 – however the top 5 causes in 1990 are neither viral nor bacterial (due to widespread use of antibiotics) but are chronic illnesses (except for Unintentional injuries) and are linked to lifestyle factors. Also Diptheria and diseases of early infancy are completely eliminated from the 1990 list due to widespread vaccination

Context for Health Psychology

Thus this leads to the context for the development of Health Psychology. In the developed countries the leading causes of death are chronic illnesses, cardiovascular disease in most part. Thus there has been an increasing awareness of the behavioral causes of illness and mortality or lifestyle factors. Changing behavior or lifestyles falls in the realm of psychology eg. Stopping smoking, beginning to exercise, changing one's diet etc. When considering lifestyle factors psychosocial aspects come into play such as culture, the social context, the economic context

That individuals are responsible for their own health is another idea fuelling health psychology. This idea comes from the western culture of individualism – therefore the focus on the individual's behavior and will power.

However in other cultures - an alternative view sees the need for policy interventions designed to support and promote health at the societal and community levels.

Individualism - works when people are empowered and have a lot of choices – and are of a relatively high socio-economic status.

Dissatisfaction with the medical model (side effects of allopathic medication, mere symptom control) is another factor playing a role in the research in health psychology.

This dissatisfaction has led to looking at health from a more holistic perspective – physical, psychological, social and spiritual perspective.

Alternative systems of medicine have gained popularity and the Indian government promotes alternative medicine and has recognized university courses in the five streams of alternative medicine which are represented by the acronym AYUSH.

AYUSH – Ayurveda, Yoga, Unani, Sidha, Homeopathic

The onion model by Dahlgren & Whitehead (as cited in Marks, 2008) visually represents the nested structure that the individual inhabits with the core attributes of age, sex and hereditary factors surrounded by individual lifestyle factors, social and community influences, living and working conditions, and socioeconomic, cultural and environmental conditions.

Health is often presumed to be merely an outcome of hereditary factors or hereditary factors interacting with lifestyle factors however in this model and through this course we will begin to appreciate the myriad factors and the complexity of their interactions that influence final health outcomes for individuals, communities and populations.

Disease Burden

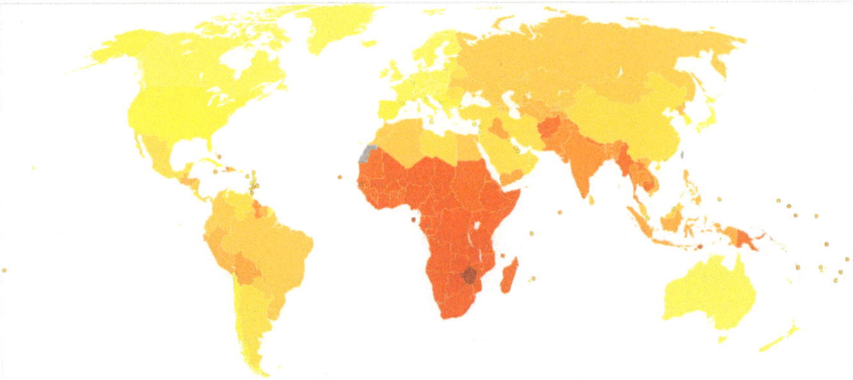

Burden of all infectious diseases, worldwide in 2004, measured in disability-adjusted life years.

Disease burden is the impact of a health problem as measured by financial cost, mortality, morbidity, or other indicators. It is often quantified in terms of quality-adjusted life years (QALYs) or disability-adjusted life years (DALYs), both of which quantify the number of years lost due to disease (YLDs). One DALY can be thought of as one year of healthy life lost, and the overall disease burden can be thought of as a measure of the gap between current health status and the ideal health status (where the individual lives to old age free from disease and disability). According to an article published in The Lancet in June 2015 low back pain and major depressive disorder were among the top ten causes of YLDs and were the cause of more health loss than diabetes, chronic obstructive pulmonary disease, and asthma combined. The study based on data from 188 countries, considered to be the largest and most detailed analysis to quantify levels, patterns, and trends in ill health and disability, concluded that "the proportion of disability-adjusted life years due to YLDs increased globally from 21.1% in 1990 to 31.2% in 2013." The environmental burden of disease is defined as the number of DALYs that can be attributed to environmental factors. These measures allow for comparison of disease burdens, and have also been used to forecast the possible impacts of health interventions. By 2014 DALYs per head were "40% higher in low-income and middle-income regions."

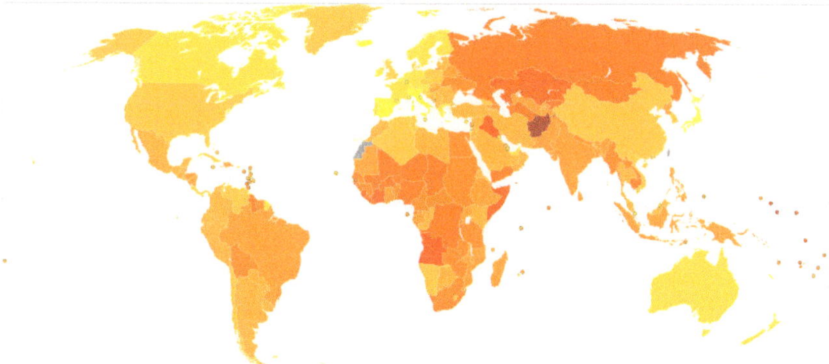

Burden of non-communicable diseases, worldwide in 2004, measured in disability-adjusted life years.

The World Health Organization (WHO) has provided a set of detailed guidelines for measuring disease burden at the local or national level. In 2004, the health issue leading to the highest YLD for both men and women was unipolar depression; in 2010, it was lower back pain. According to an article in The Lancet published in November 2014, disorders in those aged 60 years and older represent "23% of the total global burden of disease" and leading contributors to disease burden in this group in 2014 were "cardiovascular diseases (30.3%), malignant neoplasms (15.1%), chronic respiratory diseases (9.5%), musculoskeletal diseases (7.5%), and neurological and mental disorders (6.6%)."

Statistics

In 2004, the World Health Organization calculated that 1.5 billion disability-adjusted life years were lost to disease and injury.

Disease category	Percent of all YPLLs, worldwide	Percent of all DALYs, worldwide	Percent of all YPLLs, Europe	Percent of all DALYs, Europe	Percent of all YPLLs, US and Canada	Percent of all DALYs, US and Canada
Infectious and parasitic diseases, especially lower respiratory tract infections, diarrhea, AIDS, tuberculosis, and malaria	37%	26%	9%	6%	5%	3%
Neuropsychiatric conditions, such as depression	2%	13%	3%	19%	5%	28%
Injuries, especially motor vehicle accidents	14%	12%	18%	13%	18%	10%

Disease category	Percent of all YPLLs, worldwide	Percent of all DALYs, worldwide	Percent of all YPLLs, Europe	Percent of all DALYs, Europe	Percent of all YPLLs, US and Canada	Percent of all DALYs, US and Canada
Cardiovascular diseases, principally heart attacks and stroke	14%	10%	35%	23%	26%	14%
Premature birth and other perinatal deaths (infant mortality)	11%	8%	4%	2%	3%	2%
Cancer	8%	5%	19%	11%	25%	13%

History

The first study on the global burden of disease, conducted in 1990, quantified the health effects of more than 100 diseases and injuries for eight regions of the world, giving estimates of morbidity and mortality by age, sex, and region. It also introduced the DALY as a new metric to quantify the burden of diseases, injuries, and risk factors. In 2000–2002, the 1990 study was updated to include a more extensive analysis using a framework known as *comparative risk factor assessment*.

Modifiable Risk Factors

In 2006, the WHO released a report which addressed the amount of global disease that could be prevented by reducing environmental risk factors. The report found that approximately one fourth of the global disease burden, and more than one third of the burden among children, was due to modifiable environmental factors. The "environmentally-mediated" disease burden is much higher in developing countries, with the exception of certain non-communicable diseases, such as cardiovascular diseases and cancers, where the per capita disease burden is larger in developed countries. Children have the highest death toll, with more than 4 million environmentally-caused deaths yearly, mostly in developing countries. The infant death rate attributed to environmental causes is also 12 times higher in developing countries. 85 out of the 102 major diseases and injuries classified by WHO were due to environmental factors.

To measure the environmental health impact, *environment* was defined as "all the physical, chemical and biological factors external to a person, and all the related behaviours". The definition of *modifiable environment* included:

- Air, soil, and water pollution with chemicals or biological agents
- Ultraviolet and ionizing radiation
- Noise and electromagnetic fields
- Built environment
- Agricultural methods and irrigation schemes
- Man-made climate change and ecosystem degradation
- Occupational risks

- Individual behaviors, such as hand-washing and food contamination due to unsafe water or dirty hands

Certain environmental factors were excluded from this definition:

- Indoor smoke from solid fuel use
- Lead
- Mercury
- Natural climate change (as opposed to man-made climate change)
- Occupational airborne particulates or carcinogens
- Outdoor air pollution
- Sanitation and hygiene problems
- Second-hand smoke
- Solar ultraviolet radiation

Estimation

The WHO developed a methodology to quantify the health of a population using summary measures, which combine information on mortality and non-fatal health outcomes. The measures quantify either health gaps or health expectancies; the most commonly used health summary measure is the DALY.

The exposure-based approach, which measures exposure via pollutant levels, is used to calculate the environmental burden of disease. This approach requires knowledge of the outcomes associated with the relevant risk factor, exposure levels and distribution in the study population, and dose-response relationships of the pollutants.

A dose-response relationship is a function of the exposure parameter assessed for the study population. Exposure distribution and dose-response relationships are combined to yield the study population's *health impact distribution*, usually expressed in terms of incidence. The health impact distribution can then be converted into health summary measures, such as DALYs. Exposure-response relationships for a given risk factor are commonly obtained from epidemiological studies. For example, the disease burden of outdoor air pollution for Santiago, Chile was calculated by measuring the concentration of atmospheric particulate matter (PM10), estimating the susceptible population, and combining these data with relevant dose-response relationships. A reduction of particulate matter levels in the air to recommended standards would cause a reduction of about 5,200 deaths, 4,700 respiratory hospital admissions, and 13,500,000 days of restricted activity per year, for a total population of 4.7 million.

In 2002, the WHO estimated the global environmental burden of disease by using risk assessment data to develop environmentally attributable fractions (EAFs) of mortality and morbidity for 85 categories of disease. In 2007, they released the first country-by-country analysis of the impact environmental factors had on health for its then 192 member states. These country estimates were the first step to assist governments in carrying out preventive action. The country estimates were divided into three parts:

Environmental burden of disease for selected risk factors

> This presents the yearly burden, expressed in deaths and DALYs, attributable to: indoor air pollution from solid fuel use; outdoor air pollution; and unsafe water, sanitation, and hygiene. Results are calculated using the exposure-based approach.

Total environmental burden of disease for the relevant country

> The total number of deaths, DALYs per capita, and the percentage of the national burden of disease attributable to the environment represent the disease burden that could be avoided by modifying the environment as a whole.

Environmental burden by disease category

> Each country summary was broken down by the disease group, where the annual number of DALYs per capita attributable to environmental factors were calculated for each group.

Implementation and Interpretation

The public health impacts of air pollution (annual means of PM10 and ozone), noise pollution, and radiation (radon and UV), can be quantified using DALYs. For each disease, a DALY is calculated as:

DALYs = number of people with the disease × duration of the disease (or loss of life expectancy in the case of mortality) × severity (varying from 0 for perfect health to 1 for death)

Necessary data include prevalence data, exposure-response relationships, and weighting factors that give an indication of the severity of a certain disorder. When information is missing or vague, experts will be consulted in order to decide which alternative data sources to use. An uncertainty analysis is carried out so as to analyze the effects of different assumptions.

Uncertainty

When estimating the environmental burden of disease, a number of potential sources of error may arise in the measure of exposure and exposure-risk relationship, assumptions made in applying the exposure or exposure-risk relationship to the relevant country, health statistics, and, if used, expert opinions.

Generally, it is not possible to estimate a formal confidence interval, but it is possible to estimate a range of possible values the environmental disease burden may take based on different input parameters and assumptions. When more than one definition has to be made about a certain element in the assessment, multiple analyses can be run, using different sets of definitions. Sensitivity and decision analyses can help determine which sources of uncertainty affect the final results the most.

Representative examples

The Netherlands

In the Netherlands, air pollution is associated with respiratory and cardiovascular diseases, and exposure to certain forms of radiation can lead to the development of cancer. Quantification of the health impact of the environment was done by calculating DALYs for air pollution, noise, radon, UV, and indoor dampness for the period 1980 to 2020. In the Netherlands, 2–5% of the total disease burden in 2000 could be attributed to the effects of (short-term) exposure to air pollution, noise, radon, natural UV radiation, and dampness in houses. The percentage can increase to up to 13% due to uncertainty, assuming no threshold.

Among the investigated factors, long-term PM10 exposure have the greatest impact on public health. As levels of PM10 decrease, related disease burden is also expected to decrease. Noise exposure and its associated disease burden is likely to increase to a level where the disease burden is similar to that of traffic accidents. The rough estimates do not provide a complete picture of the environmental health burden, because data are uncertain, not all environmental-health relationships are known, not all environmental factors have been included, and it was not possible to assess all potential health effects. The effects of a number of these assumptions were evaluated in an uncertainty analysis.

Canada

Exposure to environmental hazards may cause chronic diseases, so the magnitude of their contribution to the Canada's total disease burden is not well-understood. In order to give an initial estimate of the environmental burden of disease for four major categories of disease, the EAF developed by the WHO, EAFs developed by other researchers, and data from Canadian public health institutions were used. Results showed a total of 10,000–25,000 deaths, with 78,000–194,000 hospitalizations; 600,000–1.5 million days spent in hospital; 1.1–1.8 million restricted activity days for sufferers of asthma; 8000–24,000 new cases of cancer; 500–2,500 babies with low birth weights; and C$3.6–9.1 billion in costs each year due to respiratory disease, cardiovascular illness, cancer, and congenital affliction associated with adverse environmental exposures.

Criticism

There is no consensus on the best measures of the public's health. This is not surprising because measurements are used to accomplish diverse functions (e.g., population health assessment, evaluation of the effectiveness of interventions, formulation of health policies, and projection of future resource need). The choice of measures may also depend on individual and societal values. Measures that only consider premature death will omit the burden of living with a disease or disability, and measures that combine both in a single measure (i.e. DALYs) need to make a judgment to the significance of these measures compared to each other. Other metrics such as economic costs will not capture pain and suffering or other broader aspects of burden.

DALYs are a simplification of a complex reality, and therefore only give a crude indication of environmental health impact. Relying on DALYs may make donors take a narrow approach to health care programs. Foreign aid is most often directed at diseases with the highest DALYs, ignoring the fact that other diseases, despite having lower DALYs, are still major contributors to disease burden. Less-publicized diseases thus have little or no funding for health efforts. For example, maternal death (one of the top three killers in most poor countries) and pediatric respiratory and intestinal infections maintain a high disease burden, and safe pregnancy and the prevention of coughs in infants do not receive adequate funding.

Healthy Lifestyle

In health care, self-care is any necessary human regulatory function which is under individual control, deliberate and self-initiated.

Some place self-care on a continuum with health care providers at the opposite end to self-care. In modern medicine, preventive medicine aligns most closely with self-care. A lack of adherence to medical advice and the onset of a mental disorder can make self-care difficult. Self-care is seen as a partial solution to the global rise in health care costs placed on governments. The notion that self-care is a fundamental pillar of health and social care means it is an essential component of a modern health care system governed by regulations and statutes.

Self-care is considered a primary form of care for patients with chronic conditions who make many day-to-day decisions, or self-manage, their illness. Self-management is critical and self-management education complements traditional patient education in primary care to support patients to live the best possible quality of life with their chronic condition. Self-care is learned, purposeful and continuous. In philosophy, self-care refers to the care and cultivation of self in a comprehensive sense, focusing in particular on the soul and the knowledge of self.

Universal Requisites

There are a number of self-care requisites applicable to all humans across all ages and necessary to fundamental human needs. For example, as humans we need to intake sufficient air, water and food; care also needs to be taken with the process of elimination and excrement. There must be a balance between rest and activity as well as between solitude and social activities. The prevention and avoidance of human hazards and participation in social groups are also requisites. Maturity requires the autonomous performance of self-care duties.

Self-care Maintenance

Self-care includes all health decisions people (as individuals or consumers) make for themselves and their families to ensure they are physically and mentally fit.

Maintaining fitness at an elderly age

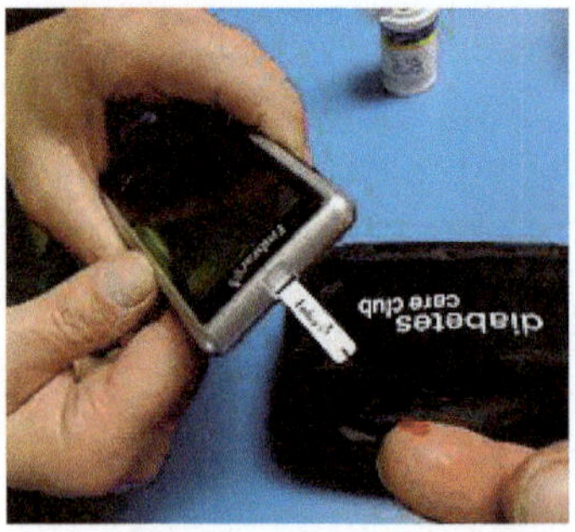

Blood sugar testing for diabetes

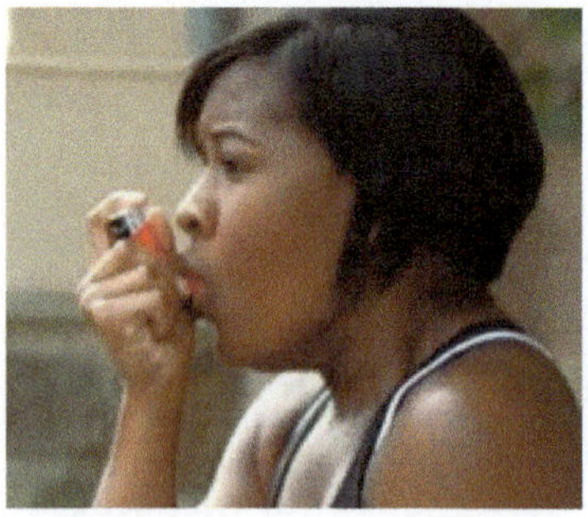

Asthma inhalers contain a medication that treats the symptoms of asthma

Self-care Maintenance Behaviors

Self-care maintenance behaviors include illness prevention, illness behaviors, and proper hygiene.

Illness prevention measures include tobacco avoidance, exercise, and diet. Tobacco use is the largest preventable cause of death and disease in the US. By avoiding or quitting tobacco use, overall health and quality of life are improved and risk of disease and premature death are reduced. The benefits of regular physical activity include weight control, reduced risk of chronic disease, strengthened bones and muscles, improved mental health, improved ability to participate in daily activities, and increased chance of living longer. The Center for Disease Control and Prevention (CDC) recommends 2 hours and thirty minutes of moderate activity each week. Examples of this include brisk walking, swimming, dancing, riding a bike, and even jumping rope. Another important aspect to self care includes eating fresh fruits and vegetables, lean meats and other proteins. Process foods should be limited. Limiting saturated fats, trans fats, sugars, and sodium will also contribute to a healthy diet.

Illness behaviors include taking medicines as prescribed and getting vaccinations. When medicines are not taken as prescribed, complications can occur. These complications include disease progression, reduced functional abilities, lower quality of life, and increased hospital visits. Vaccinations helps protect individuals from serious illnesses and complications related to vaccine-preventable diseases like pneumonia.

Hygiene is another important part of self-care maintenance. Hygiene behaviors include adequate sleep, regular oral care, and hand washing. Getting 7–8 hours of sleep each night can protect physical and mental health. Sleep deficiency increases the risk of heart disease, kidney disease, high blood pressure, diabetes, and obesity. Sleep deficiency can also lead to depression, suicide, and risk-taking behavior. Teeth brushing and personal hygiene can prevent infection.

Self-care maintenance behaviors can be influenced by external factors, such as access to healthcare and living environments. Social determinants of health play a huge role in how people take care of themselves. Access to care is one major determinant of one's ability to carry out self-care maintenance behaviors.This includes having access to transportation to visit a health care service, availability of open hours of offices/clinics, and whether or not the care is affordable. These external factors can determine a person's ability to perform self-care maintenance because a person may not be able to perform a behavior based on it's availability. Access within a one's living environment is another factor that influences self-care maintenance. An individual's environment determines whether they are able to go to the gym to exercise or go to a grocery store to buy healthy food. Living in a food desert or having limited resources that allow for physical activity would decrease the likelihood of participating in self-care maintenance behaviors.

Internal factors, such as motivation, emotions, and cognitive abilities also influence self-care maintenance behaviors. Motivation is often the driving force behind performing self-care maintenance behaviors. A person who is motivated to stay healthy and managing and/or prevent a chronic illness is more likely to be interested in performing maintenance behaviors, such as those mentioned above. Emotions are also indicative of whether a person is going to perform such behaviors. A person with depression is more likely to have a poor dietary intake low in fruits and vegetables, reduced physical activity, and poor medication adherence. An individual with impaired cognitive or functional abilities also has a diminished ability to performing self-care maintenance behaviors. Some of these behaviors, such as medication adherence, require the ability to maintain a schedule, but someone with memory impairment may have difficulty completing tasks based on memory.

Skills are also a significant aspect that influences an individual's ability to perform self-care behaviors. Individuals need to be able to plan, set goals, and make appropriate decisions regarding their health needs. In addition, self-care is influenced by an individual's attitude and belief in his or her self-efficacy. Having the confidence to perform an action and to overcome barriers is indicative of success in performing self-care behaviors. Cultural beliefs and values may also influence self-care. Self-care may be viewed as highly important in some countries or within certain cultures that value independence, but in other cultures, self-care may contradict their beliefs and values.

Social supports also influence how an individual performs self-care maintenance. Social supports include family, friends, and support groups. Support groups can be through religious groups, groups that manage chronic illnesses, or a community group. These supports can help by having people to talk to or help make decisions about your care. Individuals who live with chronic illness acknowledge that shared care can help make living with a chronic illness less stressful. If you are suffering from a chronic illness and would like to join a support group, there are resources that could be found online or offered by your primary care provider.

Living with one or more chronic illnesses can be very difficult. There are numerous medications, different specialists, and self-care maintenance behaviors that are necessary. With all of these working parts, it can be difficult to keep track of everything. The presence of co-morbid conditions makes performing self-care maintenance behaviors harder to complete. Pill burden is a huge factor in self-care maintenance of multiple chronic illnesses because many people may complain of not wanting to take all the medication or get confused regarding the schedule of their medications. As an example, a patient with diabetes would need to exercise, but if they also have COPD they easily develop shortness of breath which would cause them to stop exercising. It is important to address all the symptoms of each chronic illness an individual suffers from so that individuals with chronic illnesses can successfully perform self-care maintenance behaviors.

The benefits of living a healthy lifestyle were analyzed in the Caerphilly Heart Disease Study. Evidence showed a risk reduction in chronic diseases (including dementia and cognitive impairment) to be significantly associated with healthy lifestyles.

Self-care is also taking care of minor ailments, long term conditions, or one's own health after discharge from secondary and tertiary health care. For instances of neck pain, for example, self-care is the recommended treatment.

Patients who are better informed and more educated possess greater motivation for self-care. Individuals conduct self-care and experts and professionals support self-care to enable individuals to undertake enhanced self-care. The recognition and evaluation of symptoms is a key aspect of self-care. The main issues involved with self-care and the onset of illness are medically related such managing drug side effects, emotions and psychological issues, changes to lifestyle and knowledge acquisition to assist in decision-making.

Self-care support has crucial enabling value and considerable scope in developing countries with an already overburdened health care system. But it also has an essential role to play in affluent countries where people are becoming more conscious about their health and want to have a greater role in taking care of themselves.

To enable people to do enhanced self-care, they can be supported in various ways and by different service providers.

Methods Used to Improve Self-Care

Multifaceted interventions that tailor education to the individual are more effective than patient education alone. Approaches used to improve self-care are summarized here.

- "Teach-back" is used to gauge how much information is retained after patient teaching. Teach-back occurs when patients are asked to repeat information that was given to them. The educator checks for gaps in the patient's understanding, reinforces messages, and creates a collaborative conversation with the patient. It is important for individuals with a chronic illness to comprehend and recall information received about their condition. Teach-back education can both educate patients and assess learning. One example of how a provider can initiate teach-back is by asking, "I want to make sure that I explained everything clearly. If you were talking to your neighbor, what would you tell her/him we talked about today". This phrase protects the patient's self-esteem while placing responsibility for understanding on both the provider and patient. One study performed showed that patients with heart failure who received teach-back education had a 12% lower readmission rate compared to patients who did not receive teach-back. Although the teach-back method is effective in the short-term, there is little evidence to support its long-term effect. Long-term knowledge retention is crucial for self-care, so further research is needed on this approach.
- Habits are automatic responses to commonly encountered situations. One example of a habit is hand washing after restroom use. The main characteristic of a habit is automaticity. A habit is formed when environmental cues result in a behavior with very little conscious deliberation.
- Behavioral economics is a subset of the study of economics that examines how cognitive, social, and emotional factors play in role in an individual's economic decisions. Behavioral economics is now influencing the design of healthcare interventions aimed at improving self-care maintenance. Because humans do not always make rational decisions when it comes to self-care, behavioral economics takes into account the complexity and irrationality of human behavior.
- Motivational Interviewing is a way to engage people in critically thinking about their self-care needs. MI uses an interviewing style that focuses on the individual's goals and can be used in any context. MI is based on three psychological theories: cognitive dissonance, self-perception, and the transtheoretical model of change. MI is intended to enhance intrinsic motivation for change.
- Health coaching is another method of promoting motivation to initiate and maintain behavior change. The health coach facilitates behavior change by emphasizing personal goals, life experiences, and values.

Self-Care Monitoring

Self-care monitoring is the process of surveillance that involves measurement and perception of bodily changes. Effective self-care monitoring also requires being able to label and interpret changes in the body as normal or abnormal. Listening to your body and recognizing signs and symptoms, increasing factual knowledge towards disease or illness are all important factors. Being able to interpret and label your symptoms, understanding the process of your disease, and knowing how to act and treat accordingly allows competency in knowing when to seek further medical help.

Self-care monitoring consists of both the perception and measurement of symptoms. Symptom perception is the process of monitoring one's body for signs of changing health. This includes body awareness or body listening, recognizing symptoms relevant to health, and interpreting and labeling these symptoms. For example, a patient with diabetes may use body listening to perceive feelings of shakiness and sweating. These feelings are labeled as symptoms of low blood sugar, and the patient will decide how to act based on this information. Prompt and accurate recognition of symptoms is a necessary part of a patient's management of their health. In heart attack patients, delays in seeking treatment for worsening symptoms have been found to contribute to poor health outcomes.

Changes in health status or body function can be monitored with various tools and technologies. The range and complexity of medical devices used in both hospital and homecare settings are increasing. Certain devices are specific to a common need of a disease process. For example, various types of glucose monitors are used by patients with diabetes to track their blood sugar levels. Other devices can provide a more general set of information, such as a weight scale, blood pressure cuff, pulse oximeter, etc. Less technological tools can include organizers, charts, and diagrams to trend or keep track of things such as amount of calories, mood, vital sign measurements, and more.

Barriers to Self-Care Monitoring

A patient's ability to engage in self-care monitoring greatly impacts the progression of his/her disease. Barriers to monitoring can go unrecognized and end up interfering with effective self-care. Barriers can include knowledge deficits, undesirable self-care regimens, different instructions from multiple providers, and limitations to access related to income or disability. Psychosocial factors such as motivation, anxiety, depression, confidence can also serve as barriers.

- Cost of equipment - This is a common barrier to self-care monitoring. Certain equipment is needed to monitor symptoms, such as test strips and needles in blood glucose monitoring. The cost of equipment can be expensive for some individuals, so they are less motivated and less likely to keep track of symptoms.
- Lack of knowledge - With monitoring, it is important to understand what you're looking for and why you're doing it. For example, some individuals may not understand the implications of high blood sugars or high blood pressure. Thus, they don't feel the need to monitor it. Also, if you don't understand the importance of the monitoring, you will not do it.
- Fear of outcomes/fear of using equipment - In the example of blood glucose monitoring, some people may be afraid of needles, which will deter them from doing fingersticks to read their blood sugar. Other people may have a fear or anxiety of how results may turn out and may avoid them. For example, a person who didn't follow a diet to maintain their blood pressure or blood sugar may have a fear that it's already high and thus, doesn't want to monitor it.
- Familial/social support (or lack thereof) - Monitoring something implies doing it on a reg-

ular/frequent basis. Doing anything consistently sometimes requires reminders or a little encouragement from others.

Improving Self-Care Monitoring

Because self-care monitoring is conducted primarily by patients and their caregivers, it is necessary to work with patients closely on this topic. Providers should assess the current self-care monitoring regimen and build off this to create an individualized plan of care. Knowledge and education specifically designed for the patient's level of understating is central to self-care monitoring. When patients understand the symptoms that correspond with their disease, they can learn to recognize these symptoms early on. Then they can self-manage their disease and prevent complications.

Additional research to improve self-care monitoring is underway in the following fields:

- Mindfulness: Mindfulness and meditation, when incorporated into a one-day education program for diabetic patients, have been shown to improve diabetic control in a 3-month follow-up in comparison to those who received the education without a focus on mindfulness.
- Decision-making: How a patient's decision making capacity can be encouraged/improved with the support of their provider, leading to better self-care monitoring and outcomes.
- Self-efficacy: Self-efficacy has been shown to be more closely linked to a patient's ability to perform self-care than health literacy or knowledge.
- Wearable technology: How self-care monitoring is evolving with technology like wearable activity monitors.

Self-Care Management

Self-care management is defined as the response to signs and symptoms when they occur. Self-care management involves the evaluation of physical and emotional changes and deciding if these changes need to be addressed. Changes may occur because of illness, treatment, or the environment. Once treatment is done, it needs to be evaluated to judge whether it would be useful to do again in the future. Treatments are based on the signs and symptoms experienced. Treatments are usually specific to the illness.

Self-Care Management Behaviors

Self-care management includes recognizing symptoms, treating the symptoms, and evaluating the treatment. Self-care management behaviors are symptom- and disease-specific. For example, a patient with asthma may recognize the symptom of shortness of breath. This patient can manage the symptom by using an inhaler and seeing if their breathing improves. A patient with heart failure manages their condition by recognizing symptoms such as swelling and shortness of breath. Self-care management behaviors for heart failure may include taking a water pill, limiting fluid and salt intake, and seeking help from a healthcare provider.

Regular self-care monitoring is needed to identify symptoms early and judge the effectiveness of treatments. Some examples include:

- Inject insulin in response to high blood sugar and then re-check to evaluate if blood glucose lowered
- Use social support and healthy leisure activities to fight feelings of social isolation. This has been shown to be effective for patients with chronic lung disease

Unique Factors Influencing Self-Care Management

Access to care: Access to care is a major barrier affecting self-care management. Treatment of symptoms might require consultation with a healthcare provider. Access to the health care system is largely influenced by providers. Many people suffering from a chronic illness do not have access to providers within the health care system for several reasons. Three major barriers to care include: insurance coverage, poor access to services, and being unable to afford costs. Without access to trained health care providers, outcomes are typically worse.

Financial constraints: Financial barriers impact self-care management. The majority of insurance coverage is provided by employers. Loss of employment is frequently accompanied by loss of health insurance and inability to afford health care. In patients with diabetes and chronic heart disease, financial barriers are associated with poor access to care, poor quality of care, and vascular disease. As a result, these patients have reduced rates of medical assessments, measurements of Hemoglobin A1C (a marker that assesses blood glucose levels over the last 3 months), cholesterol measurements, eye and foot examinations, diabetes education, and aspirin use. Research has found that people in higher social classes are better at self-care management of chronic conditions. In addition, people with lower levels of education often lack resources to effectively engage in self-management behaviors.

Age: Elderly patients are more likely to rate their symptoms differently and delay seeking care longer when they have symptoms. For example, an elderly person with heart failure may experience the symptom of shortness of breath differently than someone with heart failure who is younger. There are many reasons contributing to this difference in symptom experience. Providers should be aware of the potential delay in provider-seeking behavior in elderly patients which could worsen their overall condition.

Prior experience: Prior experience contributes to the development of skills in self-care management. Experience helps the patient develop cues and patterns that they can remember and follow, leading to reasonable goals and actions in repeat situations(. A patient who has skills in self-management knows what to do during repeated symptomatic events. This could lead to them recognizing their symptoms earlier, and seeking a provider sooner.

Health care literacy: Health care literacy is another factor affecting self-care management. Health care literacy is the amount of basic health information people are able to understand. Health care literacy is the major variable contributing to differences in patient ratings of self-management support. Successful self-care involves understanding the meaning of changes in one's body. Individuals who can identify changes in their body are then able to come up with options and decide on a course of action(. Health education at the patient's literacy level can increase the patient's ability to problem solve, set goals, and acquire skills in applying practical information. A patient's literacy can also affect their rating of healthcare quality. A poor healthcare experience may cause a patient to avoid returning to that same provider. This creates a delay in acute symptom management. Providers must consider health literacy when designing treatment plans that require self-management skills.

Co-morbid conditions: A patient with multiple chronic illnesses may experience compounding effects of their illnesses. This can include worsening of one condition by the symptoms or treatment of another. People tend to prioritize one of their conditions. This limits the self-care management of their other illnesses. One condition may have more noticeable symptoms than others. Or the patient may be more emotionally connected to one illness, for example, the one they have had for a long time. If providers are unaware of the effect of having multiple illnesses, the patient's overall health may fail to improve or worsen as a result of therapeutic efforts.

Ways to Improve Self-Care Management

There are many ways for patients and healthcare providers to work together to improve the patient's self-care management. Stoplight and skill teaching allow patients and providers to work together to develop decision-making strategies.

1. Stoplight is an action plan for the daily treatment of a patient's chronic illness created by the healthcare team and the patient. It makes decision making easier by categorizing signs and symptoms and determining the appropriate actions for each set. It separates signs and symptoms into three zones:

- *Green* is the safe zone, meaning the patient's signs and symptoms are what is typically expected. The patient should continue with their daily self-care tasks, such as taking daily medications and eating a healthy diet.
- *Yellow* is the caution zone, meaning the patient's signs and symptoms should be monitored as they are abnormal, but they are not yet dangerous. Some actions may need to be taken in this zone in order to go back to the green zone, for instance taking an additional medication. The patient may need to contact their healthcare team for advice.
- *Red* is the danger zone, meaning the patient's signs and symptoms show that something is dangerously wrong. If in this category the patient needs to take actions to return to the green category, such as taking an emergency medication, as well as contact their healthcare team immediately. They may also need to contact emergency medical assistance.

The stoplight plan helps patients to make decisions about what actions to take for different signs and symptoms and when to contact their healthcare team with a problem. The patient and their provider will customize certain signs and symptoms that fit in each stoplight category.

2. Skills teaching is a learning opportunity between a healthcare provider and a patient where a patient learns a skill in self-care unique to his or her chronic illness. Some of these skills may be applied to the daily management of the symptoms of a chronic illness. Other skills may be applied when there is an exacerbation of a symptom. An exacerbation of a symptom means that the symptom is in a worsened state or is different from what the patient normally experiences. The patient should not only learn the purpose of self-care skills. It is also important to learn when to apply skills in daily management of a chronic illness and how the skill might be modified or changed when the patient experiences an exacerbation of a symptom.

For example, a patient newly diagnosed with persistent asthma might learn about taking an oral medicine for daily management, control of chronic symptoms and prevention of an asthma attack. However, there may come a time when the patient might be exposed to an environmental trigger or stress that causes an asthma attack. The patient starts to experience shortness of breath, chest tightness or wheezing. When this unexpected symptom occurs, the skill of taking daily medicines and the medicine that is taken may change. Rather than taking an oral medicine daily, a different medication is needed for quick rescue and relief of symptoms. The rescue medication works quickly with an inhaler. Knowing to choose the right medication and knowing how to take the medicine with an inhaler is a skill that is learned for the self-care management of asthma.

In skills teaching, it is important for the patient and provider to discuss skills and address any lingering questions. It is important for the patient to know when and how a skill is to be implemented, and how the skill may need to be changed when the symptom is different from normal. Learning self-care management skills for the first time in the care of a chronic illness is not easy, but with patience, practice, persistence and experience, personal mastery of self-care skills can be achieved.

Support

Self-care support can include the following:

- Self-care information on health and human body systems, lifestyle and healthy eating.
- Support to capture, manage, interpret, and report observations of daily living (ODLs), the tracking of trends, and the use of the resulting information as clues for self-care action and decision making.
- Information prescriptions providing personalised information and instructions to enable an individual to self-care and take control of their health
- Self-care and self-monitoring devices and assistive technology
- Self-care skills and life skills training programmes and courses for people
- Aid from spiritual care givers
- Advice from licensed counselors, clinical social workers, psychotherapists, pharmacists, physiotherapists and complementary therapists
- Self-care support networks which can be face to face or virtual, and made up of peers or people who want to provide support to others or receive support and information from others (including a self-care primer for provider/consumer convergence.)
- Being attuned to one's spirituality

Approaches

Self-care practices are shaped by what are seen as the proper lifestyle choices of local communities. Health-related self-care topics include;

- General fitness training and physical exercise
- Healthy diet, meals, diet foods and fasting
- Smoking cessation and avoiding alcohol abuse
- Personal hygiene
- Life extension
- Pain management
- Stress management
- Alternative medicine such as homeopathy and home remedies
- Self-help and personal development
- Self-care portals and the use of health apps

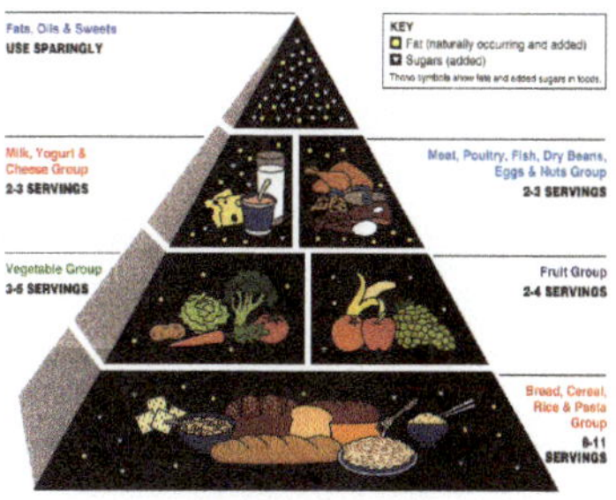

Food pyramid

Self-massage

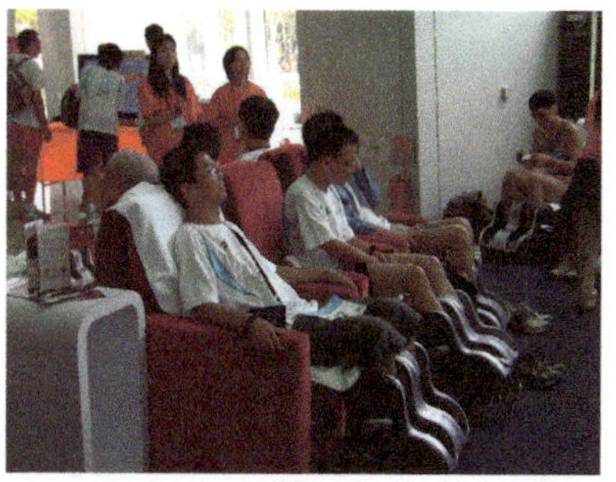

Massage with robotic massage chairs.

A lack of self-care in terms of personal health, hygiene and living conditions is referred to as self-neglect. The use of caregivers and Personal Care Assistants may be needed. An aging population is seeking greater self-care knowledge primarily within families connections and with responsibility usually belonging to the mother.

Philosophy

Michel Foucault understood the art of living (French *art de vivre*, Latin *ars vivendi*) and the care of self (French *le souci de soi*) to be central to philosophy. The third volume of his three-volume study *The History of Sexuality* is dedicated to this notion. For Foucault, the notion of *care of self* (*epimeleia heautou*) of Ancient Greek and Roman philosophy comprises an attitude towards the self, others and the world, as well as a certain form of attention. For Foucault, the pursuit of the care for one's own well-being also comprises self-knowledge (gnōthi seauton).

The self-care deficit nursing theory was developed by Dorothea Orem between 1959 and 2001. The positively viewed theory explores the use professional care and an orientation towards resources. Under Orem's model self-care has limits when its possibilities have been exhausted therefore making professional care legitimate. These deficits in self-care are seen as shaping the best role a nurse may provide. There are two phases in Orem's self-care; the investigative and decision-making phase and the production phase.

What is a Healthy Lifestyle?

The elements of a healthy lifestyle include a balanced diet, 20 minutes of exercise everyday, enough sleep, not using tobacco and coping effectively with stress. These are approximately what make up a healthy lifestyle at a basic level.

A health habit is a behavior that is firmly established and is performed automatically without conscious thought like brushing your teeth or having a bath.

Almeda County Study

This study is a classic study conducted in 1972 by Belloc and Breslow(Taylor, 1995). Alameda is a county or district in California. The researchers identified 7 healthy habits – sleeping 7-8 hours, eating breakfast, not smoking, having not more than 1 or 2 alcoholic drinks a day, exercising regularly, not being more than 10% over weight and not eating between meals.

7,000 residents of Alameda county were quizzed about their habits and a note was made of which of these 7 habits they practiced. It was found that the more health habits people practiced the fewer illnesses they had.

Nine and a half years later when a follow up study was conducted, mortality was lower among men and women who practiced these 7 habits as compared to those who practiced 0 to 3 of these habits. The effect was more pronounced for men.

Primary Prevention

Primary prevention refers to timely access to health care and preventive measures such as vaccination and frequent check ups. The goal is to combat and prevent risk factors for disease.

Health Promotion is valid at multiple levels – at a national and community level (concerning infrastructure such as piped water and sanitation and most importantly the provision of health care) at the neighborhood level (the surroundings, the amenities available), at the family level (habits practiced and inculcated) and of course at the individual level (the choices made and behaviors engaged in).

The Factors that influence the practice of health behaviors are

Demographic Variables

A study investigating the practice of 5 health habits (smoking, exercise, sleep and alcohol intake) by Gottlieb and Green (1984, in Taylor, 1995) found that health habits were being practiced by younger, better educated and wealthier people.

Age, gender, socioeconomic status, neighborhood all influence our pattern of behaviors

Socialization

How parents socialize children, the kind of habits they inculcate. Later in college peer pressure plays a strong role in influencing behavior. And the effect of the workplace. Thus this refers to the effect of family, friends, peers and other social contacts.

Emotional Factors

Stress levels & the ability to cope effectively – people who have to deal with high levels of stress – poverty, abusive spouse – it affects the control they have over their lives and hence the ability to engage in health behaviors

Self Esteem levels – people with higher levels of self esteem are more likely to value themselves enough to practice health behaviors

Goal setting and achievement – Being able to set goals and achieve them – for instance to start exercising, stop smoking, stop eating junk food etc

Cognitive Factors – Refers to beliefs, attitudes and ideas that people have with respect to health. The perceptions people have regarding certain illnesses – the severity of the threat, a sense of vulnerability to certain illnesses also affect choices made and behavior.

Access to Health Care

Timely and easy access to health care results in problems not getting out of hand or being nipped in the bud.

If basic health care is provided for all that improves the functional level of the population.

The issue of changing behaviors relevant to health is elaborated on in the chapter on health behavior.

Health Promotion

Health promotion is "the process of enabling people to increase control over their health and its determinants, and thereby improve their health", according to the World Health Organization's (WHO) 2005 Bangkok Charter for Health Promotion in a Globalized World.

Health promotion involves public policy that addresses health determinants such as income, housing, food security, employment, and quality working conditions. More recent work has used the term Health in All Policies to refer to the actions to incorporate health into all public policies. Health promotion is aligned with health equity and can be a focus of NGOs dedicated to social justice or human rights. Health literacy can be developed in schools, while aspects of health promotion such as breastfeeding promotion can depend on laws and rules of public spaces. Health promotion is focused on preventative healthcare rather than a medical model of curative care.

There is a tendency among public health officials and governments—and this is especially the case in neoliberal nations such as Canada and the USA—to reduce health promotion to health education and social marketing focused on changing behavioral risk factors.

History

The "first and best known" definition of health promotion, promulgated by the *American Journal of Health Promotion* since at least year 1986, is "the science and art of helping people change their lifestyle to move toward a state of optimal health". This definition was derived from the 1974 Lalonde report from the Government of Canada, which contained a health promotion strategy "aimed at informing, influencing and assisting both individuals and organizations so that they will accept more responsibility and be more active in matters affecting mental and physical health". Another predecessor of the definition was the 1979 *Healthy People* report of the Surgeon General of the United States, which noted that health promotion "seeks the development of community and individual measures which can help... [people] to develop lifestyles that can maintain and enhance the state of well-being".

At least two publications led to a "broad empowerment/environmental" definition of health promotion in the mid-1980s:

- In year 1984 the World Health Organization (WHO) Regional Office for Europe defined health promotion as "the process of enabling people to increase control over, and to improve, their health". In addition to methods to change lifestyles, the WHO Regional Office advocated "legislation, fiscal measures, organisational change, community development and spontaneous local activities against health hazards" as health promotion methods.
- In 1986, Jake Epp, Canadian Minister of National Health and Welfare, released *Achieving health for all: a framework for health promotion* which also came to be known as the "Epp report". This report defined the three "mechanisms" of health promotion as "self-care"; "mutual aid, or the actions people take to help each other cope"; and "healthy environments".

The WHO, in collaboration with other organizations, has subsequently co-sponsored international conferences on health promotion as follows:

- 1st International Conference on Health Promotion, Ottawa, 1986, which resulted in the "Ottawa Charter for Health Promotion". According to the Ottawa Charter, health promotion:
    - "is not just the responsibility of the health sector, but goes beyond healthy life-styles to well-being"
    - "aims at making... [political, economic, social, cultural, environmental, behavioural and biological factors] favourable through advocacy for health"
    - "focuses on achieving equity in health"
    - "demands coordinated action by all concerned: by governments, by health and other social organizations.

Workplace

Work site health focus on the prevention and the intervention that reduce the health risks of the employee. The U.S. Public Health Service recently issued a report titled "Physical Activity and Health: A Report of the Surgeon General" which provides a comprehensive review of the available scientific evidence about the relationship between physical activity and an individual's health status. The report shows that over 60% of Americans are not regularly active and that 25% are not active at all. There is very strong evidence linking physical activity to numerous health improvements. Health promotion can be performed in various locations. Among the settings that have received special attention are the community, health care facilities, schools, and worksites. Worksite health promotion, also known by terms such as "workplace health promotion," has been defined as "the combined efforts of employers, employees and society to improve the health and well-being of people at work". WHO states that the workplace "has been established as one of the priority settings for health promotion into the 21st century" because it influences "physical, mental, economic and social well-being" and "offers an ideal setting and infrastructure to support the promotion of health of a large audience".

Worksite health promotion programs (also called "workplace health promotion programs," "worksite wellness programs," or "workplace wellness programs") include exercise, nutrition, smoking cessation and stress management.

According to the Centers for Disease Control and Prevention (CDC), "Regular physical activity is one of the most effective disease prevention behaviors." Physical activity programs reduce feelings of anxiety and depression, reduce obesity (especially when combined with an improved diet), reduce risk of chronic diseases including cardiovascular disease, high blood pressure, and type 2 diabetes; and finally improve stamina, strength, and energy.

Reviews and meta-analyses published between 2005 and 2008 that examined the scientific literature on worksite health promotion programs include the following:

- A review of 13 studies published through January 2004 showed "strong evidence... for an effect on dietary intake, inconclusive evidence for an effect on physical activity, and no evidence for an effect on health risk indicators".
- In the most recent of a series of updates to a review of "comprehensive health promotion and disease management programs at the worksite," Pelletier (2005) noted "positive clinical and cost outcomes" but also found declines in the number of relevant studies and their quality.
- A "meta-evaluation" of 56 studies published 1982–2005 found that worksite health promotion produced on average a decrease of 26.8% in sick leave absenteeism, a decrease of 26.1% in health costs, a decrease of 32% in workers' compensation costs and disability management claims costs, and a cost-benefit ratio of 5.81.
- A meta-analysis of 46 studies published in 1970–2005 found moderate, statistically significant effects of work health promotion, especially exercise, on "work ability" and "overall well-being"; furthermore, "sickness absences seem to be reduced by activities promoting healthy lifestyle".
- A meta-analysis of 22 studies published 1997–2007 determined that workplace health promotion interventions led to "small" reductions in depression and anxiety.
- A review of 119 studies suggested that successful work site health-promotion programs have attributes such as: assessing employees' health needs and tailoring programs to meet those needs; attaining high participation rates; promoting self care; targeting several health issues simultaneously; and offering different types of activities (e.g., group sessions as well as print materials).

Entities and Projects by Country

Worldwide, government agencies (such as health departments) and non-governmental organizations have substantial efforts in the area of health promotion. Some of these entities and projects are:

International and Multinational

The WHO and its Regional Offices such as the Pan American Health Organization are influential in health promotion around the world. The main eight health promotion campaigns marked by WHO are World Health Day, World Tuberculosis Day, World Blood Donor Day, World Immunization Week, World Malaria Day, World No Tobacco Day, World Hepatitis Day and World AIDS Day.

The International Union for Health Promotion and Education, based in France, holds international, regional, and national conferences.

The European Union is co-funding a Joint Action on Chronic Diseases and Healthy Ageing across the Life Cycle (JA-CHRODIS) with a strong focus on health promotion.

Australia

The Australian Health Promotion Association, a professional body, was incorporated in year 1988. In November 2008, the National Health and Hospitals Reform Commission released a paper recommending a national health promotion agency. ACT Health of the Australian Capital Territory supports health promotion with funding and information dissemination. The Victorian Health Promotion Foundation (VicHealth) from the state of Victoria is "the world's first health promotion foundation to be funded by a tax on tobacco. ". The Australian Government has come up with some initiatives to help Australians achieve a healthy lifestyle. These initiatives are:

- Get Set 4 Life - Habits for Healthy Kid
- The Stephanie Alexander Kitchen Garden National Program
- Healthy Spaces and Place
- Learning from Successful Community Obesity Initiative
- Healthy Weight information and resources.

Health Promotion is strong and well-established in Australia. Since 2008 there has been a number of graduate courses people can take to be involved within Health Promotion in Australia. The government since 2008 has included an initiative that involves the Aboriginal and Torres Strait Island citizens in the preventive health sector.

Health Promotion In Australian Schools

School programs are based on curriculum documents from state and territory councils. Schools mainly focus on health issues that are being supported by funding and special events. Funding for many health issues are the main basis for school curriculum's health subject.

Health Promotion for Aboriginal and Torres Strait Islander Citizens

Aboriginal and Torres Strait Island citizens in Australia in the last couple of centuries have had poor health. The reason behind the poor health conditions is due to major events in the history of Australia, There is an increasing advancement in the promotion of health for Torres Strait Islander and Aboriginal citizens, but this cannot be achieved without the co-operation of non-indigenous

Australians. For this Health promotion to be a success the citizens of Australia need to put the history between non-indigenous and indigenous citizens behind them and co-operate as equals.

Canada

The province of Ontario appointed a health promotion minister to lead its Ministry of Health Promotion in year 2005.

The Ministry's vision is to enable Ontarians to lead healthy, active lives and make the province a healthy, prosperous place to live, work, play, learn and visit. Ministry of Health Promotion sees that its fundamental goals are to promote and encourage Ontarians to make healthier choices at all ages and stages of life, to create healthy and supportive environments, lead the development of healthy public policy, and assist with embedding behaviours that promote health.

The Canadian Health Network was a "reliable, non-commercial source of online information about how to stay healthy and prevent disease" that was discontinued in 2007.

The BC Coalition for Health Promotion is "a grassroots, voluntary non-profit society dedicated to the advancement of health promotion in British Columbia".

Ireland

Health Promotion Research in Ireland

The Health Promotion Research Centre (HPRC) at the National University of Ireland Galway was established in 1990 with support from the Department of Health to conduct health promotion related research on issues relevant to health promotion in an Irish context. The Centre is unique in that it is the only designated research centre in Ireland dedicated to health promotion. It produces high quality research of national and international significance that supports the development of best practice and policy in the promotion of health. The Centre is a World Health Organisation (WHO) Collaborating Centre for Health Promotion Research, has an active multidisciplinary research programme, and collaborates with regional, national and international agencies on the development and evaluation of health promotion interventions and strategies.

Objectives of the HPRC include:

- The generation and dissemination of health promotion research that is of national and international relevance.
- The translation of research that will lead to the development of healthy public policy and evidence-informed practice.

New Zealand

The Health Promotion Forum (HPF) of New Zealand is the national umbrella organization of over 150 organisations committed to improving health. HPF has worked with The Cancer Society in order to produce a personal development plan for health promoters, which may be helpful to inform personal development reviews, to identify the competencies of individuals and to provide ideas for future development.

The Health Promotion Agency (HPA), formed July 1, 2012, is a Crown institution that has been established under the New Zealand Public Health and Disability Amendment Act 2012. Its board has been appointed by the Minister of Health. The work of HPA is divided into three main areas:

- Promoting the wellbeing and health of the community
- Enabling health promoting initiatives and environments
- Informing the public on health promoting policies and practices

HPA has a variety of programs based around many areas of work, including alcohol, immunisation, mental health, and skin cancer prevention. The agency aims to promote the wellbeing of individuals and encourage healthy lifestyles, prevent disease, illness and injury, enable environments that support health and wellbeing, and to reduce personal, economic and social harm.

Health Workforce New Zealand (HWNZ) is an organisation that is part of the National Health Board which provides national leadership on the development of the health workforce. Some health promotional programs supported by HWNZ include education and training initiatives, and the Voluntary Bonding Scheme, which rewards medical, midwifery and nursing graduates who agree to work in hard-to-staff communities, and sonography, medical physicist and radiation therapy graduates who stay in New Zealand.

Health promotion in New Zealand has become an established approach in addressing public problems since the 1980s, through increasing use of intersectoral action, the use of public policy and mass media as promotional strategies, and the increasing control Maori have taken over the provision and purchase of health promotion services. An example of health promotional initiatives is the action put in place to reduce childhood obesity in primary schools. Research was completed to identify the barriers to improving school food environments and promoting healthy nutrition in primary schools in New Zealand.

Considerable progress has also been made in the health impact assessment (HIA) research on the impact of policies on health in New Zealand. The approach has an important contribution to make in the strengthening of health and wellbeing in policymaking in New Zealand

Sri Lanka

In 2015, the life expectancy of Sri Lankan people was 72 for male and 78 for female. The disease burden has started to shift towards non-communicable diseases related to lifestyle and environmental factors. The 2012 estimated "healthy life expectancy" at birth of all Sri Lanka population is 68 for females, 63 for males, and 65 overall.

The development of the Sri Lankan National Health Promotion Policy is related to the State Policy and Strategy for Health and the Health Master Plan 2007–2016. It emphasises advocacy and empowerment to enable individuals and communities to take control of their own health, as well as improving the management of health promotion interventions across sectors.

United Kingdom

The Royal Society for Public Health was formed in October 2008 by the merger of the Royal Society for the Promotion of Health (also known as the Royal Society of Health or RSH) and the Royal Institute of Public Health (RIPH). Earlier, July 2005 saw the publication by the Department of Health and Welsh Assembly Government of Shaping the Future of Public Health: Promoting Health in the NHS. Following discussions with the Department of Health and Welsh Assembly Government officials, the Royal Society for Public Health and three national public health bodies agreed, in 2006, to work together to take forward the report's recommendations, working in partnership with other organisations. Accordingly:

1. The Royal Society for Public Health (RSPH) leads and hosts the collaboration, and focuses on advocacy for health promotion and its workforce;
2. The Institute of Health Promotion and Education (IHPE) works with the RSPH Royal Society for Public Health to give a voice to the workforce;
3. The Faculty of Public Health (FPH) focuses on professional standards, education and training; and
4. (The UK Public Health Register (UKPHR) is responsible for regulation of the workforce.

In Northern Ireland, the government's Health Promotion Agency for Northern Ireland which was set up to "provide leadership, strategic direction and support, where possible, to all those involved in promoting health in Northern Ireland". The Health Promotion Agency for Northern Ireland was incorporated into the Public Health Agency for Northern Ireland in April 2009.

Recent work in the UK *(Delphi consultation exercise due to be published late 2009 by Royal Society of Public Health and the National Social Marketing Centre)* on relationship between health promotion and social marketing has highlighted and reinforce the potential integrative nature of the approaches. While an independent review (NCC 'It's Our Health!' 2006) identified that some social marketing has in past adopted a narrow or limited approach, the UK has increasingly taken a lead in the discussion and developed a much more integrative and strategic approach which adopts a holistic approach, integrating the learning from effective health promotion approaches with relevant learning from social marketing and other disciplines. A key finding from the Delphi consultation was the need to avoid unnecessary and arbitrary 'methods wars' and instead focus on the issue of 'utility' and harnessing the potential of learning from multiple disciplines and sources. Such an approach is arguably how health promotion has developed over the years pulling in learning from different sectors and disciplines to enhance and develop.

United States

Government agencies in the U.S. concerned with health promotion include the following:

- The Centers for Disease Control and Prevention has a Coordinating Center for Health Promotion whose mission is "Prevent disease, improve health, and enhance human potential through evidence based interventions and research in maternal and child health, chronic disease, disabilities, genomics, and hereditary disorders".
- The National Institute for Occupational Safety and Health has developed Total Worker Health, a strategy incorporating elements of occupational safety and health and health promotion, to advance the health and well-being of employees.

- The United States Army Center for Health Promotion and Preventive Medicine "provide[s] worldwide technical support for implementing preventive medicine, public health, and health promotion/wellness services into all aspects of America's Army and the Army Community".
- Nongovernmental organizations in the U.S. concerned with health promotion include:
- The Public Health Education and Health Promotion Section is an active component of the American Public Health Association.
- The National Commission for Health Education Credentialing offers the NCHEC, a competency-based tool used to measure possession, application and interpretation of knowledge in the Seven Areas of Responsibility for Health Education Specialists. The exam reflects the entry-level Sub-competencies of these Areas of Responsibility.
- The Wellness Council of America is an industry trade group that supports workplace health promotion programs.
- URAC accredits comprehensive wellness programs "that focus on health promotion, chronic disease prevention and health risk reduction".

Health Campaign

A Health campaign is a type of media campaign which attempts to promote public health by making new health interventions available. The organizers of a health campaign frequently use education along with an opportunity to participate further, such as when a vaccination campaign seeks both to educate the public about a vaccine and provide the vaccine to people who want it. When a health campaign has international relevance it may be called a global health campaign.

Examples

Health Education

Many diseases and medical problems have a "health education campaign" or "awareness campaign" associated with them. The goal of such a campaign is to make people conscious of the impact of diseases and to provide them information about the disease if they want to learn more about it.

Eradication of Infectious Diseases

Various health campaigns have taken the goal of eradicating infectious diseases. In such campaigns the organizers recruit the public to participate in the campaign by talking about it with others and encouraging others to participate.

Behavior Modification Campaign

An organization may organize a campaign which asks for participants to change their behavior in some way. Examples of such projects are smoking cessation campaigns which ask people to quit smoking, HIV prevention campaigns which ask people to do things such as use condoms to reduce

HIV infection risk, or exercise campaigns which encourage people to engage in physical activity for health.

Organizations as Campaigns

In some cases the work of an organization may itself be a health campaign. This may happen when, for example, an organization exists to provide health information or medical resources to anyone who requests them. The organization itself may conduct a series of health campaigns, and its entire operation may be called a health campaign.

References

- Stokes, J.; Noren, J.; Shindell, S. (1982-01-01). "Definition of terms and concepts applicable to clinical preventive medicine". Journal of Community Health. 8 (1): 33–41. doi:10.1007/bf01324395. ISSN 0094-5145. PMID 6764783
- Chambers, Ruth; Gill Wakley; Alison Blenkinsopp (2006). Supporting Self Care in Primary Care. Radcliffe Publishing. pp. 15, 101, 105. ISBN 1846190703. Retrieved 29 August 2013
- "Politically Active? 4 Tips for Incorporating Self-Care, US News". US News. 27 February 2017. Retrieved 5 March 2017
- Rogers, R. W. (1983). Preventive health psychology: An interface of social and clinical psychology. Journal of Social and Clinical Psychology, 1(2), 120-127. doi:10.1521/jscp.1983.1.2.120
- Mertig, Rita G. (2012). Nurses' Guide to Teaching Diabetes Self-management. Springer Publishing Company. p. 240. ISBN 0826108288. Retrieved 30 August 2013
- Dominic Tyer (28 August 2013). "UK preparing self-care portal for patients". PMLive. PMGroup Worldwide Ltd. Retrieved 31 August 2013
- Ilies, R., Dimotakis, N., & Watson, D. (2010). Mood, blood pressure, and heart rate at work: An experience-sampling study. Journal of Occupational Health Psychology, 15(2), 120-130. doi:10.1037/a0018350
- Ziguras, Christopher (2013). Self-care: Embodiment, Personal Autonomy and the Shaping of Health Consciousness. Routledge. pp. 14–15. ISBN 1134419694. Retrieved 31 August 2013
- Prevention, Centers for Disease Control and. "CDC - Workplace Health - Implementation - Physical Activity". www.cdc.gov. Retrieved 2015-09-27
- Marmot, M.G. & Theorell, T. (1988). Social class and cardiovascular disease: The contribution of work. International Journal of Health Services, 18, 659–74
- Palo Stoller, Eleanor (1998). Ory,, Marcia G.; DeFriese, Gordon H., eds. Self-care in Later Life: Research, Program, and Policy Issues. Springer Publishing Company. pp. 24–25. ISBN 0826196950. Retrieved 28 August 2013
- Health, Department of (8 August 2014). "Healthy Active". Stephanie Alexander Kitchen Garden National Program. Australian Government. Retrieved 7 April 2015
- Kompier, M.A.J.; Aust, B.; van den Berg, A.-M. & Siegrist, J. (2000). Stress prevention in bus drivers: Evaluation of 13 natural experiments. Journal of Occupational Health Psychology, 5, 32–47
- Laurin, Jacqualine (1994). "Commentary". In Kikuchi, June F.; Simmons, Helen. Developing a Philosophy of Nursing. Sage. p. 27. ISBN 0803954239. Retrieved 31 August 2013
- Health, Department of (12 August 2009). "Healthy Active". Healthy Spaces and Places. Australian Government. Retrieved 7 April 2015

2

Factors Affecting Health

Various factors such as habitat, food habits, physical activity, alcohol dependence, etc. can impact health both positively and negatively. An individual's socio-economic status and income can point to their quality of life, which plays an important part in health as well as access to health care. The section strategically encompasses and incorporates the major factors that affect health, providing a complete understanding of the subject matter.

Socioeconomic Status

Socioeconomic status (SES) is an economic and sociological combined total measure of a person's work experience and of an individual's or family's economic and social position in relation to others, based on income, education, and occupation. When analyzing a family's SES, the household income, earners' education, and occupation are examined, as well as combined income, whereas for an individual's SES only their own attributes are assessed. However, SES is more commonly used to depict an economic difference in society as a whole.

An 1880 painting by Jean-Eugène Buland showing a stark contrast in socioeconomic status

Socioeconomic status is typically broken into three levels (high, middle, and low) to describe the three places a family or an individual may fall into. When placing a family or individual into one of these categories, any or all of the three variables (income, education, and occupation) can be assessed.

Additionally, low income and education have been shown to be strong predictors of a range of physical and mental health problems, including respiratory viruses, arthritis, coronary disease, and schizophrenia. These problems may be due to environmental conditions in their workplace, or, in the case of mental illnesses, may be the entire cause of that person's social predicament to begin with.

Education in higher socioeconomic families is typically stressed as much more important, both within the household as well as the local community. In poorer areas, where food, shelter and safety are priority, education can take a backseat. Youth audiences are particularly at risk for many health and social problems in the United States, such as unwanted pregnancies, drug abuse, and obesity.

Main Factors

Income

Income refers to wages, salaries, profits, rents, and any flow of earnings received. Income can also come in the form of unemployment or worker's compensation, social security, pensions, interests or dividends, royalties, trusts, alimony, or other governmental, public, or family financial assistance.

Income can be looked at in two terms, relative and absolute. Absolute income, as theorized by economist John Maynard Keynes, is the relationship in which as income increases, so will consumption, but not at the same rate. Relative income dictates a person or family's savings and consumption based on the family's income in relation to others. Income is a commonly used measure of SES because it is relatively easy to figure for most individuals.

Income inequality is most commonly measured around the world by the Gini coefficient, where 0 corresponds to perfect equality and 1 means perfect inequality. Low income families focus on meeting immediate needs and do not accumulate wealth that could be passed on to future generations, thus increasing inequality. Families with higher and expendable income can accumulate wealth and focus on meeting immediate needs while being able to consume and enjoy luxuries and weather crises.

Education

Education also plays a role in income. Median earnings increase with each level of education. As conveyed in the chart, the highest degrees, professional and doctoral degrees, make the highest weekly earnings while those without a high school diploma earn less. Higher levels of education are associated with better economic and psychological outcomes (i.e.: more income, more control, and greater social support and networking).

Education plays a major role in skill sets for acquiring jobs, as well as specific qualities that stratify people with higher SES from lower SES. Annette Lareau speaks on the idea of concerted cultivation, where middle class parents take an active role in their children's education and development by using controlled organized activities and fostering a sense of entitlement through encouraged discussion. Laureau argues that families with lower income do not participate in this movement, causing their children to have a sense of constraint. An interesting observation that studies have noted is that parents from lower SES households are more likely to give orders to their children in their interactions while parents with a higher SES are more likely to interact and play with their children. A division in education attainment is thus born out of these two differences in child rearing. Research has shown how children who are born in lower SES households have weaker language skills compared to children raised in higher SES households. These language skills affect their abilities to learn and thus exacerbate the problem of education disparity between low and high SES neighborhoods. Lower income families can have children who do not succeed to the levels of the middle income children, who can have a greater sense of entitlement, be more argumentative, or be better prepared for adult life.

Research shows that lower SES students have lower and slower academic achievement as compared with students of higher SES. When teachers make judgments about students based on their class and SES, they are taking the first step in preventing students from having an equal opportunity for academic achievement. Educators need to help overcome the stigma of poverty. A student of low SES and low self-esteem should not be reinforced by educators. Teachers need to view students as individuals and not as a member of an SES group. Teachers looking at students in this manner will help them to not be prejudiced towards students of certain SES groups. Raising the level of instruction can help to create equality in student achievement. Teachers relating the content taught to students' prior knowledge and relating it to real world experiences can improve achievement. Educators also need to be open and discuss class and SES differences. It is important that all are educated, understand, and be able to speak openly about SES.

Occupation

Occupational prestige, as one component of SES, encompasses both income and educational attainment. Occupational status reflects the educational attainment required to obtain the job and income levels that vary with different jobs and within ranks of occupations. Additionally, it shows achievement in skills required for the job. Occupational status measures social position by describing job characteristics, decision making ability and control, and psychological demands on the job. Most of all it is the direct reflection of once country.

Occupations are ranked by the Census (among other organizations) and opinion polls from the general population are surveyed. Some of the most prestigious occupations are physicians and surgeons, lawyers, chemical and biomedical engineers, university professors, and communications analysts. These jobs, considered to be grouped in the high SES classification, provide more challenging work and greater control over working conditions but require more ability. The jobs with lower rankings include food preparation workers, counter attendants, bartenders and helpers, dishwashers, janitors, maids and housekeepers, vehicle cleaners, and parking lot attendants. The jobs that are less valued also offer significantly lower wages, and often are more laborious, very hazardous, and provide less autonomy.

Occupation is the most difficult factor to measure because so many exist, and there are so many competing scales. Many scales rank occupations based on the level of skill involved, from unskilled to skilled manual labor to professional, or use a combined measure using the education level needed and income involved.

In sum, the majority of researchers agree that income, education and occupation together best represent SES, while some others feel that changes in family structure should also be considered. With the definition of SES more clearly defined, it is now important to discuss the effects of SES on students' cognitive abilities and academic success. Several researchers have found that SES affects students' abilities.

Other Variables

Wealth

Wealth, a set of economic reserves or assets, presents a source of security providing a measure of a household's ability to meet emergencies, absorb economic shocks, or provide the means to live comfortably. Wealth reflects intergenerational transitions as well as accumulation of income and savings.

Income, age, marital status, family size, religion, occupation, and education are all predictors for wealth attainment.

The wealth gap, like income inequality, is very large in the United States. There exists a racial wealth gap due in part to income disparities and differences in achievement resulting from institutional discrimination. According to Thomas Shapiro, differences in savings (due to different rates of incomes), inheritance factors, and discrimination in the housing market lead to the racial wealth gap. Shapiro claims that savings increase with increasing income, but African Americans cannot participate in this, because they make significantly less than Americans of European descent (whites). Additionally, rates of inheritance dramatically differ between African Americans and Americans of European descent. The amount a person inherits, either during a lifetime or after death, can create different starting points between two different individuals or families. These different starting points also factor into housing, education, and employment discrimination. A third reason Shapiro offers for the racial wealth gap are the various discriminations African Americans must face, like redlining and higher interest rates in the housing market. These types of discrimination feed into the other reasons why African Americans end up having different starting points and therefore fewer assets.

Effects

Health

Recently, there has been increasing interest from epidemiologists on the subject of economic inequality and its relation to the health of populations. Socioeconomic status is an important source of health inequity, as there is a very robust positive correlation between socioeconomic status and health, other than for male homosexuals . This correlation suggests that it is not only the poor who tend to be sick when everyone else is healthy, but that there is a continual gradient, from the top to the bottom of the socio-economic ladder, relating status to health. Parents with a low socioeconomic status cannot afford many of the health care resources which is the reason that their children may have a more advanced illness because of the lack of treatment. This phenomenon is often called the "SES Gradient" or according to the World Health Organisation the "Social Gradient". Lower socioeconomic status has been linked to chronic stress, heart disease, ulcers, type 2 diabetes, rheumatoid arthritis, certain types of cancer, and premature aging.

There is debate regarding the cause of the SES Gradient. Researchers see a definite link between economic status and mortality due to the greater economic resources of the wealthy, but they find little correlation due to social status differences.

Other researchers such as Richard G. Wilkinson, J. Lynch, and G.A. Kaplan have found that socioeconomic status strongly affects health even when controlling for economic resources and access to health care. Most famous for linking social status with health are the Whitehall studies—a series of studies conducted on civil servants in London. The studies found that although all civil servants in England have the same access to health care, there was a strong correlation between social status and health. The studies found that this relationship remained strong even when controlling for health-affecting habits such as exercise, smoking and drinking. Furthermore, it has been noted that no amount of medical attention will help decrease the likelihood of someone getting type 2 diabetes or rheumatoid arthritis—yet both more common among populations with lower socioeconomic status. there is no significant relationship between SES and stress during pregnancy, while there is a significant relationship between husband's occupational status Also, there is not significant relationship between income and mother's education and the rate of pregnancy stress.

Political Participation

Political scientists have established a consistent relationship between SES and political participation.

Psychological

Home Environment

The environment of low SES children is characterized by less dialogue from parents, minimal amounts of book reading, and few instances of joint attention, the shared focus of the child and adult on the same object or event, when compared to the environment of high SES children. In contrast, infants from high SES families experience more child-directed speech. At 10 months, children of high SES hear on average 400 more words than their low SES peers.

Language ability differs sharply as a function of SES, for example, the average vocabulary size of 3-year-old children from professional families was more than twice as large as for those on welfare.

Children from lower income households had greater media access in their bedrooms but lower access to portable play equipment compared to higher income children. This eventually leads children from lower socioeconomic backgrounds to be at a disadvantage when comparing them with their counterparts in terms of access to physical activities.

Parental Interactions

In addition to the amount of language input from parents, SES heavily influences the type of parenting style a family chooses to practice. These different parenting styles shape the tone and purpose of verbal interactions between parent and child. For example, parents of high SES tend toward more authoritative or permissive parenting styles. These parents pose more open-ended questions to their children to encourage the latter's speech growth. In contrast, parents of low SES tend toward more authoritarian styles of address. Their conversations with their children contain more imperatives and yes/no questions that inhibits child responses and speech development.

Parental differences in addressing children may be traced to the position of their respective groups within society. Working class individuals often hold low power, subordinate positions in the occupational world. This standing in the social hierarchy requires a personality and interaction style that is relational and capable of adjusting to circumstances. An authoritarian style of address prepares children for these types of roles, which require a more accommodating and compliant personality. Therefore, low SES parents see the family as more hierarchical, with the parents at the top of the power structure, which shapes verbal interaction. This power differential emulates the circumstances of the working class world, where individuals are ranked and discouraged from questioning authority.

Conversely, high SES individuals occupy high power positions that call for greater expressivity. High SES parents encourage their children to question the world around them. In addition to asking their children more questions, these parents push their children to create questions of their own. In contrast with low SES parents, these individuals often view the power disparity between parent and child as detrimental to the family. Opting instead to treat children as equals, high SES conversations are characterized by a give and take between parent and child. These interactions help prepare these children for occupations that require greater expressivity.

Disparities in Language Acquisition

The linguistic environment of low and high SES children differs substantially, which affects many aspects of language and literacy development such as semantics, syntax, morphology, and phonology.

Semantics

Semantics is the study of the meaning of words and phrases. Semantics covers vocabulary, which is affected by SES. Children of high SES have larger expressive vocabularies by the age of 24 months due to more efficient processing of familiar words. By age 3, there are significant differences in the amount of dialogue and vocabulary growth between children of low and high SES. A lack of joint attention in children contributes to poor vocabulary growth when compared to their high SES peers. Joint attention and book reading are important factors that affect children's vocabulary growth. With joint attention, a child and adult can focus on the same object, allowing the child to map out words. For example, a child sees an animal running outside and the mom points to it and says, "Look, a dog." The child will focus its attention to where its mother is pointing and map the word dog to the pointed animal. Joint attention thus facilitates word learning for children.

Syntax

Syntax refers to the arrangement of words and phrases to form sentences. SES affects the production of sentence structures. Although 22- to 44-month-old children's production of simple sentence structures does not vary by SES, low SES does contribute to difficulty with complex sentence structures. Complex sentences include sentences that have more than one verb phrase. An example of a complex sentence is, "I want you to sit there". The emergence of simple sentence structures is seen as a structure that is obligatory in everyday speech. Complex sentence structures are optional and can only be mastered if the environment fosters its development.

This lag in the sentence formation abilities of low SES children may be caused by less frequent exposure to complex syntax through parental speech. Low SES parents ask fewer response-coaxing questions of their children which limits the opportunities of these children to practice more complex speech patterns. Instead, these parents give their children more direct orders, which has been found to negatively influence the acquisition of more difficult noun and verb phrases. In contrast, high SES households ask their children broad questions to cultivate speech development. Exposure to more questions positively contributes to children's vocabulary growth and complex noun phrase constructions.

Morphology

Children's grasp of morphology, the study of how words are formed, is affected by SES. Children of high SES have advantages in applying grammatical rules, such as the pluralization of nouns and adjectives compared to children of low SES. Pluralizing nouns consists of understanding that some nouns are regular and -s denotes more than one, but also understanding how to apply different rules to irregular nouns. Learning and understanding how to use plural rules is an important tool in conversation and writing. In order to communicate successfully that there is more than one dog running down the street, an -s must be added to dog. Research also finds that the gap in ability to pluralize nouns and adjectives does not diminish by age or schooling because low SES children's reaction times to pluralize nouns and adjectives do not decrease.

Phonology

Phonological awareness, the ability to recognize that words are made up different sound units, is also affected by SES. Children of low SES between the second and sixth grades are found to have low phonological awareness. The gap in phonological awareness increases by grade level. This gap is even more problematic if children of low SES are already born with low levels of phonological awareness and their environment does not foster its growth. Children who are have high phonological awareness from an early age are not affected by SES.

Positive Outcomes of Low SES

Given the large amount of research on the set backs children of low SES face, there is a push by child developmental researchers to steer research to a more positive direction regarding low SES. The goal is to highlight the strengths and assets low income families possess in raising children. For example, African American preschoolers of low SES exhibit strengths in oral narrative, or storytelling, that may promote later success in reading. These children have better narrative comprehension when compared to peers of higher SES.

Literacy Development

A gap in reading growth exists between low SES and high SES children, which widens as children move on to higher grades. Reading assessments that test reading growth include measures on basic reading skills (i.e., print familiarity, letter recognition, beginning and ending sounds, rhyming sounds, word recognition), vocabulary (receptive vocabulary), and reading comprehension skills (i.e., listening comprehension, words in context). The reading growth gap is apparent between the spring of kindergarten and the spring of first-grade, the time when children rely more on the school for reading growth and less on their parents. Initially, high SES children begin as better readers than their low SES counterparts. As children get older, high SES children progress more rapidly in reading growth rates than low SES children. These early reading outcomes affect later academic success. The further children fall behind, the more difficult it is to catch up and the more likely they will continue to fall behind. By the time students enter high school in the United States, low SES children are considerably behind their high SES peers in reading growth.

Home Environment

Home environment is one of the leading factors of a child's well being. Children living in a poor home with inadequate living conditions are more likely to be immune to illness and injuries. The disparities in experiences in the home environment children of high and low SES affect reading outcomes. The home environment is considered the main contributor to SES reading outcomes. Children of low SES status are read to less often and have fewer books in the home than their high SES peers, which suggests an answer to why children of low SES status have lower initial reading scores than their high SES counterparts upon entering kindergarten.

The home environment makes the largest contribution to the prediction of initial kindergarten reading disparities. Characteristics of the home environment include home literacy environment and parental involvement in school. Home literacy environment is characterized by the frequency with which parents engage in joint book reading with the child, the frequency with which children read books outside of school, and the frequency with which household members visited the library with the child. Parental involvement in school is characterized by attending a parent–teacher conference, attending a parent–teacher association (PTA) meeting, attending an open house, volunteering, participating in fundraising, and attending a school event. Resources, experiences, and relationships associated with the family are most closely associated with reading gaps when students reading levels are first assessed in kindergarten. The influence of family factors on initial reading level may be due to children experiencing little schooling before kindergarten—they mainly have their families to rely on their reading growth.

Family SES is also associated with reading achievement growth during the summer. Students from high SES families continue to grow in their ability to read after kindergarten and students from low SES families fall behind in their reading growth at a comparable amount. Additionally, the summer setback disproportionately affects African American and Hispanic students because they are more likely than White students to come from low SES families. Also, low SES families typically lack the appropriate resources to continue reading growth when school is not in session.

Neighborhood Influence

The neighborhood setting in which children grow up in contributes to reading disparities between low and high SES children. These neighborhood qualities include but are not limited to garbage or litter in the street, individuals selling or using drugs in the street, burglary or robbery in the area, violent crime in the area, vacant homes in the area, and how safe it is to play in the neighborhood. Low SES children are more likely to grow up in such neighborhood conditions than their high SES peers. Community support for the school and poor physical conditions surrounding the school are also associated with children's reading. Neighborhood factors help explain the variation in reading scores in school entry, and especially as children move on to higher grades. As low SES children in poor neighborhood environments get older, they fall further behind their high SES peers in reading growth and thus have a more difficult time developing reading skills at grade level.

In a study by M. Keels, it was determined that when low-income families are moved from poor neighborhoods to suburban neighborhoods, there are reductions in delinquency in children. When comparing different social statuses of families, the environment of a neighborhood turns out to be major factor in contributing to the growth of a child.

School Influence

School characteristics, including characteristics of peers and teachers, contribute to reading disparities between low and high SES children. For instance, peers play a role in influencing early reading proficiency. In low SES schools, there are higher concentrations of less skilled, lower SES, and minority peers who have lower gains in reading. The number of children reading below grade and the presence of low-income peers were consistently associated with initial achievement and growth rates. Low SES peers tend to have limited skills and fewer economic resources than high SES children, which makes it difficult for children to grow in their reading ability. The most rapid growth of reading ability happens between the spring of kindergarten and the spring of first grade. Teacher experience (number of years teaching at a particular school and the number of years teaching a particular grade level), teacher preparation to teach (based on the number of courses taken on early education, elementary education, and child development), the highest degree earned, and the number of courses taken on teaching reading all determine whether or not a reading teacher is qualified. Low SES students are more likely to have less qualified teachers, which is associated with their reading growth rates being significantly lower than the growth rates of their high SES counterparts.

Influences on Nonverbal Behavior

Michael Kraus and Dacher Keltner, in their study published in the December 2008 issue of *Psychological Science,* found that children of parents with a high SES tended to express more disengagement behaviors than their peers of low SES. In this context, disengagement behaviors included self-grooming, fidgeting with nearby objects, and doodling while being addressed. In contrast, engagement behaviors included head nods, eyebrow raises, laughter and gazes at one's partner. These cues indicated an interest in one's partner and the desire to deepen and enhance the relationship. Participants of low SES tended to express more engagement behaviors toward their conversational partners, while their high SES counterparts displayed more disengagement behaviors. Authors hypothesized that, as SES rises, the capacity to fulfill one's needs also increases. This may lead to greater feelings of independence, making individuals of high SES less inclined to gain rapport with conversational partners because they are less likely to need their assistance in the future.

Impact of Inequality and its Effects on Health

In this section we will consider the impact of inequality and its effects on health. Both financial and social inequality affect health – the effects of socio-economic status and income inequality will be covered in this lesson and in the following lesson discrimination and the effect of neighborhoods will be considered.

In this lesson we will cover the meaning and measurement of SES and the limitations of this measure. We will also look at the indices of inequality and the factors influencing health in low and high income countries.

A general pattern indicates that higher socioeconomic status (SES) is associated with better health, across time periods.

SES determines the position that individuals or groups occupy in the structure of society. SES demarcates society.

From a Marxian perspective class was determined by the ownership of capital and was characterized by an exploitative relationship between the owners of capital and those who provided labor. This is a dichotomous model.

Webber emphasized the distribution of opportunities linked to production and social honor or privilege that was independent of wealth. Social honor was linked to life style or people sharing a way of life. These opportunities determined peoples "life chances" which they could improve by collective bargaining or obtaining more skills and knowledge.

The Functionalists approach to class is that it is a natural and necessary feature of a complex society. The Functionalist view of inequality is that it is the result of "natural" forces and an indirect legitimizing of it.

The Implications of SES

SES determines lifestyles, Bourdieu (1984))(as cited in Lynch & Kaplan(2000) indicates how class is related to home décor, taste in music, food, opinions on art and desirable vacations. Thus diet and exercise and health seeking behaviors and definitely psycho social factors would necessarily also be influenced by class. Class is a pervasive influence like a lens through which you perceive the world.

The kind of resources that are available to one across ones lifetime often gets determined by class – often there is movement up and down between SES - movement down through loss of employment or retirement or illness or a accident or disaster. Upward mobility is through better jobs, opening up of the economy, better pay packages. In India the educated class has benefited from the opening up of the economy but not the uneducated class - who may have benefited marginally but in fact after liberalization – the gap between the haves and have nots has only widened. The haves or the middle class are now routinely going for foreign vacations, owning cars and buying designer clothing and branded merchandise that they never did previously.There were fewer choices available and people did not flaunt their wealth.

How is SES Measured?

The usual convention in research studies is to take a composite of income, education and occupation as a measure of SES.

Education is indicative of a privilege – a postponement of earning a living, indicative of the time and money that is available to allow people to defer earning a living. It reflects parents SES.

It is a transition from childhood to adulthood – it determines future occupation and income.

Education is usually measured as number of years of education. Although this is a conventional unit of measurement – there are certain problems with it.

- For quantity does not imply quality.
- The value of a certain education/degree in a certain culture and context may vary (for e.g. a law degree vs an engineering degree in India versus the U.S.).
- The economic returns of education may vary, some degrees having more value.
- The returns may vary according to race, ethnic and gender groups (Lynch & Kaplan, 2000).

In a stagnant society education has different implications (value knowledge for its own sake) and in a booming economy it has different implications (applied disciplines like engineering or certain techniques become valued e.g. computer applications) – there is an opportunity for upward mobility (Lynch & Kaplan,2000).

Employment creates a structure in people's lives. The lack of employment also creates a different structure. Work is a link between education and income.

Work environments vary in terms of exposure to hazardous factors – some jobs in mines or mills or nuclear plants or dump sites can be very dangerous and there is an exposure to toxins. Heat, dust, pollutants, physical stress, radiation or the probability of accidents may be part of the work environment. The mental stress of a job also has to be considered.Some jobs come with health care or health insurance like government jobs in India, which greatly improves access to health care. Women often bear the domestic burden in addition to a paid job.

Income is directly related to access to resources and material conditions, income has a documented relationship with life expectancy. Type of housing, location, food, quality and access to medical care.

The public health approach that arose in the 19th century due to the working conditions in the aftermath of the industrial revolution emphasized, clean water, shelter, adequate calories and waste removal.

Now however these basic material conditions do not determine the differences in life expectancy and health between social classes. Rather the differences may be attributed to finer gradations of material conditions such as access to cars, home ownership, a home with a garden and healthier food (Davey Smith et al 1990, Macintyre et al, 1998, Blane et al 1997 as cited in Lynch & Kaplan,2000).

In India however the basics are still relevant as many groups do not have access to them – for e.g a slum population or certain rural populations. The finer material condition differences are also relevant between the lower middle class and the upper middle class.

Shelter can be very basic to a comfortable house with a garden. Slums have tin sheet roofs that make the room into a furnace in the summer. In the rainy season the drain water mixes with the rain water spreading filth everywhere.

2000 calories can be made up of vada pav and dal chaval or a variety of fruits and vegetables and fish and chicken.

So it is not just Roti, Kapda aur Makan – however for the basics that will do with sanitation.

In Finland (Lynch et al, 1997 as cited in Lynch & Kaplan, 2000) men in low paying jobs were the most disadvantaged in terms of material resources, job insecurity, experienced more work injuries. They also tended to smoke more, get drunk more often, eat less nutritious foods and have a hostile despairing attitude.

Those groups with the lowest disposable incomes are the most exposed to multiple stressors.

Limitations

Studies that measure income at one point in time fail to capture health effects of sustained exposure of being in an income group or consider transitions in and out of income groups.

In the 45- 65 year group income reduces more steeply for those who do not have stable employment such as laborers.

Income is not the same as Wealth. Income affects access to resources but wealth is an accumulation of assets that also determines exposure to resources over and above income. Households with similar incomes may vary in terms of wealth and this is especially true for racial and ethnic groups or caste groups for India. For e.g. house ownership or membership in a club that is inherited or just inherited money as fixed deposits or shares. Liquid assets are more useful during hospitalization. Wealth is a buffer in an emergency.

Thus though many studies control for SES – this is a false effect as wealth is not being considered.

A lifecourse perspective that measures the cumulative effects from pre natal conditions and birth to infancy and childhood to adulthood and old age of exposures to harmful conditions and deprivations will be more effective in capturing the impact of SES. Lynch & Kaplan, 2000). Before birth intrauterine conditions involve maternal nutrition and exposure to toxins, during infancy and childhood, nutrition, access to healthcare & loving care are important for healthy development, during adulthood work environment (exposure to toxins, stress) and addictions (alcohol, tobacco) can lead to health problems and in old age wealth and access to good quality health care determine health outcomes .

Income Level of the Country

Do the high income countries have better health indicators than the low income countries?

That is not always the case for often countries in the low and middle income category have better health indicators than the high income countries and is reflective of their health spending and policies. For eg Cuba and Costa Rica have high life expectancy and are ranked high in terms of health indicators being low income countries whereas the U.S. ranks lower among industrialized countries.

Cuba has a public health system with universal health coverage whereas the U.S. has privatized health care and health insurance is offered as part of job benefits however many people who work part time or for minimum wage do not get health insurance and do not qualify for medicaid (the coverage for the poor) they fall thru the cracks.

There are coefficients that reflect income equality for a country. One of them is the Gini coefficient which ranges from 0 indicating perfect equality to 1 indicating perfect inequality.

The Robin Hood Index can be interpreted as the proportion of aggregate income that must be re-distributed from rich to poor households in order to maintain perfect equality.

The Robin Hood Index for India would be very high. The Robin Hood Index is more sensitive than the Gini coefficient and in a study by Kennedy et al (1996) (as cited in Kawachi, 2000) higher RHI was related to higher mortality including childhood mortality and homicide. In this study across the 50 US states a 1% increase in RHI was reflected in excess mortality of 21.7 deaths per 100,000. Thus even small reductions in inequality may have valuable public health outcomes.

RHI has also been correlated with self reported health (Kawachi et al, 1997 as cited in Kawachi, 2000).

In a study of 44 countries over 6 time periods by Asafu Adjaye (2002) it was found that level of income, inequality and education all impacted health. Among low income countries income in-equality had a greater effect because in low income countries the basics and access to health care get determined by income level whereas in the higher income countries the basics are provided for all. Also the level of savings were related to health status in low income countries – this highlights the lack of health coverage in these countries and private health care which swallows the savings.

Discrimination

In human social affairs, discrimination is treatment or consideration of, or making a distinction in favor of or against, a person or thing based on the group, class, or category to which the person or thing is perceived to belong rather than on individual attributes. This includes treatment of an individual or group, based on their actual or perceived membership in a certain group or social category, "in a way that is worse than the way people are usually treated". It involves the group's initial reaction or interaction going on to influence the individual's actual behavior towards the group leader or the group, restricting members of one group from opportunities or privileges that are available to another group, leading to the exclusion of the individual or entities based on logical or irrational decision making.

Discriminatory traditions, policies, ideas, practices, and laws exist in many countries and institutions in every part of the world, even in ones where discrimination is generally looked down upon. In some places, controversial attempts such as quotas have been used to benefit those believed to be current or past victims of discrimination—but have sometimes been called reverse discrimination. In the US, a government policy known as affirmative action was instituted to encourage employers and universities to seek out and accept groups such as African Americans and women, who have been subject to discrimination for a long time.

Etymology

The term *discriminate* appeared in the early 17th century in the English language. It is from the Latin *discriminat-* 'distinguished between', from the verb *discriminare,* from *discrimen* 'distinction', from the verb *discernere.* Since the American Civil War the term "discrimination" generally evolved in American English usage as an understanding of prejudicial treatment of an individual based solely on their race, later generalized as membership in a certain socially undesirable group or social category. "Discrimination" derives from Latin, where the verb *discrimire* means "to separate, to distinguish, to make a distinction".

Definitions

Moral philosophers have defined discrimination as *disadvantageous* treatment or consideration. This is a comparative definition. An individual need not be actually harmed in order to be discriminated against. They just need to be treated *worse* than others for some arbitrary reason. If someone decides to donate to help orphan children, but decides to donate less, say, to black children out of a racist attitude, then they would be acting in a discriminatory way despite the fact the people they discriminate against actually benefit by receiving a donation. In addition to this discrimination develops into a source of oppression. It is similar to the action of recognizing someone as 'different' so much that they are treated inhumanly and degraded.

Based on realistic-conflict theory and social-identity theory, Rubin and Hewstone have highlighted a distinction among three types of discrimination:

1. *Realistic competition* is driven by self-interest and is aimed at obtaining material resources (e.g., food, territory, customers) for the in-group (e.g., favouring an in-group in order to obtain more resources for its members, including the self).
2. *Social competition* is driven by the need for self-esteem and is aimed at achieving a positive social status for the in-group relative to comparable out-groups (e.g., favouring an in-group in order to make it better than an out-group).
3. *Consensual discrimination* is driven by the need for accuracy and reflects stable and legitimate intergroup status hierarchies (e.g., favouring a high-status in-group because it is high status).

The United Nations stance on discrimination includes the statement: "Discriminatory behaviors take many forms, but they all involve some form of exclusion or rejection." International bodies United Nations Human Rights Council work towards helping ending discrimination around the world.

United Nations Documents

Important UN documents addressing discrimination include:

- The Universal Declaration of Human Rights is a declaration adopted by the United Nations General Assembly on 10 December 1948. It states that:" *Everyone is entitled to all the rights and freedoms set forth in this Declaration, without distinction of any kind, such as race, colour, sex, language, religion, political or other opinion, national or social origin, property, birth or other status.*"
- The International Convention on the Elimination of All Forms of Racial Discrimination (ICERD) is a United Nations convention. The Convention commits its members to the elimination of racial discrimination. The convention was adopted and opened for signature by the United Nations General Assembly on 21 December 1965, and entered into force on 4 January 1969.

- The Convention on the Elimination of All Forms of Discrimination against Women (CEDAW) is an international treaty adopted in 1979 by the United Nations General Assembly. Described as an international bill of rights for women, it came into force on 3 September 1981.
- The Convention on the Rights of Persons with Disabilities is an international human rights instrument treaty of the United Nations. Parties to the Convention are required to promote, protect, and ensure the full enjoyment of human rights by persons with disabilities and ensure that they enjoy full equality under the law. The text was adopted by the United Nations General Assembly on 13 December 2006, and opened for signature on 30 March 2007. Following ratification by the 20th party, it came into force on 3 May 2008.

Types

Age

Ageism or age discrimination is discrimination and stereotyping based on the grounds of someone's age. It is a set of beliefs, norms, and values which used to justify discrimination or subordination based on a person's age. Ageism is most often directed towards old people, or adolescents and children.

Age discrimination in hiring has been shown to exist in the United States. Joanna Lahey, professor at The Bush School of Government and Public Service at Texas A&M, found that firms are more than 40% more likely to interview a young adult job applicant than an older job applicant. In Europe, Stijn Baert, Jennifer Norga, Yannick Thuy and Marieke Van Hecke, researchers at Ghent University, measured comparable ratio's in Belgium. Interestingly, they found that age discrimination is heterogeneous by the activity older candidates undertook during their additional post-educational years. In Belgium, they are only discriminated if they have more years of inactivity or irrelevant employment.

In a survey for the University of Kent, England, 29% of respondents stated that they had suffered from age discrimination. This is a higher proportion than for gender or racial discrimination. Dominic Abrams, social psychology professor at the university, concluded that ageism is the most pervasive form of prejudice experienced in the UK population.

Caste

According to UNICEF and Human Rights Watch, caste discrimination affects an estimated 250 million people worldwide. Discrimination based on caste, as perceived by UNICEF, is prevalent mainly in parts of Asia, (India, Sri Lanka, Bangladesh, China, Pakistan, Nepal, Japan), Africa and others. As of 2011, there were 200 million Dalits or Scheduled Castes (formerly known as "untouchables") in India.

Disability

Discrimination against people with disabilities in favor of people who are not is called ableism or disablism. Disability discrimination, which treats non-disabled individuals as the standard of 'normal living', results in public and private places and services, education, and social work that are built to serve 'standard' people, thereby excluding those with various disabilities. Studies have shown, employment is needed to not only provide a living but to sustain mental health and well-being. Work fulfils a number of basic needs for an individual such as collective purpose, social contact, status, and activity. A person with a disability is often found to be socially isolated and work is one way to reduce isolation.

In the United States, the Americans with Disabilities Act mandates the provision of equality of access to both buildings and services and is paralleled by similar acts in other countries, such as the Equality Act 2010 in the UK.

Employment

Ethiopian Jews protest in Israel over non-employment of Ethiopian academics.

Denying someone employment, or disallowing one from applying for a job, is often recognized as employment discrimination when the grounds for such an exclusion is not related to the requirements of the position, and protected characteristics may include age, disability, ethnicity, gender, gender identity, height, nationality, political affiliation, religion, sexual orientation, skin color, and weight.

The United States federal laws that protect against:

- Race, color and national origin discrimination include the Civil Rights Act of 1964, Executive Order Number 11478 among other numerous laws that protect people from race, color and national origin discrimination.
- Sex and gender discrimination include the Civil Rights Act of 1964 and Equal Pay Act of 1963.
- Age discrimination include the Age Discrimination in Employment Act of 1967.
- Physical and mental disability discrimination include the Americans with Disabilities Act of 1990.
- Religious discrimination include the Civil Rights Act of 1964.
- Military status discrimination include the Vietnam Era Veterans' Readjustment Assistance Act of 1974

Most other western nations have similar laws protecting these groups.

Still unrelated to the requirements of the position, only 9% of Chief Financial Officers (CFOs) are women while they are over 60% among accountants and auditors. According to a 2013 report, those who reach a high responsibility position are paid on average 16% lower than their male colleagues.

Language

Nationalists on Corsica sometimes spray-paint or shoot traffic signs in French.

Diversity of language is protected and respected by most nations who value cultural diversity. However, people are sometimes subjected to different treatment because their preferred language is associated with a particular group, class or category. Notable examples are the Anti-French sentiment in the United States as well as the Anti-Quebec sentiment in Canada targeting people who speak the French language. Commonly, the preferred language is just another attribute of separate ethnic groups.Discrimination exists if there is prejudicial treatment against a person or a group of people who speak a particular language or dialect.

Language discrimination is suggested to be labeled linguicism or logocism.Anti-discriminatory and inclusive efforts to accommodate persons who speak different languages or cannot have fluency in the country's predominant or "official" language, is bilingualism such as official documents in two languages, and multiculturalism in more than two languages.

Nationality

Discrimination on the basis of nationality is usually included in employment laws. It is sometimes referred to as bound together with racial discrimination although it can be separate. It may vary from laws that stop refusals of hiring based on nationality, asking questions regarding origin, to prohibitions of firing, forced retirement, compensation and pay, etc., based on nationality.

Discrimination on the basis of nationality may show as a "level of acceptance" in a sport or work team regarding new team members and employees who differ from the nationality of the majority of team members.

In the UAE and other GCC states, for instance, nationality is not frequently given to residents and expatriates. In the workplace, preferential treatment is given to full citizens, even though many of them lack experience or motivation to do the job. State benefits are also generally available for citizens only.

Race or Ethnicity

Racial and ethnic discrimination differentiates individuals on the basis of real and perceived racial and ethnic differences and leads to various forms of ethnic penalty. It has been official government policy in several countries, such as South Africa in the apartheid era. Discriminatory policies towards ethnic minorities include the race-based discrimination of ethnic Indians and Chinese in Malaysia After the Vietnam war, many Vietnamese refugees moved to the United States, where they face discrimination.

Anti-Arab sign in Pattaya Beach, Thailand

German warning in Germany-occupied Poland 1939 - "No entrance for Poles!"

Antisemitic graffiti in Lithuania. The signs read "Jews out" and "Hate"

An African-American child at a segregated drinking fountain on a courthouse lawn, North Carolina, US 1938.

As of 2013, aboriginal people (First Nations, Métis, and Inuit) comprise 4 percent of Canada's population, but account for 23.2 percent of the federal prison population. According to the Australian government's June 2006 publication of prison statistics, Aborigines make up 24% of the overall prison population in Australia.

In 2004, Māori made up just 15% of the total population of New Zealand but 49.5% of prisoners. Māori were entering prison at eight times the rate of non-Māori. A quarter of the people in England's prisons are from an ethnic minority. The Equality and Human Rights Commission found that in England and Wales as of 2010, a black person was five times more likely to be imprisoned than a white person. The discrepancy was attributed to "decades of racial prejudice in the criminal justice system".

In the United States, racial profiling of minorities by law-enforcement officials has been called racial discrimination. Within the criminal justice system in the United States, minorities are convicted and imprisoned disproportionately when compared to the majority. As early as 1866, the Civil Rights Act and Civil Rights Act of 1871 provided a remedy for intentional racism in employment by private employers and state and local public employers. The Civil Rights Act of 1991 expanded the damages available in Title VII cases and granted Title VII plaintiffs the right to a jury trial.

Racial discrimination in hiring has been shown to exist in the United States and in Europe. By means of their path breaking field experiment, Marianne Bertrand and Sendhil Mullainathan, showed that applications from job candidates with white-sounding names got 50 percent more callbacks for interviews than those with African-American-sounding names in the United States at the start of this millennium. A 2009 study by Devah Pager, Bruce Western, and Bart Bonikowski found that black applicants to low-wage jobs were half as likely as identically qualified white applicants to receive callbacks or job offers. More recently, Stijn Baert, Bart Cockx, Niels Gheyle and Cora Vandamme replicated and extended their field experiment in Belgium, Europe. They found that racial discrimination in the labour market is heterogeneous by the labour market tightness in the occupation: compared to natives, candidates with a foreign-sounding name are equally often invited to a job interview in Belgium if they apply for occupations for which vacancies are difficult to fill, but they have to send twice as many applications for occupations for which labor market tightness is low.

Region

Regional or geographic discrimination is discrimination based on the region in which a person lives or was born. It differs from national discrimination in that it may not be based on national borders or the country the victim lives in, but is instead based on prejudices against a specific region of one or more countries. Examples include discrimination against mainland Chinese within China, or discrimination against Americans from the south or from the north in the United States. It is often accompanied by discrimination based on accent, dialect, or cultural differences.

Religious Beliefs

Religious discrimination is valuing or treating a person or group differently because of what they do or do not believe or because of their feelings towards a given religion. For instance, the indigenous Christian population of the Balkans, known as "rayah" or "protected flock", was discriminated under the Ottoman Kanun–i–Rayah. The word is sometimes translated as 'cattle' rather than 'flock' or 'subjects' to emphasize the inferior status to the Muslim rayah.[further explanation needed]

Restrictions upon Jewish occupations were imposed by Christian authorities. Local rulers and church officials closed many professions to religious Jews, pushing them into marginal roles considered socially inferior, such as tax and rent collecting and moneylending, occupations only tolerated as a "necessary evil". The number of Jews permitted to reside in different places was limited; they were concentrated in ghettos and were not allowed to own land.

In a 1979 consultation on the issue, the United States commission on civil rights defined religious discrimination in relation to the civil rights guaranteed by the Fourteenth Amendment to the United States Constitution. Whereas religious civil liberties, such as the right to hold or not to hold a religious belief, are essential for Freedom of Religion (in the United States secured by the First Amendment), religious discrimination occurs when someone is denied " the equal protection of the laws, equality of status under the law, equal treatment in the administration of justice, and equality of opportunity and access to employment, education, housing, public services and facilities, and public accommodation because of their exercise of their right to religious freedom."

In 2015, attorney and author Roberta Kaplan stated that Kim Davis "is the clearest example of someone who wants to use a religious liberty argument to discriminate."

Sex, Sex Characteristics, Gender, and Gender Identity

Though gender discrimination and sexism refer to beliefs and attitudes in relation to the gender of a person, such beliefs and attitudes are of a social nature and do not, normally, carry any legal consequences. Sex discrimination, on the other hand, may have legal consequences. Though what constitutes sex discrimination varies between countries, the essence is that it is an adverse action taken by one person against another person that would not have occurred had the person been of another sex. Discrimination of that nature is considered a form of prejudice and in certain enumerated circumstances is illegal in many countries.

Sexual discrimination can arise in different contexts. For instance, an employee may be discriminated against by being asked discriminatory questions during a job interview, or by an employer not hiring or promoting, unequally paying, or wrongfully terminating, an employee based on their gender.

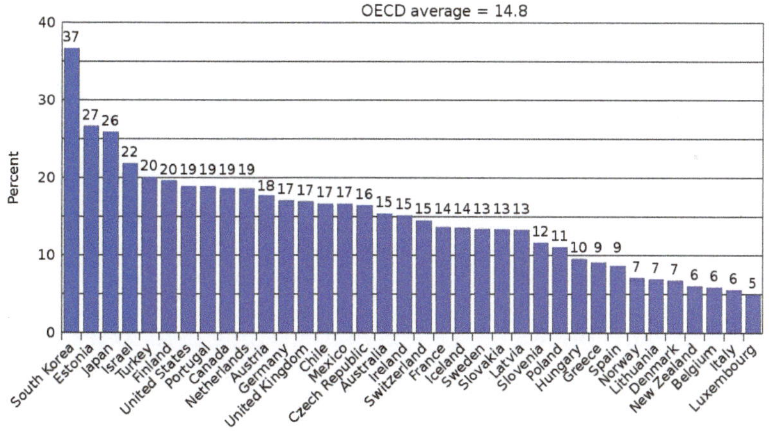

The gender gap in median earnings of full-time employees according to the OECD 2015.

Sexual discrimination can also arise when the dominant group holds a bias against the minority group. In the Wikipedian community, around 13 percent of registered users are women. This creates gender imbalances, and leaves room for systemic bias. Women are not only more harshly scrutinized, but the representation of women authors are also overlooked. Relative to men, across all source lists, women have a 2.6 greater odds of omission in Wikipedia. In an educational setting, there could be claims that a student was excluded from an educational institution, program, opportunity, loan, student group, or scholarship because of their gender. In the housing setting, there could be claims that a person was refused negotiations on seeking a house, contracting/leasing a house or getting a loan based on their gender. Another setting where there have been claims of gender discrimination is banking; for example if one is refused credit or is offered unequal loan terms based on one's gender. As with other forms of unlawful discrimination, there are two types of sex discrimination – direct discrimination and indirect discrimination. Direct sex discrimination is fairly easy to spot – 'Barmaid wanted', but indirect sex discrimination, where an unnecessary requirement puts one sex at a disproportionate disadvantage compared to the opposite sex, is sometimes less easy to spot, although some are obvious – 'Bar person wanted – must look good in a mini skirt'. Another setting where there is usually gender discrimination is when one is refused to extend their credit, refused approval of credit/loan process, and if there is a burden of unequal loan terms based on one's gender. Socially, sexual differences have been used to justify different roles for men and women, in some cases giving rise to claims of primary and secondary roles. While there are alleged non-physical differences between men and women, major reviews of the academic literature on gender difference find only a tiny minority of characteristics where there are consistent psychological differences between men and women, and these relate directly to experiences grounded in biological difference. However, there are also some psychological differences in regard to how problems are dealt with and emotional perceptions and reactions that may relate to hormones and the successful characteristics of each gender during longstanding roles in past primitive lifestyles.

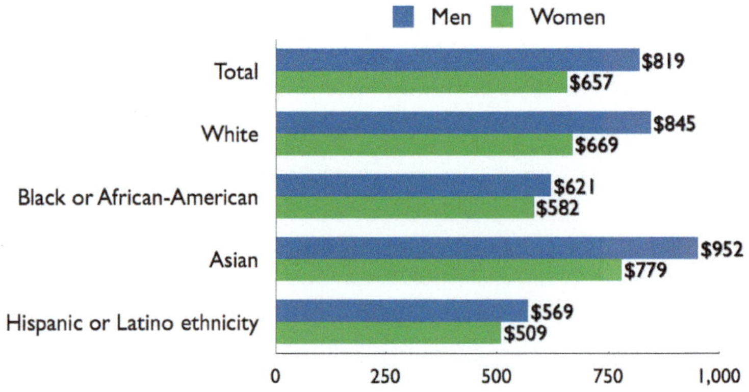

Median weekly earnings of full-time wage and salary workers, by sex, race, and ethnicity, U.S., 2009.

Unfair discrimination usually follows the gender stereotyping held by a society.

The United Nations had concluded that women often experience a "glass ceiling" and that there are no societies in which women enjoy the same opportunities as men. The term "glass ceiling" is used to describe a perceived barrier to advancement in employment based on discrimination, especially sex discrimination. In the United States in 1995, the Glass Ceiling Commission, a government-funded group, stated: "Over half of all Master's degrees are now awarded to women, yet 95% of senior-level managers, of the top Fortune 1000 industrial and 500 service companies are men. Of them, 97% are white." In its report, it recommended affirmative action, which is the consideration of an employee's gender and race in hiring and promotion decisions, as a means to end this form of discrimination. As of 2010, women accounted for 51% of workers in high-paying management, professional, and related occupations. They outnumbered men in such occupations as public relations managers, financial managers, and human resource managers.

In addition, women are found to experience a sticky floor. While a glass ceiling implies that women are less like to reach the top of the job ladder, a sticky floor is defined as the pattern that women are, compared to men, less likely to start to climb the job ladder. A sticky floor is related to gender differences at the bottom of the wage distribution. It might be explained by both employer discrimination and gender differences in career aspirations.

Intersex persons experience discrimination due to innate, atypical sex characteristics. Multiple jurisdictions now protect individuals on grounds of *intersex status* or *sex characteristics*. South Africa was the first country to explicitly add intersex to legislation, as part of the attribute of 'sex'. Australia was the first country to add an independent attribute, of 'intersex status'. Malta was the first to adopt a broader framework of 'sex characteristics', through legislation that also ended modifications to the sex characteristics of minors undertaken for social and cultural reasons.

Transgender individuals, whether male-to-female, female-to-male, or genderqueer, often experience transphobic problems that often lead to dismissals, underachievement, difficulty in finding a job, social isolation, and, occasionally, violent attacks against them. Nevertheless, the problem of gender discrimination does not stop at transgender individuals or with women. Men are often the victim in certain areas of employment as men begin to seek work in office and childcare settings traditionally perceived as "women's jobs". One such situation seems to be evident in a recent case concerning alleged YMCA discrimination and a Federal Court Case in Texas. The case actually involves alleged discrimination against both men and black people in childcare, even when they pass the same strict background tests and other standards of employment. It is currently being contended in federal court, as of fall 2009.

Discrimination in slasher films is relevant. Gloria Cowan had a research group study on 57 different slasher films. Their results showed that the non-surviving females were more frequently sexual than the surviving females and the non-surviving males. Surviving as a female slasher victim was strongly associated with the absence of sexual behavior. In slasher films, the message appears to be that sexual women get killed and only the pure women survive, thus reinforcing the idea that female sexuality can be costly.

Sexual Orientation

Protests in New York City against Uganda's Anti-Homosexuality Bill.

One's sexual orientation is a "predilection for homosexuality, heterosexuality, or bisexuality". Like most minority groups, homosexuals and bisexuals are vulnerable to prejudice and discrimination from the majority group. They may experience hatred from others because of their sexual preferences; a term for such hatred based upon one's sexual orientation is often called homophobia. Many continue to hold negative feelings towards those with non-heterosexual orientations and will discriminate against people who have them or are thought to have them. People of other uncommon sexual orientations also experience discrimination. One study found its sample of heterosexuals to be more prejudiced against asexuals than to homosexuals or bisexuals.

Employment discrimination based on sexual orientation varies by country. Revealing a lesbian sexual orientation (by means of mentioning an engagement in a rainbow organisation or by mentioning one's partner name) lowers employment opportunities in Cyprus and Greece but has, overall, no negative effect in Sweden and Belgium. In the latter country, even a positive effect of revealing a lesbian sexual orientation is found for women at their fertile ages.

Besides these academic studies, in 2009, ILGA published a report based on research carried out by Daniel Ottosson at Södertörn University College, Stockholm, Sweden. This research found that of the 80 countries around the world that continue to consider homosexuality illegal, five carry the death penalty for homosexual activity, and two do in some regions of the country. In the report, this is described as "State sponsored homophobia". This happens in Islamic states, or in two cases regions under Islamic authority. On February 5, 2005, the IRIN issued a reported titled "Iraq: Male homosexuality still a taboo." The article stated, among other things that honor killings by Iraqis against a gay family member are common and given some legal protection. In August 2009, Human Rights Watch published an extensive report detailing torture of men accused of being gay in Iraq, including the blocking of men's anuses with glue and then giving the men laxatives. Although gay marriage has been legal in South Africa since 2006, same-sex unions are often condemned as "un-African." Research conducted in 2009 shows 86% of black lesbians from the Western Cape live in fear of sexual assault.

A number of countries, especially those in the Western world, have passed measures to alleviate discrimination against sexual minorities, including laws against anti-gay hate crimes and workplace discrimination. Some have also legalized same-sex marriage or civil unions in order to grant same-sex couples the same protections and benefits as opposite-sex couples. In 2011, the United Nations passed its first resolution recognizing LGBT rights.

Drug Use

Drug use discrimination is the unequal treatment people experience because of the drugs they use. People who use or have used illicit drugs may face discrimination in employment, welfare, housing, child custody, and travel, in addition to imprisonment, asset forfeiture, and in some cases forced labor, torture, and execution. Though often prejudicially stereotyped as deviants and misfits, most drug users are well-adjusted and productive members of society. Drug prohibitions may have been partly motivated by racism and other prejudice against minorities, and racial disparities have been found to exist in the enforcement and prosecution of drug laws. Discrimination due to illicit drug use was the most commonly reported type of discrimination among Blacks and Latinos in a 2003 study of minority drug users in New York City, double to triple that due to race. People who use legal drugs such as tobacco and prescription medications may also face discrimination.

Global Marijuana March, Paris.

Ideas of self-ownership and cognitive liberty affirm rights to use drugs, whether for medicine recreation, or spiritual fulfilment. Those espousing such ideas question the legality of drug prohibition and cite the rights and freedoms enshrined in such documents as the Declaration of Independence, the U.S. Constitution and Bill of Rights, the European Convention on Human Rights, and the Universal Declaration of Human Rights, as protecting personal drug choices. They are inspired by and see themselves following in the tradition of those who have struggled against other forms of discrimination in the past.

Drug policy reform organizations such as the Drug Policy Alliance, the Drug Equality Alliance, the Transform Drug Policy Foundation, and the Beckley Foundation have highlighted the issue of stigma and discrimination in drug policy. The Partnership for Drug-Free Kids also recognizes this issue and shares on its website stories that "break through the stigma and discrimination that people with drug or drinking problems often face."

A report issued by the Global Commission on Drug Policy, critical of the global war on drugs, states, under "Undermining Human Rights, Fostering Discrimination":

Punitive approaches to drug policy are severely undermining human rights in every region of the world. They lead to the erosion of civil liberties and fair trial standards, the stigmatization of individuals and groups – particularly women, young people, and ethnic minorities – and the imposition of abusive and inhumane punishments.

Although still illegal at the federal level, about half of U.S. states have legalized marijuana for medical use and several of those states have laws, or are considering legislation, specifically protecting medical marijuana patients from discrimination in such areas as education, employment, housing, child custody, and organ transplantation.

Othering

Othering is the process by which a person or a group is placed outside of the norm, into the margins. It is a system of discrimination whereby the characteristics of a group are used to distinguish them as separate from the norm. Othering plays a fundamental role in the history and continuance of racism and other forms of discrimination. For example, by objectifying culture as something different, exotic or underdeveloped is to generalise that it is not the same as 'normal' society. Europe's colonial attitude towards the Orient exemplifies through the attitude that the East was the opposite of the West; feminine where the West was masculine, weak where the West was strong and traditional where the West was progressive. By making these generalisations and othering the East, Europe was simultaneously defining herself as the norm, further entrenching the perceived gap. Much of the process of othering relies on imagined difference, or the expectation of difference. Spatial difference can be enough to conclude that 'we' are 'here' and the 'others' are over 'there', making 'here' normal and 'there' foreign. Imagined differences serve to categorise people into groups and assign them characteristics that suit the imaginer's expectations and desires.

Reverse discrimination

Students protesting against racial quotas in Brazil: *"Quer uma vaga? Passe no vestibular!"* ("Do you want a spot? Pass the entrance exam!")

Some attempts at antidiscrimination have been criticized as reverse discrimination. In particular, minority quotas (for example, affirmative action) may discriminate against members of a dominant or majority group or other minority groups. In its opposition to race preferences, the American Civil Rights Institute's Ward Connerly stated, "There is nothing positive, affirmative, or equal about 'affirmative action' programs that give preference to some groups based on race."

Legislation

Australia

- Sex Discrimination Act 1984

Canada

- Ontario Human Rights Code 1962
- Canadian Human Rights Act 1977

Hong Kong

- Sex Discrimination Ordinance (1996)

Israel

- Prohibition of Discrimination in Products, Services and Entry into Places of Entertainment and Public Places Law, 2000
- Employment (Equal Opportunities) Law, 1988

Netherlands

- Article 137c, part 1 of Wetboek van Strafrecht prohibits insults towards a group because of its race, religion, sexual orientation (straight or gay), handicap (somatically, mental or psychiatric) in public or by speech, by writing or by a picture. Maximum imprisonment one year of imprisonment or a fine of the third category.
- Part 2 increases the maximum imprisonment to two years and the maximum fine category to 4, when the crime is committed as a habit or is committed by two or more persons.
- Article 137d prohibits provoking to discrimination or hate against the group described above. Same penalties apply as in article 137c.
- Article 137e part 1 prohibits publishing a discriminatory statement, other than in formal message, or hands over an object (that contains discriminatory information) otherwise than on his request. Maximum imprisonment is 6 months or a fine of the third category.
- Part 2 increases the maximum imprisonment to one year and the maximum fine category to 4, when the crime is committed as a habit or committed by two or more persons.
- Article 137f prohibits supporting discriminatory activities by giving money or goods. Maximum imprisonment is 3 months or a fine of the second category.
- United Kingdom
- Equal Pay Act 1970 – provides for equal pay for comparable work
- Sex Discrimination Act 1975 – makes discrimination against women or men, including discrimination on the grounds of marital status, illegal in the workplace.
- Human Rights Act 1998 – provides more scope for redressing all forms of discriminatory imbalances

United States

- Equal Pay Act of 1963 – (part of the Fair Labor Standards Act) – prohibits wage discrimination by employers and labor organizations based on sex

- Title VII of the Civil Rights Act of 1964 – broadly prohibits discrimination in the workplace including hiring, firing, workforce reduction, benefits, and sexually harassing conduct
- Fair Housing Act of 1968 prohibited discrimination in the sale or rental of housing based on race, color, national origin, religion, sex, familial status, or disability. The Office of Fair Housing and Equal Opportunity is charged with administering and enforcing the Act.
- Pregnancy Discrimination Act, which amended Title VII of the Civil Rights Act of 1964 – covers discrimination based upon pregnancy in the workplace
- Violence Against Women Act

Theories

Social theories such as egalitarianism assert that social equality should prevail. In some societies, including most developed countries, each individual's civil rights include the right to be free from government sponsored social discrimination. Due to a belief in the capacity to perceive pain or suffering shared by all animals, "abolitionist" or "vegan" egalitarianism maintains that the interests of every individual (regardless its species), warrant equal consideration with the interests of humans, and that not doing so is "speciesist".

Labeling Theory

Discrimination, in labeling theory, takes form as mental categorization of minorities and the use of stereotype. This theory describes difference as deviance from the norm, which results in internal devaluation and social stigma that may be seen as discrimination. It is started by describing a "natural" social order. It is distinguished between the fundamental principle of fascism and social democracy. The Nazis in 1930s-era Germany and the pre-1990 Apartheid government of South Africa used racially discriminatory agendas for their political ends. This practice continues with some present day governments.

Game Theory

Economist Yanis Varoufakis (2013) argues that "discrimination based on utterly arbitrary characteristics evolves quickly and systematically in the experimental laboratory", and that neither classical game theory nor neoclassical economics can explain this. Varoufakis and Shaun Hargreaves-Heap (2002) ran an experiment where volunteers played a computer-mediated, multiround hawk-dove game (HD game). At the start of each session, each participant was assigned a color at random, either red or blue. At each round, each player learned the color assigned to his or her opponent, but nothing else about the opponent. Hargreaves-Heap and Varoufakis found that the players' behavior within a session frequently developed a discriminatory convention, giving a Nash equilibrium where players of one color (the "advantaged" color) consistently played the aggressive "hawk" strategy against players of the other, "disadvantaged" color, who played the acquiescent "dove" strategy against the advantaged color. Players of both colors used a mixed strategy when playing against players assigned the same color as their own.

The experimenters then added a cooperation option to the game, and found that disadvantaged players usually cooperated with each other, while advantaged players usually did not. They state that while the equilibria reached in the original HD game are predicted by evolutionary game theory, game theory does not explain the emergence of cooperation in the disadvantaged group. Citing earlier psychological work of Matthew Rabin, they hypothesize that a norm of differing entitlements emerges across the two groups, and that this norm could define a "fairness" equilibrium within the disadvantaged group.

State vs. Free Market

State Discrimination

In the 1990s, Bhutan expelled or forced to leave its Hindu population in the name of preserving its Buddhist culture and identity.

When the "Jim Crow" racial segregation laws were enacted in the U.S., many companies disobeyed them for years, because the market automatically punishes companies that discriminate: they lose customers and get additional expenses. It took 15 years for the government to break down the resistance of the companies.

Markets Punish the Discriminator

In *The Welfare Implications of Becker's Discrimination Coefficient*, Richard S. Toikka disagrees, citing the ambivalent relations between discrimination and economic efficiency, as shown by the literature. According to Toikka the "discriminatory tastes", in Becker's explanation, was shown to be problematic because it implies discrimination is efficient. Further, the very aim of the markets is to cater efficiently for the different "tastes" of all individuals, including customers, employees, employers, and firm owners (and discrimination happens within and between all these groups). If discrimination were just another "taste", then the markets were not to punish for it. Second, microeconomic theory turns to unusual method – explicit treatment of production functions – when it analyzes discrimination. And third, the very existence of discrimination in employment (defined as wages which differ from marginal product of the discriminated employees) at the long run, contradicts perfect competition and efficiency (which imply equality of wages and the said marginal product). Hence, the very existence of discrimination at the long run, contradicts the claim that the markets function well and punish the discriminators.

Consequences of Discrimination for Health

There are economic consequences – it is not easy for certain groups to get jobs or get a useful education (for political and historical reasons) and they tend to get bogged down into poverty. Certain groups get shepherded or pushed into certain localities forming ghettos that tend to be mired in poverty and are shunned and regarded with suspicion by the mainstream even more.

Lack of access to resources such as education in turn determines job and income and residence which keep people in poverty (In India we can think of religion and caste based discrimination). The effects of poverty on health have already been discussed.

Apart from the economic aspects of prejudice is the humiliation experienced. The idea of well being is based on the concept that everyone can and ought to live a life of dignity and be free to love and achieve. Given this idea or expectation to tolerate humiliation randomly is a very stressful experience.

Discriminated groups often experience more violence in the form of beatings, attacks and homicide.

The kind of exposures of a discriminated group are different in a variety of life situations - the economic deprivation at home and work which may affect the social sphere. Exposure to toxic substances at work and also to hazardous conditions. And most importantly inadequate and inferior health care

The literature in discrimination has looked at discrimination at the individual level using measures of self reported discrimination and at the population level given institutional discrimination (Krieger, 2000). The studies reported here are American studies as there appear to be few studies in India dealing with the psychological aspects of discrimination at the individual level.

For studies at the individual level the outcome studied most often was mental health (depression and distress) and hypertension. In studying discrimination there were variations in the time period of exposure, domain of exposure, intensity and frequency of exposure, and targets of discrimination (Krieger, 2000).

Kreiger (1990, as cited in Kreiger, 2000) in a study with 50 white and 51 black women asked them -

- If they had been ever discriminated against at school, getting a job; at work; getting housing; getting medical care; from police or in the courts.
- The response format was yes or no
- They were asked about their response to unfair treatment:
- Accept as a fact of life or take action
- Talk to other or keep to self

Kreiger found that higher self reported discrimination was related to higher levels of hypertension. A few of the findings of studies at the individual level are as follows:

Krieger & Sidney (1996) with 4086 black and white men and women reported increased BP associated with self reports of discrimination .

Williams et al (1997) among 586 black and 520 white adults found that discrimination was associated with higher self rated ill health and psychological distress.

Li & Moore (1998) 1266 adults with disabilities indicated that discrimination was associated with higher chronic pain.

Perceived discrimination has been linked to mental and physical health problems.Perceived Discrimination involves a perception of discrimination based on self report without verification of actual events – though there may not be proof or evidence of the actual event – it is the person's feelings or emotions that are measured or recorded.

Findings have linked perceived discrimination with depression, psychological distress and anxiety (Williams, Neighbors & Jackson, 2003; Paradies, 2006).

In terms of physical health perceived discrimination has been linked with hypertension, self reported poor health and breast cancer as well as, risk factors such as obesity and substance use (Williams & Mohammed, 2009).

Discrimination on a daily basis or frequent exposure to discrimination may make the body more physically reactive in stressful or potentially stressful situations (Guyll, Mathews & Bromberger, 2001). Also regular discrimination becomes a chronic stressor that has a corrosive effect on the body's inner organs leading to greater susceptibility to illness or poor health.

Another pathway by which discrimination influences health is by reducing an individual's self control resources which in turn leads to unhealthy behaviors and reduced healthy behaviors. Studies indicate that discrimination is linked to smoking, alcohol and substance abuse as well as poor diabetes control and not using condoms. (as cited in Pascoe & Richman, 2009)

Thus the stress of discrimination causes peoples positive resources to be depleted and has a strong impact on their self image and self control.

Moderator variables such as social support, coping style, ethnic identity and personality variables effect on the discrimination health relationship have been studied (Pascoe & Richman, 2009).

Studies about strong ethnic identities have yielded mixed results sometimes indicating a positive protective effect and sometimes a more negative effect of discrimination on health (Pascoe & Richman, 2009).

The presence of social support has a protective effect - when people can talk about the incident and vent their feelings they are better able to deal with it. An active coping style was found to be better in dealing with discrimination (Pascoe & Richman, 2009).

The results of the meta –analysis conducted by Pascoe & Richman (2009) indicated a mean correlation of -.16 between discrimination and mental health, -.13 between discrimination and physical health, -.11 between discrimination and the stress response and -.18 with health behaviors.

Thus the pathways by which discrimination influences health are illustrated via this meta analysis. More work needs to be done to understand the nature of chronic stress and the body's response to it. Subtle forms of discrimination may produce more stress and this needs to be studied in depth.

Considering discrimination at the population level, a body of literature in India uses data from the NFHS(1,2,3) and other large data sets where the effects of caste, religion, urban-rural residence and gender inequalities for health have been examined. Results indicate regional and state differences with poorly developed states indicating more inequality than the better developed states. In a study based on data from the Morbidity and Health Care Survey (2004) (383,338 individuals) being a member of a scheduled Tribe, a scheduled caste, or being Muslim led to a higher probability of premature death, poorer health, lower treatment seeking and lower likelihood of receiving prenatal care (Borooah, 2010) controlling for education, household income and level of development of the state.

Considering, anemia, utilization of maternal healthcare, infant mortality, childhood vaccinations, and treatment of diarrhea, caste related inequalities are observed based on NFHS2 data (Nayar, 2007).

Perusing the NFHS3 data, reveals the discrimination that the scheduled tribes face in terms of being geographically isolated and how this affects their health in terms of access to health care.

In the table regarding Ante natal care –the highest percentage who had no ante natal care was the scheduled tribe group – so one can see that the negative effect of discrimination has begun before birth.

In the second table regarding institutionalized deliveries, again the scheduled tribe have the highest number of deliveries at home at 70%. There is a disadvantage at birth.

In the table about access to health care 67% scheduled tribes reported having a problem accessing health care with 44% saying the distance to health facility was a problem and 42% reporting transportation as a problem. Thus the lack of connectivity and poor roads or rather lack of them are a form of discrimination against the scheduled tribes who live in forests and mountainous areas.

However there are still many unanswered questions and unresolved issues that could only be addressed by longitudinal studies that capture the cumulative effect of discrimination. More work needs to be done to understand the nature of chronic stress and the body's response to it.

Neighborhoods and Health

In this lesson we will understand the impact of neighborhood on health. Neighborhoods are an expression of SES however there may be effects on health that are independent of SES. What specific characteristics of neighborhoods influence health is the important question that needs to be answered by research. Some empirical research has been reviewed. The importance of making specific changes that can improve the health of a neighborhood and the value of empowering residents to play a role in making these changes are discussed.

As the focus on contextual influences of health has grown, the role of neighborhoods has received attention for it has both physical and social attributes that may be related to health (Diez-Roux, 2007). Villerme as far back as 1828 demonstrated the relationship between mortality and the neighborhoods (arrondisments) in Paris, and the amount of tax paid was the influential factor rather than altitude or distance from the Seine or any other physical factor (Berkman & Kawachi, 2000). Neighborhoods are in the limelight again, for with the development of Geographical Information System (GIS), the analysis of space has become sophisticated (Diez-Roux, 2007). Neighborhoods impact health directly by influencing access to health care and indirectly by influencing behaviors (space to exercise).

The effects of policies such as housing policies or other urban planning policies (such as for e.g building flyovers or building the elevated rail in Mumbai) may impact on neighborhoods sometimes directly and sometimes indirectly. The elevated rail and the flyover at Pedder road in Mumbai is proving so difficult to build, as the well heeled denizens of that neighborhood are against it for it is perceived as destroying their peace and making their neighborhood low brow. Thus a metro that could make a difference to the millions of citizens daily commute from the north to the south will probably never get built as the rich and the powerful exert their authority to guard their neighborhoods and maintain the status quo. Thus the high rate of accidents that take place due to overcrowding in the local trains will continue impacting on mortality and injury rates.

Research indicates that living in high stress areas affected blood pressure after controlling for potentially confounding individual level factors (Harburg 1973 as cited Krieger, 2000). Many studies have reported the effect of noise pollution on children's attention spans and their ability to learn new material (Evans, 2006). In a sample of working-class, 10- to 12-year-old children in urban India the effects of chronic residential crowding were elevated blood pressure among boys and learned helplessness among girls as well as behavioral and academic problems at school and conflict with parents (Evans et al, 1988,as cited in Krieger, 2000).

In India, in urban and rural areas there are multiple levels of stratification and hence those many neighbourhoods. There are some areas that lack the basics of water, sanitation and waste removal and at the other end are opulent apartments or houses. In fact a lot of work and attention is being focused on gated communities that are attempting to create a utopian environment inside their gates, whilst being located opposite a slum. Thus the function of town planning and zoning is being taken on by the developer of such communities in the absence of liveable spaces provided by the civic authorities, for those who can pay the price.

Health outcomes such as chronic diseases, mortality, infant health and birth outcomes and mental health have been measured in association with neighbourhoods. However most of the work has been with relation to cardiovascular disease.

Defining and measuring the area and its attributes is done with GIS however GIS is only able to measure the physical attributes of space but to understand its social attributes human observers have to be relied on. Human observers are trained to report and describe how people negotiate their neighbourhoods both by observation as well as interviewing people (Diez-Roux, 2007).

To understand the clustering of people in a neighbourhood multilevel modelling could be used. For instance, where and how ghettos form and the markets and businesses that are patronized are issues that could be analyzed.

A consistent finding emerging across studies and across populations is between neighborhood deprivation and increased cardiovascular risk as assessed by morbidity, mortality or risk prevalence. These associations persist even after controlling for individual level indicators of SES (modest effects - small ICC).

Studies have linked neighborhood deprivation and poverty to individual risks of cigarette smoking (Klein Schmidt et al, 1995; Diez-Roux et al, 1997; Duncan et al 1999, as cited in Diez-Roux, 2007), to depressive symptoms (Aneshensel & Sucoff, 1996; Yen & Kaplan, 1999 , as cited in Diez-Roux, 2007), to lower quality diet (Diez-Roux et al; 1999 , as cited in Diez-Roux, 2007). Most of the work is about exercise and there is some work on diet. Attributes of the physical environment such as mixed land use (commercial and residential) street connectivity, housing density have been studied in relation with the level of physical activity (Diez-Roux, 2007).

Poor areas spatially isolated from resource rich areas may be worse off than those near such areas. For e.g. the mill area located in south Mumbai although poor are better off given their proximity to good public hospitals compared to poor areas in the north of Mumbai which are lacking in many civic amenities. Access to educational institutions, public libraries, parks, gardens and recreational spaces are much better in rich areas.

In recent work on neighborhoods the fundamental questions that are being raised are, what specific characteristic of the neighbourhood are linked to health, what are the pathways through which these characteristics influence health, the spatial scale at which they are operating and whether changing a characteristic will improve health? (Diez-Roux, 2007)

It is often not possible to study a treatment effect or vary the treatment for a research study as large scale changes to the physical environment may not be possible. However naturally occurring changes in neighbourhoods offer an opportunity to study a treatment effect as a field experiment. For e.g. a new public hospital in the area that improves access to health care, or a mall that may increase employment and also traffic and air and noise pollution. Also things like a new road that improves connectivity with other areas or an affordable gym in the locality. Thus changes in the neighbourhood may have multiple direct and indirect effects on behaviour that in turn impact on health. To make causal inferences it is also necessary to have control groups to match with the treatment or change group.

Most of the studies regarding the health effects of neighbourhoods have been cross sectional, however the effects of neighbourhoods are cumulative and need to be measured over time. Longitudinal studies will be better at revealing causal relationships between risk factors in neighbourhoods and mortality or morbidity (Diez- Roux, 2007).

Much of the research has been applied and ad hoc with very little theory guiding or driving the research. There is a need for a priori theorizing regarding the nature of the link between spatial scale and health outcomes. The development of theory fuels more research and leads to a better understanding of the area.

The wider social context in which health behaviours occur and that may influence risk factors need to be considered when developing interventions. Interventions designed at the level of the neighbourhood may be very effective for they are building on existing relationships and social capital.

Neighbourhoods are perennially changing and some changes are initiated by the residents. Often one hears of residents taking up solid waste management, recycling, developing green areas and open spaces, improving safety – thus residents are concerned about these matters that impact on their health. Thus policies need to support and empower residents to develop their neighbourhoods in conjunction with civic or municipal authorities (Diez-Roux, 2007). Sometimes policies that are unrelated to housing may impact neighbourhoods and in turn the health of residents, thus in such situations residents must be sensitized and empowered to change or create an acceptable alternative situation.

Gender Disparities in Health

Mass community health education program to educate Achham women and to challenge the region's tradition of keeping menstruating women in small, poorly ventilated sheds, which they sometimes share with cows. This tradition, also known as Chhaupadi, often compromises women's health in many different ways.

Health is the general condition of a person's mind and body, usually indicating the state of being free from illness, injury or pain. The World Health Organization (WHO) has defined health as "a state of complete physical, mental, and social well-being and not merely the absence of disease or infirmity." Identified by the *2012 World Development Report* as one of two key human capital endowments, health can influence an individual's ability to reach his or her full potential in society. Yet while gender equality has made the most progress in areas such as education and labor force participation, health inequality between men and women continues to plague many societies today. While both males and females face health disparities, girls and women experience a majority of health disparities. This comes from the fact that many cultural ideologies and practices have structured society in a way whereby women are more vulnerable to abuse and mistreatment, making them more prone to illnesses and early death. Women are also restricted from receiving many opportunities, such as education and paid labor, that can help improve their accessibility to better health care resources.

Definition of Health Disparity

Health disparity has been defined by the World Health Organization as the differences in health care received by different groups of people that are not only unnecessary and avoidable but also unfair and unjust. The existence of health disparity implies that health equity does not exist in many parts of the world. Equity in health refers to the situation whereby every individual has a fair opportunity to attain their full health potential, and that no one should be denied from achieving this potential. Overall, the term "health disparities," or "health inequalities," is widely understood as the differences in health between people who are situated at different positions in a socioeconomic hierarchy.

Gender as An Axis of Difference

Predominantly Female-bias

The social structures of many of these places perpetuate the marginalization and oppression of women in the form of cultural norms and legal codes. As a result of this unequal social order, women are usually relegated into positions where they are not only more vulnerable to suffering from health problems, but also less able to have access and control over healthcare resources than men. For example, women living in areas with a patriarchal system are often less likely to receive tertiary education or to be employed in the paid labor market due to gender discrimination. As a result, female life expectancy at birth and nutritional well-being, and immunity against communicable and non-communicable diseases, are often lower than those of men.

Disparities Against Males

While a majority of the global health gender disparities is weighted against women, there are situations in which men tend to fare poorer. One such instance is armed conflicts, where men are often the immediate victims. A study of conflicts in 13 countries from 1955 to 2002 found that 81% of all violent war deaths were male. Apart from armed conflicts, areas with high incidence of violence, such as regions controlled by drug cartels, also see men experiencing higher mortality rates. This stems from social beliefs that associate ideals of masculinity with aggressive, confrontational behavior. Lastly, sudden and drastic changes in economic environments and the loss of social safety nets, in particular social subsidies and food stamps, have also been linked to higher levels of alcohol consumption and psychological stress among men, leading to a spike in male mortality rates. This is because such situations often makes it harder for men to provide for their family, a task that has been long regarded as the "essence of masculinity."

In developed countries, overall health outcomes (such as life expectancy) are worse for men than women.

Forms of Gender Disparities

Male-female Sex Ratio

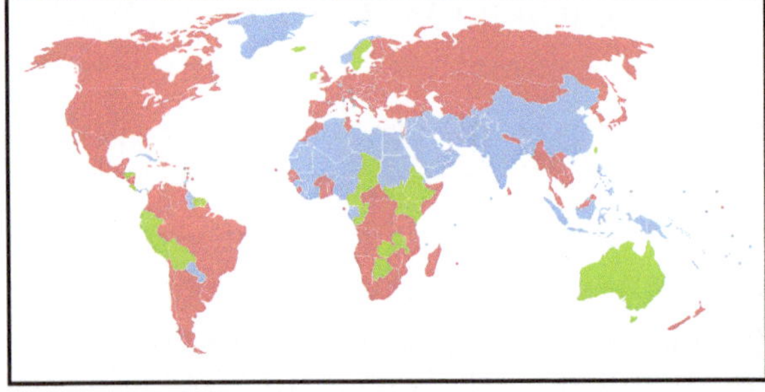

Map indicating the human sex ratio by country.

Countries with more **females** than males.

Countries with the **same** number of males and females.

Countries with more **males** than females.

No data

At birth, boys outnumber girls with the ratio of 105 or 106 male to 100 female children. However, after conception, biology favors women. Research has shown that if men and women received similar nutrition, medical attention, and general health care, women would live longer than men. This is because women, on a whole, are more resistant to diseases and less prone to debilitating genetic conditions. However, despite medical and scientific research that shows that when given the same care as males, females tend to have better survival rates than males, the ratio of women to men in developing regions such as South Asia, West Asia, and China can be as low as 0.94, or even lower. This deviation from the natural male to female sex ratio has been described by Indian philosopher and economist Amartya Sen as the "missing women" phenomenon. According to the 2012 World Development Report, the number of missing women is estimated to be about 1.5 million women per year, with a majority of the women missing in India and China.

Female Mortality

In many developing regions, women experience high levels of mortality. Many of these deaths result from maternal mortality and HIV/AIDS infection. Although only 1,900 maternal deaths were recorded in high-income nations in 2008, India and Sub-Saharan Africa experienced a combined total of 266,000 deaths from pregnancy-related causes. In Somalia and Chad, one in every 14 women die from causes related to child birth. In addition, the HIV/AIDS epidemic also contributes significantly to female mortality. The case is especially true for Sub-Saharan Africa, where women account for 60% of all adult HIV infections.

Health Outcome

Women tend to have poorer health outcomes than men for several reasons ranging from sustaining greater risk to diseases to experiencing higher mortality rates. In the Population Studies Center Research Report by Rachel Snow that compares the disability-adjusted life years (DALY) of both male and females, the global DALYs lost to females for sexually transmitted diseases such as gonorrhea and chlamydia are more than ten times greater than those of the males. Moreover, the female DALYs to male DALYs ratio for malnutrition-related diseases such as Iron-Deficiency Anemia are often close to 1.5, suggesting that poor nutrition impacts women at a much higher level than men. Additionally, in terms of mental illnesses, women are also two to three times more likely than men to be diagnosed with depression. With regards to suicidal rates, up to 80% of those who committed suicide or attempted suicide in Iran are women.

In developed countries with more social and legal gender equality, overall health outcomes can disfavor men. For example, in the United States, as of 2001, men's life expectancy is 5 years lower than women's (down from 1 year in 1920), and men die at higher rates from all top 10 causes of death, especially heart disease and stroke. Men die from suicide more frequently, though women more frequently have suicidal thoughts and the suicide attempt rate is the same for men and women. Men may suffer from undiagnosed depression more frequently, due to gender differences in the expression of emotion. American men are more likely to consume alcohol, smoke, engage in risky behaviors, and defer medical care.

Incidence of melanoma has strong gender-related differences which vary by age.

Access to Healthcare

Women tend to have poorer access to health care resources than men. In certain regions of Africa, many women often lack access to malaria treatment as well as access to resources that could protect them against Anopheles mosquitoes during pregnancy. As a result of this, pregnant women who are residing in areas with low levels of malaria transmission are still placed at two to three times higher risk than men in terms of contracting a severe malaria infection. These disparities in access to healthcare are often compounded by cultural norms and expectations imposed on women. For example, certain societies forbid women from leaving their homes unaccompanied by a male relative, making it harder for women to receive healthcare services and resources when they need it most.

Gender factors, such as women's status and empowerment (i.e., in education, employment, intimate partner relationships, and reproductive health), are linked with women's capacity to access and use maternal health services, a critical component of maternal health. Still, family planning is typically viewed as the responsibility of women, with programs targeting women and overlooking the role of men—even though men's dominance in decision making, including contraceptive use, has significant implications for family planning and access to reproductive health services.

In order to promote equity in access to reproductive health care, health programs and services should conduct analyses to identify gender inequalities and barriers to health, and determine the programmatic implications. The analyses will help inform decisions about how to design, implement, and scale up health programs that meet the differential needs of women and men.

Causes

Cultural Norms and Practices

Cultural norms and practices are two of the main reasons why gender disparities in health exist and continue to persist. These cultural norms and practices often influence the roles and behaviors that men and women adopt in society. It is these gender differences between men and women, which are regarded and valued differently, that give rise to gender inequalities as they work to systematically empower one group and oppress the other. Both gender differences and gender inequalities can lead to disparities in health outcomes and access to health care. Some of the examples provided by the World Health Organization of how cultural norms can result in gender disparities in health include a woman's inability to travel alone, which can prevent them from receiving the necessary health care that they need. Another societal standard is a woman's inability to insist on condom use by her spouse or sex partners, leading to a higher risk of contracting HIV.

Son Preference

One of the better documented cultural norms that augment gender disparities in health is the preference for sons. In India, for instance, the 2001 census recorded only 93 girls per 100 boys. This is a sharp decline from 1961, when the number of girls per 100 boys was nearly 98. In certain parts of India, such as Kangra and Rohtak the number of girls for every 100 boys can be as low as in the 70s. Additionally, low female to male numbers have also been recorded in other Asian countries – most notably in China where, according to a survey in 2005, only 84 girls were born for every 100 boys. Although this was a slight increase from 81 during 2001–2004, it is still much lower than the 93 girls per 100 boys in the late 1980s. The increasing number of unborn girls in the late 20th century has been attributed to technological advances that made pre-birth sex determination, also known as prenatal sex discernment, such as the ultrasound test more affordable and accessible to a wider population. This allowed parents who prefer a son to determine the sex of their unborn child during the early stages of pregnancy. By having early identification of their unborn child's sex, parents could practice sex-selective abortion, where they would abort the fetus if it was not the preferred sex, which in most cases is that of the female.

Additionally, the culture of son preference also extends beyond birth in the form of preferential treatment of boys. This preferential care can be manifested in many ways, such as through differential provision of food resources, attention, and medical care. Data from household surveys over the past 20 years has indicated that the female disadvantage has persisted in India and may have even worsened in some other countries such as Nepal and Pakistan.

Female Genital Mutilation

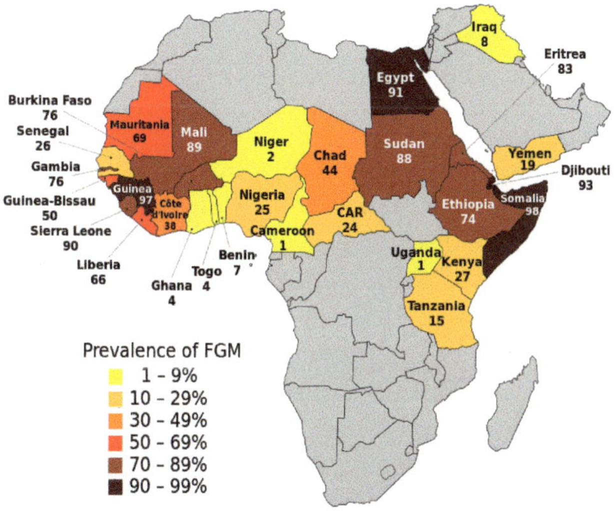

Prevalence of female genital mutilation in Africa, Yemen and Iraq

Harmful cultural practices such as female genital mutilation (FGM) also cause girls and women to face health risks. Millions of females are estimated to have undergone FGM, which involves partial or total removal of the external female genitalia for non-medical reasons. It is estimated that 92.5 million females over 10 years of age in Africa are living with the consequences of FGM. Of these, 12.5 million are girls between 10 and 14 years of age. Each year, about three million girls in Africa are subjected to FGM.

Often performed by traditional practitioners using unsterile techniques and devices, FGM can have both immediate and late complications. These include excessive bleeding, urinary tract infections, wound infection, and in the case of unsterile and reused instruments, hepatitis and HIV. In the long run, scars and keloids can form, which can obstruct and damage the urinary and genital tracts. According to a 2005 UNICEF report on FGM, it is unknown how many girls and women die from the procedure because of poor record keeping and a failure to report fatalities. FGM may also complicate pregnancy and place women at a higher risk for obstetrical problems, such as prolonged labor. According to a 2006 study by the WHO involving 28,393 women, neonatal mortality increases when women have experienced FGM; an additional ten to twenty babies were estimated to die per 1,000 deliveries.

Psychological complications are related to cultural context. Women who undergo FGM might be emotionally affected when they move outside their traditional circles and are confronted with the view that mutilation is not the norm.

Violence and Abuse

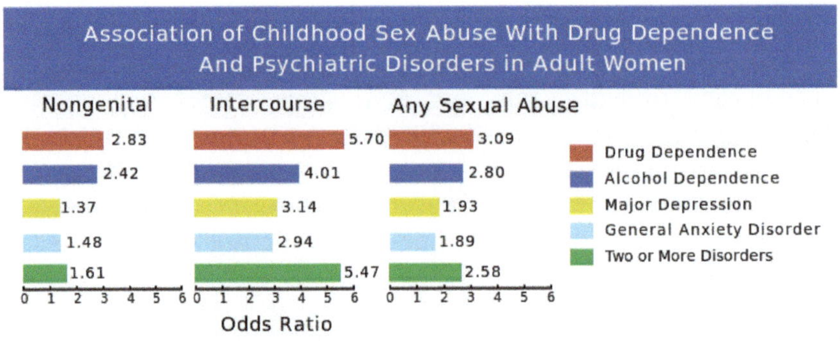

National Institute of Health: Among more than 1,400 adult females, childhood sexual abuse was associated with increased likelihood of drug dependence, alcohol dependence, and psychiatric disorders

Violence against women is a widespread global occurrence with serious public health implications. This is a result of social and gender bias. Many societies in developing nations function on a patriarchal framework, where women are often viewed as a form of property and as socially inferior to men. This unequal standing in the social hierarchy has led women to be physically, emotionally, and sexually abused by men, both as children and adults. These abuses usually constitute some form of violence. Although children of both sexes do suffer from physical maltreatment, sexual abuse, and other forms of exploitation and violence, studies have indicated that young girls are far more likely than boys to experience sexual abuse. In a 2004 study on child abuse, 25.3% of all girls surveyed experienced some form of sexual abuse, a percentage that is three times higher than that of boys (8.7%).

Such violence against women, especially sexual abuse, is increasingly being documented in areas experiencing armed conflicts. Presently, women and girls bear the brunt of social turmoil worldwide, making up an estimated 65% of the millions who are displaced and affected. Some of these places which are facing such problems include Rwanda, Kosovo, and the Democratic Republic of the Congo. This comes as a result of both the general instability around the region, as well as a tactic of warfare to intimidate enemies. Often being placed in emergency and refugee settings, girls and women alike are highly vulnerable to abuse and exploitation by military combatants, security forces, and members of rival communities.

The sexual violence and abuse of both young and adult women have both short and long-term consequences, contributing significantly to a myriad of health issues into adulthood. These range from debilitating physical injuries, reproductive health issues, substance abuse, and psychological trauma. Examples of the above categories include depression and post-traumatic stress disorder, alcohol and drug use and dependence, sexually transmitted diseases, and suicide attempts.

Abused women often have higher rates of unplanned and problematic pregnancies, abortions, neonatal and infant health issues, sexually transmitted infections (including HIV), and mental disorders (such as depression, anxiety disorders, sleep disorders and eating disorders) as compared to their non-abused peers. During peacetime, most violence against women is perpetrated by either male individuals whom them know or intimate male partners. An eleven-country study conducted by WHO between 2000 and 2003 found that, depending on the country, between 15% and 71% of women have experienced physical or sexual violence by a husband or partner in their lifetime, and 4% to 54% within the previous year. Partner violence may also be fatal. Studies from Australia, Canada, Israel, South Africa and the United States show that between 40% and 70% of female murders were carried out by intimate partners.

Other forms of violence against women include sexual harassment and abuse by authority figures (such as teachers, police officers or employers), trafficking for forced labour or sex, and traditional practices such as forced child marriages and dowry-related violence. At its most extreme, violence against women can result in female infanticide and violent death. Despite the size of the problem, many women do not report their experience of abuse and do not seek help. As a result, violence against women remains a hidden problem with great human and health care costs.

Poverty

Poverty is another factor that facilitates the continual existence of gender disparities in health. Poverty often works in tandem with various cultural norms to indirectly impact women's health. While many communities and households are not opposed to helping women attain better health through education, better nutrition, and financial stability, poverty often act as a form of barrier against gender equity in health for women. Oftentimes, due to financial constraints and limited capital, only a select few are able to receive opportunities, like education and employment, that might help them attain better health outcomes. However, cultural norms would often prioritized men in receiving these opportunities. This prioritization of males stems from the societal perception that the potential returns to both the household and the community is higher for men than women.

Healthcare System

The World Health Organization defines health systems as "all the activities whose primary purpose is to promote, restore, or maintain health". However, factors outside of healthcare systems can influence the impact healthcare systems have on the health of different demographics within a population. This is because healthcare systems are known to be influenced by social, cultural and economic frameworks. As a result, health systems are regarded as not only "producers of health and health care", but also as "purveyors of a wider set of societal norms and values," many of which are biased against women.

In the Women and Gender Equity Knowledge Network's Final Report to the WHO Commission on Social Determinants of Health in 2007, health systems in many countries were noted to have been unable to deliver adequately on gender equity in health. One explanation for this issue is that many healthcare systems tend to neglect the fact that men and women's health needs can be very different. In the report, studies have found evidence that the healthcare system can promote gender disparities in health through the lack of gender equity in terms of the way women are regarded - as both consumers (users) and producers (carers) of health care services. For instance, healthcare systems tend to regard women as objects rather than subjects, where services are often provided to women as a means of something else rather on the well-being of women. In the case of reproductive health services, these services are often provided as a form of fertility control rather than as care for women's well-being. Additionally, although the majority of the workforce in health care systems are female, many of the working conditions remain discriminatory towards women. Many studies have shown that women are often expected to conform to male work models that ignore their special needs, such as childcare or protection from violence. This significantly reduces the ability and efficiency of female caregivers providing care to patients, particularly female ones.

Structural Gender Oppression

Structural gender inequalities in the allocation of resources, such as income, education, health care, nutrition and political voice, are strongly associated with poor health and reduced well-being. Very often, such structural gender discrimination of women in many other areas has an indirect impact on women's health. For example, because women in many developing nations are less likely to be part of the formal labor market, they often lack access to job security and the benefits of social protection, including access to health care. Additionally, within the formal workforce, women often face challenges related to their lower status, where they suffer workplace discrimination and sexual harassment. Studies have shown that this expectation of having to balance the demands of paid work and work at home often give rise to work-related fatigue, infections, mental ill-health and other problems, which results in women faring poorer in health.

Women's health is also put at a higher level of risk as a result of being confined to certain traditional responsibilities, such as cooking and water collection. Being confined to unpaid domestic labor not only reduces women's opportunities to education and formal job employment (both of which can indirectly contribute to better health in the long run), but also potentially expose women to higher risk of health issues. For instance, in developing regions where solid fuels are used for cooking, women are exposed to a higher level of indoor air pollution due to extended periods of cooking and preparing meals for the family. Breathing air tainted by the burning of solid fuels is estimated to be responsible for 641,000 of the 1.3 million deaths of women worldwide each year due to chronic obstructive pulmonary disorder (COPD).

In some settings, structural gender inequity is associated with particular forms of violence, marginalization, and oppression against females. This includes violent assault by men, child sexual abuse, strict regulation of women's behavior and movement, female genital mutilation, and exploitative, forced labor. Women and girls are also vulnerable to less well-documented forms of abuse or exploitation, such as human trafficking or "honor killings" for perceived behavioral transgressions and deviation of their social roles. These acts are associated with a wide range of health problems in women such as physical injuries, unwanted pregnancies, abortions, mental disorders such as depression, and anxiety, substance abuse, and sexually transmitted infections, all of which can potentially lead to premature death.

The ability of women to utilize health care is also heavily influenced by other forms of structural gender inequalities. These include unequal restriction on one's mobility and behavior, as well as unequal control over financial resources. Many of these social gender inequalities can impact the way women's health is regarded, which can in turn determine the level of access women have to healthcare services and the extent by which households and the larger community are willing to invest in women's health issues.

Other Axes of Oppression

Uninsured Children by Poverty Status, Household Income, Age, Race and Hispanic Origin and Nativity in the United States in 2009.

Apart from gender discrimination, other axes of oppression also exist in society to further marginalize certain groups of women, especially those who are living in poverty or of minority status in which they live.

Race and Ethnicity

Race is a well known axis of oppression, where people of color tend to suffer more from structural violence. For people of color, race can serve as a factor, in addition to gender, that can further influence one's health negatively. Studies have shown that in both high-income and low-income countries, levels of maternal mortality may be up to three times higher among women of disadvantaged ethnic groups than among white women. In a study on race and mother-death within the USA, the maternal mortality rate for African Americans is close to four times higher than that of white women. Similarly in South Africa, the maternal mortality rate for black/African women and women of color is approximately 10 and 5 times greater respectively than that of white/European women.

Socioeconomic Status

Although women around the world share many similarities in terms of the health-impacting challenges, there are also many distinct differences that arise from their varying states of socioeconomic conditions. The type of living conditions in which women live is largely associated with not only their own socioeconomic status, but also that of their nation.

At every single age category, women in high income countries tend to live longer and are less likely to suffer from ill health than and premature mortality than those in low income countries. Death rates in high-income countries are also very low among children and younger women, where most deaths occur after the age of 60 years. In low-income countries however, the death rates at young ages are much higher, with most death occurring among girls, adolescents, and younger adult women. Data from 66 developing countries show that child mortality rates among the poorest 20% of the population are almost double those in the top 20%. The most striking health outcome difference between rich and poor countries is maternal mortality. Presently, an overwhelming proportion of maternal mortality is concentrated within the nations that are suffering from poverty or some other form of humanitarian crises, where 99% of the more than half a million maternal deaths every year occur. This comes from the fact that institutional structures which could protect women's health and well-being are either lacking or poorly developed in these places.

The situation is similar within countries as well, where the health of both girls and women is critically affected by social and economic factors. Those who are living in poverty or of lower socioeconomic status tend to perform poorly in terms of health outcomes. In almost all countries, girls and women living in wealthier households experience lower levels of mortality and higher usage of health care services than those living in the poorer households. Such socioeconomic status-related health disparities is present in every nation around the world, including developed regions.

Management

The Fourth World Conference on Women asserts that men and women share the same right to the enjoyment of the highest attainable standard of physical and mental health. However, women are disadvantaged due to social, cultural, political and economic factors that directly influence their health and impede their access to health-related information and care. In the 2008 World Health Report, the World Health Organization stressed that strategies to improve women's health must take full account of the underlying determinants of health, particularly gender inequality. Additionally, specific socioeconomic and cultural barriers that hamper women in protecting and improving their health must also be addressed.

Gender Mainstreaming

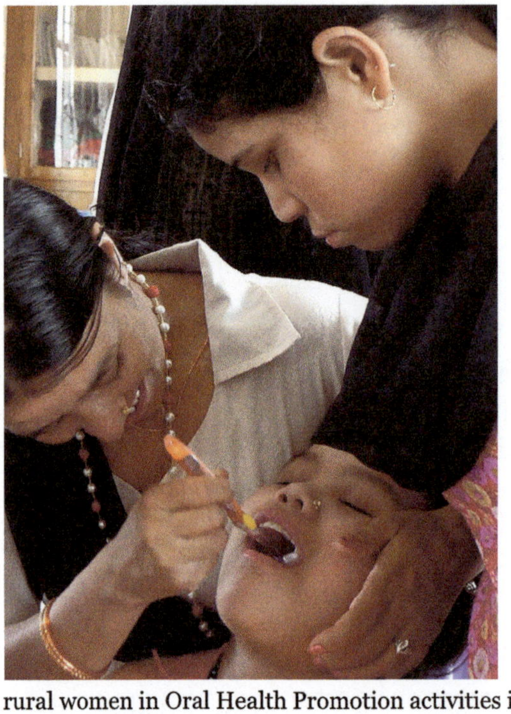

Training rural women in Oral Health Promotion activities in Nepal

Gender mainstreaming was established as a major global strategy for the promotion of gender equality in the Beijing Platform for Action from the Fourth United Nations World Conference on Women in Beijing in 1995. Gender mainstreaming is defined by the United Nations Economic and Social Council in 1997 as follows:

"Mainstreaming a gender perspective is the process of assessing the implications for women and men of any planned action, including legislation, policies or programmes, in all areas and at all levels. It is a strategy for making women's as well as men's concerns and experiences an integral dimension of the design, implementation, monitoring and evaluation of policies and programmes in all political, economic and societal spheres so that women and men benefit equally and inequality is not perpetuated. The ultimate aim is to achieve gender equality."

Over the past few years, "gender mainstreaming" has become a preferred approach for achieving greater health parity between men and women. It stems from the recognition that while technical strategies are necessary, they are not sufficient in alleviating gender disparities in health unless the gender discrimination, bias and inequality that in organizational structures of governments and organizations – including health systems - are being challenged and addressed. The gender mainstreaming approach is a response to the realisation that gender concerns must be dealt with in every aspect of policy development and programming, through systematic gender analyses and the implementation of actions that address the balance of power and the distribution of resources between women and men. In order to address gender health disparities, gender mainstreaming in health employs a dual focus. First, it seeks to identify and address gender-based differences and inequalities in all health initiatives; and second, it works to implement initiatives that address women's specific health needs that are a result either of biological differences between women and men (e.g. maternal health) or of gender-based discrimination in society (e.g. gender-based violence; poor access to health services).

Sweden's new public health policy, which came into force in 2003, has been identified as a key example of mainstreaming gender in health policies. According to the World Health Organization, Sweden's public health policy is designed to address not only the broader social determinants of health, but also the way in which gender is woven into the public health strategy. The policy specifically highlights its commitment to address and reduce gender-based inequalities in health.

Female Empowerment

The United Nations has identified the enhancement of women's involvement as way to achieve gender equality in the realm of education, work, and health. This is because women play critical roles as caregivers, formally and informally, in both the household and the larger community. Within the United States, an estimated 66% of all caregivers are female, with one-third of all female caregivers taking care of two or more people According to the World Health Organization, it is important that approaches and frameworks that are being implemented to address gender disparities in health acknowledge the fact that majority of the care work is provided by women. A meta-analysis of 40 different women's empowerment projects found that increased female participation have led to a broad range of quality of life improvements. These improvements include increases in women's advocacy demands and organization strengths, women-centered policy and governmental changes, and improved economic conditions for lower class women.

In Nepal, a community-based participatory intervention to identify local birthing problems and formulating strategies has been shown to be effective in reducing both neonatal and maternal mortality in a rural population. Community-based programs in Malaysia and Sri Lanka that used well-trained midwives as front-line health workers also produced rapid declines in maternal mortality.

In this lesson we look at differences in health status and outcome that are attributed to gender and the factors responsible for or influencing these differences.

The traditional view was that women report more health problems but have lower mortality (Verbrugge, 1985). This was believed to be the typical pattern in developed countries. In developing countries due to lack of access to healthcare the higher risk that women face due to childbirth results in higher mortality, thus mortality rates are somewhat similar for males and females. In India the life expectancy for males and females have reversed with females now indicating lower rates of mortality at 66.9 years as compared with males at 63.7 years since it equalized in 1981.

The difference in mortality rates may be ascribed to a combination of biological, environmental and social factors. In terms of the biological make up chromosomes and hormones play a role in influencing illness and death rates. Males have a genetic makeup that is a XY chromosome pair, X inherited from the mother and Y from the father whereas females have a genetic make up of XX that is they inherit an X chromosome from each parents. Chromosomes contain genes and males are more likely to be at risk for X linked disorders such as colour blindness and haemophilia as they do not have a back up copy of the damaged gene on the other chromosome as females are likely to have. Thus males have a disadvantage when it comes to X linked disorders and have a higher probability of inheriting them.

Males and females are exposed to different sex hormones in the endocrine system. Females are exposed to estrogen and progesterone whilst males are exposed to testosterone. Estrogen has been documented as having a protective effect for women as it guards against cardiovascular disease. Women are exposed to estrogen during their menarche and until menopause are protected against cardiovascular disease. Men on the other hand lack these protective benefits of estrogen and are exposed to testosterone which be implicated with hypertension and cardiac problems although this research is not conclusive.

Male mortality is higher for cardiovascular disease, COPD, cancer, accidents, suicide and homicide (U.S Death Rates, 1998 as cited in Arber, 1999). As far as environmental factors are considered the differential exposure hypothesis proposes that men and women have a differential exposure to resources. Women are less likely to be employed, have lower incomes, be engaged in domestic labour and be a single parent (Denton & Walters, 1999). Women are more likely to live in poverty than men especially in their later years. Given their lower levels of employment and lower paying employment their health coverage would also be poorer (in terms of insurance or employee benefits). Males however are more likely to be exposed to hazardous working conditions where they are exposed to risk from accidents as well as toxins (in coal mines, construction sites, chemical factories, cement factories, fertilizer and pesticides for farmers).This is especially true for developing countries, where safety standards are poor. Men are also more vulnerable to road accidents as they drive more often.

Gender differences in social and behavioral factors also impact on health differences. The most important difference in lifestyle is that more men tend to smoke and drink (Denton & Walters, 1999). Smoking is related to hypertension and lung cancer and is a big health risk factor. Men are more likely to binge drink than women thus putting themselves at greater risk than women who maybe more moderate drinkers. Men are more likely to eat an unbalanced diet and be overweight. Women are more likely to be physically inactive as compared to men (Denton & Walters, 1999). Women have slightly lower levels of self esteem but higher levels of social support.

According to the differential vulnerability hypotheses a high income, full time employment, caring for a family and having social support are more important predictors of good health for women. Also men and women tend to react differently to stress, with women seeking social support and men more likely to smoke or drink.

The traditional view that women have poorer health (in developed countries) is being revised. For when class and age are factored in, the differences in health seem less large. It is necessary to revisit the question or issue of gender differences in morbidity from time to time with better analytical tools for the situation is changing. The new finding that has emerged is that there are no gender differences in self assessed health in the older age group although women have a higher level of functional disability (Arber, 1999).

There are more women in the older age groups than men given their higher life expectancy. Thus controlling for age is important. The variable of class also is vital as more women in the older age group are poorer. Marital status is implicated with residential living (elderly homes) more women above 65 are widowed and hence more women live in residential establishments than men who are still married (Arber, 1999).Class differences impact on self reported health for both males and female with people in professional occupations rating their health as better. Class as measured in terms of occupation as well as income and house ownership all pointed in the same direction (Arber, 1999). After controlling for age, class, income and functional disability older women were found to have more positive self assessment of health (Arber, 1999).

Women's Health

Women's health refers to the health of women, which differs from that of men in many unique ways. Women's health is an example of population health, where health is defined by the World Health Organization as "a state of complete physical, mental and social well-being and not merely the absence of disease or infirmity". Often treated as simply women's reproductive health, many groups argue for a broader definition pertaining to the overall health of women, better expressed as "The health of women". These differences are further exacerbated in developing countries where women, whose health includes both their risks and experiences, are further disadvantaged.

Although women in industrialised countries have narrowed the gender gap in life expectancy and now live longer than men, in many areas of health they experience earlier and more severe disease with poorer outcomes. Gender remains an important social determinant of health, since women's health is influenced not just by their biology but also by conditions such as poverty, employment, and family responsibilities. Women have long been disadvantaged in many respects such as social and economic power which restricts their access to the necessities of life including health care, and the greater the level of disadvantage, such as in developing countries, the greater adverse impact on health.

Women's reproductive and sexual health places a unique burden on them. Even in developed countries pregnancy and childbirth are associated with substantial risks to women with maternal mortality accounting for more than a quarter of a million deaths per year, with large gaps between the developing and developed countries. Comorbidity from other non reproductive disease such as cardiovascular disease contribute to both the mortality and morbidity of pregnancy, including preeclampsia. Sexually transmitted infections have serious consequences for women and infants, with mother-to-child transmission leading to outcomes such as stillbirths and neonatal deaths, and pelvic inflammatory disease leading to infertility. In addition infertility from many other causes, birth control, unplanned pregnancy, unconsensual sexual activity and the struggle for access to abortion create other burdens for women.

While the rates of the leading causes of death, cardiovascular disease, cancer and lung disease, are similar in women and men, women have different experiences. Lung cancer has overtaken all other types of cancer as the leading cause of cancer death in women, followed by breast cancer, colorectal, ovarian, uterine and cervical cancers. While smoking is the major cause of lung cancer, amongst nonsmoking women the risk of developing cancer is three times greater than amongst nonsmoking men. Despite this, breast cancer remains the commonest cancer in women in developed countries, and is one of the more important chronic diseases of women, while cervical cancer remains one of the commonest cancers in developing countries, associated with human papilloma virus (HPV), an important sexually transmitted disease. HPV vaccine together with screening offers the promise of controlling these diseases. Other important health issues for women include cardiovascular disease, depression, dementia, osteoporosis and anemia. A major impediment to advancing women's health has been their underrepresentation in research studies, an inequity being addressed in the United States and other western nations by the establishment of centers of excellence in women's health research and large scale clinical trials such as the Women's Health Initiative.

Definitions and Scope

Women's experience of health and disease differ from those of men, due to unique biological, social and behavioural conditions. Biological differences vary all the way from phenotype to the cellular, and manifest unique risks for the development of ill health. The World Health Organization (WHO) defines health as "a state of complete physical, mental and social well-being and not merely the absence of disease or infirmity". Women's health is an example of population health, the health of a specific defined population.

Women's health has been described as "a patchwork quilt with gaps". Although many of the issues around women's health relate to their reproductive health, including maternal and child health, genital health and breast health, and endocrine (hormonal) health, including menstruation, birth control and menopause, a broader understanding of women's health to include all aspects of the health of women has been urged, replacing "Women's Health" with "The Health of Women". The WHO considers that an undue emphasis on reproductive health has been a major barrier to ensuring access to good quality health care for all women. Conditions that affect both men and women, such as cardiovascular disease, osteoporosis, also manifest differently in women. Women's health issues also include medical situations in which women face problems not directly related to their biology, such as gender-differentiated access to medical treatment and other socioeconomic factors. Women's health is of particular concern due to widespread discrimination against women in the world, leaving them disadvantaged.

A number of health and medical research advocates, such as the Society for Women's Health Research in the United States, support this broader definition, rather than merely issues specific to human female anatomy to include areas where biological sex differences between women and men exist. Women also need health care more and access the health care system more than do men. While part of this is due to their reproductive and sexual health needs, they also have more chronic non-reproductive health issues such as cardiovascular disease, cancer, mental illness, diabetes and osteoporosis. Another important perspective is realising that events across the entire life cycle (or life-course), from *in utero* to aging effect the growth, development and health of women. The life-course perspective is one of the key strategies of the World Health Organization.

Global Perspective

Gender differences in susceptibility and symptoms of disease and response to treatment in many areas of health are particularly true when viewed from a global perspective. Much of the available information comes from developed countries, yet there are marked differences between developed and developing countries in terms of women's roles and health. The global viewpoint is defined as the "area for study, research and practice that places a priority on improving health and achieving health equity for all people worldwide". In 2015 the World Health Organisation identified the top ten issues in women's health as being cancer, reproductive health, maternal health, human immunodeficiency virus (HIV), sexually transmitted infections, violence, mental health, non communicable diseases, youth and aging.

Life Expectancy

Women's life expectancy is greater than that of men, and they have lower death rates throughout life, regardless of race and geographic region. Historically though, women had higher rates of mortality, primarily from maternal deaths (death in childbirth). In industrialised countries, particularly the most advanced, the gender gap narrowed and was reversed following the industrial revolution. Despite these differences, in many areas of health, women experience earlier and more severe disease, and experience poorer outcomes.

Despite these differences, the leading causes of death in the United States are remarkably similar for men and women, headed by heart disease, which accounts for a quarter of all deaths, followed by cancer, lung disease and stroke. While women have a lower incidence of death from unintentional injury and suicide, they have a higher incidence of dementia..

The major differences in life expectancy for women between developed and developing countries lie in the childbearing years. If a woman survives this period, the differences between the two regions become less marked, since in later life non-communicable diseases (NCDs) become the major causes of death in women throughout the world, with cardiovascular deaths accounting for 45% of deaths in older women, followed by cancer (15%) and lung disease (10%). These create additional burdens on the resources of developing countries. Changing lifestyles, including diet, physical activity and cultural factors that favour larger body size in women, are contributing to an increasing problem with obesity and diabetes amongst women in these countries and increasing the risks of cardiovascular disease and other NCDs.

Social and Cultural Factors

Women's health is positioned within a wider body of knowledge cited by, amongst others, the World Health Organisation, which places importance on gender as a social determinant of health. Women's health is affected not just by their biology, but also by their social conditions, such as poverty, employment, and family responsibilities.

Women have traditionally been disadvantaged in terms of economic and social status and power, which in turn reduces their access to the necessities of life including health care. Despite recent improvements in western nations, women remain disadvantaged with respect to men. The gender gap in health is even more acute in developing countries where women are relatively more disadvantaged. In addition to gender inequity, thre remain specific disease processes uniquely associated with being a woman which create specific challenges in both prevention and health care.

Logo of Sustainable Development Goal 5: Gender Equality

Even after succeeding in accessing health care, women have been discriminated against, a process that Iris Young has called "internal exclusion", as opposed to "external exclusion", the barriers to access. This invisibility effectively masks the grievances of groups already disadvantaged by power inequity, further entrenching injustice.

Behavioral differences also play a role, in which women display lower risk taking including consume less tobacco, alcohol, and drugs, reducing their risk of mortality from associated diseases, including lung cancer, tuberculosis and cirrhosis. Other risk factors that are lower for women include motor vehicle accidents. Occupational differences have exposed women to less industrial injuries, although this is likely to change, as is risk of injury or death in war. Overall such injuries contributed to 3.5% of deaths in women compared to 6.2% in the United States in 2009. Suicide rates are also less in women.

The social view of health combined with the acknowledgement that gender is a social determinant of health inform women's health service delivery in countries around the world. Women's health services such as Leichhardt Women's Community Health Centre which was established in 1974 and was the first women's health centre established in Australia is an example of women's health approach to service delivery.

Women's health is an issue which has been taken up by many feminists, especially where reproductive health is concerned and the international women's movement was responsible for much of the adoption of agendas to improve women's health.

Biological Factors

Women and men differ in their chromosomal makeup, protein gene products, genomic imprinting, gene expression, signaling pathways, and hormonal environment. All of these necessitate caution in extrapolating information derived from biomarkers from one sex to the other. Women are particularly vulnerable at the two extremes of life. Young women and adolescents are at risk from STIs, pregnancy and unsafe abortion, while older women often have few resources and are disadvantaged with respect to men, and also are at risk of dementia and abuse, and generally poor health.

Reproductive and Sexual Health

5

Improve Maternal Health

Logo of Millennium Development Goal 5: Improving Maternal and Reproductive health

Women experience many unique health issues related to reproduction and sexuality and these are responsible for a third of all health problems experienced by women during their reproductive years (aged 15–44), of which unsafe sex is a major risk factor, especially in developing countries. Reproductive health includes a wide range of issues including the health and function of structures and systems involved in reproduction, pregnancy, childbirth and child rearing, including antenatal and perinatal care. Global women's health has a much larger focus on reproductive health than that of developed countries alone, but also infectious diseases such as malaria in pregnancy and non-communicable diseases (NCD). Many of the issues that face women and girls in resource poor regions are relatively unknown in developed countries, such as female genital cutting, and further lack access to the appropriate diagnostic and clinical resources.

Maternal Health

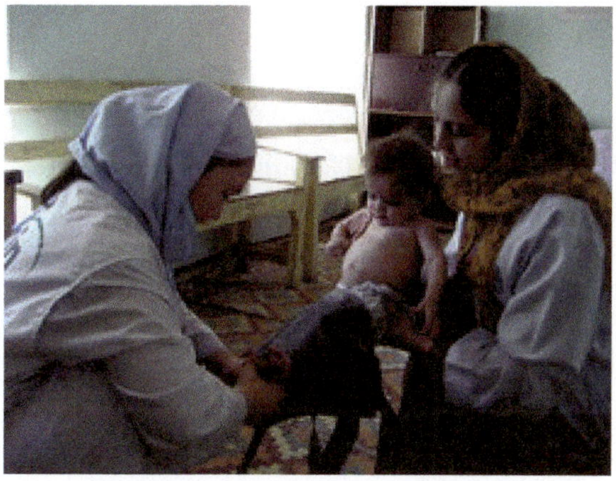

Maternal health clinic in Afghanistan

Pregnancy presents substantial health risks, even in developed countries, and despite advances in obstetrical science and practice. Maternal mortality remains a major problem in global health and is considered a sentinel event in judging the quality of health care systems. Adolescent pregnancy represents a particular problem, whether intended or unintended, and whether within marriage or a union or not. Pregnancy results in major changes in a girl's life, physically, emotionally, socially and economically and jeopardises her transition into adulthood. Adolescent pregnancy, more often than not, stems from a girl's lack of choices. or abuse. Child marriage is a major contributor worldwide, since 90% of births to girls aged 15–19 occur within marriage.

Maternal Death

In 2013 about 289,000 women (800 per day) in the world died due to pregnancy-related causes, with large differences between developed and developing countries. Maternal mortality in western nations had been steadily falling, and forms the subject of annual reports and reviews. Yet, between 1987 and 2011, maternal mortality in the United States rose from 7.2 to 17.8 deaths per 100,000 live births, this is reflected in the Maternal Mortality Ratio (MMR). By contrast rates as high as 1,000 per birth are reported in the rest of the world, with the highest rates in Sub-Saharan Africa and South Asia, which account for 86% of such deaths. These deaths are rarely investigated, yet the World Health Organization considers that 99% of these deaths, the majority of which occur within 24 hours of childbirth, are preventable if the appropriate infrastructure, training, and facilities were in place. In these resource-poor countries, maternal health is further eroded by poverty and adverse economic factors which impact the roads, health care facilities, equipment and supplies in addition to limited skilled personnel. Other problems include cultural attitudes towards sexuality, contraception, child marriage, home birth and the ability to recognise medical emergencies. The direct causes of these maternal deaths are hemorrhage, eclampsia, obstructed labor, sepsis and unskilled abortion. In addition malaria and AIDS complicate pregnancy. In the period 2003–2009 hemorrhage was the leading cause of death, accounting for 27% of deaths in developing countries and 16% in developed countries.

Non-reproductive health remains an important predictor of maternal health. In the United States, the leading causes of maternal death are cardiovascular disease (15% of deaths), endocrine, respiratory and gastrointestinal disorders, infection, hemorrhage and hypertensive disorders of pregnancy.

In 2000, the United Nations created Millennium Development Goal (MDG) 5 to improve maternal health. Target 5A sought to reduce maternal mortality by three quarters from 1990 to 2015, using two indicators, 5.1 the MMR and 5.2 the proportion of deliveries attended by skilled health personnel (physician, nurse or midwife). Early reports indicated MDG 5 had made the least progress of all MDGs. By the target date of 2015 the MMR had only declined by 45%, from 380 to 210, most of which occurred after 2000. However this improvement occurred across all regions, but the highest MMRs were still in Africa and Asia, although South Asia witnessed the largest fall, from 530 to 190 (64%). The smallest decline was seen in the developed countries, from 26 to 16 (37%). In terms of assisted births, this proportion had risen globally from 59 to 71%. Although the numbers were similar for both developed and developing regions, there were wide variations in the latter from 52% in South Asia to 100% in East Asia. The risks of dying in pregnancy in developing countries remains fourteen times higher than in developed countries, but in Sub-Saharan Africa, where the MMR is highest, the risk is 175 times higher. In setting the MDG targets, skilled assisted birth was considered a key strategy, but also an indicator of access to care and closely reflect mortality rates. There are also marked differences within regions with a 31% lower rate in rural areas of developing countries (56 vs. 87%), yet there is no difference in East Asia but a 52% difference in Central Africa (32 vs. 84%). With the completion of the MDG campaign in 2015, new targets are being set for 2030 under the Sustainable Development Goals campaign. Maternal health is placed under Goal 3, Health, with the target being to reduce the global maternal mortality ratio to less than 70. Amongst tools being developed to meet these targets is the WHO Safe Childbirth Checklist.

Improvements in maternal health, in addition to professional assistance at delivery, will require routine antenatal care, basic emergency obstetric care, including the availability of antibiotics, oxytocics, anticonvulsants, the ability to manually remove a retained placenta, perform instrumented deliveries, and postpartum care. Research has shown the most effective programmes are those focussing on patient and community education, prenatal care, emergency obstetrics (including access to cesarean sections) and transportation. As with women's health in general, solutions to maternal health require a broad view encompassing many of the other MDG goals, such as poverty and status, and given that most deaths occur in the immediate intrapartum period, it has been recommended that intrapartum care (delivery) be a core strategy. New guidelines on antenatal care were issued by WHO in November 2016.

Complications of Pregnancy

In addition to death occurring in pregnancy and childbirth, pregnancy can result in many non-fatal health problems including obstetrical fistulae, ectopic pregnancy, preterm labor, gestational diabetes, hyperemesis gravidarum, hypertensive states including preeclampsia, and anemia. Globally, complications of pregnancy vastly outway maternal deaths, with an estimated 9.5 million cases of pregnancy-related illness and 1.4 million near-misses (survival from severe life-threatening complications). Complications of pregnancy may be physical, mental, economic and social. It is estimated that 10–20 million women will develop physical or mental disability every year, resulting from complications of pregnancy or inadequate care. Consequently, international agencies have developed standards for obstetric care.

Obstetrical Fistula

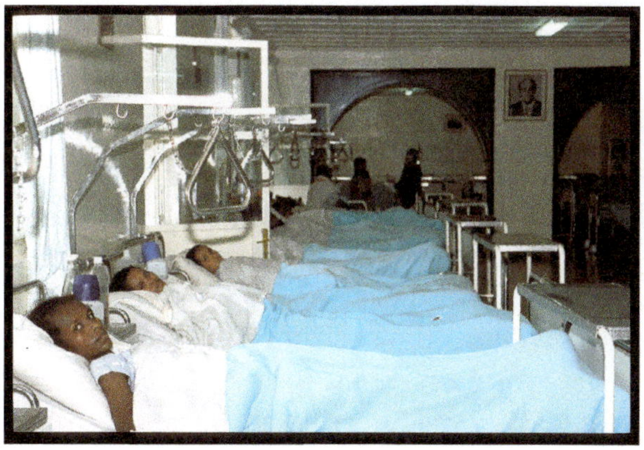

Women in an Ethiopian fistula hospital

Of near miss events, obstetrical fistulae (OF), including vesicovaginal and rectovaginal fistulae, remain one of the most serious and tragic. Although corrective surgery is possible it is often not available and OF is considered completely preventable. If repaired, subsequent pregnancies will require cesarian section. While unusual in developed countries, it is estimated that up to 100,000 cases occur every year in the world, and that about 2 million women are currently living with this condition, with the highest incidence occurring in Africa and parts of Asia. OF results from prolonged obstructed labor without intervention, when continued pressure from the fetus in the birth canal restricts blood supply to the surrounding tissues, with eventual fetal death, necrosis and expulsion. The damaged pelvic organs then develop a connection (fistula) allowing urine or feces, or both, to be discharged through the vagina with associated urinary and fecal incontinence, vaginal stenosis, nerve damage and infertility. Severe social and mental consequences are also likely to follow, with shunning of the women. Aprt from lack of access to care, causes include young age, and malnourishment. The UNFPA has made prevention of OF a priority and is the lead agency in the Campaign to End Fistula, which issues annual reports and the United Nations observes May 23 as the International Day to End Obstetric Fistula every year. Prevention includes discouraging teenage pregnancy and child marriage, adeaquate nutrition, and access to skilled care, including caesarian section.

Contraception

Family Planning Association: Kuala Terengganu, Malaysia

The ability to determine if and when to become pregnant, is vital to a woman's autonomy and well being, and contraception can protect girls and young women from the risks of early pregnancy and older women from the increased risks of unintended pregnancy. Adequate access to contraception can limit multiple pregnancies, reduce the need for potentially unsafe abortion and reduce maternal and infant mortality and morbidity. Some barrier forms of contraception such as condoms, also reduce the risk of STIs and HIV infection. Access to contraception allows women to make informed choices about their reproductive and sexual health, increases empowerment, and enhances choices in education, careers and participation in public life. At the societal level, access to contraception is a key factor in controlling population growth, with resultant impact on the economy, the environment and regional development. Consequently, the United Nations considers access to contraception a human right that is central to gender equality and women's empowerment that saves lives and reduces poverty, and birth control has been considered amongst the 10 great public health achievements of the 20th century.

To optimise women's control over pregnancy, it is essential that culturally appropriate contraceptive advice and means are widely, easily, and affordably available to anyone that is sexually active, including adolescents. In many parts of the world access to contraception and family planning services is very difficult or non existent and even in developed counties cultural and religious traditions can create barriers to access. Reported usage of adequate contraception by women has risen only slightly between 1990 and 2014, with considerable regional variability. Although global usage is around 55%, it may be as low as 25% in Africa. Worldwide 222 million women have no or limited access to contraception. Some caution is needed in interpreting available data, since contraceptive prevalence is often defined as "the percentage of women currently using any method of contraception among all women of reproductive age (*i.e.*, those aged 15 to 49 years, unless otherwise stated) who are married or in a union. The "in-union" group includes women living with their partner in the same household and who are not married according to the marriage laws or customs of a country." This definition is more suited to the more restrictive concept of family planning, but omits the contraceptive needs of all other women and girls who are or are likely to be sexually active, are at risk of pregnancy and are not married or "in-union".

Three related targets of MDG5 were adolescent birth rate, contraceptive prevalence and unmet need for family planning (where prevalence+unmet need = total need), which were monitored by the Population Division of the UN Department of Economic and Social Affairs. Contraceptive use was part of Goal 5B (universal access to reproductive health), as Indicator 5.3. The evaluation of MDG5 in 2015 showed that amongst couples usage had increased worldwide from 55% to 64%. with one of the largest increases in Subsaharan Africa (13 to 28%). The corollary, unmet need, declined slightly worldwide (15 to 12%). In 2015 these targets became part of SDG5 (gender equality and empowerment) under Target 5.6: Ensure universal access to sexual and reproductive health and reproductive rights, where Indicator 5.6.1 is the proportion of women aged 15–49 years who make their own informed decisions regarding sexual relations, contraceptive use and reproductive health care.

There remain significant barriers to accessing contraception for many women in both developing and developed regions. These include legislative, administrative, cultural, religious and economic barriers in addition to those dealing with access to and quality of health services. Much of the attention has been focussd on preventing adolescent pregnancy. The Overseas Development Institute (ODI) has identified a number of key barriers, on both the supply and demand side, including internalising socio-cultural values, pressure from family members, and cognitive barriers (lack of knowledge), which need addressing. Even in developed regions many women, particularly those who are disadvantaged, may face substantial difficulties in access that may be financial and geographic but may also face religious and political discrimination. Women have also mounted campaigns against potentially dangerous forms of contraception such as defective intrauterine devices (IUD)s, particularly the Dalkon Shield.

Abortion

Abortion is the intentional termination of pregnancy, as compared to spontaneous termination (miscarriage). Abortion is closely allied to contraception in terms of women's control and regulation of their reproduction, and is often subject to similar cultural, religious, legislative and economic constraints. Where access to contraception is limited, women turn to abortion. Consequently, abortion rates may be used to estimate unmet needs for contraception. However the available procedures have carried great risk for women throughout most of history, and still do in the developing world, or where legal restrictions force women to seek clandestine facilities. Access to safe legal abortion places undue burdens on lower socioeconomic groups and in jurisdictions that create significant barriers. These issues have frequently been the subject of political and feminist campaigns where differing viewpoints pit health against moral values.

Women demonstrate for abortion rights, Dublin, 2012

Globally, there were 87 million unwanted pregnancies in 2005, of those 46 million resorted to abortion, of which 18 million were considered unsafe, resulting in 68,000 deaths. The majority of these deaths occurred in the developing world. The United Nations considers these avoidable with access to safe abortion and post-abortion care. While abortion rates have fallen in developed countries, but not in developing countries. Between 2010–2014 there were 35 abortions per 1000 women aged 15–44, a total of 56 million abortions per year. The United nations has prepared recommendations for health care workers to provide more accessible and safe abortion and post-abortion care. An inherent part of post-abortion care involves provision of adequate contraception.

Sexually transmitted infections

Important sexual health issues for women include Sexually transmitted infections (STIs) and female genital cutting (FGC). STIs are a global health priority because they have serious consequences for women and infants. Mother-to-child transmission of STIs can lead to stillbirths, neonatal death, low-birth-weight and prematurity, sepsis, pneumonia, neonatal conjunctivitis, and congenital deformities. Syphilis in pregnancy results in over 300,000 fetal and neonatal deaths per year, and 215,000 infants with an increased risk of death from prematurity, low-birth-weight or congenital disease.

Diseases such as chlamydia and gonorrhoea are also important causes of pelvic inflammatory disease (PID) and subsequent infertility in women. Another important consequence of some STIs such as genital herpes and syphilis increase the risk of acquiring HIV by three-fold, and can also influence its transmission progression. Worldwide, women and girls are at greater risk of HIV/AIDS. STIs are in turn associated with unsafe sexual activity that is often unconsensual.

Female Genital Cutting

Traditional African midwife explaining the risks of FGC for childbirth at a community meeting

Female genital cutting (also referred to as female genital mutilation) is defined by the World health Organization (WHO) as "all procedures that involve partial or total removal of the external female genitalia, or other injury to the female genital organs for non-medical reasons". It has sometimes been referred to as female circumcision, although this term is misleading because it implies it is analogous to the circumcision of the foreskin from the male penis. Consequently, the term mutilation was adopted to emphasise the gravity of the act and its place as a violation of human rights. Subsequently, the term cutting was advanced to avoid offending cultural sensibility that would interfere with dialogue for change. To recognise these points of view some agencies use the composite female genital mutilation/cutting (FMG/C).

It has affected more than 200 million women and girls who are alive today. The practice is concentrated in some 30 countries in Africa, the Middle East and Asia. FGC affects many religious faiths, nationalities, and socioeconomic classes and is highly controversial. The main arguments advanced to justify FGC are hygiene, fertility, the preservation of chastity, an important rite of passage, marriageability and enhanced sexual pleasure of male partners. The amount of tissue removed varies considerably, leading the WHO and other bodies to classify FGC into four types. These range from the partial or total removal of the clitoris with or without the prepuce (clitoridectomy) in Type I, to the additional removal of the labia minora, with or without excision of the labia majora (Type II) to narrowing of the vaginal orifice (introitus) with the creation of a covering seal by suturing the remaining labial tissue over the urethra and introitus, with or without excision of the clitoris (infibulation). In this type a small opening is created to allow urine and menstrual blood to be discharged. Type 4 involves all other procedures, usually relatively minor alterations such as piercing.

While defended by those cultures in which it constitutes a tradition, FGC is opposed by many medical and cultural organizations on the grounds that it is unnecessary and harmful. Short term health effects may include hemorrhage, infection, sepsis, and even result in death, while long term effects include dyspareunia, dysmenorrhea, vaginitis and cystitis. In addition FGC leads to complications with pregnancy, labor and delivery. Reversal (defibulation) by skilled personnel may be required to open the scarred tissue. Amongst those opposing the practice are local grassroots groups, and national and international organisations including WHO, UNICEF, UNFPA and Amnesty International. Legislative efforts to ban FGC have rarely been successful and the preferred approach is education and empowerment and the provision of information about the adverse health effects as well the human rights aspects.

Progress has been made but girls 14 and younger represent 44 million of those who have been cut, and in some regions 50% of all girls aged 11 and younger have been cut. Ending FGC has been considered one of the necessary goals in achieving the targets of the Millennium Development Goals, while the United Nations has declared ending FGC a target of the Sustainable Development Goals, and for February 6 to known as the International Day of Zero Tolerance for Female Genital Mutilation, concentrating on 17 African countries and the 5 million girls between the ages of 15 and 19 that would otherwise be cut by 2030.

Infertility

In the United States, infertility affects 1.5 million couples. Many couples seek assisted reproductive technology (ART) for infertility. In the United States in 2010, 147,260 in vitro fertilization (IVF) procedures were carried out, with 47,090 live births resulting. In 2013 these numbers had increased to 160,521 and 53,252. However, about a half of IVF pregnancies result in multiple-birth deliveries, which in turn are associated with an increase in both morbidity and mortality of the mother and the infant. Causes for this include increased maternal blood pressure, premature birth and low birth weight. In addition, more women are waiting longer to conceive and seeking ART.

Child Marriage

Poster addressing the 2014 London Girl Summit dealing with FGM and Child Marriage

Child marriage (including union or cohabitation) is defined as marriage under the age of eighteen and is an ancient custom. In 2010 it was estimated that 67 million women, then, in their twenties had been married before they turned eighteen, and that 150 million would be in the next decade, equivalent to 15 million per year. This number had increased to 70 million by 2012. In developing countries one third of girls are married under age, and 1:9 before 15. The practice is commonest in South Asia (48% of women), Africa (42%) and Latin America and the Caribbean (29%). The highest prevalence is in Western and Sub-Saharan Africa. The percentage of girls married before the age of eighteen is as high as 75% in countries such as Nigeria. Most child marriage involves girls. For instance in Mali the ratio of girls to boys is 72:1, while in countries such as the United States the ratio is 8:1. Marriage may occur as early as birth, with the girl being sent to her husbands home as early as age seven.

There are a number of cultural factors that reinforce this practice. These include the child's financial future, her dowry, social ties and social status, prevention of premarital sex, extramarital pregnancy and STIs. The arguments against it include interruption of education and loss of employment prospects, and hence economic status, as well as loss of normal childhood and its emotional maturation and social isolation. Child marriage places the girl in a relationship where she is in a major imbalance of power and perpetuates the gender inequality that contributed to the practice in the first place. Also in the case of minors, there are the issues of human rights, non-consensual sexual activity and forced marriage and a 2016 joint report of the WHO and Inter-Parliamentary Union places the two concepts together as Child, Early and Forced Marriage (CEFM), as did the 2014 Girl Summit. In addition the likely pregnancies at a young age are associated with higher medical risks for both mother and child, multiple pregnancies and less access to care with pregnancy being amongst the leading causes of death amongst girls aged 15–19. Girls married under age are also more likely to be the victims of domestic violence.

There has been an international effort to reduce this practice, and in many countries eighteen is the legal age of marriage. Organizations with campaigns to end child marriage include the United Nations and its agencies, such as the Office of the High Commissioner for Human Rights, UNFPA, UNICEF and WHO. Like many global issues affecting women's health, poverty and gender inequality are root causes, and any campaign to change cultural attitudes has to address these. Child marriage is the subject of international conventions and agreements such as The Convention on the Elimination of All Forms of Discrimination against Women (CEDAW, 1979) (article 16) and the Universal Declaration of Human Rights and in 2014 a summit conference (Girl Summit) co-hosted by UNICEF and the UK was held in London to address this issue together with FGM/C. Later that same year the General Assembly of the United Nations passed a resolution, which *inter alia.*

Urges all States to enact, enforce and uphold laws and policies aimed at preventing and ending child, early and forced marriage and protecting those at risk, and ensure that marriage is entered into only with the informed, free and full consent of the intending spouses (5 September 2014)

Amongst non-governmental organizations (NGOs) working to end child marriage are Girls not Brides, Young Women's Christian Association (YWCA), the International Center for Research on Women (ICRW) and Human Rights Watch (HRW). Although not explicitly included in the original Millennium Development Goals, considerable pressure was applied to include ending child marriage in the successor Sustainable Development Goals adopted in September 2015, where ending this practice by 2030 is a target of SDG 5 Gender Equality. While some progress is being made in reducing child marriage, particularly for girls under fifteen, the prospects are daunting. The indicator for this will be the percentage of women aged 20–24 who were married or in a union before the age of eighteen. Efforts to end child marriage include legislation and ensuring enforcement together with empowering women and girls. To raise awareness, the inaugural UN International Day of the Girl Child[a] in 2012 was dedicated to ending child marriage.

Menstrual Cycle

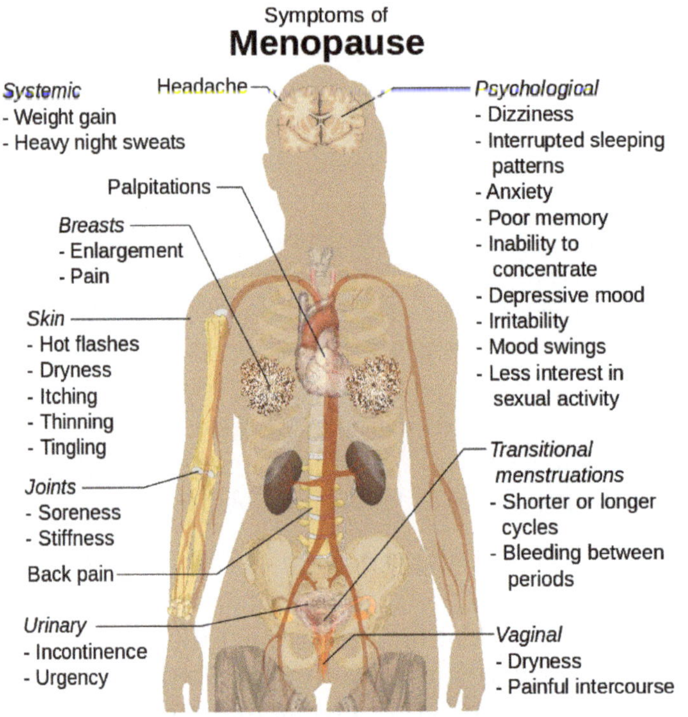

Women's menstrual cycles, the approximately monthly cycle of changes in the reproductive system, can pose significant challenges for women in their reproductive years (the early teens to about 50 years of age). These include the physiological changes that can effect physical and mental health, symptoms of ovulation and the regular shedding of the inner lining of the uterus (endometrium) accompanied by vaginal bleeding (menses or menstruation). The onset of menstruation (menarche) may be alarming to unprepared girls and mistaken for illness. Menstruation can place undue burdens on women in terms of their ability to participate in activities, and access to menstrual aids such as tampons and "sanitary pads". This is particularly acute amongst poorer socioeconomic groups where they may represent a financial burden and in developing countries where menstruation can be an impediment to a girl's education.

Equally challenging for women are the physiological and emotional changes associated with the cessation of menses (menopause or climacteric). While typically occurring gradually towards the end of the fifth decade in life marked by irregular bleeding the cessation of ovulation and menstruation is accompanied by marked changes in hormonal activity, both by the ovary itself (oestrogen and progesterone) and the pituitary gland (follicle stimulating hormone or FSH and luteinizing hormone or LH). These hormonal changes may be associated with both systemic sensations such as hot flashes and local changes to the reproductive tract such as reduced vaginal secretions and lubrication. While menopause may bring relief from symptoms of menstruation and fear of pregnancy it may also be accompanied by emotional and psychological changes associated with the symbolism of the loss of fertility and a reminder of aging and possible loss of desirability. While menopause generally occurs naturally as a physiological process it may occur earlier (premature menopause) as a result of disease or from medical or surgical intervention. When menopause occurs prematurely the adverse consequences may be more severe.

Other Reproductive and Sexual Health Issues

Other reproductive and sexual health issues include sex education, puberty, sexuality and sexual function. Women also experience a number of issues related to the health of their breasts and genital tract, which fall into the scope of gynaecology.

Non-reproductive Health

Women and men have different experiences of the same illnesses, especially cardiovascular disease, cancer, depression and dementia, and are more prone to urinary tract infections than men.

Cardiovascular Disease

Cardiovascular disease is the leading cause of death (30%) amongst women in the United States, and the leading cause of chronic disease amongst them, affecting nearly 40% (Gronowski and Schindler, Tables I and IV). The onset occurs at a later age in women than in men. For instance the incidence of stroke in women under the age of 80 is less than that in men, but higher in those aged over 80. Overall the lifetime risk of stroke in women exceeds that in men. The risk of cardiovascular disease amongst those with diabetes and amongst smokers is also higher in women than in men. Many aspects of cardiovascular disease vary between women and men, including risk factors, prevalence, physiology, symptoms, response to intervention and outcome.

Cancer

Women and men have approximately equal risk of dying from cancer, which accounts for about a quarter of all deaths, and is the second leading cause of death. However the relative incidence of different cancers varies between women and men. In the United States the three commonest types of cancer of women in 2012 were lung, breast and colorectal cancers. In addition other important cancers in women, in order of importance, are ovarian, uterine (including endometrial and cervical cancers (Gronowski and Schindler, Table III). Similar figures were reported in 2016. While cancer death rates rose rapidly during the twentieth century, the increase was less and later in women due to differences in smoking rates. More recently cancer death rates have started to decline as the use of tobacco becomes less common. Between 1991 and 2012, the death rate in women declined by 19% (less than in men). In the early twentieth century death from uterine (uterine body and cervix) cancers was the leading cause of cancer death in women, who had a higher cancer mortality than men. From the 1930s onwards, uterine cancer deaths declined, primarily due to lower death rates from cervical cancer following the availability of the Papanicolaou (Pap) screening test. This resulted in an overall reduction of cancer deaths in women between the 1940s and 1970s, when rising rates of lung cancer led to an overall increase. By the 1950s the decline in uterine cancer left breast cancer as the leading cause of cancer death till it was overtaken by lung cancer in the 1980s. All three cancers (lung, breast, uterus) are now declining in cancer death rates, but more women die from lung cancer every year than from breast, ovarian, and uterine cancers combined. Overall about 20% of people found to have lung cancer are never smokers, yet amongst nonsmoking women the risk of developing lung cancer is three times greater than amongst men who never smoked.

In addition to mortality, cancer is a cause of considerable morbidity in women. Women have a lower lifetime probability of being diagnosed with cancer (38% vs 45% for men), but are more likely to be diagnosed with cancer at an earlier age.

Breast Cancer

Breast cancer is the secondest common cancer in the world and the commonest amongst women, as well as being amongst the ten commonest chronic diseases of women, and a substantial contributor to loss of quality of life (Gronowski and Schindler, Table IV). Globally, it accounts for 25% of all cancers. In 2016, breast cancer is the commonest cancer diagnosed amongst women in both developed and developing countries, accounting for nearly 30% of all cases, and worldwide accounts for one and a half million cases and over half a million deaths, being the fifth commonest cause of cancer death overall and the second in developed regions. Geographic variation in incidence is the opposite of that of cervical cancer, being highest in Northern America and lowest in Eastern and Middle Africa, but mortality rates are relatively constant, resulting in a wide variance in case mortality, ranging from 25% in developed regions to 37% in developing regions, and with 62% of deaths occurring in developing countries.

Cervical Cancer

Globally, cervical cancer is the fourth commonest cancer amongst women, particularly those of lower socioeconomic status. Women in this group have reduced access to health care, high rates of child and forced marriage, parity, polygamy and exposure to STIs from multiple sexual contacts of male partners. All of these factors place them at higher risk. In developing countries, cervical cancer accounts for 12% of cancer cases amongst women and is the second leading cause of death, where about 85% of the global burden of over 500,000 cases and 250,000 deaths from this disease occurred in 2012. The highest incidence occurs in Eastern Africa, where with Middle Africa, cervical cancer is the commonest cancer in women. The case fatality rate of 52% is also higher in developing countries than in developed countries (43%), and the mortality rate varies by 18-fold between regions of the world.

Cervical cancer is associated with human papillomavirus (HPV), which has also been implicated in cancers of the vulva, vagina, anus, and oropharynx. Almost 300 million women worldwide have been infected with HPV, one of the commoner sexually transmitted infections, and 5% of the 13 million new cases of cancer in the world have been attributed to HPV. In developed countries, screening for cervical cancer using the Pap test has identified pre-cancerous changes in the cervix, at least in those women with access to health care. Also an HPV vaccine programme is available in 45 countries. Screening and prevention programmes have limited availability in developing countries although inexpensive low technology programmes are being developed, but access to treatment is also limited. If applied globally, HPV vaccination at 70% coverage could save the lives of 4 million women from cervical cancer, since most cases occur in developing countries.

Ovarian Cancer

By contrast, ovarian cancer, the leading cause of reproductive organ cancer deaths, and the fifth commonest cause of cancer deaths in women in the United States, lacks an effective screening programme, and is predominantly a disease of women in industrialised countries. Because it is largely asymptomatic in its earliest stages, more than 50% of women have stage III or higher cancer (spread beyond the ovaries) by the time they are diagnosed, with a consequent poor prognosis.

Mental Health

Almost 25% of women will experience mental health issues over their lifetime. Women are at higher risk than men from anxiety, depression, and psychosomatic complaints. Globally, depression is the leading disease burden. In the United States, women have depression twice as often as men. The economic costs of depression in American women are estimated to be $20 billion every year. The risks of depression in women have been linked to changing hormonal environment that women experience, including puberty, menstration, pregnancy, childbirth and the menopause. Women also metabolise drugs used to treat depression differently to men. Suicide rates are less in women than men (<1% vs. 2.4%), but are a leading cause of death for women under the age of 60.

Dementia

The prevalence of Alzheimer's Disease in the United States is estimated at 5.1 million, and of these two thirds are women. Furthermore, women are far more likely to be the primary caregivers of adult family members with depression, so that they bear both the risks and burdens of this disease. The lifetime risk for a woman of developing Alzeimer's is twice that of men. Part of this difference may be due to life expectancy, but changing hormonal status over their lifetime may also play a par as may differences in gene expression. Deaths due to dementia are higher in women than men (4.5% of deaths vs. 2.0%).

Bone Health

Osteoporosis ranks sixth amongst chronic diseases of women in the United States, with an overall prevalence of 18%, and a much higher rate involving the femur, neck or lumbar spine amongst women (16%) than men (4%), over the age of 50 (Gronowski and Schindler, Table IV). Osteoporosis is a risk factor for bone fracture and about 20% of senior citizens who sustain a hip fracture die within a year. The gender gap is largely the result of the reduction of estrogen levels in women following the menopause. Hormone Replacement Therapy (HRT) has been shown to reduce this risk by 25–30%, and was a common reason for prescribing it during the 1980s and 1990s. However the Women's Health Initiative (WHI) study that demonstrated that the risks of HRT outweighed the benefits has since led to a decline in HRT usage.

Anaemia

Anaemia is a major global health problem for women. Women are affected more than men, in which up to 30% of women being found to be anaemic and 42% of pregnant women. Anaemia is linked to a number of adverse health outcomes including a poor pregnancy outcome and impaired cognitive function (decreased concentration and attention). The main cause of anaemia is iron deficiency. In United States women iron deficiency anaemia (IDA) affects 37% of pregnant women, but globally the prevalence is as high as 80%. IDA starts in adolescence, from excess menstrual blood loss, compounded by the increased demand for iron in growth and suboptimal dietary intake. In the adult woman, pregnancy leads to further iron depletion.

Violence

Women experience structural and personal violence differently than men. The United Nations has defined violence against women as:

> *"Any act of gender-based violence that results in, or is likely to result in, physical, sexual or mental harm or suffering to women, including threats of such acts, coercion or arbitrary deprivation of liberty, whether occurring in public or in private life." —United Nations, Declaration on the Elimination of Violence against Women, 1993.*

Violence against women may take many forms, including physical, sexual, emotional and psychological and may occur throughout the life-course. Structural violence may be embedded in legislation or policy, or be systematic misogyny by organisations against groups of women. Perpetrators of personal violence include state actors, strangers, acquaintances, relatives and intimate partners and manifests itself across a spectrum from discrimination, through harassment, sexual assault and rape, and physical harm to murder (femicide). It may also include cultural practices such as female genital cutting.

Non-fatal violence against women has severe implications for women's physical, mental and reproductive health, and is seen as not simply isolated events but rather a systematic pattern of behaviour that both violates their rights but also limits their role in society and requires a systematic approach.

The World Health Organisation (WHO) estimates that 35% of women in the world have experienced physical or sexual violence over their lifetime and that the commonest situation is intimate partner violence. 30% of women in relationships report such experience, and 38% of murders of women are due to intimate partners. These figures may be as high as 70% in some regions. Risk factors include low educational achievement, a parental experience of violence, childhood abuse, gender inequality and cultural attitudes that allow violence to be considered more acceptable.

Violence was declared a global health priority by the WHO at its assembly in 1996, drawing on both the United Nations Declaration on the elimination of violence against women (1993) and the recommendations of both the International Conference on Population and Development (Cairo, 1994) and the Fourth World Conference on Women (Beijing, 1995) This was followed by its 2002 World Report on Violence and Health, which focusses on intimate partner and sexual violence. Meanwhile, the UN embedded these in an action plan when its General Assembly passed the Millennium Declaration in September 2000, which resolved *inter alia* "to combat all forms of violence against women and to implement the Convention on the Elimination of All Forms of Discrimination against Women". One of the Millennium Goals (MDG 3) was the promotion of gender equality and the empowerment of women, which sought to eliminate all forms of violence against women as well as implementing CEDAW. This recognised that eliminating violence, including discrimination was a prerequisite to achieving all other goals of improving women's health. However it was later criticised for not including violence as an explicit target, the "missing target". In the evaluation of MDG 3, violence remained a major barrier to achieving the goals. In the successor Sustainable Development Goals, which also explicitly list the related issues of discrimination, child marriage and genital cutting, one target is listed as "Eliminate all forms of violence against all women and girls in the public and private spheres" by 2030.

UN Women believe that violence against women "is rooted in gender-based discrimination and social norms and gender stereotypes that perpetuate such violence", and advocate moving from supporting victims to prevention, through addressing root and structural causes. They recommend programmes that start early in life and are directed towards both genders to promote respect and equality, an area often overlooked in public policy. This strategy, which involves broad educational and cultural change, also involves implementing the recommendations of the 57th session of the UN Commission on the Status of Women (2013). To that end the 2014 UN International Day of the Girl Child was dedicated to ending the cycle of violence. In 2016, the World Health Assembly also adopted a plan of action to combat violence against women, globally.

Women in Health Research

Women's Health Initiative logo

Changes in the way research ethics was visualised in the wake of the Nuremberg Trials (1946), led to an atmosphere of protectionism of groups deemed to be vulnerable that was often legislated or regulated. This resulted in the relative underrepresentation of women in clinical trials. The position of women in research was further compromised in 1977, when in response to the tragedies resulting from thalidomide and diethylstilbestrol (DES), the United States Food and Drug Administration (FDA) prohibited women of child bearing years from participation in early stage clinical trials. In practice this ban was often applied very widely to exclude all women. Women, at least those in the child bearing years, were also deemed unsuitable research subjects due to their fluctuating hormonal levels during the menstrual cycle. However, research has demonstrated significant biological differences between the sexes in rates of susceptibility, symptoms and response to treatment in many major areas of health, including heart disease and some cancers. These exclusions pose a threat to the application of evidence-based medicine to women, and compromise to care offered to both women and men.

The increasing focus on Women's Rights in the United States during the 1980s focused attention on the fact that many drugs being prescribed for women had never actually been tested in women of child-bearing potential, and that there was a relative paucity of basic research into women's health. In response to this the National Institutes of Health (NIH) created the Office of Research on Women's Health (ORWH) in 1990 to address these inequities. In 1993 the National Institutes of Health Revitalisation Act officially reversed US policy by requiring NIH funded phase III clinical trials to include women. This resulted in an increase in women recruited into research studies. The next phase was the specific funding of large scale epidemiology studies and clinical trials focussing on women's health such as the Women's Health Initiative (1991), the largest disease prevention study conducted in the US. Its role was to study the major causes of death, disability and frailty in older women. Despite this apparent progress, women remain underrepresented. In 2006 women accounted for less than 25% of clinical trials published in 2004, A follow up study by the same authors five years later found little evidence of improvement. Another study found between 10–47% of women in heart disease clinical trials, despite the prevalence of heart disease in women. Lung cancer is the leading cause of cancer death amongst women, but while the number of women enrolled in lung cancer studies is increasing, they are still far less likely to be enrolled than men.

One of the challenges in assessing progress in this area is the number of clinical studies that either do not report the gender of the subjects or lack the statistical power to detect gender differences. These were still issues in 2014, and further compounded by the fact that the majority of animal studies also exclude females or fail to account for differences in sex and gender. for instance despite the higher incidence of depression amongst women, less than half of the animal studies use female animals. Consequently, a number of funding agencies and scientific journals are asking researchers to explicitly address issus of sex and gender in their research.

A related issue is the inclusion of pregnant women in clinical studies. Since other illnesses can exist concurrently with pregnancy, information is needed on the response to and efficacy of interventions during pregnancy, but ethical issues relative to the fetus, make this more complex. This gender bias is partly offset by the iniation of large scale epidemiology studies of women, such as the Nurses' Health Study (1976), Women's Health Initiative and Black Women's Health Study.

Women have also been the subject of abuse in health care research, such as the situation revealed in the Cartwright Inquiry in New Zealand (1988), in which research by two feminist journalists revealed that women with cervical abnormalities were not receiving treatment, as part of an experiment. The women were not told of the abnormalities and several later died.

National and International Initiatives

Logo of UN Sustainable Development Goals

In addition to addressing gender inequity in research, a number of countries have made women's health the subject of national initiatives. For instance in 1991 in the United States, the Department of Health and Human Services established an Office on Women's Health (OWH) with the goal of improving the health of women in America, through coordinating the women's health agenda throughout the Department, and other agencies. In the twenty first century the Office has focussed on underserviced women. Also, in 1994 the Centers for Disease Control and Prevention (CDC) established its own Office of Women's Health (OWH), which was formally authorised by the 2010 Affordable Health Care Act (ACA).

Internationally, many United Nations agencies such as the World Health Organization (WHO), United Nations Population Fund (UNFPA) and UNICEF maintain specific programs on women's health, or maternal, sexual and reproductive health. In addition the United Nations global goals address many issues related to women's health, both directly and indirectly. These include the 2000 Millennium Development Goals (MDG) and their successor, the Sustainable Development Goals adopted in September 2015, following the report on progress towards the MDGs (*The Millenium Development Goals Report 2015*). For instance the eight MDG goals, eradicating extreme poverty and hunger, achieving universal primary education, promoting gender equality and empowering women, reducing child mortality rates, improving maternal health, combating HIV/AIDS malaria and other diseases, ensuring environmental sustainability, and developing a global partnership for development, all impact on women's health, as do all seventeen SDG goals, in addition to the specific SDG5: Achieve gender equality and empower all women and girls.

Goals and Challenges

Research is a priority in terms of improving women's health. Research needs include diseases unique to women, more serious in women and those that differ in risk factors between women and men. The balance of gender in research studies needs to be balanced appropriately to allow analysis that will detect interactions between gender and other factors. Gronowski and Schindler suggest that scientific journals make documentation of gender a requirement when reporting the results of animal studies, and that funding agencies require justification from investigators for any gender inequity in their grant proposals, giving preference to those that are inclusive. They also suggest it is the role of health organisations to encourage women to enroll in clinical research. However, there has been progress in terms of large scale studies such as the WHI, and in 2006 the Society for Women's Health Research founded the Organization for the Study of Sex Differences (OSSD) and the journal *Biology of Sex Differences* to further the study of sex differences.

Women receiving health education in India

Research findings can take some time before becoming routinely implemented into clinical practice. Clinical medicine needs to incorporate the information already available from research studies as to the different ways in which diseases affect women and men. Many "normal" laboratory values have not been properly established for the female population separately, and similarly the "normal" criteria for growth and development. Drug dosing needs to take gender differences in drug metabolism into account.

Globally, women's access to health care remains a challenge, both in developing and developed countries. In the United States, before the Affordable Health Care Act came into effect, 25% of women of child bearing age lacked health insurance. In the absence of adequate insurance, women are likely to avoid important steps to self care such as routine physical examination, screening and prevention testing, and prenatal care. The situation is aggravated by the fact that women living below the poverty line are at greater risk of unplanned pregnancy, unplanned delivery and elective abortion. Added to the financial burden in this group are poor educational achievement, lack of transportation, inflexible work schedules and difficulty obtaining child care, all of which function to create barriers to accessing health care. These problems are much worse in developing countries. Under 50% of childbirths in these countries are assisted by healthcare providers (*e.g.* midwives, nurses, doctors) which accounts for higher rates of maternal death, up to 1:1,000 live births. This is despite the WHO setting standards, such as a minimum of four antenatal visits. A lack of healthcare providers, facilities, and resources such as formularies all contribute to high levels of morbidity amongst women from avoidable conditions such as obstetrical fistulae, sexually transmitted diseases and cervical cancer.

These challenges are included in the goals of the Office of Research on Women's Health, in the United States, as is the goal of facilitating women's access to careers in biomedicine. The ORWH believes that one of the best ways to advance research in women's health is to increase the proportion of women involved in healthcare and health research, as well as assuming leadership in government, centres of higher learning, and in the private sector. This goal acknowledges the glass ceiling that women face in careers in science and in obtaining resources from grant funding to salaries and laboratory space. The National Science Foundation in the United States states that women only gain half of the doctorates awarded in science and engineering, fill only 21% of full-time professor positions in science and 5% of those in engineering, while earning only 82% of the remuneration their male colleagues make. These figures are even lower in Europe.

Women are more likely to be exposed to violence, both physical and mental. Women in a patriarchal society are oppressed and have to obey orders or face the consequences which may often involve physical violence. They have to contend with violence in the domestic realm which is a routine occurrence as well as violence in times of turbulence from outsiders as they are vulnerable targets.

Women are also exposed to sexual violence as victims of rape, child sexual abuse and in the marital context. The implications of these forms of violence that women are victims of, is that they are often unable to seek help or health care and have to quietly tolerate it (NFHS3). There is no balm for the mental violence in any case other than social support from the natal family if at all. Domestic violence has been documented as risk factor for depression in women in both developed and developing countries (Perriera et al,2011). Thus with domestic violence which is often repetitive there is actual bodily harm that is often untended to and the more grave repercussion which is the loss of hope or despair that leads to depression which in turn affects physical health.

Women in developing countries are likely to marry early, as early as in adolescence.The median age of marriage in India is 17.2 , 46% of the women in the 18 -29 year age group got married before 18 (the legal age) in India (NFHS 3). Early marriage implies an early sexual initiation that they may not be ready for. It also exposes them to the risk of sexual infections. Marriage may expose them to harassment from in laws as well as the husband. Girls who marry young are often poor and marriage implies a life of drudgery and oppression.

Early marriage implies early pregnancy often in their teens. The implications of early pregnancy are threatening for both mother and foetus. A teenager's body may not be ready for pregnancy especially given that they are poor and probably underweight. Their body mass index is too low to carry a full term pregnancy; they are still just recovering from puberty and are very anaemic. There is a high risk of complications given these factors. Teenage pregnancies are linked to low birth weight babies even when mother's weight and socioeconomic status were controlled (WHO, 2013).

Socially and psychologically they may be unprepared for motherhood and may resent it. The risk of complications with the baby and birth defects is high given the context of poor medical care and poor ante natal care. The likelihood of post partum depression is higher for teens given the multiple risk factors.

Childbirth is an additional health risk factor for women. About 800 women die from pregnancy related complications every day (WHO, 2013). India's maternal mortality rate is 230 per 100,000 live births and it ranks 56th in the world. Most of these deaths are preventable and reflect poor access to health care compounded with poverty and anemia.

Why are there so many deaths at childbirth and why are all these young girls having babies? Why not wait until they are older and wiser? After all conception can be delayed with contraception! Again we come back to the issue of lack of access to health care and a strong cultural norm for women to prove their fertility as soon as possible. Women are very reluctant to use contraception before their first pregnancy thus lowering the age of first birth (Kulkarni, 2007).Despite the safe methods available to males, it is the invasive methods of the pill and IUD are prescribed to women and it becomes the responsibility of women to prevent preganancies. Both the pill and IUD have side effects that are rarely communicated to women by the authorities. However women have an even more exaggerated perception of the side effects in the absence of communication about this. After achieving the desired family size it is the woman who undergoes a permanent sterilization rather than the man for whom it is a simple procedure. Due to the lack of availability of safe contraception many women use abortion as a contraceptive method. Many abortions are carried outside a medical setting by people who are not medically qualified and it ends in either death or severe septic infections that put the woman in grave danger. Although abortion is legal in India, many women attempt an unsafe abortion because they may be doing it without consulting the spouse or in- laws or they may lack access to health care especially in rural areas.

Women all over the developing world are exposed to fumes from stoves and suffer from higher rates of Chronic Obstructive Pulmonary Disorder (COPD). The houses are small and lack ventilation and henceget filled with smoke. It is also a grave risk factor for infants who are always in the house and are exposed to the smoke.

The one issue that consistently emerges across all these concerns, is the lack of access to health care. Women particularly in developing countries may have additional obstacles to accessing health care as it may be very far away, they may lack transportation, they may not be allowed to go so far, they may not feel empowered to ask to seek care, they may not perceive it as not that important given the obstacles and let things slide until it is very bad.

In India, women's health begins with a risk to being born at all , given the prevalence female foeticide. In some districts across India the sex ratio has become very skewed with males outnumbering females by more than 200-300 (NFHS, 3) . This has led to buying women for sex /marriage and reducing women to property.This has led to ill treatment of women.

Women in general and especially in the poorer section are neglected and deprived of resources and opportunities that are reserved for male children. They are treated as secondary citizens and this impacts on the health care that would be available to them. In a study about the sex of siblings it was found that having sisters was advantageous to a child irrespective of its own sex, as the resources were shared in a more advantageous way as opposed to having brothers (Garg & Morduch, 1998).

Girls would be likely to have a higher rate of disabilities due to neglect and those with disabilities would be treated with disdain. They would not be trained in any skill or given an opportunity to be treated.

In terms of research in health and medicine there is a tradition of having male participants thus women participants have been underrepresented. Thus medical knowledge about women is still being researched given the different hormonal make ups.

The culture of patriarchy restricts women's freedom and education and employment (the right to vote or drive in some Arab countries). This oppression can be a risk factor for depression.

Prevalence of depression is higher among women (WHO 2001) due to hormonal reasons but this may also be due to cultural reasons. Some Women are likely to develop post partum depression. Depression results in a loss of productivity and in post partum cases also affects the health and nutrition of the infant. There is very little treatment available to women in this condition in developing countries and it is necessary to address this problem as depression is projected as having the highest burden of disease by 2030 according to the WHO.

Food and Health

Food and eating are vital to living. What we eat, how we eat and when we eat to a great extent are determined by culture and region. 'We are what we eat' is a phrase oft heard and refers to the effect of diet on health. In this chapter we will attempt to understand the influences on our diets and its influences on our health.

From an evolutionary perspective, it is interesting to see how our diets have evolved and are constantly evolving. Early homo sapiens were hunter gatherers and lived in small bands and foraged for food. For the most part they survived on roots and berries and seasonal fruit. Meat was available only when they managed to make a kill with their primitive weapons. Thus the pattern that emerges is that they expended enormous energy in searching for food and were not always guaranteed of returns. Their diet was varied but not very dense in calories. The impact of people on the environment was minimal given that the population was very small and resources were relatively abundant .

Genetically we have not changed much since the time of our hunter gatherer ancestors however our lifestyles and culture have no similarity with theirs (apart from the hunter gatherer tribes that still exist in isolated pockets). It has been estimated that the average daily energy expenditure for a 65kg male is 4.4 MJ among hunter gatherers as opposed to 3.5MJ for a person in post industrial society (Powles, 1992 as cited in Marks et al, 2000). Women were always responsible for most of the food related activities (gathering plant produce) bringing water and child rearing , thus the difference in energy expenditure is probably greater for women (Fieldhouse, 1996 as cited in Marks et al, 2000). Among Kung Bushmen, the child is carried by the mother for 2,400 kms in the first two years of life (Powles, 1992 as cited in Marks et al, 2000). For thousands of years of evolution the capacity to store fat was an advantage as it helped people tide over times of shortage. However this characteristic has now become a risk factor for chronic diseases that may not have previously existed.

The hunter gatherer era was followed by the development of agriculture, the cultivation of grains and the breeding of livestock. Food became routinely available including meat.Population density increased as people began to lead a settled life and villages and towns developed. With settlements, sanitation as well as social problems due to ownership arose. Diet became less varied and average levels of activity decreased. Bowel and respiratory infections increased and epidemics spread due to increased density. Disputes over territory led to wars (Marks et al, 2000).

The agricultural era was followed by the industrial revolution which changed lives dramatically with the invention of electricity, mechanized labor saving devices, transport – rail and air travel. The energy expended for food reduced further as people now only walked or drove to the nearest market where everything was abundantly available for a price.

Current society is a post industrial society that is characterized by the availability of information via the internet. Now people can order groceries online and even meals online without expending any energy.Increased food consumption and decreased energy expenditure characterizes this era resulting in obesity and overweight.

Diet and Health

How does diet impact health? What is a balanced diet? A balanced diet contains carbohydrates, proteins, fats, minerals, vitamins and fiber which are recommended to be consumed in proportions on the basis of the food pyramid.

A Meta-analysis was conducted by Keys et al (1998) of 5 prospective studies comparing mortality rates of vegetarians versus non vegetarians. Participants were followed for an average of 10.6 yrs and 8,330 deaths occurred. Results indicated a death rate ratio for ischemic heart disease was .76 for vegetarians. The reduction in mortality for vegetarians was significant at lower ages.

Cholesterol is type of lipid present in meat and dairy and eggs. It is also produced by the body however when it is in excess it forms plaques that block the arteries that lead to atherosclerosis or the hardening of arteries. Atherosclerosis is a risk factor for hypertension and coronary heart disease. There are two forms of cholesterol - Low Density Lipoprotein (LDL) and High Density Lipoprotein (HDL).

Another aspect of diet that has a known relationship with health is salt which is implicated in hypertension. Law et al (1991) in 24 populations correlated blood pressure and salt intake – a highly significant relationship was found that increased with age. There are high levels of salt in processed foods and snack foods.

Sugar is another element that is implicated with poor health. High sugar intake is associated with obesity, type 2 diabetes and dental carries. Sugar is cheap and pervasive and is added to many processed foods to make things taste better, however it is potentially dangerous as it interferes with the hunger and satiety signals in the brain (Lustig, Schmidt & Brindis, 2012). It is also highly addictive.

Psychological, Cultural and Social Aspects of Food

The preference for foods develop and can be modified by conditioning and early experience. According to Capaldi (1996) food preferences may develop or get modified By the following aspects:

- Mere exposure – is being exposed to the taste or experiencing it in childhood or before birth via the amniotic fluid in the mothers womb. Babies whose mother's diets include garlic are more open to the flavor of garlic later as mother's milk is flavored with garlic.
- Flavour-flavour learning refers to pairing a new flavor with an experienced flavor usually a sweet taste – since mother's milk is sweet and babies seem to prefer a sweet taste.
- Flavour –nutrient learning refers to pairing of a new flavor with a nutrient such as protein which leads to the flavor being preferred (maybe because it causes satiety).
- Taste aversion learning refers to when a new taste is paired with nausea or vomiting the new flavor is rejected or people develop an aversion to it (an allergy to prawns).

Why is there an Emotional Association with Food?

It starts with the early childhood environment and memories of who fed us and the taste and smell of the food becomes associated with the feeling of being loved or cared for and a sense of security. For Indians the smell of plain dal and rice with ghee probably brings back childhood memories. Certain foods have an emotional connotation for people learn by association the connection with a particular occasion (festivals).

The olfactory tract (the bundle of nerves carrying the olfactory stimuli) goes directly to the mid brain very close to the amygdala and hippocampus which are centers of emotion and memory. The olfactory sense, unlike vision and hearing which go the cortical areas goes directly to the mid brain (inside) this is because olfaction is evolutionarily a very primitive (old) sense. Olfaction or odours are related to both fear as well as sexual arousal. Hence flavor which is entwined with the sense of smell can provoke emotion and memories.

Chocolate – there are alcoholics and then there are chocoholics. Chocolate creates an intense craving – but why does that happen?

There is a certain molecule in the body that has been relatively recently discovered called Anandamide (after Sanskrit ananda or bliss) which binds with certain receptors that create a very very mild high. Now compounds in dark chocolate that resemble anandamide have been discovered that explains the feeling of a happy glow that follows after eating a piece of chocolate (Tomaso et al, 1996). We probably crave that feeling when we crave chocolate.

Stress

How does stress affect our eating? Sometimes if it is too severe we may not eat and loose our appetite, but sometimes when it is moderate and we are busy coping with it we may crave fatty foods and binge on salty fried snacks without even being aware of it. Stress increases the appetite and comfort foods are eaten as they are rewarding and give you a calm feeling. It is a signal to our body that we have tanked up on energy and hence it shuts of the stress response (Marano, 2003).

Food Craving

We crave certain foods – where do these cravings come from? Stress may direct us to more calorie dense food – but the pervasive food imagery we are surrounded by also stimulates the craving. Pictures or advertisements of ice cream or cake or talking about it or seeing someone eat it stimulate craving. Thus the environment also plays a role in determining our eating.

What is the Role of Culture in Influencing Our Diet?

Culture and region influence the ingredients of a cuisine, what is locally available is what is a dominant part of the cuisine. Coastal areas in India all use coconut and fish. Where there is wheat – people eat it (Punjabis eat rotis) and where there is rice people eat that like China or South India. The style of cooking is also influenced by the culture – the kind of utensils used whether food is steamed or baked in a oven or on a tava.

Rules and values concerning food and eating vary across cultures, in India, cooking and making fresh food is emphasized as opposed to the American culture which is more dependent on processed foods. Rules about eating – where you sit, the etiquette to be followed all add to the eating experience.

The social environment – the family eats together or the kids eat in front of the television or everybody eats whenever its convenient for them influences how and what you eat. The conversation that accompanies the meal does influence how you eat and your mood and your digestion.

Advertising and the Food Industry

We are surrounded by stimuli of food imagery in television adds, magazine adds, on billboards at shops. Some people and children maybe more vulnerable to these messages and maybe more influenced by them

What is the influence of food advertising on children?

The Food Standards Agency report(2003 ,as cited in Marks et al, 2000) highlighted that advertising focused on children for sugared breakfast cereal, soft drinks, sweets and savory snacks influences their purchase and consumption.

The food industry is already a saturated market therefore they will keep advertising – to grow especially, in the developing country markets which they see as untapped. (The Maggi and Knor noodles and soup are constantly being advertised on children's channels projecting it as children's food in India).

The childhood obesity epidemic in America is not a mystery given the culture's heavy dependence on processed foods. Their schools have vending machines with candy bars and soft drinks which are now being removed. Americans consume a lot of sugar hence they also have a lot of tooth decay.

That brings us to the obesity issue. Obesity is the excessive accumulation of body fat – over 20% above one's ideal weight. Obesity is associated with atherosclerosis, hypertension, diabetes, some forms of cancer, gall bladder disease and arthritis. It is also implicated in risk of heart trouble, complications in surgery, anesthesia & childbearing. Obesity is associated with early mortality.

What are the Factors Affecting Obesity?

Genetic Predisposition that interacts with the immediate environment

Childhood Eating Habits – if bingeing on sweets and fatty foods were part of growing up or if they were completely deprived of them which can lead to overeating in adulthood.

Emotional Factors such as stress or depression can be triggers for eating comfort foods.

Attitudes towards weight and weight loss – whether it is perceived as impossible or people have a positive attitude to exercise and weight loss.

Social environments – family and friends and their attitudes and their weight exert an influence on people. The pervasiveness of processed foods that are flooding the urban market and making their way into people's regular diets is another factor. Many mothers and women see it as a convenience, given their rushed schedules. Frozen fries and smileys have become birthday party staples in some groups

Cultural environnent – in many cultures being overweight is valued and women who are big have high social status (Botswana). In some cultures like India women putting on weight after child-birth is seen as normal but in other cultures there is a strong motivation to loose the weight.

Treating Obesity

Dieting, Surgery (bariatric surgery – where the stomach is reduced in size),Appetite –Suppressing Drugs and Behavior Modification to change eating habits and reward patterns that exclude food are the varied options to treat obesity.

The Multimodal Approach that is a combination of the above strategies is the most effective.

While the western world concerns itself with the obesity pandemic in India and other developing countries malnutrition continues to be a problem.

Malnutrition

Malnourishment is linked to half of all child deaths and is also responsible for 35% of the disease burden of children below 5 and 11% of total global DALYs (Black et al, 2008). In India according to the third National Family Health Survey (2005-6) 48% of children under the age of 5 are stunted, 20% are wasted and 43% are underweight.

Low birth weight and or stunting in the first two years are associated with lower adult height, fewer years of schooling and lower income as adults (from longitudinal studies across 5 countries including India) (Victora, 2008).

In a study aimed at identifying the predictors of child malnutrition, the factors highlighted were having a body mass index below normal for the mother, being below the poverty line, being illiterate, having no media exposure, being underage at the first birth, and not breast feeding within the first hour of birth (Nair, 2007). Strategies to improve nutrition (quantity & quality) for all categories of the population with an emphasis on child bearing women and children in the 0-5 category will be giant step in the direction of preventive health care.

Health Food

Health food is food considered normally beneficial to to human health a normal healthy diet required for human nutrition. No human being the same as any other, different dietary practices can be considered healthy by different people.

Foods marketed as "healthy" may be natural foods, organic foods, whole foods, and sometimes vegetarian or dietary supplements. Such products are sold in health food stores or in the health/organic sections of supermarkets.

Health Claims

In the United States, health-related claims on nutrition facts labels are regulated by the U.S. Food and Drug Administration (FDA), while advertising is regulated by the Federal Trade Commission.

According to the FDA, "Health claims describe a relationship between a food, food component, or dietary supplement ingredient, and reducing risk of a disease or health-related condition".

In general, claims of health benefits for specific foodstuffs have not been evaluated by national regulatory agencies. Additionally, research funded by manufacturers or marketers that may form the basis of such marketing claims has been shown to result in more favorable results than independently funded research.

While there is no precise definition for "health food", the United States Food and Drug Administration has warned food manufacturers against labeling foods as being "healthy" when they have a high sugar, salt, or fat content.

Examples

Fruit Juice Smoothie preparation

The following is a non-exhaustive list of foods that have been considered healthy:

- Apple cider vinegar, a fruit vinegar considered a health food
- Broccoli sprouts
- Certain cereal products:
    - Corn flakes, patented food invented in 1894
    - Digestive biscuit, English baked good from 1851, containing fiber and sometimes sodium bicarbonate
    - Graham cracker, cracker made with whole grain Graham flour (1829)
    - Graham bread, a type of whole wheat bread
    - Granola, a food made from mixed, toasted grains
    - Granula, the first manufactured breakfast cereal (1863)
    - Grape-Nuts, an American breakfast cereal made from baked and ground grain (1897)
    - Muesli, breakfast cereal of rolled oats, fruit and nuts, made by a Swiss doctor (1900)
    - Shredded wheat, whole wheat cereal (1893)
- Eggplant, hosts of vitamin and minerals, and also contains important phytonutrients
- Herbal extract, plants, often medicinal that are concentrated and standardized
- Herbal teas
- Honey, a naturally occurring whole sweetener
- Malt, whole sprouted barley
- Meat analogue, a dietary alternative to meat, found in some vegetarian and vegan diets
- Molasses, black strap molasses has been sold as a health food
- Certain oils, including olive oil and fish oil
- Postum, a coffee alternative from 1895
- Yogurt, traditional cultured milk product

Physical Exercise

Physical exercise is any bodily activity that enhances or maintains physical fitness and overall health and wellness. It is performed for various reasons, including increasing growth and development, preventing aging, strengthening muscles and the cardiovascular system, honing athletic skills, weight loss or maintenance, and also enjoyment. Frequent and regular physical exercise boosts the immune system and helps prevent "diseases of affluence" such as cardiovascular disease, type 2 diabetes, and obesity. It may also help prevent stress and depression, increase quality of sleep and act as a non-pharmaceutical sleep aid to treat diseases such as insomnia, help promote or maintain positive self-esteem, improve mental health, maintain steady digestion and treat constipation and gas, regulate fertility health, and augment an individual's sex appeal or body image, which has been found to be linked with higher levels of self-esteem. Childhood obesity is a growing global concern, and physical exercise may help decrease some of the effects of childhood and adult obesity. Some care providers call exercise the "miracle" or "wonder" drug—alluding to the wide variety of benefits that it can provide for many individuals. Aside from the health advantages, these benefits may include different social rewards for staying active while enjoying the environment of one's culture. Many individuals choose to exercise publicly outdoors where they can congregate in groups, socialize, and appreciate life.

Running in water

Weight training

In the United Kingdom two to four hours of light activity are recommended during working hours. This includes walking and standing. In the United States, the CDC/ACSM consensus statement and the Surgeon General's report states that every adult should participate in moderate exercise, such as walking, swimming, and household tasks, for a minimum of 30 minutes daily.

Classification

Exercise in space: Astronaut Daniel Tani, Expedition 16 flight engineer, works out at the Unity node of the International Space Station using the short bar of the Interim Resistive Exercise Device (IRED) to perform pull-ups to increase his upper body strength while in a microgravity environment.

Physical exercises are generally grouped into three types, depending on the overall effect they have on the human body:

- Aerobic exercise is any physical activity that uses large muscle groups and causes the body to use more oxygen than it would while resting. The goal of aerobic exercise is to increase cardiovascular endurance. Examples of aerobic exercise include cycling, swimming, brisk walking, skipping rope, rowing, hiking, playing tennis, continuous training, and long slow distance training.
- Anaerobic exercise, which includes strength and resistance training, can firm, strengthen, and tone muscles, as well as improve bone strength, balance, and coordination. Examples of strength moves are push-ups, pull-ups, lunges, and bicep curls using dumbbells. Anaerobic exercise also include weight training, functional training, eccentric training, Interval training, sprinting, and high-intensity interval training increase short-term muscle strength.
- Flexibility exercises stretch and lengthen muscles. Activities such as stretching help to improve joint flexibility and keep muscles limber. The goal is to improve the range of motion which can reduce the chance of injury.

Physical exercise can also include training that focuses on accuracy, agility, power, and speed.

Sometimes the terms 'dynamic' and 'static' are used. 'Dynamic' exercises such as steady running, tend to produce a lowering of the diastolic blood pressure during exercise, due to the improved blood flow. Conversely, static exercise (such as weight-lifting) can cause the systolic pressure to rise significantly (during the exercise).

Health Effects

Physical exercise is important for maintaining physical fitness and can contribute to maintaining a healthy weight, regulating digestive health, building and maintaining healthy bone density, muscle strength, and joint mobility, promoting physiological well-being, reducing surgical risks, and strengthening the immune system. Some studies indicate that exercise may increase life expectancy and the overall quality of life. People who participate in moderate to high levels of physical exercise have a lower mortality rate compared to individuals who by comparison are not physically active. Moderate levels of exercise have been correlated with preventing aging by reducing inflammatory potential. The majority of the benefits from exercise are achieved with around 3500 metabolic equivalent (MET) minutes per week. For example, climbing stairs 10 minutes, vacuuming 15 minutes, gardening 20 minutes, running 20 minutes, and walking or bicycling for transportation 25 minutes on a daily basis would *together* achieve about 3000 MET minutes a week. A lack of physical activity causes approximately 6% of the burden of disease from coronary heart disease, 7% of type 2 diabetes, 10% of breast cancer and 10% of colon cancer worldwide. Overall, physical inactivity causes 9% of premature mortality worldwide.

Fitness

Individuals can increase fitness following increases in physical activity levels. Increases in muscle size from resistance training is primarily determined by diet and testosterone. This genetic variation in improvement from training is one of the key physiological differences between elite athletes and the larger population. Studies have shown that exercising in middle age leads to better physical ability later in life.

Cardiovascular System

The beneficial effect of exercise on the cardiovascular system is well documented. There is a direct correlation between physical inactivity and cardiovascular mortality, and physical inactivity is an independent risk factor for the development of coronary artery disease. Low levels of physical exercise increase the risk of cardiovascular diseases mortality.

Children who participate in physical exercise experience greater loss of body fat and increased cardiovascular fitness. Studies have shown that academic stress in youth increases the risk of cardiovascular disease in later years; however, these risks can be greatly decreased with regular physical exercise. There is a dose-response relation between the amount of exercise performed from approximately 700 to 2000 kcal of energy expenditure per week and all-cause mortality and cardiovascular disease mortality in middle-aged and elderly populations. The greatest potential for reduced mortality is in the sedentary who become moderately active. Studies have shown that since heart disease is the leading cause of death in women, regular exercise in aging women leads to healthier cardiovascular profiles. Most beneficial effects of physical activity on cardiovascular disease mortality can be attained through moderate-intensity activity (40% to 60% of maximal oxygen uptake, depending on age). Persons who modify their behavior after myocardial infarction to include regular exercise have improved rates of survival. Persons who remain sedentary have the highest risk for all-cause and cardiovascular disease mortality. According to the American Heart Association, exercise reduces blood pressure, LDL and total cholesterol, and body weight. It increases HDL cholesterol, insulin sensitivity, and exercise tolerance.

Immune System

Although there have been hundreds of studies on exercise and the immune system, there is little direct evidence on its connection to illness. Epidemiological evidence suggests that moderate exercise has a beneficial effect on the human immune system; an effect which is modeled in a J curve. Moderate exercise has been associated with a 29% decreased incidence of upper respiratory tract infections (URTI), but studies of marathon runners found that their prolonged high-intensity exercise was associated with an increased risk of infection occurrence. However, another study did not find the effect. Immune cell functions are impaired following acute sessions of prolonged, high-intensity exercise, and some studies have found that athletes are at a higher risk for infections. Studies have shown that strenuous stress for long durations, such as training for a marathon, can suppress the immune system by decreasing the concentration of lymphocytes. The immune systems of athletes and nonathletes are generally similar. Athletes may have slightly elevated natural killer cell count and cytolytic action, but these are unlikely to be clinically significant.

Vitamin C supplementation has been associated with lower incidence of URTIs in marathon runners.

Biomarkers of inflammation such as C-reactive protein, which are associated with chronic diseases, are reduced in active individuals relative to sedentary individuals, and the positive effects of exercise may be due to its anti-inflammatory effects. In individuals with heart disease, exercise interventions lower blood levels of fibrinogen and C-reactive protein, an important cardiovascular risk marker. The depression in the immune system following acute bouts of exercise may be one of the mechanisms for this anti-inflammatory effect.

Cancer

A systematic review evaluated 45 studies that examined the relationship between physical activity and cancer survivorship. According to the study results "There was consistent evidence from 27 observational studies that physical activity is associated with reduced all-cause, breast cancer–specific, and colon cancer–specific mortality".

Epigenetic Effects

Physical exercise was correlated with a lower methylation frequency of two tumor suppressor genes, CACNA2D3 and L3MBTL. Hypermethylation of CACNA2D3 is associated with gastric cancer, while hypermethylation of L3MBTL is associated with breast cancer, brain tumors and hematological malignancies. A recent study indicates that exercise results in reduced DNA methylation at CpG sites on genes associated with breast cancer.

Cancer Cachexia

Physical exercise is becoming a widely accepted non-pharmacological intervention for the prevention and attenuation of cancer cachexia. "Cachexia is a multiorganic syndrome associated with cancer, characterized by inflammation, body weight loss (at least 5%) and muscle and adipose tissue wasting". Exercise triggers the activation of the transcriptional coactivator peroxisome proliferator-activated receptor gamma coactivator-1α (PGC-1α), which suppresses FoxO- and NF-κB-dependent gene transcription during muscle atrophy that is induced by fasting or denervation; thus, PGC-1α may be a key intermediate responsible for the beneficial antiatrophic effects of physical exercise on cancer cachexia. The exercise-induced isoform PGC-1α4, which can repress myostatin and induce IGF1 and hypertrophy, is a potential drug target for treatment of cancer cachexia. Other factors, such as JUNB and SIRT1, that maintain skeletal muscle mass and promote hypertrophy are also induced with regular physical exercise.

Neurobiological

The neurobiological effects of physical exercise are numerous and involve a wide range of interrelated effects on brain structure, brain function, and cognition. A large body of research in humans has demonstrated that consistent aerobic exercise (e.g., 30 minutes every day) induces persistent improvements in certain cognitive functions, healthy alterations in gene expression in the brain, and beneficial forms of neuroplasticity and behavioral plasticity; some of these long-term effects include: increased neuron growth, increased neurological activity (e.g., c-Fos and BDNF signaling), improved stress coping, enhanced cognitive control of behavior, improved declarative, spatial, and working memory, and structural and functional improvements in brain structures and pathways associated with cognitive control and memory. The effects of exercise on cognition have important implications for improving academic performance in children and college students, improving adult productivity, preserving cognitive function in old age, preventing or treating certain neurological disorders, and improving overall quality of life.

People who regularly perform aerobic exercise (e.g., running, jogging, brisk walking, swimming, and cycling) have greater scores on neuropsychological function and performance tests that measure certain cognitive functions, such as attentional control, inhibitory control, cognitive flexibility, working memory updating and capacity, declarative memory, spatial memory, and information processing speed. Aerobic exercise is also a potent antidepressant and euphoriant; as a result, consistent exercise produces general improvements in mood and self-esteem.

Regular aerobic exercise improves symptoms associated with a variety of central nervous system disorders and may be used as an adjunct therapy for these disorders. There is clear evidence of exercise treatment efficacy for major depressive disorder and attention deficit hyperactivity disorder. A large body of preclinical evidence and emerging clinical evidence supports the use of exercise therapy for treating and preventing the development of drug addictions. Reviews of clinical evidence also support the use of exercise as an adjunct therapy for certain neurodegenerative disorders, particularly Alzheimer's disease and Parkinson's disease. Regular exercise is also associated with a lower risk of developing neurodegenerative disorders. Regular exercise has also been proposed as an adjunct therapy for brain cancers.

Depression

Physical exercise has established efficacy as an antidepressant in individuals with depression and current medical evidence supports the use of exercise as both a preventive measure against and an adjunct therapy with antidepressant medication for depressive disorders. A July 2016 meta-analysis concluded that physical exercise improves overall quality of life in individuals with depression relative to controls. One systematic review noted that yoga may be effective in alleviating symptoms of prenatal depression. The biomolecular basis for exercise-induced antidepressant effects is believed to be a result of increased neurotrophic factor signaling, particularly brain-derived neurotrophic factor.

Continuous aerobic exercise can induce a transient state of euphoria, colloquially known as a "runner's high" in distance running or a "rower's high" in crew, through the increased biosynthesis of at least three euphoriant neurochemicals: anandamide (an endocannabinoid), β-endorphin (an endogenous opioid), and phenethylamine (a trace amine and amphetamine analog).

A systematic review noted that, although limited, some evidence suggests that the duration of engagement in a sedentary lifestyle is positively correlated with a risk of developing an anxiety disorder or experiencing anxiety symptoms. It noted that additional research is needed in order to confirm these findings.

Sleep

A 2010 review of published scientific research suggested that exercise generally improves sleep for most people, and helps sleep disorders such as insomnia. The optimum time to exercise *may* be 4 to 8 hours before bedtime, though exercise at any time of day is beneficial, with the possible exception of heavy exercise taken shortly before bedtime, which may disturb sleep. There is, in any case, insufficient evidence to draw detailed conclusions about the relationship between exercise and sleep.

According to a 2005 study, exercise is the most recommended alternative to sleeping pills for resolving insomnia. Sleeping pills are more costly than to make time for a daily routine of staying fit, and may have dangerous side effects in the long run. Exercise can be a healthy, safe and inexpensive way to achieve more and better sleep.

Excessive Exercise

Too much exercise can be harmful. Without proper rest, the chance of stroke or other circulation problems increases, and muscle tissue may develop slowly. Extremely intense, long-term cardiovascular exercise, as can be seen in athletes who train for multiple marathons, has been associated with scarring of the heart and heart rhythm abnormalities. Specifically, high cardiac output has been shown to cause enlargement of the left and right ventricle volumes, increased ventricle wall thickness, and greater cardiac mass. These changes further result in myocardial cell damage in the lining of the heart, leading to scar tissue and thickened walls. During these processes, the protein troponin increases in the bloodstream, indicating cardiac muscle cell death and increased stress on the heart itself.

Inappropriate exercise can do more harm than good, with the definition of "inappropriate" varying according to the individual. For many activities, especially running and cycling, there are significant injuries that occur with poorly regimented exercise schedules. Injuries from accidents also remain a major concern, whereas the effects of increased exposure to air pollution seem only a minor concern.

In extreme instances, over-exercising induces serious performance loss. Unaccustomed overexertion of muscles leads to rhabdomyolysis (damage to muscle) most often seen in new army recruits. Another danger is overtraining, in which the intensity or volume of training exceeds the body's capacity to recover between bouts. One sign of Overtraining Syndrome (OTS) is suppressed immune function, with an increased incidence of upper respiratory tract infection (URTI). An increased incidence of URTIs is also associated with high volume/intensity training, as well as with excessive exercise (EE), such as in a marathon.

Stopping excessive exercise suddenly may create a change in mood. Exercise should be controlled by each body's inherent limitations. While one set of joints and muscles may have the tolerance to withstand multiple marathons, another body may be damaged by 20 minutes of light jogging. This must be determined for each individual.

Too much exercise may cause a woman to miss her periods, a symptom known as amenorrhea. This is a very serious condition which indicates a woman is pushing her body beyond its natural boundaries.

Mechanism of Effects

Skeletal Muscle

Resistance training and subsequent consumption of a protein-rich meal promotes muscle hypertrophy and gains in muscle strength by stimulating myofibrillar muscle protein synthesis (MPS) and inhibiting muscle protein breakdown (MPB). The stimulation of muscle protein synthesis by resistance training occurs via phosphorylation of the mechanistic target of rapamycin (mTOR) and subsequent activation of mTORC1, which leads to protein biosynthesis in the ribosome via phosphorylation of mTORC1's immediate targets (the p70S6 kinase and the translation repressor protein 4EBP1). The suppression of muscle protein breakdown following food consumption occurs primarily via increases in plasma insulin; however, a suppression of MPB of comparable magnitude has also been shown to occur in humans from a sufficient elevation of plasma β-hydroxy β-methylbutyric acid.

Aerobic exercise induces mitochondrial biogenesis and an increased capacity for oxidative phosphorylation in the mitochondria of skeletal muscle, which is one mechanism by which aerobic exercise enhances submaximal endurance performance. These effects occur via an exercise-induced increase in the intracellular AMP:ATP ratio, thereby triggering the activation of AMP-activated protein kinase (AMPK) which subsequently phosphorylates peroxisome proliferator-activated receptor gamma coactivator-1α (PGC-1α), the master regulator of mitochondrial biogenesis.

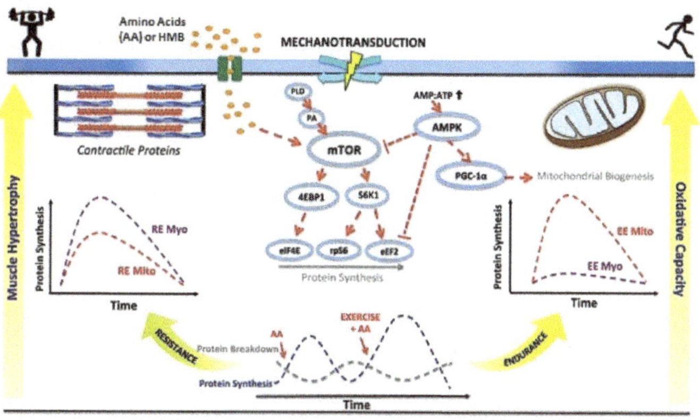

Diagram of the molecular signaling cascades that are involved in myofibrillar muscle protein synthesis and mitochondrial biogenesis in response to physical exercise and specific amino acids or their derivatives (primarily L-LEUCINE and HMB). Many amino acids derived from food protein promote the activation of mTORC1 and increase protein synthesis by signaling through Rag GTPases.

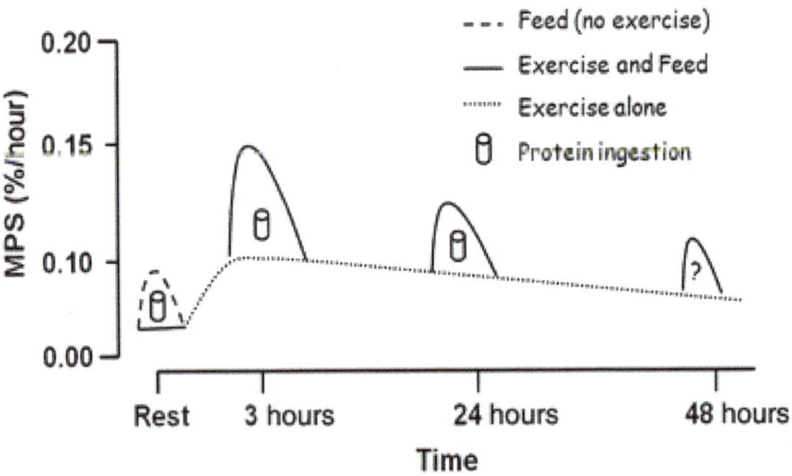

Resistance training stimulates muscle protein synthesis (MPS) for a period of up to 48 hours following exercise (shown by dotted line). Ingestion of a protein-rich meal at any point during this period will augment the exercise-induced increase in muscle protein synthesis (shown by solid lines).

Other Peripheral Organs

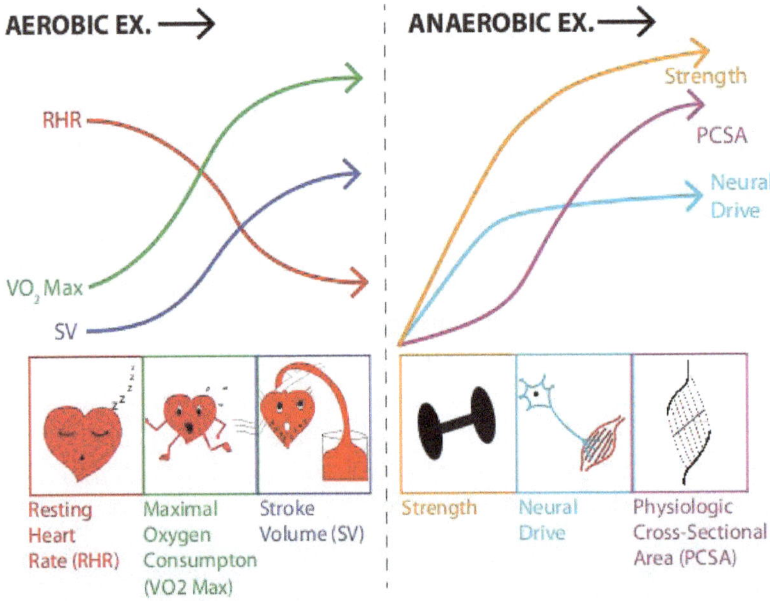

Summary of long-term adaptations to regular aerobic and anaerobic exercise.

Developing research has demonstrated that many of the benefits of exercise are mediated through the role of skeletal muscle as an endocrine organ. That is, contracting muscles release multiple substances known as myokines which promote the growth of new tissue, tissue repair, and multiple anti-inflammatory functions, which in turn reduce the risk of developing various inflammatory diseases. Exercise reduces levels of cortisol, which causes many health problems, both physical and mental. Endurance exercise before meals lowers blood glucose more than the same exercise after meals. There is evidence that vigorous exercise (90–95% of VO_2 max) induces a greater degree of physiological cardiac hypertrophy than moderate exercise (40 to 70% of VO_2 max), but it is unknown whether this has any effects on overall morbidity and/or mortality. Both aerobic and anaerobic exercise work to increase the mechanical efficiency of the heart by increasing cardiac volume (aerobic exercise), or myocardial thickness (strength training). Ventricular hypertrophy, the thickening of the ventricular walls, is generally beneficial and healthy if it occurs in response to exercise.

Central Nervous System

The persistent long-term neurobiological effects of regular physical exercise are believed to be mediated by transient exercise-induced increases in the concentration of neurotrophic factors (e.g., BDNF, IGF-1, VEGF, and GDNF) and other biomolecules in peripheral blood plasma, which subsequently cross the blood–brain barrier and blood–cerebrospinal fluid barrier and bind to their associated receptors in the brain. Upon binding to their receptors in cerebral vasculature and brain cells (i.e., neurons and glial cells), these biomolecules trigger intracellular signaling cascades that lead to neuroplastic biological responses – such as neurogenesis, synaptogenesis, oligodendrogenesis, and angiogenesis, among others – which ultimately mediate the exercise-induced improvements in cognitive function.

Public Health Measures

Multiple component community-wide campaigns are frequently used in an attempt to increase a population's level of physical activity. A 2015 Cochrane review, however, did not find evidence supporting a benefit. The quality of the underlying evidence was also poor. However, there is some evidence that school-based interventions can increase activity levels and fitness in children. Another Cochrane review found some evidence that certain types of exercise programmes, such as those involving gait, balance, co-ordination and functional tasks, can improve balance in older adults. Following progressive resistance training, older adults also respond with improved physical function. Survey of brief interventions promoting physical activity found that they are cost-effective, although there are variations between studies.

Environmental approaches appear promising: signs that encourage the use of stairs, as well as community campaigns, may increase exercise levels. The city of Bogotá, Colombia, for example, blocks off 113 kilometers (70 mi) of roads on Sundays and holidays to make it easier for its citizens to get exercise. These pedestrian zones are part of an effort to combat chronic diseases, including obesity.

To identify which public health strategies are effective, a Cochrane overview of reviews is in preparation.

Physical exercise was said to decrease healthcare costs, increase the rate of job attendance, as well as increase the amount of effort women put into their jobs.

Children will mimic the behavior of their parents in relation to physical exercise. Parents can thus promote physical activity and limit the amount of time children spend in front of screens which may decrease the risk of childhood obesity.

Overweight children who participate in physical exercise experience greater loss of body fat and increased cardiovascular fitness. According to the Centers for Disease Control and Prevention in the United States, both children and adults should do 60 minutes or more of physical activity each day. Implementing physical exercise in the school system and ensuring an environment in which children can reduce barriers to maintain a healthy lifestyle is essential.

Exercise Trends

Jumping fitness exercise

Worldwide there has been a large shift towards less physically demanding work. This has been accompanied by increasing use of mechanized transportation, a greater prevalence of labor saving technology in the home, and fewer active recreational pursuits. Personal lifestyle changes however can correct the lack of physical exercise.

Research in 2015 indicates integrating mindfulness to physical exercise interventions increases exercise adherence, self-efficacy and also has positive effects both psychologically and physiologically.

Social and Cultural Variation

Exercising looks different in every country, as do the motivations behind exercising. In some countries, people exercise primarily indoors, and in others, people exercise primarily outdoors. People may exercise for personal enjoyment, health and well-being, social interactions, competition or training, etc. These differences could potentially be attributed to geographic location, social tendencies, or otherwise.

In Colombia, citizens value and celebrate the outdoor environments of their country. In many instances, they utilize outdoor activities as social gatherings to enjoy nature and their communities. In Bogotá, Colombia, a 70-mile stretch of road known as the Ciclovía is shut down each Sunday for bicyclists, runners, rollerbladers, skateboarders and other exercisers to work out and enjoy their surroundings.

Similarly to Colombia, citizens of Cambodia tend to exercise socially outside. In this country, public gyms have become quite popular. People will congregate at these outdoor gyms not only to utilize the public facilities, but also to organize aerobics and dance sessions, which are open to the public.

Sweden has also begun developing outdoor gyms, called *utegym*. These gyms are free to the public and are often placed in beautiful, picturesque environments. People will swim in rivers, use boats, and run through forests to stay healthy and enjoy the natural world around them. This is especially possible in Sweden due to its geographical location.

Chinese exercise, particularly in the retired community, seems to be socially grounded. In the mornings, dances are held in public parks; these gatherings may include Latin dancing, ballroom dancing, tango, or even the jitterbug. Dancing in public allows people to interact with those with whom they would not normally interact, allowing for both health benefits and social benefits.

These sociocultural variations in physical exercise show how people in different geographic locations and social climates have varying motivations and methods of exercising. Physical exercise can improve health and well-being, as well as enhance community ties and appreciation of natural beauty.

Nutrition and Recovery

Proper nutrition is as important to health as exercise. When exercising, it becomes even more important to have a good diet to ensure that the body has the correct ratio of macronutrients while providing ample micronutrients, in order to aid the body with the recovery process following strenuous exercise.

Active recovery is recommended after participating in physical exercise because it removes lactate from the blood more quickly than inactive recovery. Removing lactate from circulation allows for an easy decline in body temperature, which can also benefit the immune system, as an individual may be vulnerable to minor illnesses if the body temperature drops too abruptly after physical exercise.

History

The benefits of exercise have been known since antiquity. Marcus Cicero, around 65 BCE, stated: "It is exercise alone that supports the spirits, and keeps the mind in vigor."

Several mass exercise movements were started in the early twentieth century to realise the benefits of exercise. The first and most significant of these in the UK was the Women's League of Health and Beauty founded in 1930 by Mary Bagot Stack that had 166,000 members in 1937.

However, the link between physical health and exercise (or lack of it) was only discovered in 1949 and reported in 1953 by a team led by Jerry Morris. Dr. Morris noted that men of similar social class and occupation (bus conductors versus bus drivers) had markedly different rates of heart attacks, depending on the level of exercise they got: bus drivers had a sedentary occupation and a higher incidence of heart disease, while bus conductors were forced to move continually and had a lower incidence of heart disease. This link had not previously been noted and was later confirmed by other researchers.

Other Animals

Physical exercise has been shown to benefit a wide range of other mammals, as well as salmon, juvenile crocodiles, and at least one species of bird.

However, several studies have shown that lizards display no benefit from exercise, leading them to be termed "metabolically inflexible". Indeed, damage from overtraining may occur following weeks of forced treadmill exercise in lizards.

A number of studies of both rodents and humans have demonstrated that individual differences in both ability and propensity for exercise (i.e., voluntary exercise) have some genetic basis.

Several studies of rodents have demonstrated that maternal or juvenile access to wheels that allow voluntary exercise can increase the propensity to run as adults. These studies further suggest that physical activity may be more "programmable" than food intake.

The recommended exercise routine is aerobic exercise everyday for 20 minutes and anaerobic exercise twice or thrice a week.

The documented benefits of aerobic exercise include

- increased efficiency of cardio respiratory system (lungs and heart)
- improved circulation and reduced blood pressure
- increased red blood cells – oxygen transportation
- improved muscle strength
- increased soft tissue and joint flexibility
- improved glucose tolerance
- increased longevity

According to the US surgeon general's report (DHHS, 1996 , as cited in Marks et al., 2008) it was estimated that physical inactivity leads to 400,000 preventable deaths (17%) per year. Physical inactivity also impacts on morbidity especially cardiovascular disease, hypertension and diabetes of which there may be a premature onset due to physical inactivity.

Mental Health

Plante & Rodin (1990) review suggests that physical activity improves mood and well being and reduces anxiety, depression and stress in healthy populations.

The biological pathways that mediate this effect are:

- increases in body temperature due to exercise result in short term tranquilizing effects
- reduction in resting muscle activity potential after exercise helps release tension
- enhances neurotransmission of noradrenalin, serotonin and dopamine leading to improved mood.
- releases endorphins (natural opiates) (enhanced feeling well being) (Plante & Rodin, 1990).

The psychological pathways that mediate this effect are:

- Physical fitness provides people with a sense of mastery, control and self sufficiency

- Triggers an altered and more relaxed state of consciousness
- Provides distraction, or time out from unpleasant cognitions emotions and behavior
- Repeated pairing of the physical symptoms of the sympathetic ns in the absence of distress results in improved psychological functioning (Plante & Rodin, 1990).

Thus the effects of exercise are not limited only to the body but also affect psychological processes which in turn affect general mental health.

In a year long longitudinal study of adolescents who exercised by Brown & Siegel (1988) it was found that the negative impact of stressful life events on health declined as exercise levels increased. The negative effects of stress on ill health have been documented; that exercise can have a protective effect against stress has important implications for both physical and mental health.

Exercise and Cognition

Castelli et al (2007) in a study with 259 3-5th graders found an association between their performance on field exercise routine and math and reading scores on standardized tests. The children with the best performance on the field exercises also had the best math and reading scores.

Researchers have found that in animal models exercising rats indicated higher levels of Brain derived neurotrophic factor (BDNF) than control rats Farmer et al 2004).

IGF-1 (insulin like growth factor1) crosses the blood brain barrier into the brain and orders the production of several chemicals including BDNF

BDNF is associated with neurogenesis (birth of new neurons) and exercise increases BDNF levels in the hippocampus -an area associated with memory and learning (Cotman & Berchtold 2002; Neeper at al 1995).

According to Vaynman et al (2004) "A brain low on BDNF shuts itself off to new information"

Blood Volume to the brain increases as a result of exercise which increases blood flow in the brain.

Astrocytes increase with exercise. Astrocytes are glial cells in the central nervous system that play a supporting role and help in myelination and repair. Thus these functions are also maintained with exercise.

Exercise and Aging

In a study by Larson et al (2006)1,740 men and women above the age of 65 were asked about their levels of physical activity and related factors such as diet, lifestyle, health and smoking and drinking were taken into account. They were followed for 6.2 years - it was found that the incidence rate for Alzheimer's dementia was significantly higher for those who exercised fewer than 3 times a week.

Alzheimer's and vascular dementia may get postponed with regular exercise.

Cognitive Function

Aging brains benefit from exercise and show the effects of BDNF – older adults who exercised fared better on cognitive tests.

Safdara, et al. (2011) in a study with rats who had malfunctioning mitochondria (which causes premature aging) were divided into 2 groups, one that exercised and one that didn't otherwise their environments were similar. The exercise group ran on a wheel for 45 min 3 times a week. which by human standards is like running 6.2 miles. This continued for 5 months. When they were compared the sedentary rats were bald, frail and dying the running rats were youthful with full pelts of dark fur and all their muscle mass and brain volume intact.

Who are these people who exercise regularly?

What are the factors that predict regular exercise? (Marks et al, 2000)

Gender – women are less active than men especially through adolescence and adulthood even if the levels of activity were similar in childhood. In India especially among the middle class sometimes women have very low levels of physical activity.

SES – people from the lower SES have higher activity levels because of their jobs which may be manual however they are less likely to voluntarily exercise as compared to those from a higher SES. In the British Whitehall study it was found that 95% of men at the highest grade exercised as opposed to 69% at the lowest grade.

Education impacts on activity levels data from the Center for Disease control in the U.S (2008) indicates that almost half of those with less than a high school education do not exercise as opposed to only 15% of college graduates.

Family can have an impact on exercise behavior. There is a norm of exercise and time is made for it and members may engage in an activity together. Families where most of the members exercise, may perceive themselves as athletic and feel responsible for their health.

Self efficacy beliefs – refers to the individual's confidence or sense of mastery or control over a particular behavior (Bandura's Social Learning Theory, 1986). Self efficacy has been found to be related to higher levels of exercising. Research has looked at barrier self efficacy (self efficacy to overcome barriers to regular exercise) and scheduling self –efficacy.

Characteristics of the Setting

How does location or the physical situation affect exercise?

The physical surroundings include weather (extreme temperatures are unpleasant to exercise in). In the U.S. there are heated gyms and in India there are air conditioned gyms for those who can afford it. That brings us to the issue of cost, what are the costs incurred to exercise – do you to travel a long way to get to a open space, how expensive are gyms, are there other activities that can be engaged in easily?

Walkability of neighborhoods - Mixed land use results in a mix of destinations to walk to (walk to the grocery etc). Street connectivity and neighborhood aesthetics also encourage walking. Safety concerns are another important factor that influence how much people walk and use open spaces.

Exercise facilities or open spaces in the neighborhood are another vital factor in determining levels of activity.

In a study by Zenk et al (2009) on characteristics of the Neighborhood Environment and Adherence to a Walking Intervention in African American Women most of the above factors were considered. Results revealed that the availability of indoor walking spaces in their neighborhood predicted adherence to the intervention program. Thus women may feel safer in an indoor facility and it gives them the flexibility of time to exercise at a later time in the evening when they are free from household reponsibilities .

Social and Cultural Norms

In certain societies there is a norm to exercise or be physically fit such as the U.S. or the Scandinavian countries or Germany whereas in other developing societies this norm may not be there as neither leisure time nor facilities are available and it is not important as opposed to earning a living. In the developing countries the elite would follow western norms in keeping with their lifestyle. Urban middleclass women would be more likely to exercise than their counterparts in small towns or rural areas.

Encouraging Physical Activity

Given the value of physical activity in reducing and postponing morbidity, one can see it's larger implications for productivity, for lowered costs in healthcare and optimal functioning.

Thus there is an effort to increase levels of physical activity at the population level in developed countries. Programs that have been effective were home based and encouraged walking and had frequent professional contact (Marks et al, 2000).

Effort needs to be directed to creating a habit of regular exercise among the young as well as high risk populations.

Those forms of exercise that are indigenous to the culture are more likely to succeed such as yoga or kabbadi or cricket in India. That yoga has become an international craze but is not as widely practiced in India is telling.

Exercise that is fun and has some socializing involved is more likely to be effective in terms of people being regular about it (walking with friends or playing badminton with them) . Home based, informal, moderate intensity, walking for e.g – would be most likely to succeed.

Interventions need to focus on how to prevent relapse as most people tend to relapse after a while. Some of the strategies suggested by Robinson & Rogers (1994) is providing cues that remind people of the program, combining behavioral and cognitive strategies, providing rewards and punishments and increasing people's belief that they have control over the design and conduct of the program.

Alcohol and Health

Short-term effects of alcohol consumption include intoxication and dehydration. Long-term effects of alcohol consumption include changes in the metabolism of the liver and brain and alcoholism. Alcohol intoxication affects the brain, causing slurred speech, clumsiness, and delayed reflexes. Alcohol stimulates insulin production, which speeds up glucose metabolism and can result in low blood sugar, causing irritability and possibly death for diabetics. A 2014 World Health Organization report found that harmful alcohol consumption caused about 3.3 million deaths annually worldwide.

However, some effects of alcohol consumption are beneficial. Although even moderate alcohol consumption increased the risk of death in younger people, it has been shown to *decrease* the risk of death for individuals ages 55+ (due to decreased risk of ischemic heart disease).

The median lethal dose of alcohol in test animals is a blood alcohol content of 0.45%. This is about six times the level of ordinary intoxication (0.08%), but vomiting or unconsciousness may occur much sooner in people who have a low tolerance for alcohol. The high tolerance of chronic heavy drinkers may allow some of them to remain conscious at levels above 0.40%, although serious health hazards are incurred at this level.

Alcohol also limits the production of vasopressin (ADH) from the hypothalamus and the secretion of this hormone from the posterior pituitary gland. This is what causes severe dehydration when alcohol is consumed in large amounts. It also causes a high concentration of water in the urine and vomit and the intense thirst that goes along with a hangover.

Stress, hangovers, and the oral contraceptive pill may increase the desire for alcohol because these things will lower the level of testosterone and alcohol will acutely elevate it. Tobacco has the same effect of increasing the craving for alcohol.

Short-term Effects

The short-term effects of alcohol consumption range from a decrease in anxiety and motor skills at lower doses to unconsciousness, anterograde amnesia, and central nervous system depression at higher doses. Cell membranes are highly permeable to alcohol, so once alcohol is in the bloodstream it can diffuse into nearly every cell in the body.

The concentration of alcohol in blood is measured via blood alcohol content (BAC). The amount and circumstances of consumption play a large part in determining the extent of intoxication; for example, eating a heavy meal before alcohol consumption causes alcohol to absorb more slowly. Hydration also plays a role, especially in determining the extent of hangovers. After excessive drinking, unconsciousness can occur and extreme levels of consumption can lead to alcohol poisoning and death (a concentration in the blood stream of 0.40% will kill half of those affected). Alcohol may also cause death indirectly, by asphyxiation from vomit.

Alcohol can greatly exacerbate sleep problems. During abstinence, residual disruptions in sleep regularity and sleep patterns are the greatest predictors of relapse.

Long-term Effects

The long-term effects of alcohol consumption range from cardioprotective health benefits for low to moderate alcohol consumption in industrialized societies with higher rates of cardiovascular disease to severe detrimental effects in cases of chronic alcohol abuse. Health effects associated with large levels of alcohol intake include an increased risk of alcoholism, malnutrition, chronic pancreatitis, alcoholic liver disease and cancer. In addition, damage to the central nervous system and peripheral nervous system can occur from chronic alcohol abuse. The long-term use of alcohol is capable of damaging nearly every organ and system in the body. The developing adolescent brain is particularly vulnerable to the toxic effects of alcohol. In addition, the developing fetal brain is also vulnerable, and fetal alcohol spectrum disorders (FASDs) may result if pregnant mothers consume alcohol.

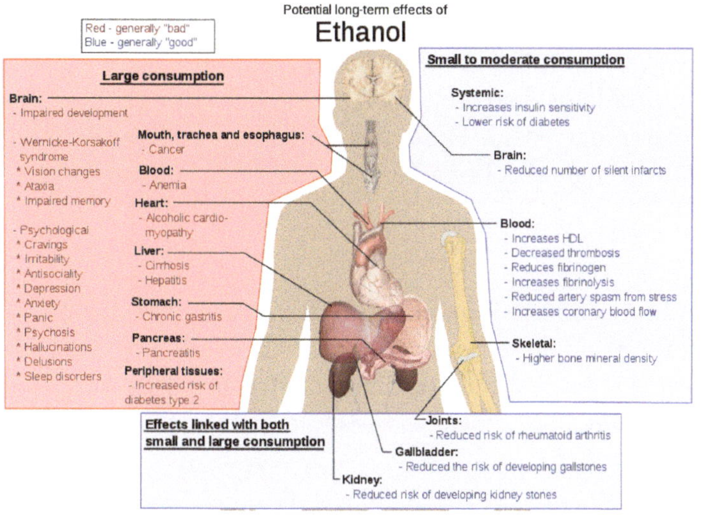

Cardiovascular Disease

A study published in the British Medical Journal on 10 July 2014 investigated the correlation between human variants of the ADH1B gene, which codes for the ADH1B enzyme (Alcohol dehydrogenase 1B), and cardiovascular health. The study concluded that carriers of one specific variant of this gene (A-allele of ADH1B rs1229984), which is associated with lower alcohol consumption, '...had a more favourable cardiovascular profile and a reduced risk of coronary heart disease than those without the genetic variant.' The study's authors extrapolated from this finding to suggest that '...reduction of alcohol consumption, even for light to moderate drinkers, is beneficial to health.'

This study contradicts previous findings on the causal relationship between light alcohol consumption and cardiovascular health, and has been criticized on its methodology by members of the International Scientific Forum on Alcohol Research, which stated in its analysis that '...[there are] questions about making generalized statements about the effects of alcohol on disease based on results from the analysis of a single nucleotide polymorphism of a gene.'

Moreover, the study fails to explain or discount previous findings that show a causal link between alcohol intake and cardiovascular health that can not be accounted for by genetic predisposition alone.

Pregnancy

Medical organizations strongly discourage drinking alcohol during pregnancy. Alcohol passes easily from the mother's bloodstream through the placenta and into the bloodstream of the fetus, which interferes with brain and organ development. Alcohol can affect the fetus at any stage during pregnancy, but the level of risk depends on the amount and frequency of alcohol consumed. Regular heavy drinking and binge drinking (four or more drinks on any one occasion) pose the greatest risk for harm, but lesser amounts can cause problems as well. There is no known safe amount or safe time to drink during pregnancy.

Prenatal alcohol exposure can lead to fetal alcohol spectrum disorders (FASDs). The most severe form of FASD is fetal alcohol syndrome (FAS). Problems associated with FASD include facial anomalies, low birth weight, stunted growth, small head size, delayed or uncoordinated motor skills, hearing or vision problems, learning disabilities, behavior problems, and inappropriate social skills compared to same-age peers. Those affected are more likely to have trouble in school, legal problems, participate in high-risk behaviors, and develop substance use disorders themselves.

Breastfeeding

The NHS states that minor amounts of alcohol do not make breastfeeding dangerous. However, it can be better to wait for a couple of hours before breastfeeding or express the milk into a bottle before drinking. Researchers have shown that intoxicated breastfeeding reduces the average milk expression but poses no immediate threat to the child as the amount of transferred alcohol is insignificant.

Alcohol Expectations

Alcohol expectations are beliefs and attitudes that people have about the effects they will experience when drinking alcoholic beverages. They are just largely beliefs about alcohol's effects on a person's behaviors, abilities, and emotions. Some people believe that if alcohol expectations can be changed, then alcohol abuse might be reduced. Men tend to become more aggressive in laboratory studies in which they are drinking only tonic water but believe that it contains alcohol. They also become less aggressive when they believe they are drinking only tonic water, but are actually drinking tonic water that contains alcohol.

The phenomenon of alcohol expectations recognizes that intoxication has real physiological consequences that alter a drinker's perception of space and time, reduce psychomotor skills, and disrupt equilibrium. The manner and degree to which alcohol expectations interact with the physiological short-term effects of alcohol, resulting in specific behaviors, is unclear.

A single study found that if a society believes that intoxication leads to sexual behavior, rowdy behavior, or aggression, then people tend to act that way when intoxicated. But if a society believes that intoxication leads to relaxation and tranquil behavior, then it usually leads to those outcomes. Alcohol expectations vary within a society, so these outcomes are not certain.

People tend to conform to social expectations, and some societies expect that drinking alcohol will cause disinhibition. However, in societies in which the people do not expect that alcohol will disinhibit, intoxication seldom leads to disinhibition and bad behavior.

Alcohol expectations can operate in the absence of actual consumption of alcohol. Research in the United States over a period of decades has shown that men tend to become more sexually aroused when they think they have been drinking alcohol, — even when they have not been drinking it.

Women report feeling more sexually aroused when they falsely believe the beverages they have been drinking contained alcohol (although one measure of their physiological arousal shows that they became less aroused).

Drug Treatment Programs

Most addiction treatment programs encourage people with drinking problems to see themselves as having a chronic, relapsing disease that requires a lifetime of attendance at 12-step meetings to keep in check. However, some people do not develop lifelong problems.

Alcohol Abuse

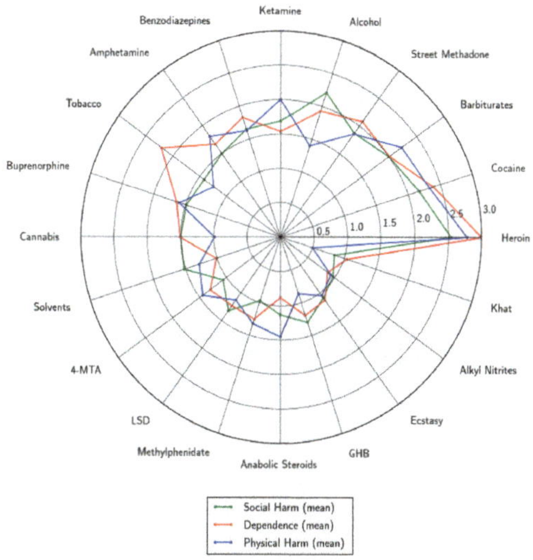

Addiction experts in psychiatry, chemistry, pharmacology, forensic science, epidemiology, and the police and legal services engaged in delphic analysis regarding 20 popular recreational drugs. Alcohol was ranked 6th in dependence, 11th in physical harm, and 2nd in social harm.

Alcohol Abuse Prevention Programs

The Army at Fort Drum has taken the "0-0-1-3" and exchanged it for the new "0-1-2-3" described in the Prime-For-Life Program, which highlights the ill effects of alcohol abuse as more than just an individual's "driving while intoxicated." The Prime-For-Life program identifies alcohol abuse to be a health and impairment problem, leading to adverse legal as well as health outcomes associated with misuse.

The 0-1-2-3 now represents low-risk guidelines:

- 0 – Zero drinks for those driving a vehicle.
- 1 – One drink per hour
- 2 – No more than two drinking sessions per week
- 3 – Not to exceed three drinks on any one day

Recommended Maximum Intake

Binge drinking is becoming a major problem in the UK. Advice on weekly consumption is avoided in United Kingdom.

Since 1995 the UK government has advised that regular consumption of three to four units a day for men and or two to three units for women, would not pose significant health risks. However, consistently drinking more than four units a day (for men) and three units (women), is not advisable.

Previously (from 1992 until 1995), the advice was that men should drink no more than 21 units per week, and women no more than 14. (The difference between the sexes was due to the typically lower weight and water-to-body-mass ratio of women.) This was changed because a government study showed that many people were in effect "saving up" their units and using them at the end of the week, a phenomenon referred to as binge drinking. The Times reported in October 2007 that these limits had been "plucked out of the air" and had no scientific basis.

Sobriety

A midshipman is subjected to a random breathalyzer test to determine sobriety.

Sobriety is the condition of not having any measurable levels, or effects from mood-altering drugs. According to WHO "Lexicon of alcohol and drug terms..." sobriety is continued abstinence from psychoactive drug use. Sobriety is also considered to be the natural state of a human being given at a birth. In a treatment setting, sobriety is the achieved goal of independence from consuming or craving mind-altering substances. As such, sustained abstinence is a prerequisite for sobriety. Early in abstinence, residual effects of mind-altering substances can preclude sobriety. These effects are labeled "PAWS", or "post acute withdrawal syndrome". Someone who abstains, but has a latent desire to resume use, is not considered truly sober. An abstainer may be subconsciously motivated to resume drug use, but for a variety of reasons, abstains (e.g. such as a medical or legal concern precluding use). Sobriety has more specific meanings within specific contexts, such as the culture of Alcoholics Anonymous, other 12 step programs, law enforcement, and some schools of psychology. In some cases, sobriety implies achieving "life balance".

Injury

Injury is defined as damage or harm that is done or sustained. The potential of injuring oneself or others can be increased after consuming alcohol due to the certain short term effects related to the substance such as lack of coordination, blurred vision, and slower reflexes to name a few. Due to these effects the most common injuries include head, fall, and vehicle related injuries. These include a range of soft tissue damage and fractures. A study was conducted between November 1, 2001 and June 30, 2002 of patients admitted to The Ulster Hospital in Northern Ireland with fall related injuries. They found that 113 of those patients admitted to that hospital during that had consumed alcohol recently and that the injury severity was higher for those that had consumed alcohol compared to those that hadn't. Another study showed that 21% of patients admitted to the Emergency Department of the Bristol Royal Infirmary had either direct or indirect alcohol related injuries. If these figures are extrapolated it shows that the estimated number of patients with alcohol related injuries are over 7000 during the year at this ED alone.

Genetic Differences

Alcohol Flush and Respiratory Reactions

Alcohol flush reaction is a condition in which an individual's face or body experiences flushes or blotches as a result of an accumulation of acetaldehyde, a metabolic byproduct of the catabolic metabolism of alcohol. It is best known as a condition that is experienced by people of Asian descent. According to the analysis by HapMap Project, the rs671 allele of the ALDH2 gene responsible for the flush reaction is rare among Europeans and Africans, and it is very rare among Mexican-Americans. 30% to 50% of people of Chinese and Japanese ancestry have at least one ALDH*2 allele. The rs671 form of ALDH2, which accounts for most incidents of alcohol flush reaction worldwide, is native to East Asia and most common in southeastern China. It most likely originated among Han Chinese in central China, and it appears to have been positively selected in the past. Another analysis correlates the rise and spread of rice cultivation in Southern China with the spread of the allele. The reasons for this positive selection aren't known, but it's been hypothesized that elevated concentrations of acetaldehyde may have conferred protection against certain parasitic infections, such as *Entamoeba histolytica*.

The same SNP allele of ALDH2, also termed glu487lys, and the abnormal accumulation of acetaldehyde following the drinking of alcohol, is associated with the alcohol-induced respiratory reactions of rhinitis and asthma that occur in Eastern Asian populations.

Metabolism of alcohol (ethanol) to acetaldehyde (ethanal) and then acetic acid (ethanoic acid)

American Indian Alcoholism

While little detailed genetic research has been done, it has been shown that alcoholism tends to run in families with possible involvement of differences in alcohol metabolism and the genotype of alcohol-metabolizing enzymes.

Genetics and Amount of Consumption

Having a particular genetic variant (A-allele of ADH1B rs1229984) is associated with non-drinking and lower alcohol consumption. This variant is also associated with favorable cardiovascular profile and a reduced risk of coronary heart disease compared to those without the genetic variant, but it is unknown whether this may be caused by differences in alcohol consumption or by additional confounding effects of the genetic variant itself.

Gender differences

Alcoholism

Based on combined data from SAMHSA's 2004-2005 National Surveys on Drug Use & Health, the rate of past year alcohol dependence or abuse among people aged 12 or older varied by level of alcohol use: 44.7% of past month heavy drinkers, 18.5% binge drinkers, 3.8% past month non-binge drinkers, and 1.3% of those who did not drink alcohol in the past month met the criteria for alcohol dependence or abuse in the past year. Males had higher rates than females for all measures of drinking in the past month: any alcohol use (57.5% vs. 45%), binge drinking (30.8% vs. 15.1%), and heavy alcohol use (10.5% vs. 3.3%), and males were twice as likely as females to have met the criteria for alcohol dependence or abuse in the past year (10.5% vs. 5.1%). Over time the difference between males and females has narrowed. According to a 2016 systematic review, for those born at the end of the 20th century men were 1.1 times as likely as women to drink alcohol at all, 1.2 times as likely to drink to problematic levels, and 1.3 times as likely to develop health problems from drinking.

Sensitivity

Several biological factors make women more vulnerable to the effects of alcohol than men.

- Body fat. Women tend to weigh less than men, and—pound for pound—a woman's body contains less water and more fatty tissue than a man's. Because fat retains alcohol while water dilutes it, alcohol remains at higher concentrations for longer periods of time in a woman's body, exposing her brain and other organs to more alcohol.
- Enzymes. Women have lower levels of two enzymes—alcohol dehydrogenase and aldehyde dehydrogenase—that metabolize (break down) alcohol in the stomach and liver. As a result, women absorb more alcohol into their bloodstreams than men.
- Hormones. Changes in hormone levels during the menstrual cycle may also affect how a woman metabolizes alcohol.

Metabolism

Females demonstrated a higher average rate of elimination (mean, 0.017; range, 0.014-0.021 g/210 L) than males (mean, 0.015; range, 0.013-0.017 g/210 L). Female subjects on average had a higher percentage of body fat (mean, 26.0; range, 16.7-36.8%) than males (mean, 18.0; range, 10.2-25.3%).

Depression

The link between alcohol consumption, depression, and gender was examined by the Centre for Addiction and Mental Health (Canada). The study found that women taking antidepressants consumed more alcohol than women who did not experience depression as well as men taking antidepressants. The researchers, Dr. Kathryn Graham and a PhD Student Agnes Massak analyzed the responses to a survey by 14,063 Canadian residents aged 18–76 years. The survey included measures of quantity, frequency of drinking, depression and antidepressants use, over the period of a year. The researchers used data from the GENACIS Canada survey, part of an international collaboration to investigate the influence of cultural variation on gender differences in alcohol use and related problems. The purpose of the study was to examine whether, like in other studies already conducted on male depression and alcohol consumption, depressed women also consumed less alcohol when taking anti-depressants. According to the study, both men and women experiencing depression (but not on anti-depressants) drank more than non-depressed counterparts. Men taking antidepressants consumed significantly less alcohol than depressed men who did not use antidepressants. Non-depressed men consumed 436 drinks per year, compared to 579 drinks for depressed men not using antidepressants, and 414 drinks for depressed men who used antidepressants. Alcohol consumption remained higher whether the depressed women were taking anti-depressants or not. 179 drinks per year for non-depressed women, 235 drinks for depressed women not using antidepressants, and 264 drinks for depressed women who used antidepressants. The lead researcher argued that the study "suggests that the use of antidepressants is associated with lower alcohol consumption among men suffering from depression. But this does not appear to be true for women."

Effects of Alcohol on Health

Alcohol is an element of lifestyle that may impact health. In this chapter we will consider the units to measure alcohol - what is moderate, what is excessive – the health effects of excessive alcohol, the benefits if any of moderate drinking, the theories of alcohol addiction,the alcohol scenario in India, the approach to addiction and how to resolve it.

According to the British System 1 Unit is equal to 8gms of alcohol which is equivalent to 1glass of wine or1/2 pint of beer or a single measure of spirits (25ml). 2 to 3 units a day or 14 to 21 units a week is considered within the moderate range whereas 4-5 units a day or 35 units a week is in the heavy or excessive range (as cited in Marks et al, 2000).

The health risks from heavy drinking are liver cirrhosis and acute pancreatitis, irreversible neurological damage and increased risk of cardiovascular disease and certain cancers. The risks to pregnant women from alcohol are spontaneous abortion and there is greater risk of having low birth weight babies and having babies with Foetal Alcohol Syndrome (FAS is a syndrome characterized by mental retardation and characteristic looks).

According to the British Department of Health there has been a 4-5 fold increase in deaths from chronic liver disease from 1970 to 2000 and over 9 fold increase among young men and women(Marks et al.,2000).

Acute pancreatitis more than doubled between 1963 to 1998, with more increases in the younger population (Goldacre & Roberts, 2004).

Are There Benefits of Light to Moderate Drinking?

One keeps hearing/reading about the benefits of light to moderate drinking in the popular press so much so that it makes one wonder whether it is time to begin having a daily tipple in the interest of health.

Let us review the literature available – studies have reported that moderate drinking is associated with reduced risk of stroke (Berger et al, 1999) and lower incidence of dementia (Ruitenberg et al,

2002). However 2 reviews of all the studies concluded that when appropriate statistical controls are made for confounding effects there is no evidence that abstinence is associated with greater mortality risk than light drinking (Fillmore et al 1998, Hart et al 1999). Confounding effects refer to factors such as lifestyle, prior health, and all possible factors that could affect the relationship between health outcome and drinking.

Other Problems Associated with Drinking

Apart from health problems alcohol dependence often may disguise or be symptomatic of a mental health problem such as depression or anxiety. Among the lower Ses, people may use alcohol to self medicate their condition, lacking awareness of the condition itself.

Existing difficulties such as family conflicts tend to get worse. Unemployment and lowered career prospects also become a concern. Thus drinking to resolve a problem only adds to the problem.

Accidents

Drunk driving accounts for a large number of traffic accidents all over the world. Alcohol appears to be implicated in falls, fires, drowning incidents and industrial and household accidents as seen in emergency room records.

Crime

Homicide, domestic violence, and other violence are associated with alcohol.

Theories

There are three basic classes of theories: genetic, disease and learning theories.

Genetic Theories

It has been observed that alcohol problems tend to run in families. However that is not enough to conclude that it is genetic, as nurture or environment and learning also play a major role in families. The role of inheritance is usually studied using twin studies and comparing monozygotic twins to dizygotic twins, most studies indicate a higher concordance rate for MZ twins for alcohol dependence although MZ twins tend to spend more time with each other than DZ twins and that needs to be considered. Studies also found a higher concordance rate among twins that were adopted thus pointing to the role of genes however specific genetic pathways have not been established beyond doubt. The contribution of genes and the environment are so finely interwoven that it is very difficult to untangle their respective contributions or specify their interactions (Marks et al., 2000).

Addiction, Disease and Dependency Theories

The individual with an alcohol problem is perceived as a victim of disease, of addiction. According to Disease theories some individuals have a predisposition to become alcoholic - based on both genetic as well as psychological counts. The Alcohol dependence syndrome is conceptualized as a psycho-physiological disorder that is characterized by all the signs of any addiction (– interferes with other aspects of life etc..)(Marks et al., 2000).

Learning Theories

Operant Conditioning refers to a form of learning where the behavior is followed by an immediate reinforcement which is much more effective in producing learning than delayed reinforcement.

Alcohol which has a small positive reinforcement of reduced anxiety may be rewarding enough to develop into a strong habit. As is the case with any addictive behaviors – the pleasurable effects occur immediately while unpleasant consequences occur after a delay.The issue of the rewards not being worth the problems or costs incurred gets explained by this immediate reward versus delayed punishment schedule.

Classical Conditioning uses the compensatory conditioned response model whereby the homeostatic mechanism of the body activates the nervous system in response to the depressing effect of alcohol. The homeostatic response is conditioned to stimuli normally associated with drinking. If you are in a bar but not drinking one would experience this unpleasant state excessive activation. There is not enough research however to support this explanation.

Social Learning Theory (Bandura, 1977) focuses on learning by imitation. Thus the behavior of role models in the immediate psychological environment becomes salient. Those with low self efficacy (self confidence) are more likely to imitate undesirable behavior. Parents, respected older peers and high status colleagues are important role models for drinking (Marks et al., 2000).

Helping people overcome alcohol addiction is a challenging endeavor – the first step is getting them to acknowledge that there is a problem and seek help.

There are government and private Rehabilitation centers where people are helped to overcome their addiction by treating withdrawal symptoms and being counseled.

Alcoholics Anonymous is a self help group of recovered alcoholics who help other alcoholics become abstinent. It is based on a 12 step program.

Counseling and Psychotherapy attempts to create an insight into the drinking problem to enable people to change their behavior.

Cognitive Behavior Therapy – is a particular style of therapy based on cognitive and behavioral principles. Motivation enhancement therapy uses a gentle approach to inculcate change by improving self esteem and self efficacy.

Relapse prevention therapy works on creating skills to deal with relapse and not give up but go back to abstaining. Relapse is one of the major problems of any behavior change programs. Any de- addiction program that has a relapse component built in is far more effective than those lacking a relapse component (Marks et al, 2008).

Prevention

High Taxation of all alcoholic beverages and restricting access such as opening hours for bars, where and when alcohol is sold, strict enforcement of age permits. This would result in lowering the consumption of alcohol as has been seen, however the drinks industry has a strong lobby and is very influential in preventing such legislations (Marks et al, 2000).

Bans on advertising and sponsorship would be another effective measure in reducing the salience and popularity with the young. However the drinks industry overcomes this by promoting another product under the same brand name such as soda or CDs or bottled water with advertising that is implying an elevated lifestyle (as related to alcohol).

The drinks industry have their own research arm that is very influential in lobbying with governments such as The Portman Group in the U.K and the International Center for Alcohol Policies in the U.S. Both these groups are established with the objective of reducing harm caused by alcohol but they actively oppose legislations against increases in taxation and curbing advertising and propose health education initiatives, thus placing the complete burden responsibility on the shoulders of the individual while they exempt the the government and the drinks industry of any responsibility (Marks et al, 2000).

Health Education Initiatives to increase awareness about the harmful heath effects of alcohol addiction can be carried out at all levels and via the media to confront the advertising from the drinks industry.

Stress and the Immune System

Many studies suggest that stress has an impact on the immune system, however this relationship is moderated or influenced by many other factors such as base health levels, lifestyle, nutrition, and even factors such as access to healthcare.

As early as 1919, Ishigami (as cited in Taylor, 1995) found that immune functioning is suppressed during times of excitement – he noticed a decrease in phagocytic activity of Tuberculosis patients when emotionally excited.

Now a large volume of literature confirms this early finding that emotion impacts on the immune system. Stressors that have been manipulated in the laboratory also change or impact immune functioning. Studies with animals that keep them in cold water or expose them to loud noise or electric shock or separate them from the mother indicate reduced lymphocytes

The immune system is plugged into or connects with the endocrine system and the nervous system thus one can see the relationship between emotion, stress and the immune system

The effect of stress on the immune system has been recorded among humans as well. Children are more likely to develop infectious diseases when the family is under stress (Boyce et al, 1977 as cited in Taylor, 1995), daily hassles are also related to suppressed immune functioning (Levy et al, 1989 as cited in Taylor, 1995). However there are individual differences in the immune response to stress. Those who react to a stressor with a more intense stress response were more likely to show decreased immune functioning (Manuck et al, 1991 as cited in Taylor, 1995).

The reaction to a stressor in the laboratory may result in increased T and NK cells (in the short run) however exposure to a stressor over a longer period results in suppression of the immune system (Taylor, 1995). Thus the reaction to acute and chronic stressors differ as you may have observed. Exposure to chronic stress results in wear and tear of the internal organs.

Students have been found to have reduced NK cell activity during exams (Glaser et al, 1985, 1992 as cited in Taylor, 1995). A number of studies conclude that academic stress impacts on immunity. During periods of academic stress sleep is compromised and other health behaviours are compromised (increased junk food, may not eat properly, stop exercising). Thus there are multiple pathways that impact on the immune system.

Can Changes in Relationships Impact on the Immune System?

Maternal Separation at an early stage for animals as well as humans results in deprivation of mother's milk as well as contact comfort. The mother passes her immunity to the infant via breast milk, thus being deprived of it results in a poorly developed immune system.

Being in a bad marriage is a chronic stressor and relationships that are characterized by hostile conflict have a negative impact on the immune system. Separation and divorce are also associated with suppressed immune functioning. Divorced men as compared to married counterparts were more distressed and reported falling ill more often (Kiecolt-Glaser et al, 1988). According to this study initiators were less distressed and had better health and immunity indicators than non initiators.

Caregivers for the terminally ill such as cancer patients or Alzheimer's patients experience chronic stress coping with the challenges of the care giving role as well as coming to terms with the imminent loss of a loved one. In a study by Kiecolt-Glaser (1987) caregivers for the terminally ill showed suppressed immune functioning.

Death of a loved one

> Studies have shown that some immune parameters are compromised after bereavement or the death of a loved one. Bereavement when followed by depression results in greater negative impact on the immune indicators rather than when bereavement is not followed by depression (Irwin et al, 1986, 1987 as cited in Taylor, 1995).

Loneliness

> For lonely people some of the immune parameters are compromised and they also have worse health outcomes than people who are not lonely(Glaser et al, 1985, as cited in Taylor, 1995).

Does stress directly affect the immune system or is it mediated via negative emotions such as depression which may follow the stressful event?

Literature indicates that when the death of a loved one is followed by depression the impact on immunological indicators is more severe than when not followed by depression.

From a meta analysis (a quantitative review of a number of studies) Herbert & Cohen (1993) concluded that clinical depression was associated with large alterations in cellular immunity. The biggest effect was seen in those who were older and hospitalized. Depression influences lifestyle (nutrition, exercise, substance use – smoking, drinking and drugs, sleeping patterns etc) which in turn influences immunity. When people are depressed , their regular patterns change, they become apathetic, loose interest in their daily tasks and find no pleasure in anything. Sometimes people may oversleep or suffer from insomnia, they may either overeat or loose their appetite, they may stop exercising and even stop going out (do not get exposed to sunlight), they may overdo smoking, drinking or drugs and withdraw from social contact. Thus depression may influence the immune system via the behavioral route as well.

However the question regarding whether the immune differences between depressed and non depressed individuals are related to differences in actual health outcomes has not been researched (Herbert & Cohen, 1993). So do people with compromised immune parameters fall ill more often or do they take longer to recover ?- these indicators have not been recorded or measured.

Most of the studies that measure immune indices such as cell counts have not linked these parameters with actual reported illness. Whether suppressed immune parameters translate into more infections and longer periods of illness is not clear. To study this connection, longitudinal studies would be required to see the effects over time whether suppressed immunity results in illness later or whether frequent stressors have a cumulative effect or what sort of pattern emerges over time. Thus the need for longitudinal studies that link the measures of immune parameters after stressful events to actual illness are required in the future.

Occupational Stress

Occupational stress is stress related to one's job. Occupational stress often stems from unexpected responsibilities and pressures that do not align with a person's knowledge, skills, or expectations, inhibiting one's ability to cope. Occupational stress can increase when workers do not feel supported by supervisors or colleagues, or feel as if they have little control over work processes.

Models

Because stress results from the complex interactions between a large system of interrelated variables, there are several psychological theories and models that address occupational stress.

Person Environment Fit Model: This model "suggests that the match between a person and their work environment is key in influencing their health. For healthy conditions, it is necessary that employees' attitudes, skills, abilities and resources match the demands of their job, and that work environments should meet workers' needs, knowledge, and skills potential. Lack of fit in either of these domains can cause problems, and the greater the gap or misfit (either subjective or objective) between the person and their environment, the greater the strain as demands exceed abilities, and need exceeds supply. These strains can relate to health related issues, lower productivity, and other work problems. Defense mechanisms, such as denial, reappraisal of needs, and coping, also operate in the model, to try and reduce subjective misfit"

Job Characteristics Model: This model "focuses on important aspects of job characteristics, such as skill variety, task identity, task significance, autonomy, and feedback. These characteristics are proposed to lead to 'critical psychological states' of experienced meaningfulness, and experienced responsibility and knowledge of outcomes. It is proposed that positive or negative work characteristics give rise to mental states which lead to corresponding cognitive and behavioral outcomes, e.g. motivation, satisfaction, absenteeism, etc. In conjunction with the model, Hackman and Oldham (1980) developed the Job Diagnostic Survey, a questionnaire for job analysis, which implies key types of job-redesign including combining tasks, creating feedback methods, job enrichment, etc."

Diathesis-Stress Model: This model looks at behaviors as a susceptibility burden together with stress from life experiences. It is useful to distinguish stressful job conditions or stressors from an individual's reactions or strains. Strains can be mental, physical or emotional. Occupational stress can occur when there is a discrepancy between the demands of the environment/workplace and an individual's ability to carry out and complete these demands. Often a stressor can lead the body to have a physiological reaction that can strain a person physically as well as mentally. A variety of factors contribute to workplace stress such as excessive workload, isolation, extensive hours worked, toxic work environments, lack of autonomy, difficult relationships among coworkers and management, management bullying, harassment and lack of opportunities or motivation to advancement in one's skill level.

Jobs-Demand Resources Model: This model posits that strain are a response to imbalance between demands of one's job and the resources he or she has to deal with those demands.

- Job demands: the physical, psychological, social, or organizational aspects of a job that require sustained physical and/or psychological effort or skills. Therefore, they are associated with expenditure of time and energy.
- Job resources: the physical, psychological, social, or organizational aspects of the job that aid in achieving work goals; reduce job demands and the associated physiological and psychological cost; stimulate personal growth, learning, and development.

Effort-Reward Imbalance Model: This model focuses on the reciprocal relationship between efforts and rewards at work. "More specifically, the ERI Model claims that work characterized by both high efforts and low rewards represents a reciprocity deficit between high 'costs' and low 'gains', which could elicit negative emotions in exposed employees. The accompanying feelings may cause sustained strain reactions. So, working hard without receiving adequate appreciation or being treated fairly are examples of a stressful imbalance. Another assumption of the ERI Model concerns individual differences in the experience of effort-reward imbalance. It is assumed that employees characterized by a motivational pattern of excessive job-related commitment and a high need for approval (i.e., overcommitment) will respond with more strain reactions to an effort-reward imbalance, in comparison with less overcommitted people."

Origins

Sources of occupational stress come from:

- a toxic work environment
- negative workload
- isolation
- types of hours worked
- role conflict & role ambiguity

- lack of autonomy, career development barriers
- difficult relationships with administrators and/or coworkers
- managerial bullying
- towing to the wrong gates
- harassment,
- and organizational climate.

These individual sources demonstrate that stress can occur specifically when a conflict arises from the job demands of the employee and the employee itself. If not handled properly, the stress can become distress.

1. Coping: the ability of the employee coping with the specific hours worked, the level of productive rate expected, the physical environment, as well as the expectancy of the work desired by management. For instance, research shows that night shifts in particular has a high possibility of negative impact towards the health of the employee. In relation to this, approximately 20 percent of night shift workers have experienced psycho-physiological dysfunctions, including heart diseases. Extreme factors can affect the competence levels of employees.
2. Role in the organization: associated with the hierarchical ranking of that particular employee within the organization. Upper management is entitled to oversee the overall functioning of the organization. This causes potential distress as the employee must be able to perform simultaneous tasks.
3. Career development: Security of their occupation, promotion levels, etc. are all sources of stress, as this business market in terms of technology of economic dominance is ever-changing.
4. Interpersonal relationships within the workplace: The workplace is a communication and interaction based industry. These relationships (either developed or developing) can be problematic or positive. Common stressors include harassment, discrimination, biased opinions, hearsay, and other derogatory remarks.
5. Organizational climate or structure: The overall communication, management style, and participation among groups of employees are variables to be considered. In essence, the resultant influence of the high participation rate, collaborative planning, and equally dispersed responsibilities provides a positive effect on stress reduction, improved work performance, job satisfaction, and decreased psychosomatic disorders.

Prevalence

Distress is a prevalent and costly problem in today's workplace. About one-third of workers report high levels of stress. 20-30% of workers in different sectors of the European Union reported in 2007 that they believed work-related stress was potentially affecting their health. Three-quarters of employees believe the worker has more on-the-job stress than a generation ago. In Great Britain, a sixth of the workforce experiences occupational stress every year. Evidence also suggests that distress is the major cause of turnover in organizations. With continued distress at the workplace, workers will develop psychological and physiological dysfunctions and decreased motivation in excelling in their position. Increased levels of job stress are determined by the awareness of having little control but lots of demands in the work area. Occupational stress and its sequelae represent the majority of work-related illnesses causing missed work days. Those in the protective services, transportation and materials moving, building grounds cleaning and maintenance, and healthcare are more susceptible to both work injuries and illnesses, as well as work-related stress.

Negative Health Effects

Stress-related disorders encompass a broad array of conditions, including psychological disorders (e.g., depression, anxiety, post-traumatic stress disorder) and other types of emotional strain (e.g., dissatisfaction, fatigue, tension, etc.), maladaptive behaviors (e.g., aggression, substance abuse), and cognitive impairment (e.g., concentration and memory problems). In turn, these conditions may lead to poor work performance, higher absenteeism, less work productivity or even injury. "If untreated, consistently high stress can become a chronic condition, which can exacerbate existing mental health conditions and chronic physical conditions (diabetes, hypertension, weak immune system). These conditions not only diminish the well-being of workers and increase the employer's health benefits expenses, they contribute to increased injury incidence. Consistently high levels of stress increase the risk of occupational injury. A study of light/short haul truckers, a group that experiences high rates of injury and mental health issues, found that frequent stress increased the odds of occupational injury by 350%."

Job stress is also associated with various biological reactions that may lead ultimately to compromised health, such as cardiovascular disease, or in extreme cases death. Due to the high pressure and demands in the work place the demands have been shown to be correlated with increased rates of heart attack, hypertension and other disorders. In New York, Los Angeles, and London, among other municipalities, the relationship between job stress and heart attacks is acknowledged.

Problems at work are more strongly associated with health complaints than are any other life stressor-more so than even financial problems or family problems. Occupational stress accounts for more than 10% of work-related health claims. Many studies suggest that psychologically demanding jobs that allow employees little control over the work process increase the risk of cardiovascular disease. Research indicates that job stress increases the risk for development of back and upper-extremity musculoskeletal disorders. Other disorders that can be caused or exacerbated by occupational stress include sleep disorders, headache, mood disorders, upset stomach, hypertension, high cholesterol, autoimmune disease, cardiovascular disease, depression, and anxiety. Stress at work can also increase the risk of acquiring an infection and the risk of accidents at work.

High levels of stress are associated with substantial increases in health service utilization. Workers who report experiencing stress at work also show excessive health care utilization. In a 1998 study of 46,000 workers, health care costs were nearly 50% greater for workers reporting high levels of stress in comparison to "low risk" workers. The increment rose to nearly 150%, an increase of more than $1,700 per person annually, for workers reporting high levels of both stress and depression. Health care costs increase by 200% in those with depression and high occupational stress. Additionally, periods of disability due to job stress tend to be much longer than disability periods for other occupational injuries and illnesses.

Physiological reactions to stress can have consequences for health over time. Researchers have been studying how stress affects the cardiovascular system, as well as how work stress can lead to hypertension and coronary artery disease. These diseases, along with other stress-induced illnesses tend to be quite common in American work-places. There are four main physiological reactions to stress:

- Blood is shunted to the brain and large muscle groups, and away from extremities, skin, and organs that are not currently serving the body.
- An area near the brain stem, known as the reticular activating system, goes to work, causing a state of keen alertness as well as sharpening of hearing and vision.
- Energy-providing compounds of glucose and fatty acids are released into the bloodstream.
- The immune and digestive systems are temporarily shut down.

Gender

Frustrated man at a desk

Men and women are exposed to many of the same stressors. Although men and women might not differ in overall strains, women are more likely to experience psychological distress, whereas men experience more physical strain. Desmarais and Alksnis suggest two explanations for the greater psychological distress of women. First, the genders may differ in their awareness of negative feelings, leading women to express and report strains, whereas men deny and inhibit such feelings. Second, the demands to balance work and family result in more overall stressors for women that leads to increased strain.

The Kenexa Research Institute released a global survey of almost 30,000 workers which showed that females suffered more workplace distress than their male counterparts. According to the survey, women's stress level were 10% higher for those in supervisory positions, 8% higher stress in service and production jobs than men, and 6% higher in middle and upper management than men in the same position.

Causes

Job stress results from various interactions of the worker and the environment of the work they perform their duties. Location, gender, environment, and many other factors contribute to the buildup of stress. Job stress results from the interaction of the worker and the conditions of work. Views differ on the importance of worker characteristics versus working conditions as the primary cause of job stress. The differing viewpoints suggest different ways to prevent stress at work. Differences in individual characteristics such as personality and coping skills can be very important in predicting whether certain job conditions will result in stress. In other words, what is stressful for one person may not be a problem for someone else. This viewpoint underlies prevention strategies that focus on workers and ways to help them cope with demanding job conditions. In general, occupational stress is caused by a mismatch between perceived effort and perceived reward, and/or a sense of low control in a job with high demands. Low social support at work and job insecurity can also increase occupational stress. Psychosocial stressors are a major cause of occupational stress.

Working Conditions

Although the importance of individual differences cannot be ignored, scientific evidence suggests that certain working conditions are stressful to most people. Such evidence argues for a greater emphasis on working conditions as the key source of job stress, and for job redesign as a primary prevention strategy. Large surveys of working conditions, including conditions recognized as risk factors for job stress, were conducted in member states of the European Union in 1990, 1995, and 2000. Results showed a time trend suggesting an increase in work intensity. In 1990, the percentage of workers reporting that they worked at high speeds at least one-quarter of their working time was 48%, increasing to 54% in 1995 and to 56% in 2000. Similarly, 50% of workers reported they work against tight deadlines at least one-fourth of their working time in 1990, increasing to 56% in 1995 and 60% in 2000. However, no change was noted in the period 1995–2000 (data not collected in 1990) in the percentage of workers reporting sufficient time to complete tasks.

Workload

In an occupational setting, dealing with workload can be stressful and serve as a stressor for employees. There are three aspects of workload that can be stressful.

- Quantitative workload or overload: Having more work to do than can be accomplished comfortably.
- Qualitative workload: Having work that is too difficult.
- Underload: Having work that fails to use a worker's skills and abilities.

Workload as a work demand is a major component of the demand-control model of stress. This model suggests that jobs with high demands can be stressful, especially when the individual has low control over the job. In other words, control serves as a buffer or protective factor when demands or workload is high. This model was expanded into the demand-control-support model that suggests that the combination of high control and high social support at work buffers the effects of high demands.

As a work demand, workload is also relevant to the job demands-resources model of stress that suggests that jobs are stressful when demands (e.g., workload) exceed the individual's resources to deal with them.

Long Hours

A substantial percentage of Americans work very long hours. By one estimate, more than 26% of men and more than 11% of women worked 50 hours per week or more in 2000. These figures represent a considerable increase over the previous three decades, especially for women. According to the Department of Labor, there have been a rise in increasing amount of hours in the work place by employed women, an increase in extended work weeks (>40 hours) by men, and a considerable increase in combined working hours among working couples, particularly couples with young children.

Evidence of occupational stress due to an individual's status in the workplace

Status

A person's status in the workplace can also affect levels of stress. While workplace stress has the potential to affect employees of all categories; those who have very little influence to those who make major decisions for the company. However, less powerful employees (that is, those who have less control over their jobs) are more likely to suffer stress than powerful workers. Managers as well as other kinds of workers are vulnerable to work overload.

Economic Factors

Economic factors that employees are facing in the 21st century have been linked to increased stress levels. Researchers and social commentators have pointed out that the computer and communications revolutions have made companies more efficient and productive than ever before. This boon in productivity however, has caused higher expectations and greater competition, putting more stress on the employee.

The following economic factors may lead to workplace stress:

- Pressure from investors, who can quickly withdraw their money from company stocks.
- The lack of trade and professional unions in the workplace.
- Inter-company rivalries caused by the efforts of companies to compete globally
- The willingness of companies to swiftly lay off workers to cope with changing business environments.

Bullying

Bullying in the workplace can also contribute to stress. This can be broken down into five different categories:

- Threat to profession status
- Threat to personal status
- Isolation
- Excess work
- Destabilization i.e. lack of credit for work, meaningless tasks etc.

This in effect can create a hostile work environment for the employees that, which in turn, can affect their work ethic and contribution to the organization.

Narcissism and Psychopathy

Thomas suggests that there tends to be a higher level of stress with people who work or interact with a narcissist, which in turn increases absenteeism and staff turnover. Boddy finds the same dynamic where there is corporate psychopath in the organisation.

Workplace Conflict

Interpersonal conflict among people at work has been shown to be one of the most frequently noted stressors for employees. Conflict has been noted to be an indicator of the broader concept of workplace harassment. It relates to other stressors that might co-occur, such as role conflict, role ambiguity, and workload. It also relates to strains such as anxiety, depression, physical symptoms, and low levels of job satisfaction.

Sexual Harassment

Women are more likely than men to experience sexual harassment, especially for those working in traditionally masculine occupations. In addition, a study indicated that sexual harassment negatively affects workers' psychological well-being. Another study found that level of harassment at workplaces lead to differences in performance of work related tasks. High levels of harassment were related to the worst outcomes, and no harassment was related to least negative outcomes. In other words, women who had experienced a higher level of harassment were more likely to perform poorly at workplaces.

Occupational group

Lower occupational groups are at higher risk of work-related ill health than higher occupational groups. This is in part due to adverse work and employment conditions. Furthermore, such conditions have greater effects on ill-health to those in lower socio-economic positions.

Effects

Stressful working conditions can lead to three types of strains: Behavioral (e.g., absenteeism or poor performance), physical (e.g., headaches or coronary heart disease), and psychological (e.g., anxiety or depressed mood). Physical symptoms that may occur because of occupational stress include fatigue, headache, upset stomach, muscular aches and pains, weight gain or loss, chronic mild illness, and sleep disturbances. Psychological and behavioral problems that may develop include anxiety, irritability, alcohol and drug use, feeling powerless and low morale. The spectrum of effects caused by occupational stress includes absenteeism, poor decision making, lack of creativity, accidents, organizational breakdown or even sabotage. If exposure to stressors in the workplace is prolonged, then chronic health problems can occur including stroke. An examination was of physical and psychological effects of workplace stress was conducted with a sample of 552 female blue collar employees of a microelectronics facility. It was found that job-related conflicts were associated with depressive symptoms, severe headaches, fatigue, rashes, and other multiple symptoms. Studies among the Japanese population specifically showed a more than 2-fold increase in the risk of total stroke among men with job strain (combination of high job demand and low job control). Those in blue-collar or maual labor jobs are more likely to develop heart disease compared to those in white-collar jobs. Along with the risk of stroke, stress can raise the risk of high blood pressure, immune system dysfunction, coronary artery disease. Prolonged occupational stress can lead to occupational burnout. Occupational stress can also disrupt relationships.

The effects of job stress on chronic diseases are more difficult to ascertain because chronic diseases develop over relatively long periods of time and are influenced by many factors other than stress. Nonetheless, there is some evidence that stress plays a role in the development of several types of chronic health problems—including cardiovascular disease, musculoskeletal disorders, and psychological disorders. Job stress and strain has been associated with poor mental health and wellbeing over a 12 year period.

Occupational stress has negative effects for organizations and employers. Occupational stress is the cause of approximately 40% of turnover and 50% of workplace absences. The annual cost of occupational stress and its effects in the US is estimated to be over $60 billion to employers and $250–300 billion to the economy.

Prevention

A combination of organizational change and stress management is often the most useful approach for preventing stress at work. Both organizations and employees can employ strategies at organizational and individual levels. Generally, organizational level strategies include job procedure modification and employee assistance programs (EAP). Individual level strategies include taking vacation. Getting a realistic job preview to understand the normal workload and schedules of the job will also help people to identify whether or not the job fit them.

How an Organization Can Prevent Job Stress

- Ensure that the workload is in line with workers' capabilities and resources.
- Design jobs to provide meaning, stimulation, and opportunities for workers to use their skills.
- Clearly define workers' roles and responsibilities.
- To reduce workplace stress, managers may monitor the workload given out to the employees. Also while they are being trained they should let employees understand and be notified of stress awareness.
- Give workers opportunities to participate in decisions and actions affecting their jobs.
- Improve communications-reduce uncertainty about career development and future employment prospects.
- Provide opportunities for social interaction among workers.
- Establish work schedules that are compatible with demands and responsibilities outside the job.
- Combat workplace discrimination (based on race, gender, national origin, religion or language).
- Bringing in an objective outsider such as a consultant to suggest a fresh approach to persistent problems.
- Introducing a participative leadership style to involve as many subordinates as possible to resolve stress-producing problems.
- Encourage work-life balance through family-friendly benefits and policies

An insurance company conducted several studies on the effects of stress prevention programs in hospital settings. Program activities included (1) employee and management education on job stress, (2) changes in hospital policies and procedures to reduce organizational sources of stress, and (3) the establishment of employee assistance programs. In one study, the frequency of medication errors declined by 50% after prevention activities were implemented in a 700-bed hospital. In a second study, there was a 70% reduction in malpractice claims in 22 hospitals that implemented stress prevention activities. In contrast, there was no reduction in claims in a matched group of 22 hospitals that did not implement stress prevention activities.

Telecommuting is another way organizations can help reduce stress for their workers. Employees defined telecommuting as "an alternative work arrangement in which employees perform tasks elsewhere that are normally done in a primary or central workplace, for at least some portion of their work schedule, using electronic media to interact with others inside and outside the organization." One reason that telecommuting gets such high marks is that it allows employees more control over how they do their work. Telecommuters reported more job satisfaction and less desire to find a new job. Employees that worked from home also had less stress, improved work/life balance and higher performance rating by their managers.

A systematic review of stress-reduction techniques among healthcare workers found that cognitive behavioral training lowered emotional exhaustion and feelings of lack of personal accomplishment.

Signs and Symptoms of Excessive Job and Workplace Stress

Signs and symptoms of excessive job and workplace stress include:

• Feeling anxious, irritable, or depressed	• Muscle tension or headaches
• Apathy, loss of interest in work	• Stomach problems
• Problems sleeping	• Social withdrawal
• Fatigue	• Loss of sex drive
• Trouble concentrating	• Using alcohol or drugs to cope

Both yoga and mindful-based stress reduction have been shown to reduce work-related stress. Nursings participating in cognitive behavioral interventions less perceived stress, a greater sense of coherence, and increased mood.

Expanding Research on Stress: Contemporary opinions hold that jobs designed to support skill variety, task identity, significance, autonomy, and feedback, while providing for existence and growth needs, will sustain a healthier, greater satisfied workforce.

For team-oriented work environments, Patrick Lencioni's The Five Dysfunctions of a Team profiles the behavior of cohesive teams:

1. They trust one another
2. They engage in unfiltered conflict around ideas
3. They commit to decisions and plans of action
4. They hold one another accountable for delivering against those plans
5. They focus on the achievement of collective results.

For immediate individual stress management, rudimentary mental coping strategies may be adopted in the work environment.

References

- Baert, S., Norga, J., Thuy, Y., Van Hecke, M. (In press) Getting Grey Hairs in the Labour Market: An Alternative Experiment on Age Discrimination Journal of Economic Psychology
- Leigh, A., Jencks, C., & Smeeding, T.M. (2009). Nolan, B., Salverda, W., & Smeeding, T.M., eds. The Oxford Handbook of Economic Inequality (PDF). ISBN 9780199606061
- Nussbaum, M. C. (2004). "Women's Education: A Global Challenge". Signs: Journal of Women in Culture and Society. 29 (2): 325–355. doi:10.1086/378571
- Wilkinson, Richard; Pickett, Kate (2009). The Spirit Level: Why More Equal Societies Almost Always Do Better. Allen Lane. p. 352. ISBN 978-1-84614-039-6

- "Drug Discrimination and the case against Casey Hardison". Transform Drug Policy Foundation. Retrieved 2015-06-30
- Drydakis, N. (2014) Sexual Orientation Discrimination in the Cypriot Labour Market: Distastes or Uncertainty? International Journal of Manpower, 35, 720-744
- Clark, Eve (2009). First Language Acquisition. New York, NY: Cambridge University Press. pp. 44–46. ISBN 978-0-521-51413-2
- Hager, Paul. "The Drug War and the Constitution". paulhager.org. Retrieved 2015-06-30. Transcript of a speech given at the 1991 Indiana Civil Liberties Union Conference at Indiana University
- Flanigan J (October 2012). "Three arguments against prescription requirements". Journal of Medical Ethics. 38 (10): 579–86. doi:10.1136/medethics-2011-100240. PMID 22844026
- Markus, H.; Conner, A (2013). Clash!: 8 cultural conflicts that make us who we are. New York, NY: Hudson Street Press. pp. 89–112. ISBN 1101623608
- Richey, Warren (2005-10-31). "On docket: religious freedom vs. drug laws". Christian Science Monitor. Retrieved 2015-07-01
- Jennifer Roback, "The Political Economy of Segregation: The Case of Segregated Streetcars." Journal of Economic History 56, no. 4 (December 1986): 893–917
- Thompson, Neil (2016-05-12). Anti-Discriminatory Practice: Equality, Diversity and Social Justice. Palgrave Macmillan. ISBN 9781137586667
- Emily Dufton (Mar 28, 2012). "The War on Drugs: Should It Be Your Right to Use Narcotics?". The Atlantic. Retrieved 2015-07-01
- Vlassoff, C (March 2007). "Gender differences in determinants and consequences of health and illness.". Journal of health, population, and nutrition. 25 (1): 47–61. PMC 3013263. PMID 17615903
- Szalavitz, Maia (2012-08-06). "Human Rights Watch: Hundreds of Thousands Still Tortured in Name of Drug Treatment". Time. Retrieved 2015-07-01

3

Health Communication: An Integrated Study

Through health communication, many health-related events can be propagated among the public. It is a method to improve health literacy and health choice. The central motive of this practice is the idea that prevention is a better measure in fighting diseases than curing diseases. Health communication has been shown to be more effective than support or control groups. The section also delves into the concepts of fear appeal, health education, health literacy etc. This chapter has been carefully written to provide an easy understanding of the varied facets of health communication.

Health Communication

Health communication is the study and practice of communicating promotional health information, such as in public health campaigns, health education, and between doctor and patient. The purpose of disseminating health information is to influence personal health choices by improving health literacy.

Because effective health communication must be tailored for the audience and the situation, research into health communication seeks to refine communication strategies to inform people about ways to enhance health or to avoid specific health risks. Academically, health communication is a discipline within communication studies.

Health communication may variously seek to:

- increase audience knowledge and awareness of a health issue
- influence behaviors and attitudes towards a health issue
- demonstrate healthy practices
- demonstrate the benefits of behavior changes to public health outcomes
- advocate a position on a health issue or policy
- increase demand or support for health services
- argue against misconceptions about health

Establishment

The term was generated when members of an ICA, International Communication Association, interest group adopted the term. Interdisciplinary marriage between health and communication was certainly a common-law relationship long before the term "health communication" was introduced. (Stacks & Salween, page 489) The research of health communication surrounds the development of effective messages about health, the dissemination of health-related information through broadcast, print, and electronic media, and the role of inter personal relationships in health communities. At the core of all of the communication is the idea of health and the emphasis of health. The goal of health communication research is to identify and provide better and more effective communication strategies that will improve the overall health of society.

Research

There are many purposes and reasons why health communication research is important and how it betters the health care field. The training programs of Health Care Professionals, or HCP, can be adapted and developed based on health communication research. (Stacks & Salween, 495) Due to there being a diverse culture that makes up the group of patients within the health care field, communication to other cultures has been taught and has been made a focus in health care training classes. Research suggests that nonverbal and verbal communication between health care professionals and patient can lead to improved patient outcomes. According to Stacks and Salween on page 496 some health care facilities, like hospitals are providing training and education materials to patients. The goal of hospitals doing this is to allow for patients to have a better outcome due to better communication skills. Over the years, there has been much research done on health communication. For example, researchers want to know if people are more effectively motivated by a positive message versus a negative message. Researchers examine ideas like, are people better motivated by ideas of wealth and safety or an idea of illness and death. Researchers are examining which dimensions of persuasive incentives are most influential: physical health versus economic, versus psychological, versus moral, versus social. (Stacks & Salween, 497) Impact of the Health Campaign-After research has been conducted and analyzed on the effects of health communication, it can be concluded that a health communication campaign that is requiring a behavior change causes the desired behavior change in about 7%-10% or more in the people who are in the campaign site than those who are in the control group. Also, the effects are stronger for adoption of a new behavior than cessation of a current behavior, about 12% higher.

When assessing how affective a health campaign is, the key determinant is the degree of audience reception, the quality and quantity of the message, the dissemination channels, and the larger communication environment. It is possible that an audience can be more receptive to some messages than others. The media channel and how the message is reached by the audience can affect the effectiveness of the health campaign. (Stacks & Salween page 498)

The efforts and effects of health messages and communication are often counter affected by alcohol and tobacco commercials. The advertisement for these items is often made to be glamorous and will contradict what was said in the health campaign. This can lead to the efforts of the health communication seem to be pointless.

Training

Health communication professionals are specifically trained in methods and strategies for effective communication of public health messages, with qualifications in research, strategic development, and evaluating effectiveness. Health communication is taught in master's and doctoral programs. The Coalition for Health Communication maintains a list of such programs.

Scholars and practitioners in health communication are often trained in disciplines such as communication studies, sociology, psychology, public health, or medicine and then focus within their field on either health or communication. Practitioners are pragmatic and draw from social-scientific scholarship, theories from the humanities, and professional fields such as education, management, law and marketing (Maibach 2008). Professionals trained in health communication encounter a wide range of employment opportunities spanning between the public, private, and volunteer sectors and have the opportunity for a large amount of career mobility. Examples of jobs in each of these categories include federal, state, and local health departments in the public sector, Pharmaceutical companies and large corporations in the private sector, and various non-profit organizations such as the American Cancer Society and the American Heart Association in the volunteer sector.

Overview

International Communication Association officially recognized health communication in 1975; in 1997, the American Public Health Association categorised health communication as a discipline of Public Health Education and Health Promotion.

Careers in the field of health communication range widely between the public, private, and volunteer sectors and professionals of health communication are distinctively trained to conduct communication research, develop successful and repeatable campaigns for health promotion and advocacy, and to evaluate how effective these strategies have been for future campaigns.

Clear communication is essential to successful public health practice at every level of the ecological model; intrapersonal, interpersonal, group, organizational, and societal. In each instance of health communication, there must be careful deliberation concerning the appropriate channel for messages to best reach the target audience, ranging from face-to-face interactions to television, Internet, and other forms of mass media. The recent explosion of new Internet communication technologies, particularly through the development of health websites (such as MedlinePlus, Healthfinder, and WebMD), online support groups (such as the Association for Cancer Online Resources), web portals, tailored information systems, telehealth programs, electronic health records, social networking, and mobile devices (cell phones, PDAs, etc.) means that the potential media are ever changing.

The social and cultural contexts in which health communication occurs are also widely diverse and can include (but are not limited to) homes, schools, doctor's offices, and workplaces, and messages must consider the variant levels of health literacy and education of their audience, as well as demographics, values, socioeconomic issues, and many other factors that may influence effective communication.

Strategies and Methods

Tailoring a health message is one strategy for persuasive health communication. For messages of health communication to reach selected audiences accurately and quickly, health communication professionals must assemble a collection of superior and audience appropriate information that target population segments. Understanding the audience for the information is critical to effective delivery.

Communication is an enigma that is detrimental to the healthcare world and to the resulting health of a patient. Communication is an activity that involves oral speech, voice, tone, nonverbal body language, listening and more. It is a process for a mutual understanding to come at hand during interpersonal connections. A patient's communication with their healthcare team and vice versa, affects the outcome of their health. Strong, clear, and positive relationships with physicians can chronically improve and increase the condition of a certain patient. Through two approaches, the biomedical model and the biopsychosocial model; this can be successfully achieved. Evidence has shown that communication and its traditions have altered throughout the years. With the use of many new discoveries and the changes within our technology market, communication has severely improved and become instantaneous.

Communicators need to continually synthesize knowledge from a range of other scholarly disciplines including marketing, psychology, and behavioural sciences. Once this information has been collected, professionals can choose from a variety of methods and strategies of communication that they believe would best convey their message. These methods include campaigns, entertainment advocacy, media advocacy, new technologies, and interpersonal communication.

Campaigns

Health Communication campaigns are arguably the most utilized and effective method for spreading public health messages, especially in endorsing disease prevention (e.g. cancer, HIV/AIDS) and in general health promotion and wellness (e.g. family planning, reproductive health). The Institute of Medicine argues that health communication campaigns tend to organize their message for a diverse audience in one of three ways:

- By catering to the common denominator within the audience
- By creating one central message and then later making systematic alterations in order to better reach a certain audience segment, while retaining the same central message
- By creating distinctly different messages for different audience segments

Both the Centers for Disease Control and Prevention and scholars of health communication emphasize the importance of strategic planning throughout a campaign. This includes a variety of steps to ensure a well-developed message is being communicated:

- Reviewing background information to define what the problem is and who is affected by the problem
- Setting communication objectives and proposing a plan to meet the wanted outcome
- Analyze the target audience by determining interests, attitudes, behaviors, benefits, and barriers
- Select channels and materials for communication in relation to what will most effectively reach audiences
- Develop and pretest message concepts to determine understanding, acceptance, and reaction to the message
- Implement communication with selected audience and monitor exposures and reactions to the message

- Assess the outcome and evaluate the effectiveness and impact of the campaign, noting if changes need to be made

Historical Campaigns

American Smallpox Epidemic

In 1721, health communication was used to mitigate the smallpox epidemic in Boston. Cotton Mather, a political leader, used pamphlets and speeches to promote inoculation of smallpox. Alcohol abuse has been a problem within society for about as long as alcohol has been around. In the 19th century, the Women's Christian Temperance Union led a movement against alcohol abuse. They utilized mass communication to communicate the desired message. News papers and magazines allowed for the promotion of the anti-alcohol movement.

Cardiovascular Disease

Three-community study and the five-city project were experimental campaigns to inform middle-aged men about the causes of cardiovascular disease. Health messages were communicated via television, radio, newspaper, cookbooks, booklets, and bus cards. The three "communities" comprised three experimental communication strategies: a media-only campaign, a media campaign supplemented with face-to-face communication, and a no-intervention control group. The experimented revealed that after one year, the most informed at-risk men were those in the second experimental group: they men consumed the media campaign and were attended by a health care provider.

Communication Channels

Entertainment Media

Using the entertainment industry as a platform for advocating health information and education is a communication strategy that has become increasingly popular. The most utilized strategy is for health communication professionals to create partnerships with storyline creators so that public health information can be incorporated into within the plot of a television show. The Centers for Disease Control and Prevention has formed a strong partnership with Hollywood, Health, and Society, at the University of Southern California Norman Lear Center to continue to produce new storylines on television and in film studios that will help to promote public health information. Some of the resources provided with this partnership include comprehensive "tip sheets" to provide writers with easy to access and trustworthy information on health issues, and meetings and panels to discuss new information and resources. Some of the most notable examples of this method of communication in recent years have been with the films *Contagion* and *I Am Legend* in understanding the spread of disease, *NBC's* series *Parenthood* in Asperger's Syndrome, and with the *CW's* series *90210* and spreading cancer awareness.

Writers and storyline developers have an increased motivation to continue to incorporate public health information into their scripts with the creation of the Sentinel for Health Awards in 2000, which honors storylines that effectively promote health topics and audience awareness of public health issues. Surveys conducted by Porter Novelli in 2001 reported many interesting statistics on the effectiveness of this strategy, such as that over half of regular prime time and daytime drama viewers have reported that they have learned something about health promotion or disease prevention from a TV show. Amongst this data, minority groups are significantly represented with well over half of African American and Hispanic viewers stating that they had either taken some form of preventative action after hearing about a health issue on TV, or that a TV storyline helped them to provide vital health information to a friend or family member.

Direct Marketing

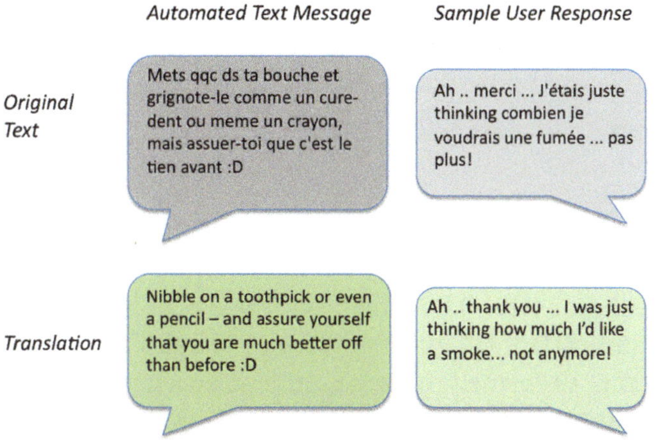

Some health organizations manage text messaging services to help people avoid smoking

Media advocacy use strategic mass media tools combined with widespread organization in order to advocate for healthy public policies or lifestyles. This can include the use of text messaging and email to spread messages from person to person, and using social networking venues to promote health information to a wide ranging audience. As technologies expand, the platforms for health communication through media advocacy will undoubtedly expand as well.

Interpersonal Communication

Health communication relies on strong interpersonal communications in order to influence health decisions and behaviours. The most important of these relationships are the connection and interaction between an individual and their health care provider (e.g., physician, therapist, pharmacist) and an individual's social support system (family, friends, community). These connections can positively influence the individual's decision to make healthy choices. Patients are more prone to listen when they feel invested emotionally into the situation. If they feel as if they understand what is being said, they are more prone to make objective decisions based on the information heard.

Applications

Health communication has become essential in promoting the general public health in myriad situations. One of health communication's most important applications has been throughout major Environmental events (e.g. hurricanes, flooding, tornados) and addressing the affected audience's questions and needs quickly and efficiently, keeping the protection of public health and the forefront of their message. Health communication professionals are constantly working to improve this type of risk communication in order to be prepared in the case of an emergency.

Another increasingly important application of health communication has been in reaching students in the college community. The National College Health Assessment has measured that 92.5% of college students reported being in "good, very good, or excellent health", however college students seem to battle serious problems with stress, depression, substance abuse, and a general lack of nutrition in comparison to other age groups and audiences. Professionals in health communication are actively striving for new ways to reach this at-risk audience in order to raise standards of public health in the college setting and to promote a healthier life style amongst students.

Challenges

Health communication faces many challenges. While problems can be attributed to many factors, some of the most essential issues have to do with the gap between health literacy and health communication, flaws in communicating through the mass media, and a lack of trained professionals.

Literacy-communication Gap

One of the most pertinent challenges health communication faces is the general gap that has formed between the population's health literacy and the use of health communication. While the goal is that health communication will effectively *lead* to health literacy, issues such as the use of unexplained medical jargon, ill-formed messages, and often a general educational gap have created a gap. Specifically, studies have been done amongst elderly populations in America to illustrate a common audience who is left at a disadvantage due to this issue. The older adults comprise an age group that generally suffers from the most chronic health conditions in comparison to other age groups, however studies have shown that even this group have difficulty understanding written health materials, understanding health care and policies, and generally do not comprehend medical jargon. Such shortfallings of health communication may lead to increased hospitalizations, the inability to respond to and manage a disease or medical condition, and a generally declining health status.

In some populations, health-related websites (e.g., WebMD) and online support groups (e.g., Association for Cancer Online Resources) have increased access to health information.

Mass Media

Mass communication is used to promote beneficial changes in behavior among members of populations. A major criticism of the use of mass media as a method of health communication is the unfortunate ability for false and misinformed messages to spread quickly through the mass media, before they have the chance to be disputed by professionals. This issue may generate unwarranted panic amongst those who receive the messages and be an issue as technology continues to advance. An example of this may be observed in the ongoing distrust of vaccinations due to the publication of numerous messages that wrongly link the childhood measles-mumps-rubella (MMR) vaccination with the development and onset of Autism. The speed with which this message spread due to new social networking technologies caused many parents to distrust vaccinations and therefore forgo having their children receive the vaccine. Although this panic has been ferociously labeled as fictitious, many still harbor a lingering suspicion towards vaccinations and refuse them, which has caused an immediate public health concern.

Behavior Change (Public Health)

Behavior change is a central objective in public health interventions, with an increased focus on prevention prior to onset of disease. This is particularly important in low and middle income countries, where efficiency of health spending and costs and benefits of health interventions has come under increased scrutiny in recent decades. Behavior change in public health is also known as Social and Behavior Change Communication (SBCC).

Background

Health conditions and infections are associated with risky behaviors. Tobacco use, alcoholism, multiple sex partners, substance use, reckless driving, obesity, or unprotected sexual intercourse are some examples. Human beings have, in principle, control over their conduct. Behavior modification can contribute to the success of self-control, and health-enhancing behaviors. Risky behaviors can be eliminated including physical exercise, weight control, preventive nutrition, dental hygiene, condom use, or accident prevention. Health behavior change refers to the motivational, volitional, and action based processes of abandoning such health-compromising behaviors in favor of adopting and maintaining health-enhancing behaviors. Addiction that is assoociated with risky behavior may have a genetic component.

One emerging concept in the American health system is that of small, manageable changes. It is not necessary to make sweeping, drastic alterations to one's whole lifestyle in order to see benefit. Dietary and exercise contexts, in particular show the benefit of moderate, slow changes. For example, behavior change steps to include more physical activity can improve ones life expectancy, control weight, and boost mental health. It is also known to reduce the chance of some diseases such as type 2 diabetes, cardiovascular disease, and some cancers. Healthy behaviors and practices during youth, particularly in school settings, is far more cost-effective than waiting until unhealthy behaviors are entrenched. A study of the Toward No Tobacco program, which was designed to prevent cigarette use among middle and high school students, found that for every dollar invested in school tobacco prevention programs, almost $20 in future medical care costs would be saved.

Theories

Behavior change programs tend to focus on a few behavioral change theories which gained ground in the 1980s. These theories share a major commonality in defining individual actions as the locus of change. Behavior change programs that are usually focused on activities that help a person or a community to reflect upon their risk behaviors and change them to reduce their risk and vulnerability are known as interventions. Examples include: "Transtheoretical (Stages of Change) Model of Behavior Change", "theory of reasoned action", "health belief model", "theory of planned behavior", diffusion of innovation", and the health action process approach. Developments in health behavior change theories since the late 1990s have focused on incorporating disparate theories of health behavior change into a single unified theory.

Tools

- Care groups are groups of 10–15 volunteer, community-based health educators who regularly meet together.

- Barrier Analysis is a rapid assessment tool used in behavior change projects to identify behavioral determinants.
- Community-led total sanitation is a behaviour change tool used in the sanitation sector for mainly rural settings in developing countries with the aim to stop open defecation. The method uses shame, disgust and to some extent peer pressure which leads to the "spontaneous" construction and long-term use of toilets after an initial triggering process has taken place.

Behavior Change Communication (BCC)

Behavior change communication, or BCC, is an approach to behavior change focused on communication. It is also known as Social and Behavior Change Communication, or SBCC. The assumptions is that through communication of some kind, individuals and communities can somehow be persuaded to behave in ways that will make their lives safer and healthier. BCC was first employed in HIV and TB prevention projects. More recently, its ambit has grown to encompass any communication activity whose goal is to help individuals and communities select and practice behavior that will positively impact their health, such as immunization, cervical cancer check up, employing single-use syringes, etc.

Examples

- Johns Hopkins Center for Communication Programs specializes in health-related BCC (behavior change communication) programs, primarily in developing countries. It includes programs in reproductive health and family planning, malaria, and HIV/AIDS.
- Development Media International uses mass media to promote healthy behaviors in Burkina Faso, DRC and Mozambique.
- Young 1ove provides information to youth to reduce the spread of HIV/AIDS in Botswana.

Fear Appeal

Fear appeal is a term used in psychology, sociology and marketing. It generally describes a strategy for motivating people to take a particular action, endorse a particular policy, or buy a particular product, by arousing fear. A well-known example in television advertising was a commercial employing the musical jingle: "Never pick up a stranger, pick up Prestone anti-freeze." This was accompanied by images of shadowy strangers (hitchhikers) who would presumably do one harm if picked up. The commercial's main appeal was not to the positive features of Prestone anti-freeze, but to the fear of what a "strange" brand might do.

A fear appeal is a persuasive message that attempts to arouse fear in order to divert behavior through the threat of impending danger or harm. It presents a risk, presents the vulnerability to the risk, and then may, or may not suggest a form of protective action.

It is assumed that through a fear appeal the perception of threatening stimuli creates fear arousal. The state of fear is believed to be an unpleasant emotional state that involves physiological arousal that motivates cognitive, affective, and behavioral responses directed towards alleviating the threat or reducing fear. There are many different theoretical models of fear appeal messages. They include: the extended parallel process model, the drive theory, the subjective expected utility theory, the protection motivation theory, the health belief model, the theory of reasoned action, and the transtheoretical model. These models are widely used in substance abuse campaigns, sexual health programs, and many other general health contexts. The persuasive effect of fear appeals is thought to be influenced by several factors such as individual characteristics, self-efficacy, perception of norms, fear strength, perceived threat, perception of treatment efficacy, and defense mechanisms. Mixed results have been produced from studies that attempt to demonstrate the effectiveness of fear appeals for behavior modification, and a recent meta-analysis recommended extreme caution in the use of fear appeals.

Models

Over the last half century, a substantial amount of research has been done on the influence of fear on persuasion. A multitude of theories and models of fear appeals, also known as cognitive mediating processes, have been derived from this research. The goal of each of these has been to conceptualize the influence of fear on persuasion so as to better understand how to employ it in addressing the public on a number of social issues.

Extended Parallel Process Model

The extended parallel process model (EPPM) is a theory that explains how cognitive and emotional mechanisms trigger distinct motivational and coping responses such as fear control and danger control responses. Fear control responses minimize fear through emotional coping that generates reassurance through denial of the threat or derogation of the persuasive message. Fear control is a process of denial that does not involve physically averting behavior to the perceived threat. Danger control is a cognitive process also oriented towards reducing the presented threat. However, unlike fear control response, danger control response may prompt protective action. Thus according to the extended parallel process model, the experience of fear is considered an emotional reaction, and the perceptions of threat are a set of cognitions. The extended parallel process model differs from many other fear appeal arguments because it suggests that that fear arousal and danger control processes are distinct processes where fear arousal need not precede the danger control process that underpin precautionary behaviors.

It is predicted that a fear appeal will initiate a dominant response of either fear control or danger control processes. The extended parallel process model concludes that that cognitions (attitudes, intentions, and behavior changes) result in fear appeal success via the danger control process. It also concludes that fear appeals fail when the fear emotion is reduced via the fear control process.

Defensive avoidance is an example of a fear control response that leads to the failure of fear appeals.

Drive Theory

Emotional tension is a key characteristic of drive theory. According to the theory, a threat that portrays the negative consequences of non-compliance to a recommended behavior is expected to create fear. In order to relieve the emotional tension of the threat, the "drive" state motivates behavior conduct that reduces the tension. According to the drive theory, it is expected that the greater the fear, the greater the compliance to message recommendations.

Research has not produced consistent empirical results supporting the drive reduction model. For example, a dental hygiene presentation to a group of high school students reported greater change in attitudes using mild rather than strong fear appeals. When repeated, the reverse effect was true: greater attitude and behavior change occurred when a strong fear appeal was used, versus a moderate or weak fear appeal.

Subjective Expected Utility Theory

The subjective expected utility theory has been applied to contexts beyond fear appeals. In the context of a fear appeal, the subjective expected utility theory predicts that a fear appeal is successful when the individual believes that the benefits in risk reduction outweigh the expected cost of acting. To assess the efficacy of a fear appeal respondents would be asked about the likelihood and severity of harmful outcomes of risk involved. The proposed severity is considered under the conditions of the current behavior and then under the alternative behavior. The efficacy is perceived through the effectiveness of the respondents answer. The subjective expected utility theory is unlike other theories of fear appeal because it does not describe the emotional process involved in fear reduction. It is only used to predict the relative likelihood of action. As previously stated, the subjective expected utility theory can be applied to various contexts such as predicting retirement and child-bearing.

Protection Motivation Theory

The protection motivation theory is an attitude-based model. It holds that a fear appeal argument initiates a cognitive assessment process that considers the severity of the threatened event, the probability of the occurrence of the event, and the efficacy of a recommended behavior response. According to the theory, the cognitive assessment processes enhance a fear appeal when it provokes protection motivation. Protection motivation is a variable that arouses, sustains, and directs the suggested behavior to avoid danger. In absence of protection motivation, the recommended protective action is judged to be ineffective in averting the threat or impossible to undertake then no intention to act will result. The protection motivation theory predicts that preventative actions will be preferred in a high threat situation when the self-efficacy and the efficacy of the recommended action are both high. Conversely, it is expected that maladaptive actions will be maintained when there is a high threat but the efficacy perceptions are low.

The protection motivation theory has been applied to analyzing the efficacy of health campaigns such as those encouraging self-breast examinations for detecting breast cancer. Studies found that perceptions of threat concerning breast cancer prompted adaptive actions, such as performing self-examinations, and maladaptive actions, such as to avoid thinking about breast cancer.

Health Belief Model

The health belief model predicts that perceived susceptibility and severity of a risk motivates individuals to engage in preventive actions, and the type of preventative action depends on the perceived benefits and hindrances of performing the action.

A fear argument based on the health belief model is typically presented in terms of the likelihood and severity of health consequences if the current behavior is not changed. With the health belief model, it is unclear whether self-efficacy is directly considered a cost of performing a suggested action because occasionally, a fear appeal is thought to be less effective if a difficulty of acting is considered a cost of acting.

Theory of Reasoned Action

According to the theory of reasoned action, acting on fear appeals begins by consideration of a wider range of consequences of continuing the current behavior beyond the threat of health risks. It also considers a wider range of consequences of the suggested behavior beyond the costs and reduced health risks. The projected consequences vary depending on the situation. The theory of reasoned action differs from other theories because it also incorporates a social influence factor in predicting the efficacy of fear appeals. The social influence is determined by normative beliefs and the desires of other relevant people to perform the given behavior.

The theory of reasoned action has been applied to alcohol, tobacco, and other drug campaigns. For example, it has helped identify the importance of peer pressure and the normative belief of parents as variables for improving school-based drug campaigns. Although the theory of reasoned action has been shown to be a strong predictive utility of social behavior, it is considered to be deficient in explaining behavior change.

Transtheoretical Model

A transtheoretical model of fear appeals explains a dynamic process of health behavior change. Its structure is based on the assumption that behavior change is a systematic process involving a series of stages referred to as stages of change. It also holds that the transition between stages involves a rational coping process referred to as processes of change. The stages of change are: pre-contemplation, contemplation, preparation, action, and maintenance. According to the transtheoretical model, movement through the different stages involves a process called decision balance. Decision balance takes into account the potential gains and costs resulting from the new behavior. It is believed that an individual will not change or continue a behavior unless they perceive advantages to outweigh the disadvantages.

Pre-contemplation

The pre-contemplation stage is a period in which individuals have no intentions to stop a risky behavior or start a healthy behavior. This may be due to a lack in knowledge of the risk involving their current behavior, or an unwillingness to acknowledge that their behavior puts them at risk. The process of change from the pre-contemplation phase to the contemplation phase includes the response of conscious raising, dramatic relief, and an environmental reevaluation process to the argument.

Contemplation

The second stage is contemplation. It is the stage at which an individual is actively considering stopping risky behavior or starting a healthy behavior. It is predicted that individuals will remain at this stage for a long period of time due to the difficulty in evaluating the advantages and disadvantages of behavior change. The process of change to the following stage is expedited by self-re-evaluation.

Preparation

This is the third stage at which individuals have been persuaded and commit to change their behavior. The process of change to the action stage involves a self-liberation process in which the fear appeal influences a changed behavior.

Action

Action is the stage at which the individual engages in behavior change. They have tried to stop their risky behavior. The process of change that helps facilitate progression includes behavioral processes, such as reinforcement management, helping relationships, counterconditioning, and stimulus control.

Maintenance

Maintenance is the final stage for changing risky behavior. This is the stage at which individuals adopt healthy behavior into their lifestyle, and try to prevent regression into the risk behavior. Regression is possible at any point of the stages.

The transtheoretical model has been used to structure various programs for smoking cessation, alcohol abstinence, sunscreen use, dietary change, and contraceptive use.

Factors that Affect its Efficacy

"The ultimate goal of fear appeals is to effectively promote reflective message processing and to influence individual affect towards the message". Individual perceptual differences towards the fear appeal are factors that govern the efficacy of the fear appeal. Researchers have examined several variables that have been thought, at one time or another, to influence the persuasive effect of fear appeals. These factors include: individual characteristics, risk perception, perception of self-efficacy, perception of treatment efficacy, perception of norms, the strength of the fear elicited, perceived threat, and defense mechanisms. The results of the research have demonstrated that various, and sometimes multiple factors, affect the efficacy of fear appeals depending on the method used and the individual.

Individual Characteristics

Also of interest in the fear appeals literature has been the contribution of individual characteristics. The goal has been to understand which individual differences in personality or psychological traits contribute or detract from the effectiveness of the fear appeal. Individual moderating variables studied thus far include trait anxiety, age, ethnicity, gender, coping style, locus of control, self-esteem, perceived vulnerability, need for cognition and uncertainty orientation. Of these, uncertainty orientation and need for cognition have been found to interact with the level of threat. Uncertainty orientation is an individual's characteristic response to uncertainty. That is, whether one attends to or avoids and ignores the source of the uncertainty. Those with an uncertainty orientation tend to be more motivated to deeply process the information presented as the personal relevance increases, whereas those with a certainty orientation will actively avoid it. Some early studies examined other characteristics, such as individual thresholds for fear arousal, to see if they moderated the effect of fear on persuasion. A study by Janis and Feshbach (1954) found that those with lower fear arousal thresholds were the least compelled to act by the high fear appeals, as they tended to react with defensive control responses. Lower threshold subjects were also more easily persuaded by counterarguments following the fear appeal. Trait anxiety has also been the subject of some of the early research, which has since been found to have no discernible effect on persuasion.

Perception of Self-efficacy

The self-efficacy theory states that all processes of psychological change alter the level and strength of self-efficacy. Self-efficacy is enhanced by performance accomplishments, vicarious experience, verbal persuasion, and physiological states. Self-efficacy can also be enhanced by the perceived dependability of the source. The level of self-efficacy an individual has is believed to influence their choice of behavior as well as the amount of time, and the amount of effort expended on that behavior. If the individual does not believe that he or she is capable of averting the threat, it is likely that denial or other defensive responses will be produced in order to lower the fear. The fear of threatening situations may have an adverse effect on the efficacy of a fear appeal. An intimidating situation may cause an individual to believe that he/she is incapable of performing the suggested preventative behaviors that will lead to avoidance behaviors. Bandura's research has demonstrated a positive correlation between changes in behavior and changes in self-efficacy expectance. He found that behavioral transformations are caused by changes in self-efficacy.

Research done by others have revealed "a positive, linear effect of fear on overall intentions and behavior", especially when the messages endorse people's self-efficacy. This effect is more positive when behaviors are performed on one-time basis instead of repeatedly. However, other researchers also pointed out that in the context of self-efficacy need to be considered carefully in relation to other stratefies. The use of other persuative techniques such as behavioral trainings might counteract against the efficacy of fear appeal in isolation.

Performance Accomplishments

According to the theory of self-efficacy, performance accomplishments are related to the success of personal experience. When strong efficacy expectations are established, then the impact of occasional failures are reduced. If self-efficacy is established, it tends to generalize to other situations. Vicarious experience is the observation of others who have performed threatening activities. If others are observed to successfully perform threatening activities, then self-efficacy is expected to increase because the social comparison will reinforce the perception that the behavior can be achieved through effort.

Verbal Persuasion

Verbal persuasion is widely used because of the potentially persuasive influence of suggestion. The influence of suggestion is expected to boost individual self-efficacy. Research has shown that the effects of verbal persuasion may not prevail through a long history of failure. It has been shown to create an enduring sense of self-efficacy in situations where aid is given to facilitate successful action. Failures have a negative effect because it discredits the persuaders and undermines the individual's self-efficacy.

Emotional Arousal

Depending on the circumstances, stressful situations can lessen the feeling of personal competency. Poor performance, for example is usually associated with a state of high arousal. Fear-provoking thoughts can cause an individual to overestimate the intensity of a threatening situation. According to the self-efficacy theory, diminishing emotional arousal can reduce avoidance behavior. Physiological arousal has been predicted to have both positive and negative effects on beneficial or negative coping behaviors. A positive perception of an aroused state may energize, while a negative perception of an aroused state may inhibit coping behaviors.

Physiological Arousal

Physiological arousal has been predicted to have both positive and negative effects on beneficial or negative coping behaviors. A positive perception of an aroused state may energize, while a negative perception of an aroused state may inhibit coping behaviors.

Perception of Treatment Efficacy

Perceived treatment efficacy is also referred to as response-outcome expectancies. It is conceptualized as a person's estimate that a given behavior will lead to certain outcomes. Perception of treatment efficacy differs from self-efficacy because an individual's belief in their ability to perform the suggested actions does not influence their behavior it is the perceived outcome that determines an individual's actions. The enactment of sustained long-term behaviors intended by the fear appeal communication is strongly influenced by the individual perception of treatment efficacy. The extent to which an individual perceives the protection of the recommended action against the health risk determines whether they are persuaded to perform the recommended course of action. A positive perception of treatment efficacy is internalized by the emphasis of the positive aspects of the recommended action. Perceived treatment efficacy is possibly the most integral element of an effectively persuasive fear appeal, and more predictive of action than fear arousal, is perceived efficacy. Some research has found that perceived efficacy is more predictive of intention to change behavior than other elements of perceived threat.

Perception of Norms

Even if a health behavior is portrayed as harmful, the behavior may not be altered by fear inducing communication if the individual is convinced that the behavior is common practice. The behavior is unlikely to be changed if the individual's social group models or reinforces the actions. In this case, there may also be a false perception of norms. Reinforcement of the negative health behavior by the common social group decreases the effectiveness of the fear appeal.

Example: In a study of alcohol abuse on college campuses, students demonstrated heavy alcohol use in response to their peer groups that reinforced the behavior. Students who abused alcohol also believed that their peers were even heavier users than they actually were. Those who believed that heavy intoxication was an element of campus culture may be at a greater risk for personal alcohol abuse due to the desire to conform to the perceived norm.

Fear Strength

The strength of the fear elicited by the message is also an important determinant of the subject's intentions to change the target behavior. Fear strength is distinct from threat severity in that, as mentioned before, fear strength is related to the emotion of fear, whereas threat severity is considered to be an entirely cognitive process. Some early research found that higher levels of fear produced defensive reactions, compelling the researchers to caution that low or moderate levels were the most effective. With rare exception, strength of the fear elicited has been consistently found to be positively correlated with behavior change. This positive linear correlation is ubiquitous in fear appeal research and has laid to rest the curvilinear relationship implied by some of the earliest research. Strength of fear has been found to be positively correlated, as expected, with arousal. Early research has found that low fear appeal strength was the most persuasive. Strength of fear alone is not enough to motivate change in behavior as strong fear with no recommended action, or a recommended action that is not easily performed, may result in the exact opposite effect. According to Sternthal and Craig, fear strength affects attitude change more than it does intentions. They argue that although persuasion increases when fear rises from low to moderate levels, when rising from moderate to high levels, it actually decreases.

Some have even gone so far as to argue that fear is an entirely unnecessary component of an effective appeal as perceived efficacy is more predictive of intention to change behavior than either element of perceived threat. The tendency for higher levels of fear to raise defensive control responses, it is argued, suggests that fear is not useful and that efficacy may be able to bring about intention and behavior change by itself. Another argument states that since higher levels of personal efficacy are necessary, the target of the fear appeal who is most likely to act is one who is most likely to change his behavior to begin with. The implication is that another tact (other than fear) is necessary.

Perceived Threat

Perceived threat is thought to be an important moderator in the process of fear evoked persuasion. It consists of both the perceived severity of the threat and the perceived susceptibility to it.

Perceived susceptibility, sometimes referred to as perceived vulnerability, is thought to be key in motivating an individual to act in response to a fear appeal. It is the perception of the probability and extent to which he/she might experience the threat. Perceived severity, however, is the degree to which the person believes that they will be harmed if the threat is experienced. These threat components form the perceptual trigger for the fear reaction. Higher levels of perceived susceptibility have been found to increase the degree to which people are critical of the message. An example of a fear appeal of a message that emphasizes perceived severity would be the quote "AIDS leads to death". These threat components form the perceptual trigger for fear reaction. Higher levels of perceived susceptibility have been found to increase the degree to which people are critical of the message. However, subjects report more positive thoughts about the recommendation and negative emotions associated with the threat when susceptibility is high. Higher levels of perceived susceptibility are associated with greater intention to change behavior in the manner recommended in the fear appeal message, and are a strong determinant of intentions and behavior, even in the face of weak arguments. It is thought that when perceived susceptibility is high, defense motivations prevent even poor information or weak arguments from detracting from the message's impact on intention. As influential as it appears to be, susceptibility has still been found in some cases to have a much less direct effect on motivation to act on the message than, for instance, self efficacy beliefs or response efficacy.

Perceived severity, the extent to which the individual believes he/she will be adversely affected by the threat has a significant effect on persuasion. A statement that emphasizes the seriousness of a threat would be a statement directed towards a targeted population. An example would be, "You're at-risk for AIDS because you share needles while using intravenous drugs". In some cases, persuasion has been found to be aided by lowering severity, the majority of the fear appeal research has found just the opposite. However, it is important to distinguish perceived severity of the threat from the actual fear elicited. The former is considered to be an entirely cognitive process, while the latter is an emotional process. Some have even argued that cognitive processes in the context of fear appeals are more important than emotional ones. Research has found that the effect of fear on intentions is mediated by the perceived severity. That is, fear does not act directly on intentions, but increases the level of perceived severity, which in turn raises intentions to act on the message. Indeed, the strength of the fear appeal is believed to be positively correlated with the perceived severity of the threat. Severity seems to produce the strongest effects on perceptions.

Defense Mechanisms

The previous components are thought to determine what response an individual has to the message. One of these potential reactions to the fear appeal that is of the most negative consequence is that of the defensive fear control reaction. In response to the fear appeal, an individual may form the intent to change their behavior. However, when either self or response efficacy is low, the individual, perceiving that they are unable to avert the threat, may rely on defensive avoidance to lower their fear. Some have argued that fear appeals are unnecessary as defensive avoidance reactions have been found in some studies to be positively correlated with strength of fear and negatively with perceived efficacy. The required balance of fear and efficacy levels has been the subject of much research, with some finding that moderate to high levels of fear are unnecessary in changing intentions. In fact, they argue, what is important is the ratio of these to each other. Gore and Bracken (2005) found that even with low levels of threat, they were able to take individuals who had started to exhibit defensive fear control reactions to move toward danger control (intention change) reactions. Another way of defending yourself against fear appeals is prior knowledge, according to one study, individuals are less likely to be influenced by a fear appeal if they have prior knowledge.

Examples

This is your brain on drugs, the D.A.R.E. program, abstinence-only sex education, deprogramming.

Ethical Considerations

A number of ethical concerns regarding the use of fear appeals have been raised, leading to widespread debate regarding the acceptability of their use. For example, it has been questioned whether it is ethical to expose large numbers of people to potentially distressing messages without their consent. Hastings, Stead and Webb question whether it is ethically acceptable to expose an entire population to a distressing message intended for a specific subset of that population. For example, a fear appeal message stressing the likelihood of premature death for individuals who smoke may also reach the children of people who smoke, leading to avoidable anxiety in such groups.

Further to this, it is evident that anxiety responses may not even be helpful when elicited in the target group. This is because, while anxiety can motivate positive health behaviour, it can also be maladaptive, as some individuals form a defensive response to mitigate the negative feeling arising from the fear appeal. While there have been mixed results regarding whether fear appeals elicit a defense response, it is important to note that studies exploring this relationship are done in a laboratory setting free of external distractions and where participants are told to focus on the health messages. It may be that people may have stronger defense responses in real life situations where they must navigate a complex range of competing messages and where they have the option of ignoring the message or looking for competing explanations. In addition to this, no studies have followed responses to fear appeals over the longer term, and it possible that repetition of fear appeals may lead to habituation and annoyance, therefore cause individuals to tune out to the messages of the health promotion campaign. Furthermore, even if they do work, some authors question whether it is ethical to frighten people in to behaving in a certain way, as this may compromise their autonomy by manipulating their beliefs.

A concern has also been raised that fear appeals serve to contribute to the widening of health disparities. This is because certain individuals are more likely to develop the maladaptive responses mentioned above. Empirical research suggests that fear appeals work best for individuals with high levels of self-efficacy, and that maladaptive responses are more likely in those with low self-efficacy. This means that fear appeals work best for those who are equipped, both physically and psychologically, to take appropriate action. Individuals who do not have the resources for health behaviour change are often those who already have negative health status. For example, people who regularly engage in behaviours which are damaging to health (e.g. smoking and other drug use) have been found to typically have lower self-efficacy than others. Therefore, it seems that, in addition to having the potential to cause harm, this harm is more likely to affect groups that would most benefit from health behaviour change, therefore contributing to the widen of health disparities.

There is also a concern that fear appeals give rise to stigmatisation of those who are seen to be already suffering the negative consequences of the undesirable behaviour. For example, injury prevention campaigns often rely on emphasising the negative consequences of potentially becoming disabled. Wang hypothesises that when becoming disabled is portrayed as unacceptable, so is being disabled, adding to the stigmatisation of disabled individuals. For example, in responses to a poster campaign stating that “Last year, 1057 teenagers got so drunk they couldn’t stand up. Ever.” presented alongside a picture of a wheelchair, disabled participants in Wang’s study felt that this held them up as an example of how not to be. One participant said “I feel it’s an attack on my self esteem and dignity.”

Health Belief Model

The health belief model (HBM) is a psychological health behavior change model developed to explain and predict health-related behaviors, particularly in regard to the uptake of health services. The health belief model was developed in the 1950s by social psychologists at the U.S. Public Health Service and remains one of the best known and most widely used theories in health behavior research. The health belief model suggests that people's beliefs about health problems, perceived benefits of action and barriers to action, and self-efficacy explain engagement (or lack of engagement) in health-promoting behavior. A stimulus, or cue to action, must also be present in order to trigger the health-promoting behavior.

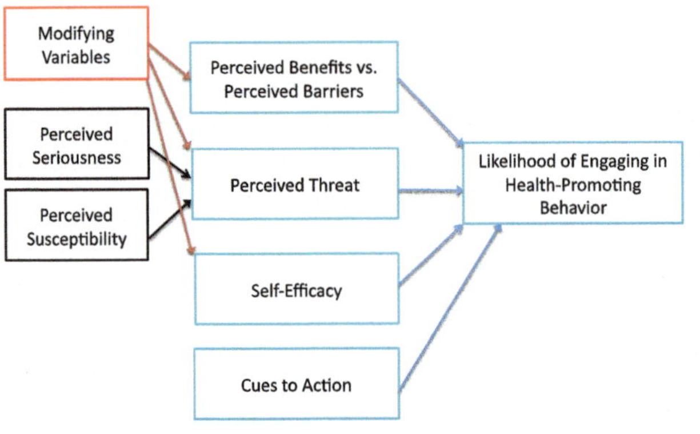

The health belief model

History

One of the first theories of health behavior, the health belief model was developed in the 1950s by social psychologists Irwin M. Rosenstock, Godfrey M. Hochbaum, S. Stephen Kegeles, and Howard Leventhal at the U.S. Public Health Service to better understand the widespread failure of screening programs for tuberculosis. The health belief model has been applied to predict a wide variety of health-related behaviors such as being screened for the early detection of asymptomatic diseases and receiving immunizations. More recently, the model has been applied to understand patients' responses to symptoms of disease, compliance with medical regimens, lifestyle behaviors (e.g., sexual risk behaviors), and behaviors related to chronic illnesses, which may require long-term behavior maintenance in addition to initial behavior change. Amendments to the model were made as late as 1988 to incorporate emerging evidence within the field of psychology about the role of self-efficacy in decision-making and behavior.

Theoretical Constructs

The following constructs of the health belief model are proposed to vary between individuals and predict engagement in health-related behaviors (e.g., getting vaccinated, getting screened for asymptomatic diseases, exercising).

Health belief model chart (smoking as an example)				
Modifying Variables (age, gender, race, economy, characteristics)	Perceived Severity + Perceived Susceptibility	perceived benefit - perceived barriers	Cues to Action	taking action (or not)
(base score for this person's health)	(base score as to the belief that smoking will harm one's health)	(base score for smoking behavior)		

Perceived Severity

Perceived severity refers to the subjective assessment of the severity of a health problem and its potential consequences. The health belief model proposes that individuals who perceive a given health problem as serious are more likely to engage in behaviors to prevent the health problem from occurring (or reduce its severity). Perceived seriousness encompasses beliefs about the disease itself (e.g., whether it is life-threatening or may cause disability or pain) as well as broader impacts of the disease on functioning in work and social roles. For instance, an individual may perceive that influenza is not medically serious, but if he or she perceives that there would be serious financial consequences as a result of being absent from work for several days, then he or she may perceive influenza to be a particularly serious condition.

Perceived Susceptibility

Perceived susceptibility refers to subjective assessment of risk of developing a health problem. The health belief model predicts that individuals who perceive that they are susceptible to a particular health problem will engage in behaviors to reduce their risk of developing the health problem. Individuals with low perceived susceptibility may deny that they are at risk for contracting a particular illness. Others may acknowledge the possibility that they could develop the illness, but believe it is unlikely. Individuals who believe they are at low risk of developing an illness are more likely to engage in unhealthy, or risky, behaviors. Individuals who perceive a high risk that they will be personally affected by a particular health problem are more likely to engage in behaviors to decrease their risk of developing the condition.

The combination of perceived severity and perceived susceptibility is referred to as perceived threat. Perceived severity and perceived susceptibility to a given health condition depend on knowledge about the condition. The health belief model predicts that higher perceived threat leads to higher likelihood of engagement in health-promoting behaviors.

Perceived Benefits

Health-related behaviors are also influenced by the perceived benefits of taking action. Perceived benefits refer to an individual's assessment of the value or efficacy of engaging in a health-promoting behavior to decrease risk of disease. If an individual believes that a particular action will reduce susceptibility to a health problem or decrease its seriousness, then he or she is likely to engage in that behavior regardless of objective facts regarding the effectiveness of the action. For example, individuals who believe that wearing sunscreen prevents skin cancer are more likely to wear sunscreen than individuals who believe that wearing sunscreen will not prevent the occurrence of skin cancer.

Perceived Barriers

Health-related behaviors are also a function of perceived barriers to taking action. Perceived barriers refer to an individual's assessment of the obstacles to behavior change. Even if an individual perceives a health condition as threatening and believes that a particular action will effectively reduce the threat, barriers may prevent engagement in the health-promoting behavior. In other words, the perceived benefits must outweigh the perceived barriers in order for behavior change to occur. Perceived barriers to taking action include the perceived inconvenience, expense, danger (e.g., side effects of a medical procedure) and discomfort (e.g., pain, emotional upset) involved in engaging in the behavior. For instance, lack of access to affordable health care and the perception that a flu vaccine shot will cause significant pain may act as barriers to receiving the flu vaccine.

Modifying Variables

Individual characteristics, including demographic, psychosocial, and structural variables, can affect perceptions (i.e., perceived seriousness, susceptibility, benefits, and barriers) of health-related behaviors. Demographic variables include age, sex, race, ethnicity, and education, among others. Psychosocial variables include personality, social class, and peer and reference group pressure, among others. Structural variables include knowledge about a given disease and prior contact with the disease, among other factors. The health belief model suggests that modifying variables affect health-related behaviors indirectly by affecting perceived seriousness, susceptibility, benefits, and barriers.

Cues to Action

The health belief model posits that a cue, or trigger, is necessary for prompting engagement in health-promoting behaviors. Cues to action can be internal or external. Physiological cues (e.g., pain, symptoms) are an example of internal cues to action. External cues include events or information from close others, the media, or health care providers promoting engagement in health-related behaviors. Examples of cues to action include a reminder postcard from a dentist, the illness of a friend or family member, and product health warning labels. The intensity of cues needed to prompt action varies between individuals by perceived susceptibility, seriousness, benefits, and barriers. For example, individuals who believe they are at high risk for a serious illness and who have an established relationship with a primary care doctor may be easily persuaded to get screened for the illness after seeing a public service announcement, whereas individuals who believe they are at low risk for the same illness and also do not have reliable access to health care may require more intense external cues in order to get screened.

Self-efficacy

Self-efficacy was added to the four components of the health belief model (i.e., perceived susceptibility, seriousness, benefits, and barriers) in 1988. Self-efficacy refers to an individual's perception of his or her competence to successfully perform a behavior. Self-efficacy was added to the health belief model in an attempt to better explain individual differences in health behaviors. The model was originally developed in order to explain engagement in one-time health-related behaviors such as being screened for cancer or receiving an immunization. Eventually, the health belief model was applied to more substantial, long-term behavior change such as diet modification, exercise, and smoking. Developers of the model recognized that confidence in one's ability to effect change in outcomes (i.e., self-efficacy) was a key component of health behavior change.

Empirical Support

The health belief model has gained substantial empirical support since its development in the 1950s. It remains one of the most widely used and well-tested models for explaining and predicting health-related behavior. A 1984 review of 18 prospective and 28 retrospective studies suggests that the evidence for each component of the health belief model is strong. The review reports that empirical support for the health belief model is particularly notable given the diverse populations, health conditions, and health-related behaviors examined and the various study designs and assessment strategies used to evaluate the model. A more recent meta-analysis found strong support for perceived benefits and perceived barriers predicting health-related behaviors, but weak evidence for the predictive power of perceived seriousness and perceived susceptibility. The authors of the meta-analysis suggest that examination of potential moderated and mediated relationships between components of the model is warranted.

Applications

The health belief model has been used to develop effective interventions to change health-related behaviors by targeting various aspects of the model's key constructs. Interventions based on the health belief model may aim to increase perceived susceptibility to and perceived seriousness of a health condition by providing education about prevalence and incidence of disease, individualized estimates of risk, and information about the consequences of disease (e.g., medical, financial, and social consequences). Interventions may also aim to alter the cost-benefit analysis of engaging in a health-promoting behavior (i.e., increasing perceived benefits and decreasing perceived barriers) by providing information about the efficacy of various behaviors to reduce risk of disease, identifying common perceived barriers, providing incentives to engage in health-promoting behaviors, and engaging social support or other resources to encourage health-promoting behaviors. Furthermore, interventions based on the health belief model may provide cues to action to remind and encourage individuals to engage in health-promoting behaviors. Interventions may also aim to boost self-efficacy by providing training in specific health-promoting behaviors, particularly for complex lifestyle changes (e.g., changing diet or physical activity, adhering to a complicated medication regimen). Interventions can be aimed at the individual level (i.e., working one-on-one with individuals to increase engagement in health-related behaviors) or the societal level (e.g., through legislation, changes to the physical environment).

Limitations

The health belief model attempts to predict health-related behaviors by accounting for individual differences in beliefs and attitudes. However, it does not account for other factors that influence health behaviors. For instance, habitual health-related behaviors (e.g., smoking, seatbelt buckling) may become relatively independent of conscious health-related decision making processes. Additionally, individuals engage in some health-related behaviors for reasons unrelated to health (e.g., exercising for aesthetic reasons). Environmental factors outside an individual's control may prevent engagement in desired behaviors. For example, an individual living in a dangerous neighborhood may be unable to go for a jog outdoors due to safety concerns. Furthermore, the health belief model does not consider the impact of emotions on health-related behavior. Evidence suggests that fear may be a key factor in predicting health-related behavior.

The theoretical constructs that constitute the health belief model are broadly defined. Furthermore, the health belief model does not specify how constructs of the model interact with one another. Therefore, different operationalizations of the theoretical constructs may not be strictly comparable across studies.

Research assessing the contribution of cues to action in predicting health-related behaviors is limited. Cues to action are often difficult to assess, limiting research in this area. For instance, individuals may not accurately report cues that prompted behavior change. Cues such as a public service announcement on television or on a billboard may be fleeting and individuals may not be aware of their significance in prompting them to engage in a health-related behavior. Interpersonal influences are also particularly difficult to measure as cues.

Behaviour Change

As Aristotle put it "We are what we repeatedly do". We are defined by our behavior and our behavior becomes our identity. According to the behaviorist school of psychology – behavior is the main focus of study as it is observable and can be measured as opposed to thoughts, beliefs, sensations or emotions. In the realm of health, behavior plays an important role whether it is practicing health habits or addictions or going for regular check ups.

This chapter will focus on the modification of health related behavior. It will discuss attitude change, cognitive behavioral approaches, relapse prevention, Stages of Change, self empowerment approach, community approach and social engineering. At the end there is a section on public health messages.

Attitude change focuses on changing people's attitudes regarding risky behaviors and inculcating positive attitudes towards new healthy behaviors – regular dental check ups or exercising. Attitude is seen as a precursor to behavior. Information appeals and fear appeals are used to influence attitudes and will be discussed in detail in the section on public health messages. Two attitude theories based on health beliefs, the Health Belief Model and the Theory of Reasoned Action will be described in this section.

The Health Belief Model (Hochbaum, 1958, Rosenstock, 1966 as cited in Taylor, 1995)The two important beliefs that influence behavior are Belief in a Health Threat and the Belief that a specific Health Behavior can reduce threat. Belief in a Health Threat is further influenced by general health values, specific beliefs about vulnerability and beliefs about the severity of the disorder. Belief that a specific health behavior can reduce threat is influenced by the belief that a specific measure can be effective against a specific threat and the belief that health measure exceeds the cost. Any behavior could be considered for e.g smoking - if you believe smoking causes cancer – this will depend on your general health values – health is important, specific belief about vulnerability – it causes lung cancer – my cousin who smoked developed lung cancer, beliefs about severity of the disorder – cancer is a terminal illness – it is a deadly disease, causes suffering. Belief that specific health behavior can reduce threat - avoiding smoking can lower the risk of lung cancer and that the link between smoking and lung cancer is higher than the link between air pollution and lung cancer. The costs of giving up smoking are minor as compared to avoiding the risk of cancer. If all these beliefs are aligned then the behavior of giving up smoking may occur.

Theory of Reasoned Action (Fishbein & Ajzen, 1975)

According to the Theory of Reasoned Action (TRA), intention is a far more accurate predictor of behavior than attitude, therefore the theory proposes that attitude and subjective norms influence intention which in turn influences behavior. Attitude is influenced by beliefs about the outcomes of behavior and evaluations of those beliefs. Subjective Norms are influenced by normative beliefs (beliefs of important others with respect to the belief) and the motivation to comply with those beliefs. This theory can be used in any cultural setting – since the beliefs are elicited from the local population.

This theory can be applied to any behavior and it has been applied to a wide variety of behaviors from voting behavior, to smoking, to condom use and contraceptive use behavior. If it is applied to contraceptive behavior – then if your beliefs about contraception was that it prevents having too many children – children are a cost and therefore contraception is a good thing. The normative beliefs may be that mother in law does not want you to use it and will not allow it, husband may be undecided but will go with mother in law if it is a choice and motivation to comply is the extent you want to do what your mother in law and husband want you to do. If you want to please them then it is unlikely you will intend to use contraception in the near future.

Cognitive Behavioral Approaches

People are actively negotiating the world around them and hence are interpreting and constructing their environment at a cognitive level. Thus behavior is influenced by external stimuli as well as how one thinks about them. Thus both beliefs as well as behavior are important with respect to changing behavior. Some of the cognitive behavioral approaches that we will discuss are Self Observation and Monitoring, Classical conditioning, Systematic Desensitization and Modeling.

Self Observation and Monitoring

The first step is to discriminate the target behavior (internal sensation or urge to smoke or the urge to overeat for e.g.). The second step is to record the frequency of the behavior and chart its pattern (Abel et al., 1987 as cited in Taylor, 1995).By monitoring the behavior one can record the antecedents and consequents of the behavior. By attending to the behavior, one develops insight into when and why it occurs for e.g. the urge to smoke is the highest when one is bored or one needs a break or between meals. Thus the person can make a conscious effort to do something else at these times. Attention by itself may not be enough to change behavior but it is the beginning and can be used effectively with other methods.

Classical Conditioning

In this technique an unconditioned response or the behavior in question is paired with a conditioned stimulus that results in learning by association. In the case of changing behaviors in the health realm, an unpleasant response is conditioned to the behavior such as drinking or smoking or taking drugs which needs to be changed. Antabuse is a drug that is administered along with alcohol and it produces extreme nausea. Thus the experience of drinking gets paired with the unpleasant experience of queasiness. The taste of alcohol gets associated with nausea and gastric discomfort and revulsion to it develops. However the person would have to decide to take such a drug and may just decide not to use it. To administer it without the person's consent would be unethical and hence it is a difficult situation.

On the other hand certain behaviors such as exercise or regular check ups could be reinforced with positive consequences that will instill the behavior.

Systematic Desensitization

Systematic desensitization is a technique based on classical conditioning and was developed to treat anxiety disorders. It consists of learning to pair or associate a relaxation response with the anxiety arousing stimulus. The relaxation response consists of deep breathing and progressive muscle relaxation. Progressive muscle relaxation is a process of systematically working from head to toe to relax all the muscles one at a time resulting in a deep state of relaxation. Deep breathing also has the effect of calming the body and lowering heart rate. Addictive behaviors such as smoking and drinking are often engaged in, in response to anxiety, which may often be unconscious. Thus the idea is to get people to realize when they feel the urge to smoke or drink or eat fatty foods and engage in the relaxation response to deal with the craving. Thus the craving is countered with the relaxation response. For instance when a person who is quitting smoking is with friends who are smoking or an alcoholic who is in a similar situation the relaxation response can be used to counter feelings of anxiety or stress (feeling of compulsion). This technique could be especially effective in dealing with relapse prevention.

Modeling

Modeling is a concept from social learning theory where learning takes place by imitation. In the case of changing undesirable behaviours and initiating desirable behaviors – the behaviour of a suitable model can be imitated. For instance in support groups where people in a similar situation get together to cope with a problem, certain effective behaviors can be learnt. Alcoholics Annonymous is a group where recovering alcoholics are supported by others who have recovered and are abstaining from alcohol – they act as role models for those trying to overcome their drinking problem.

Self Control of Behaviour

Certain cognitive behaviour techniques are based on the person's exertion of self control. Thus the person practices these techniques themselves with some outside help. Some of these techniques are discussed below:

Contingency Contracting

The use of reinforcement to develop or extinguish behavior is operant conditioning and is very effective when the rewards and punishments are controlled externally. When reinforcement is brought under the person's control, reward is administered but self punishment is rarely administered. People rarely self administer punishment as they will tell themselves this the last time, or will justify their behaviour and attribute it to external causes. Thus in Contingency Contracting the punishment is contracted out to the therapist or a friend. The person makes a contract with the therapist or friend that if they engage in the undesirable behaviour that a certain previously agreed upon punishment will be administered to them. Monetary fines cold be imposed or

An effective punishment is one that hurts the person and hence they learn not to repeat the undesired behavior.

Cognitive Restructuring

Since Cognitive behaviour techniques are based on a combination of changing thoughts and beliefs as well as behaviour (Meichenbaum & Cameron, 1974 as cited in Taylor, 1995).Some techniques focus more exclusively on the cognitive aspect. In this technique the therapist helps clients to change their negative self talk and replace it with more positive statements that help develop self efficacy and self esteem. Thus individuals learn to monitor their behaviour and become aware of when they engage in negative self talk and use positive statements to replace it.

Skills Training

Social skills training or assertiveness training are skills that are actively developed to help people to overcome negative behaviours and develop positive behaviours. These skills help to reduce anxiety and negotiate social situations that they could not previously.

Relapse Prevention

Most behaviour change programs fail due to its participants relapsing into their previous behaviour (McCaul et al, 1992 as cited in Taylor, 1995). Relapse is a part of behaviour change. It is not easy to change a habit once and for all and most people tend to go back to them unconsciously when stressed. Especially with addictive behaviours, there is a tendency to relapse when under stress.

Incidents such as a break up in a relationship, a setback at work, disappointments, stress at work or being in a situation that was associated with the behaviour (friends who smoke) may lead to relapse. Relapsing leads to a feeling of loss of self control and guilt and a feeling that you can never quit successfully. If people are made aware that relapse is a normal part of all behaviour change and that it tends to happen in certain circumstances – they become more vigilant and react less to the relapse and may see what is needed to be able to improve self control. Thus programs that have a relapse prevention component are more effective than those that don't. Another effective strategy is to have booster sessions – after the prevention program is completed every 2 months a counseling session with participants can help them reiterate their goals and focus on self control. Programs that include a stress management component are more effective in providing people the skills needed to negotiate challenges (Marlatt & George, 1988 as cited in Taylor, 1995).

Stages of Health Behaviour Change (Prochaska, DiClemente & Norcross, 1992 as cited in Taylor, 1995)

This model describes long term behaviour change as an upward spiral that includes the stages of precontemplation, contemplation, preparation, action, maintenance which may continue until relapse occurs and the spiral begins again with precontemplation and goes through the steps until the next relapse. This cycle continues until the person reaches the stage of termination which is the final stage at which there is no more relapse. This model gives us a sense of the dynamic and continuous nature of behaviour change that may incorporate many relapses before the behaviour changes for good.

We have reviewed a number of behaviour change techniques where the responsibility for change was located in the individual. However there are circumstances of risk that overwhelm the individual's responsibility in maintaining healthy behaviours.

Limitations

A criticism of these behaviour change technique is that contextual factors are not considered. Factors such as socio-economic status, urban –rural residence, access to health care, education are important contextual factors that undermine individual responsibility to some extent. Much of the research is oriented in a way as to assume a common value system and rationality between those promoting the change and the people. Often people on whom this change or behaviour is imposed don't see the point of it (contraceptive use for instance or tobacco cessation). The change initiatives often work top down with a government agenda to reduce tobacco use or increase contraceptive use and can be authoritative without understanding the people's perspectives. Such programs are based on rationality (such as governments needs to reduce health care spending) however in many cases people's behaviours are irrational and cannot be made to function rationally.

The Self Empowerment Approach

In this approach individuals and groups are helped to gain increased control over physical, social and internal environments. This is especially focused on oppressed groups. Participatory learning techniques such as problem solving, client centered counseling, assertiveness training and social skills training are imparted with the goal of empowering people to resolve their own problems. Health education and HIV prevention for young people have used a self empowerment approach (Abraham & Sheeran, 1994 as cited in Marks et al, 2008).

The idea is to create awareness about issues and create a spirit of self efficacy or confidence that enables behaviour change. Case studies where the self empowerment approach has been used however has shown that there isn't much change in behavior across the group and they are less successful than the individual based methods.The limitations of this approach is that the techniques that are used to empower are practiced in an artificial setting and do not always translate into the real setting- for eg assertiveness training with a women's group may not translate into assertiveness in the home with the mother in law or husband. The focus is still on the individual. The assumption that healthy choices are rational choices is still there as in the previous individual level techniques. The assumption of shared rationality is still being made. Another issue is also that the behaviour change is slow to manifest and may happen with a lag and may manifest itself in the next generation.

Collective Action/Community Development Approach

In this approach the responsibility lies with the community rather than the individual. At a point in time there is a consciousness within a community of the social and economic obstacles that impede growth. In this approach the focus is on democratic participation from stating objectives to planning taking the community's needs into consideration, planning for resources, allocating tasks to as many people as possible and reviewing progress in a public forum periodically. The idea is to make it everybody's project.

However in such circumstances there is bound to be conflict with the existing power structure which will resist any attempts to share power. Whoever becomes involved with the work becomes powerful and hence different from the others even if they were not previously so. The concept of community is problematic as people have multiple identities with conflicting desires – gender, caste, age even within a village. Studies using this method have not been very effective in achieving behaviour change as powerful others often do not participate.

Is there any method that is effective?

Social Engineering refers to modifying the environment in ways that affect an individual's ability to practice a health behaviour. Social engineering solutions include providing purified water to people or banning smoking in public places and banning drugs like cocaine and heroin, lowering the speed limit, helmet safety laws, preventing advertising of tobacco and alcohol, regulations regarding seat belt use. In this case the individual is left with very little choice or responsibility, the behaviour becomes the default behaviour.

At the level of the nation or the community – legislations can be passed to make the environment healthier and help people lead more healthy lives. The media can be used to influence people towards making healthier choices especially children who are suggestible and vulnerable to advertising. Information resources on health can be made available to all. Facilities that facilitate development of health habits such as open spaces and parks that encourage people to exercise, relatively cheap fruits and vegetables which are organic, minimal marketing of tobacco and alcohol. And most important of all, the provision of good health care for all.

Thus in this chapter we have looked at behaviour change at the individual level both through conditioning and social learning techniques as well as through the self empowerment approach. Change at the community level through collective action or collective behaviour has been discussed. And social engineering or changing the environment through infrastructural changes and legislations has also been discussed. Every discipline favors a different approach with psychologists focusing on conditioning and social learning techniques and social activists and social workers on the self empowerment approach and the collective action approach, whereas activists, lawyers, academicians and hopefully politicians on the social engineering approach. Each approach has its ideology and language and methods however for effective and real change to occur an eclectic approach of whatever it takes needs to be adopted and public opinion and support need to be harnessed for it.

Framing Health Messages

Health messages are used, to convey information at the most basic level but also aim to change attitudes, opinions and behaviour. Are these messages effective, how are they framed, what has social science theory to say – these are some of the questions that we will attempt to discuss in this chapter.

How can people be persuaded to change their attitude through messages?

For messages to be persuasive they have to be salient, vivid and accessible.

Salience refers to how much an object stands out in relation to its context. Some of the factors that make an object salient are novelty (something new catches people's attention),being perceptually figural (stands out in the field of perception), unusual, extremely negative (people tend to focus more on negative information) or relevant to the person. The higher the salience the more likely it will capture the attention of a person.

Vividness refers to the clarity or intensity of the stimulus. The emotionality of the message, its imagery (visual quality), its proximity in a sensory (visual, auditory characteristics) temporal and spatial way all contribute to its vividness.

Accessibility refers to how frequently or recently the construct/category was activated. Thus messages that are easily and frequently remembered are better or more effective messages (Fiske & Taylor, 1991).

The Yale Attitude Change Approach (Hovland, Janis & Kelley, 1953) focuses on three elements- the source of the message (expertise, prestige, attractiveness of the source), the message (quality of the arguments, presenting both sides of the argument) and the nature of the audience (age, friendly/hostile, social class). A source that is perceived as an expert is perceived as more credible. Prestige and attractiveness also contribute towards increasing the persuasiveness of the message. Hence in advertising you see a fair number of doctors and dentists and mothers (experts) for some products and then celebrities (prestige & attractiveness) for other products. Strong arguments are persuasive and presenting both sides of the argument is more effective than a one sided message as people may feel that they are being persuaded and they do not prefer such arguments.

A younger audience is more likely to be persuaded as they may not have stable opinions, and the quality of the message would have to differ depending on the audience's socioeconomic characteristics.

How does the way we process information interact with the message in influencing us?

Heuristic-Systematic Model (Chaiken, 1980)

When we are exposed to stimuli from the outside world we may use two types of processing heuristic or systematic. Heuristic is a short cut. Heuristic processing is based on a short cut that has been learnt in the past like a rule of thumb. Often we are exposed to a lot of information and have to respond quite quickly and in cases where the information is not very important to us we tend to use the heuristic style.

Systematic processing refers to a more reasoned step-by-step approach and is used when the issue is personally relevant and has important consequences. This is the long route and people make a list of pros and cons regarding the issue and give the issue more attention and thought. It is also used when one is solely responsible for message evaluation (for the family/department) and in the case where one disagrees with the majority position.

Thus often people may not be paying attention to messages and processing it at a heuristic level depending on the message and its perceived relevance and their motivation. Thus for health messages they need to be made more relevant and personal for people to process them at a systematic level.

The Elaboration Likelihood Model (Petty & Cacioppo, 1981)

This model proposes two routes – the central route and the peripheral route of attitude change. The central route specifies active and careful thinking of the issue and is similar to systematic processing. The peripheral route refers to superficial attitude change that occurs due to casual processing without much thought. In the peripheral route not much attention is being paid but it is not necessarily heuristic. People are motivated to hold correct attitudes and hence with sufficient motivation and ability they will pay attention to the arguments.

Thus again we see that the type of issue and the motivation of the audience interact to determine the route that is used. People are more careful and process important issues systematically or via the central route when the issue is pertinent and has personal consequences as opposed to issues they perceive as trivial or irrelevant that are processed via the peripheral route.

To change attitudes regarding health behavior messages that have been found to be effective are those that are short, clear, direct and colorful and vivid. An anecdote or individual story tends to be vivid and captures the audiences' attention. The message must discuss both sides of the issue – as this gives the message more credibility and it is perceived as more honest and less persuasive. For e.g. while promoting contraceptives the side effects of particular methods must be listed which eventually will increase contraceptive use rather than not talking about the side effects which people fear anyway. And finally the source must be expert, prestigious and trustworthy - hence the doctors and dentists and doctors who are also mothers are often models for health related product advertisements.

How Effective are Fear Appeals?

The literature on fear appeals was mixed with some studies indicating the effectiveness of fear appeals and some studies finding that the effects of fear appeals were short lived. Some of the issues in fear appeals are the level of emotion that is aroused, perceived threat (cognition - thought), perceived efficacy regarding the relevant response needed to avoid the threat. A distinction in the literature is made between danger control and fear control, danger control refers to controlling threat versus controlling emotion which is fear control and the distinct processes used in each.

A meta-analysis of fear appeals by Witte & Allen (2000) concluded that

- Vivid language and imagery increase perception of severity/threat
- Personalistic language is more effective in creating attitude change
- Strong severity & susceptibility message create attitude, intention and behavior change
- Strong fear appeals effective only when accompanied by strong efficacy messages
- Individual differences and Demographic factors do not play a role
- Danger control responses and Fear control responses must be assessed in evaluations

Thus fear-inducing messages can be effective in creating attitude change, provided that a clear solution is proposed with it. When an answer is provided people feel a sense of efficacy and feel like they can do whatever is necessary (go in for voluntary testing for HIV given that there is a provision for free treatment).

Balbir Pasha ko AIDS hoga kya

This was a mass media campaign launched by Population Services International (PSI) India Wing from November 2002 to February 2003. A combination of communication channels such as billboards, posters in trains and buses, television and radio messages and newspapers were used to address 12 port communities in India. This campaign focused on changing behavior outcomes in the areas of increased condom usage, partner reduction, treatment seeking for sexually transmitted infections and increased use of voluntary counseling and testing services. Prior to the campaign, research indicated that there were high HIV rates and faulty risk perception. The campaign was based on the concept of vicarious learning (Bandura's Social Learning Theory) and the fictional character of Balbir Pasha was created as a behavioral model for consumers to relate to, learn from and empathize. By gradually unraveling each of the scenarios in an approachable and familiar manner the campaign managed to build interest, personalize HIV and bring the topic into the public sphere. Based on recall of the campaign and message and an increase in the number of phone calls to the hotline number provided – the campaign was deemed a success (PSI, 2003).

In a paper by Dorfman, Wallack & Woodruff (2000), the notion of social justice as being the guiding ethic of public health as opposed to market justice is discussed. In this paper the notion of social justice is contrasted with the notion of market justice pushed by corporate firms. Mere individual responsibility for health is no longer the accepted norm and there is a recognition, of the environmental factors that provide the parameters for individual behaviour.

Market justice is concerned with individualism and self-interest and limited government interference and limited obligations to public good whereas social justice is concerned with shared responsibility, governmental involvement and the idea that basic benefits should be assured. According to conglomerates that are involved with tobacco, alcohol, processed snacks and beverages, individuals are free agents and are not forced to use these products, which is partially true but only partially. For some people (middle and upper classes) have more real choices than others (lower classes). The values of individual freedom must be balanced with the values of common good, one of which is health.

Framing

Dorfman and colleagues (2005) discuss two types of frames – conceptual frames and news frames. People have templates in their head about various activities, objects, relationships and this template or schema as we know it in psychology helps us imbue new stimulus with meaning. We relate new incoming information with respect to pre existing schemas.

Lakoff (1996)describes three conceptual levels for framing public health messages, level 1 is the level of overarching values – such as fairness, responsibility, equity that are pivotal to social change. Level 2 is the particular issue being addressed such as tobacco, worker safety. Level 3 is to do with the details of policy and strategy for achieving change. A message could be generated at any level however a message that includes level one has the most impact as it pitches the issue boldly and puts it in stark contrast against the market justice values of the corporate giants. A message should include all levels with level 1 setting the frame . Here is an example based on these conceptual levels for providing health insurance to contract labour.

Some workers get health benefits and sick leave whereas others who labour with their bodies to build the houses and factories of the modern world, get negligible benefits with very little compensation for injuries that handicap them for life, no sick leave and zero health insurance. Do they not have the right to health just like other workers and even more so given that their work often compromises their health ? The employees association and the state governments must create adequate health insurance for contract labourers.

News framing refers to the framing of health stories at a very individual or personalistic level rather than defining the problem in its wider context and suggesting institutional involvement in creating solutions.

Tobacco has gone from being an individual responsibility to a public health issue so it has been reframed in terms of common good, responsibility for the vulnerable (non smokers exposed to passive smoke) and commitment to larger goals of protecting health (cancer prevention) by banning smoking in public places as well as offices, restaurants which required legislations and government interference. This has changed the moral overtones of smoking as well.

Thus all the other issues could be reframed in this perspective such as alcohol, housing etc. However when there is an attempt to create environmental change it results in a shift in responsibility that is resisted by the status quo – the corporate firms, the government and other beneficiaries.

The guidelines to frame an effective message involves three questions that create frames that are associate values with strategies (Dorfman, Wallack & Woodruff, 2005).

- What's wrong?
- Why does it matter?
- What should we do about it?

What's wrong?

This is a clear statement of the problem and should focus on one aspect of the problem.

Why does it matter?

Here the value from level 1 comes in.

What should we do about it?

A clear concrete solution – maybe a policy objective or the need for a regulation must be proposed. Often the proposed solution is vague and the built up momentum is dissipated. The proposed solution may not be the best, its limitations may be mentioned but yet the value of a clear plan is vital to create any change. The change may not be actual but the idea gradually gains momentum in time and results in immense public pressure to bring about a legislation.

Health Education

Health education is a profession of educating people about health. Areas within this profession encompass environmental health, physical health, social health, emotional health, intellectual health, and spiritual health.

Two boys in rural Laos take a clear interest in a book about intestinal parasites.

Health education can be defined as the principle by which individuals and groups of people, learn to behave in a manner conducive to the promotion, maintenance, or restoration of health. However, as there are multiple definitions of health, there are also multiple definitions of health education. The Joint Committee on Health Education and Promotion Terminology of 2001 defined Health Education as "any combination of planned learning experiences based on sound theories that provide individuals, groups, and communities the opportunity to acquire information and the skills needed to make quality health decisions."

The World Health Organization defined Health Education as "compris[ing] [of] consciously constructed opportunities for learning involving some form of communication designed to improve health literacy, including improving knowledge, and developing life skills which are conducive to individual and community health."

The Role of Health Education Specialists

From the late nineteenth to the mid-twentieth century, the aim of public health was controlling the harm from infectious diseases, which were largely under control by the 1950s. By the mid 1970s it was clear that reducing illness, death, and rising health care costs could best be achieved through a focus on health promotion and disease prevention. At the heart of the new approach was the role of a health educator A health educator is "a professionally prepared individual who serves in a variety of roles and is specifically trained to use appropriate educational strategies and methods to facilitate the development of policies, procedures, interventions, and systems conducive to the health of individuals, groups, and communities" (Joint Committee on Terminology, 2001, p. 100). In January 1978 the Role Delineation Project was put into place, in order to define the basic roles and responsibilities for the health educator. The result was a Framework for the Development of Competency-Based Curricula for Entry Level Health Educators (NCHEC, 1985). A second result was a revised version of A Competency-Based Framework for the Professional Development of Certified Health Education Specialists (NCHEC,1996). These documents outlined the seven areas of responsibilities which are shown below.

Responsibility I: Assessing Individual and Community Needs for Health Education

- Provides the foundation for program planning
- Determines what health problems might exist in any given groups
- Includes determination of community resources available to address the problem
- Community Empowerment encourages the population to take ownership of their health problems
- Includes careful data collection and analysis

Responsibility II: Plan Health Education Strategies, Interventions, and Programs

- Actions are based on the needs assessment done for the community
- Involves the development of goals and objectives which are specific and measurable
- Interventions are developed that will meet the goals and objectives
- According to Rule of Sufficiency, strategies are implemented which are sufficiently robust, effective enough, and have a reasonable chance of meeting stated objectives

Responsibility III: Implement Health Education Strategies, Interventions, and Programs

- Implementation is based on a thorough understanding of the priority population
- Utilize a wide range of educational methods and techniques

Responsibility IV: Conduct Evaluation and Research Related to Health Education

- Depending on the setting, utilize tests, surveys, observations, tracking epidemiologicaldata, or other methods of data collection

- Health Educators make use of research to improve their practices.

Responsibility V: Administer Health Education Strategies, Interventions, and Programs

- Administration is generally a function of the more experienced practitioner
- Involves facilitating cooperation among personnel, both within and between programs

Responsibility VI: Serve as a Health Education Resource Person

- Involves skills to access needed resources, and establish effective consultative relationships.

Responsibility VII: Communicate and Advocate for Health and Health Education

- Translates scientific language into understandable information
- Address diverse audience in diverse settings
- Formulates and support rules, policies and legislation
- Advocate for the profession of health education

Motivation

Education for health begins with people. It hopes to motivate them with whatever interests they may have in improving their living conditions. Its aim come is to develop in them a sense of responsibility for health conditions for themselves as individuals, as members of families, and as communities. In communicable disease control, health education commonly includes an appraisal of what is known by a population about a disease, an assessment of habits and attitudes of the people as they relate to spread and frequency of the disease, and the presentation of specific means to remedy observed deficiencies.

Health education is also an effective tool that helps improve health in developing nations. It not only teaches prevention and basic health knowledge but also conditions ideas that re-shape everyday habits of people with unhealthy lifestyles in developing countries. This type of conditioning not only affects the immediate recipients of such education but also future generations will benefit from an improved and properly cultivated ideas about health that will eventually be ingrained with widely spread health education. Moreover, besides physical health prevention, health education can also provide more aid and help people deal healthier with situations of extreme stress, anxiety, depression or other emotional disturbances to lessen the impact of these sorts of mental and emotional constituents, which can consequently lead to detrimental physical effects.

Credentialing

Credentialing is the process by which the qualifications of licensed professionals, organizational members or an organization are determined by assessing the individuals or group background and legitimacy through a standardized process. Accreditation, licensure, or certifications are all forms of credentialing.

In 1978, Helen Cleary, the president of the Society for Public Health Education (SOPHE) started the process of certification of health educators. Prior to this, there was no certification for individual health educators, with exception to the licensing for school health educators. The only accreditation available in this field was for school health and public health professional preparation programs.

Her initial response was to incorporate experts in the field and to promote funding for the process. The director if the Division of Associated Health Professions in the Bureau of Health Manpower of the Department of Health, Education, and Welfare, Thomas Hatch, became interested in the project. To ensure that the commonalities between health educators across the spectrum of professions would be sufficient enough to create a set of standards, Dr. Cleary spent a great amount of time to create the first conference called the Bethesda Conference. In attendance were interested professionals who covered the possibility of creating credentialing within the profession.

With the success of the conference and the consensus that the standardization of the profession was vital, those who organized the conference created the National Task Force in the Preparation and Practice of Health Educators. Funding for this endeavor became available in January 1979, and role delineation became a realistic vision for the future. They presented the framework for the system in 1981 and published entry-level criteria in 1983. Seven areas of responsibility, 29 areas of competency and 79 sub-competencies were required of health education professionals for approximately 20 years for entry-level educators.

In 1986 a second conference was held in Bethesda, Maryland to further the credentialing process. In June 1988, the National Task Force in the Preparation and Practice of Health Educators became the National Commission for Health Education Credentialing, Inc. (NCHEC). Their mission was to improve development of the field by promoting, preparing and certifying health education specialists. The NCHEC has three division boards that included preparation, professional development and certification of health educator professionals. The third board, which is called the Division Board of Certification of Health Education Specialist (DBCHES), has the responsibility of developing and administering the CHES exam. An initial certification process allowed 1,558 individuals to be chartered into the program through a recommendation and application process. The first exam was given in 1990.

In order for a candidate to sit for an exam they must have either a bachelor's, master's, or doctoral degree from an accredited institution, and an official transcript that shows a major in health education, Community Health Education, Public Health Education, or School Health Education, etc. The transcript will be accepted if it reflects 25 semester hours or 37 quarter hours in health education preparation and covers the 7 responsibilities covered in the framework.

In 1998 a project called the Competencies Update Project (CUP) began. The purpose of the CUP project was to up-date entry-level requirements and to develop advanced-level competences. Through research the CUP project created the requirements for three levels, which included entry-level, Advanced I and Advanced II educators.

Recently the Master Certified Health Education Specialist (MCHES) was created. The MCHES exam measures the knowledge of the advanced levels and sub levels of the Seven Areas of Responsibilities. The first MCHES exam was given in October 2011.

In order to be eligible to take the MCHES exam you must have at least a master's degree in health education or related discipline along with a least 25 credit hours related to health education. In addition, five years of documented information of practice in health education and two recommendations of past/present supervisors must be provided. A vitae/resume must also be submitted.

The Competency Update Project (CUP), 1998-2004 revealed that there were higher levels of health education practitioners, which is the reasoning for the advancements for the MCHES. Many health educators felt that the current CHES credential was an entry-level exam.

Teaching

In the United States some forty states require the teaching of health education. A comprehensive health education curriculum consists of planned learning experiences which will help students achieve desirable attitudes and practices related to critical health issues. Some of these are: emotional health and a positive self image; appreciation, respect for, and care of the human body and its vital organs; physical fitness; health issues of alcohol, tobacco, drug use and abuse; health misconceptions and myths; effects of exercise on the body systems and on general well being; nutrition and weight control; sexual relationships and sexuality, the scientific, social, and economic aspects of community and ecological health; communicable and degenerative diseases including sexually transmitted diseases; disaster preparedness; safety and driver education; factors in the environment and how those factors affect an individual's or population's Environmental health (ex: air quality, water quality, food sanitation); life skills; choosing professional medical and health services; and choices of health careers.

The National Center for Education Statistics share that 99% of public schools conduct some type of nutrition education. For each grade from kindergarten through eighth, 50 percent or more of all schools have district or state requirements for students to receive nutrition education. However, only 40 percent have these requirements for ninth and tenth grades; and about 20 percent for eleventh and twelfth grades. The issue still lies with the content and thoroughness that is being taught. Topics taught in a most all of the schools are: the relationship between diet and health, finding and choosing healthy foods, nutrients and their food sources, the Food Guide Pyramid, and the Dietary Guidelines and goals. However, with the exception of the Food Guide Pyramid, less than half of schools cover these topics thoroughly. Overall, schools focus on increasing students' knowledge about what is meant by good nutrition, with less emphasis on influencing students' motivation, attitudes, and eating behaviors. Four of the five topics covered by more than 90 percent of all schools are related to knowledge. With the exception of finding and choosing healthy foods, less than one-third of schools provide thorough coverage of topics related to motivation, attitudes, and eating behaviors. Not often are there teachers specific for nutrition.

Health Education Code of Ethics

The Health Education Code of Ethics has been a work in progress since approximately 1976, begun by the Society of Public Health Education (SOPHE). Various Public Health and Health Education organizations such as the American Association of Health Education (AAHE), the Coalition of National Health Education Organizations (CNHEO), SOPHE, and others collaborated year after year to devise a unified standard of ethics that health educators would be held accountable to professionally. In 1995, the National Commission for Health Education Credentialing, Inc. (NCHEC) proposed a profession-wide standard at the conference: Health Education Profession in the Twenty-First Century: Setting the Stage. Post-conference, an ethics task force was developed with the purpose of solidifying and unifying proposed ethical standards. The document was eventually unanimously approved and ratified by all involved organizations in November 1999 and has since then been used as the standard for practicing health educators.

"The Code of Ethics that has evolved from this long and arduous process is not seen as a completed project. Rather, it is envisioned as a living document that will continue to evolve as the practice of Health Education changes to meet the challenges of the new millennium."

Health Education Code of Ethics

PREAMBLE: The Health Education profession is dedicated to excellence in the practice of promoting individual, family, organizational, and community health. The Code of Ethics provides a framework of shared values within which Health Education is practiced. The responsibility of each Health Educator is to aspire to the highest possible standards of conduct and to encourage the ethical behavior of all those with whom they work.

Article I: Responsibility to the Public A Health Educator's ultimate responsibility is to educate people for the purpose of promoting, maintaining, and improving individual, family, and community health. When a conflict of issues arises among individuals, groups, organizations, agencies, or institutions, health educators must consider all issues and give priority to those that promote wellness and quality of living through principles of self-determination and freedom of choice for the individual.

Article II: Responsibility to the Profession Health Educators are responsible for their professional behavior, for the reputation of their profession, and for promoting ethical conduct among their colleagues.

Article III: Responsibility to Employers Health Educators recognize the boundaries of their professional competence and are accountable for their professional activities and actions.

Article IV: Responsibility in the Delivery of Health Education Health Educators promote integrity in the delivery of health education. They respect the rights, dignity, confidentiality, and worth of all people by adapting strategies and methods to the needs of diverse populations and communities.

Article V: Responsibility in Research and Evaluation Health Educators contribute to the health of the population and to the profession through research and evaluation activities. When planning and conducting research or evaluation, health educators do so in accordance with federal and state laws and regulations, organizational and institutional policies, and professional standards.

Article VI: Responsibility in Professional Preparation Those involved in the preparation and training of Health Educators have an obligation to accord learners the same respect and treatment given other groups by providing quality education that benefits the profession and the public.

All versions of the document are available on the Coalition of National Health Education's. The National Health Education Code of Ethics is the property of the Coalition of National Health Education.

National Organizations for Public Health/Health Education

American Public Health Association (APHA) APHA is the main voice for public health advocacy that is the oldest organization of public health since 1872. The American Public Health Association aims to "protect all Americans and their communities from preventable, serious health threats and strives to assure community-based health promotion and disease preventions." Any individual can become a member and benefit in online access and monthly printed issues of The Nation's Health and the American Journal of Public Health

Society for Public Health Education (SOPHE) The mission of SOPHE is to provide global leadership to the profession of health education and health promotion and to promote the health of society through advances in health education theory and research, excellence in professional preparation and practice, and advocacy for public policies conducive to health, and the achievement of health equity for all. Membership is open to all who have an interest in health education and or work in health education in schools, medical care settings, worksites, community-based organizations, state/local government, and international agencies. Founded in 1950, SOPHE publishes 2 indexed, peer-reviewed journals, Health Education & Behavior and Health Promotion Practice.

American School Health Association (ASHA) The American School Health Association was founded in 1972 by a group of physicians that already belonged to the American Public Health Association. This group specializes in school-aged health specifically. Over the years it has snowballed and now includes any person that can be a part of a child's life, from dentists, to counselors and school nurses. The American School Health Association mission "is to protect and promote the health of children and youth by supporting coordinated school health programs as a foundation for school success."

American Association of Health Education/American Alliance for Health, Physical Education, Recreation, and Dance (AAHE/AAHPERD) The AAHE/AAHPERD is said to be the largest organization of professionals that supports physical education; which includes leisure, fitness, dance, and health promotion. That is only a few; this incorporates all that is physical movement. This organization is an alliance with five national associations and six districts and is there to provide a comprehensive and coordinated array of resources to help support practitioners to improve their skills and always be learning new things. This organization was first stated in November 1885. William Gilbert Anderson had been out of medical school for two years and was working with many other people that were in the gymnastic field. He wanted them to get together to discuss their field and this organization was created. Today AAHPERD serves 25,000 members and has its headquarters in Reston, Virginia.

Eta Sigma Gamma (ESG) Eta Sigma Gamma is a national health education organization founded in 1967 by three professor from Ball State University. The mission of ESG is to promote public health education by improving the standards, ideals, capability, and ethics of public health education professionals. The three key points of the organization are to teach, research, and provide service to the members of the public health professionals. Some of the goals that the Eta Stigma Gamma targets are support planning and evaluation of future and existing health education programs, support and promote scientific research, support advocacy of health education issues, and promote professional ethics.

American College Health Association (ACHA) The American College Health Association originally began as a student health association in 1920, but then in 1948 the association changed the name to what its known today. The principal interest of the ACHA is to promote advocacy and leadership to colleges and universities around the country. Other part of the mission's association is to encourage education, communication, and services to students and campus community in general. The association also promotes advocacy and research. The American College Health Association has three types of membership: institutions of higher education, individual members who are interested in the public health profession, and susbtain members which are profitable and non-profitable organization. The ACHA is connected to 11 organizations located in six regions around the country. Currently, the American College Health Association serves 900 educative institutions and about 2400 individual members in the United States.

Directors of Health Promotion and Education (DHPE) Founded in 1946 as one of the professional groups of the Health Education Profession. The main goal of the HEPE is to improve the health education standards in any public health agency. As well, build networking opportunities among all public health professionals as a media to communicate ideas for implementing health programs, and to keep accurate information about the latest health news. The DHPE also focus to increase public awareness of health education and promotion by creating and expanding methods of existing health programs that will improve the quality of health. The Directors of Health Promotion and Education is linked to the Association of State and Territorial Health Officials (ASTHO) to "work on health promotion and disease prevention".

National Commission for Health Education Credentialing (NCHEC)

The National Commission for Health Education Credentialing NCHEC is the national accrediting organization for health educators, promoting the certified and master certified health education specialist (CHES and MCHES, respectively) credential. Many government and private sector jobs require that the health educator have at least the CHES credential as a prerequisite qualification for work. NCHEC also administers the affirmation of approved continuing education to maintain these credentials. Both CHES and MCHES are required to take at least 75 continuing education contact hours (CECH) every five years to be recertified. The provision and administration of the CHES credential represents the major strategy of NCHEC to fulfill its mission to "improve the practice of health education and to serve the public and profession of health education by certifying health education specialists, promoting professional development, and strengthening professional preparation and practice." NCHEC's quarterly newsletter is "The CHES Bulletin."

Health Education Career Opportunities

The terms Public Health Educator, Community Health Educator or Health Educator are all used interchangeable to describe an individual who plans implements and evaluates health education and promotion programs. These individuals play a crucial role in many organizations in various settings to improve our nations health. Just as a Community health educator works work toward population health, a school Health educator generally teaches in our Schools. A community health educator is typically focused on their immediate community striving to serve the public.

Health Care Settings: these include hospitals (for-profit and public), medical care clinics, home health agencies, HMOs and PPOs. Here, a health educator teaches employees how to be healthy. Patient education positions are far and few between because insurance companies do not cover the costs.

Public Health Agencies: are official, tax funded, government agencies. They provide police protection, educational systems, as well as clean air and water. Public health departments provide health services and are organized by a city, county, state, or federal government.

School Health Education: involves all strategies, activities, and services offered by, in, or in association with schools that are designed to promote students' physical, emotional, and social development. School health involves teaching students about health and health related behaviors. Curriculum and programs are based on the school's expectations and health.

Non Profit Voluntary Health Agencies: are created by concerned citizens to deal with health needs not met by governmental agencies. Missions include public education, professional education, patient education, research, direct services and support to or for people directly affected by a specific health or medical problem. Usually funded by such means as private donations, grants, and fund-raisers.

Higher Education: typically two types of positions health educators hold including academic, or faculty or health educator in a student health service or wellness center. As a faculty member, the health educator typically has three major responsibilities: teaching, community and professional service, and scholarly research. As a health educator in a university health service or wellness center, the major responsibility is to plan, implement, and evaluate health promotion and education programs for program participants.

Work site Health Promotion: is a combination of educational, organizational and environmental activities designed to improve the health and safety of employees and their families. These work site wellness programs offer an additional setting for health educators and allow them to reach segments of the population that are not easily reached through traditional community health programs. Some work site health promotion activities include: smoking cessation, stress management, bulletin boards, newsletters, and much more.

Independent Consulting and Government Contracting: international, national, regional, state, and local organizations contract with independent consultants for many reasons. They may be hired to assess individual and community needs for health education; plan, implement, administer and evaluate health education strategies; conduct research; serve as health education resource person; and or communicate about and advocate for health and health education. Government contractors are often behind national health education programs, government reports, public information web sites and telephone lines, media campaigns, conferences, and health education materials.

Influential Individuals in Health Education: Past and Present

Dorothy Bird Nyswander

Dr. Nyswander was born September 29, 1894. She earned her bachelor's and master's degree at the University of Nevada and received her Doctorate in educational psychology at Berkeley. She is a founder of the School of Public Health at the University of California at Berkeley. Dr. Nysawnder pursued her interest in public health at the Works Progress Administration during the depression. She served with the Federal Works Agency contributing to the establishment of nursery schools and child care centers to accommodate young mothers working in defense plants. She set up these centers in 15 northeastern states. This did not happen quickly so she advocated all over the nation to train people to act as foster parents for the children of working women. Dr. Nyswander became the director of the City health Center in Astoria, Queens in 1939. She spent her time as director promoting the idea of New York City keeping an eye on the health of children. They would do this by keeping records that would follow them to whatever school they might move to. She wrote "Solving School Health Problems" which is an analysis of the health issues in New York children. This is still used in public health education courses today.

Mayhew Derryberry

Dr. Derryberry was born December 25, 1902 and earned his bachelor's degree in chemistry and mathematics at the University of Tennessee. He began his career in 1926 with the American Child Health Association as the director of one of the first large-scale studies of the health status of the nation's schoolchildren. A year after his work with the American Child Health Association he earned his master's degree in education and psychology at Columbia University. He then went on to earn his doctorate and moved to the New York City Health Department as the secretary to the sanitary superintendent. He finally moved to Washington DC and joined the US Public Health Service as a senior public health analyst. He became chief of the Public Health Service and began assembling a team of behavioral scientists. They studied the nexus of behavior, social factors, and disease. Two scientists and Derryberry conducted the study of the role of health beliefs in explaining utilization of public health screening services. This work contributed to the development of the Health Belief Model. This provided an important theoretical foundation for modern health education. His legacy was very important because he engaged behavioral and social scientists in the problems of public health and gave importance to the role of that health education plays on human health.

Elena Sliepcevich

Elena Sliepcevich was a leading figure in the development of health education both as an academic discipline and a profession. She graduated from the University of Ireland in 1939 and received her master's degree from the University of Michigan in 1949. She received her doctorate in physical education from Springfield College in 1955. After completing her schooling, Elena Sliepcevich worked at Ohio State University in 1961 as a professor of health education. There she helped direct the School Health Education Study from 1961 to 1969, and most health education curricula used in schools today are based on the ten conceptual areas identified by the School Health Education Study. These ten areas of focus include community health, consumer health, environmental health, family life, mental and emotional health, injury prevention and safety, nutrition, personal health, prevention and control of disease, and drug use and abuse.

Helen Agnes Cleary

Helen Cleary was born March 28, 1914, at Petersburg, South Australia. She trained as a nurse at the Broken Hill and District Hospital in New South Wales. She became a general nurse in 1941, and an obstetric nurse in 1942. She joined the Royal Australian Air Force Nursing Service as a sister on November 15, 1943. Along with other RAAF nurses, she would partake in evacuations throughout New Guinea and Borneo, which earned the nurses the nickname "the flying angels", and were also known as the "glamor girls" of the air force. In April 1945, she was ranked No. 2 Medical Air Evacuation Transport Unit, and began bringing thousands of Australian and British servicemen from prisoner-of-war camps after Japan had surrendered. She and other nurses cared for many patients who suffered from malnutrition and dysentery. During the Korean War, Cleary was charge sister on the RAAF, where she organized medical evacuations of Australians from Korea, fought for better treatment and conditions of the critically wounded, and nursed recently exchanged Prisoners of War. On August 18, 1967, Ms. Cleary was made honorary nursing sister to Queen Elizabeth II. She had been appointed an associate of the Royal Red Cross in 1960, and became a leading member in 1968 for her contributions to the training of medical staff, and for maintaining "the high ideals of the nursing profession". She retired on March 28, 1969, and later died on August 26, 1987.

Delbert Oberteuffer

A long time health educator, Delbert Oberteuffer definitely made his mark on the physical education and health education world. He was born in Portland, Oregon in 1902 where he remained through college, attending the University of Oregon receiving his bachelor's degree. His next step took him to the prestigious Columbia University where he obtained his Masters of Arts and Doctor of Philosophy Degree. He furthered his education by becoming a professor at Ohio State University where he taught from 1932 until 1966. During his time there, he was head of the Men's Physical Education Department for 25 years. After years of hard work, he was rewarded with numerous jobs including the President of the American School Health Association and The College of Physical Education Association. He died in 1981 at the age of 79. He was survived by his wife, Katherine, and his son, Theodore K. Oberteuffer.

Howard Hoyman

Howard Hoyman is mainly recognized for his work in sex education and introductions of ecology concepts. He is credited for developing the original sex education program for students in grades 1 through 12. The model Hoyman created heavily influenced the thinking of many health educators. Hoyman received his bachelor's degree from Ohio State University in 1931. He then went on to earn his master's degree in 1932 and Doctorate in 1945 from the University of Colombia. Throughout his career he wrote over 200 articles and was honored many times by multiple organizations such as Phi Beta Kappa and the American Public Health Association. Dr. Hoyman retired in 1970 as A Professor Emeritus.

Lloyd Kolbe

Lloyd Kolbe received his B.S. form Towson University and then received his Ph.D. and M.Ed. from the University of Toledo during the 1970s. Dr. Kolbe played a huge role in the development of many health programs applied to the daily life of different age groups. He received the award for Excellence in Prevention and Control of Chronic Disease, which is the highest recognition in his department of work, for his work forming the Division of Adolescent and School Health. Dr. Kolbe was the Director of this program for 15 years. He has also taken time to write and publish numerous books such as *Food marketing to Children and Youth and School* as well as *Terrorism Related to Advancing and Improving the Nation's Health.*

Robert Morgan Pigg

University of Florida professor, Robert Morgan Pigg, started his health career in 1969 when he received his bachelor's degree in Health, Physical Education, and Recreation from Middle Tennessee State University. A year later he received his M.Ed; also from Middle Tennessee University before moving on to Indian University where he obtained his H.S.D. in 1974 and his M.P.H. in 1980. He held many jobs at numerous Universities including Western Kentucky University, University of Georgia, Indiana University, and the University of Florida where he currently resides today. Pigg's main focus of interest is the promotion of health towards children and adolescents. After spending 20 years as Editor for the Journal of Health, he was given the job as Department Chair in 2007 for The University of Florida.

Linda Rae Murray

Linda Rae Murray holds her MD, and MPH. Currently she is the Chief Officer for the Ambulatory & Community Health Network. She was elected president November 2009. Dr. Murray has served in a number of Medical settings her most recent being Medical Director of the federally funded health center, Winfield Moody, serving the Cabrini–Green public housing project in Chicago. She has also been an active member of the board of national organizations. Along with this she served as Chief Medical Officer in primary care for the twenty three primary care and community health centers. Today Murray serves as the Chief Medical Officer for the Cook County Health & Hospital system. Dr. Murray has also been a voice for social justice and health care as a basic human right for over forty years.

Mark J. Kittleson

Mark J. Kittleson is a professor at New Mexico State University for Public Health Education. His interests include Educational Technology and Behaviorism; he attended the University of Akron and received his PhD in Health Education. Dr. Kittleson has experience as owner and founder of the HEDIR a place where people can hold discussions related to health and health education. His honors and awards consist of Scholar of the Year, American Association of Health Education 2008 and he is a member of the American Association of Health Education.

Elaine Auld

Elaine Auld has been a leading figure for over more than 30 years in the health education field. She attended the University of Michigan, MPH, and Health Behavior/Health Education, from 1976 to 1978 Elaine is the chief executive officer for the Society for Public Health Education (SOPHE) and has had many contributions in health promotion and health communications. She has been a certified health specialist since 1989 and in 1996 was an adviser to the first Health Education Graduate Standards. Elaine was involved with the Competency Update Project (CUP), which provided standards for the health education profession. Elaine's interest and work are related to health education credentialing and standards, workforce development, public policy, and health equity. For the last decade Elaine has been a site visitor for the Council on Education for Public Health, and also strengthened the accreditation and preparation of future health specialists, which is key to an overall healthy well-being. Elaine has received two awards U of MI SPH Alumni of the Year Award in 2010 and SOPHE Distinguished Fellow in 2008.

Susan Wooley

Susan Wooley received her bachelor's degree from Case Western Reserve University, a master's degree in health education from the University of North Carolina at Greensboro, and a Ph.D. in health education from Temple University. Susan is the executive director of the American School Health Association and has been a member to ASHA for 31 years. She co-edited Health Is Academic: A Guide to Coordinated School Health Programs and co-authored Give It a Shot, a Toolkit for Nurses and Other Immunization Champions Working with Secondary Schools. Susan has had many previous jobs such as CDC's Division of Adolescent and School Health, Delaware State College, American Association for Health Education and Delaware Department of Public Instruction and is also a certified health specialist. Wooley spent four years on a curriculum development project for elementary schools, Science for Life and Living: Integrating Science, Technology and Health. Now Susan oversees the day-to-day operations of a national professional association and provides consultation and technical assistance to others working toward health education.

Health Education Worldwide

There are many countries which developed a Health Education curriculum. For example:

Romania

Since 2001, the Ministry of Education, Research, Youth and Sports developed a national curriculum on Health Education. The National Health Education Programme in Romanian Schools was considered as being a priority for the intervention of the GFATM (Global Fund) and UN Agencies.

Japan

Shokuiku is the Japanese term for "food education". The law defines it as the "acquisition of knowledge about food and nutrition, as well as the ability to make appropriate decisions through practical experience with food, with the aim of developing people's ability to live on a healthy diet".

It was initiated by Sagen Ishizuka, a famous military doctor and pioneer of the macrobiotic diet. Following the introduction of Western fast food in the late 20th century, the Japanese government mandated education in nutrition and food origins, starting with the Basic Law of Shokuiku in 2005, and followed with the School Health Law in 2008. Universities have established programs to teach shokuiku in public schools, as well as investigating its effectiveness through academic study.

Major concerns that led to the development of shokuiku law include:

- Schoolchildren skipping breakfast.

- Children purchasing meals at a convenience store instead of eating with their parents.
- Families not eating meals together.

Classes in shokuiku will study the processes of making food, such as farming or fermentation; how additives create flavor; and where food comes from.

Poland

Health education in Poland is not mandatory, but research has shown that even with implantation of health education that the adolescents of Poland were still not choosing to live a health lifestyle. Health education is still needed in Poland, but the factor of what is actually available, especially in rural areas, and what is affordable affects the decisions more than what is healthy.

Taiwan

The Health education in Taiwan focus on multiple topic, this included but not limit to

- Education for student to enhance its health satue
- assists parents to use health resources,information
- Teach student to understand specific diseases & known basic medical knowledge
- help adolescents to handle currency problem,those such as menstruation, erection

Health Literacy

Health literacy is the ability to obtain, read, understand and use healthcare information to make appropriate health decisions and follow instructions for treatment. There are multiple definitions of health literacy, in part, because health literacy involves both the context (or setting) in which health literacy demands are made (e.g., health care, media, internet or fitness facility) and the skills that people bring to that situation (Rudd, Moeykens, & Colton, 1999). Studies reveal that only 12 percent of the adults in the U.S. have proficient health literacy. This means 77 million adults have basic or below basic health literacy. These individuals have difficulty with common health tasks including reading the label of a prescribed drug. Low health literacy reduces the success of treatment and increases the risk of medical error. Health literacy is essential to promote healthy individuals and communities.

Various interventions, such as simplified information and illustrations, avoiding jargon, "teach back" methods and encouraging patients' questions, have improved health behaviors in persons with low health literacy. Health literacy is of continued and increasing concern for health professionals, as it is a primary factor behind health disparities. The proportion of adults aged 18 and over in the U.S., in the year 2010, who reported that their health care providers always explained things so they could understand them was about 60.6%. This number increased 1% from 2007 to 2010. The Healthy People 2020 initiative of the United States Department of Health and Human Services has included it as a pressing new topic, with objectives for addressing it in the decade to come.

Society as a whole is responsible for improving health literacy, but most importantly the healthcare, public health professionals, and the public health systems.

Characteristics

Plain Language

In order to have a population that understands health terms and can make proper health decisions, the language used by health professionals has to be a level that others who are not in the medical field can understand. Health professionals must know their audience in order to better serve their patient. The language used by these professionals should be plain language. Plain language is a strategy for making written and oral information easier to understand; it is communication that users can understand the first time they read or hear it.

Some key elements of plain language include:

- Organizing information so most important points come first
- Breaking complex information into understandable chunks
- Using simple language and defining technical terms
- Using active voice
- Using lists and tables to make complex material easier to understand

If health practitioners use plain language and ask their patients to teach back what they were told, individuals will be better able to take action, protect their health and wellness, and the health system will have better health outcomes.

Factors

Many factors determine the health literacy level of health education materials or other health interventions: reading level, numeracy level, current state of health, language barriers, cultural appropriateness, format and style, sentence structure, use of illustrations, interactiveness of intervention, and numerous other factors will affect how easily health information is understood and followed.

A study of 2,600 patients conducted in 1995 by two US hospitals found that between 26% and 60% of patients could not understand medication directions, a standard informed consent or basic health care materials.

History

The young and multidisciplinary field of health literacy emerged from two expert groups; physicians, other health providers, and health educators, and Adult Basic Education (ABE) and English as a Second Language (ESL) practitioners. Physicians are a source of groundbreaking patient comprehension and compliance studies. Adult Basic Education / English for Speakers of Languages Other Than English (ABE/ESOL) specialists study and design interventions to help people develop reading, writing, and conversation skills and increasingly infuse curricula with health information to promote better health literacy. A range of approaches to adult education brings health literacy skills to people in traditional classroom settings, as well as where they work and live.

Biomedical Approach

The biomedical approach to health literacy that became dominant (in the U.S.) during the 1980s and 1990s often depicted individuals as lacking, or "suffering" from, low health literacy, assumed that recipients are passive in their possession and reception of health literacy, and believed that models of literacy and health literacy are politically neutral and universally applicable. This approach is found lacking when placed in the context of broader ecological, critical, and cultural approaches to health. This approach has produced, and continues to reproduce, numerous correlational studies.

Where there are adequate levels of health literacy, that is where the population has sufficient knowledge and skills and where members of a community have the confidence to guide their own health, people are able to stay healthy, recover from illness and live with disease or disability.

McMurray states that health literacy is important in a community as it addresses health inequities, as those at the lower levels of health literacy are often the ones who live in lower socio-economic communities. Being aware of information relevant to improving their health, or how to access health resources creates higher levels of disadvantage. For some people, a lack of education and health literacy that would flow from education prevents them from becoming empowered at any time in their lives.

A more robust view of health literacy includes the ability to understand scientific concepts, content, and health research; skills in spoken, written, and online communication; critical interpretation of mass media messages; navigating complex systems of health care and governance; and knowledge and use of community capital and resources, as well as using cultural and indigenous knowledge in health decision making (Nutbeam, 2000; Ratzan, 2001; Zarcadoolas, Pleasant, & Greer, 2002). This view sees health literacy as a social determinant of health that offers a powerful opportunity to reduce inequities in health.

This perspective defines health literacy as the wide range of skills, and competencies that people develop over their lifetimes to seek out, comprehend, evaluate, and use health information and concepts to make informed choices, reduce health risks, and increase quality of life (Zarcadoolas, Pleasant, & Greer, 2006). While definitions vary in wording, they all fall within the conceptual framework offered in this definition.

Defining health literacy in that manner builds the foundation for a multi-dimensional model of health literacy built around four central domains:

- fundamental literacy,
- scientific literacy,
- civic literacy, and
- cultural literacy.

There are several tests, which have verified reliability in the academic literature that can be administered in order to test one's health literacy. Some of these tests include the Medical Term Recognition Test (METER), which was developed in the United States (2 minute administration time) for the clinical setting. The METER includes many words from the Rapid Estimate of Adult Literacy in Medicine (REALM) test. The Short Assessment of Health Literacy in Spanish and English populations (SAHL-S&E) uses word recognition and multiple choice questions to test a person's comprehension. The CHC-Test is a test used to measure critical health competencies, which consists of 72 items and is designed to test a person's understanding of medical concepts, literature searching, basic statistics and design of experiments and samples.

Patient Safety and Outcomes

According to an Institute of Medicine (2004) report, low health literacy negatively affects the treatment outcome and safety of care delivery. The lack of health literacy affects all segments of the population. Although it is disproportionate in certain demographic groups, such as the elderly, ethnic minorities, recent immigrants and persons with low general literacy, it does not only affect the; it is an issue for all racial and ethnic groups. Anyone can face health literacy challenges including people with strong literacy skills. Nevertheless, elderlies, ethnic minorities, recent immigrants and people with low general literacy, have a higher risk of hospitalization and longer hospital stays, are less likely to comply with treatment, are more likely to make errors with medication, and are more ill when they seek medical care.

The mismatch between a clinician's level of communication and a patient's ability to understand can lead to medication errors and adverse medical outcomes. Health literacy skills are not only a problem in the public. Health care professionals (doctors, nurses, public health workers) can also have poor health literacy skills, such as a reduced ability to clearly explain health issues to patients and the public. A well arranged layout, pertinent illustrations, and intuitive format can improve the usability of health care literature. This in turn can help in effective communication between health care providers and patients and their families.

Risk Identification

Identifying patients at risk due to low health literacy is productive. Health behaviors such as correct medication use, taking advantage of health screening and effective preventive measures such as exercise and smoking cessation improved when low literacy patients were given visual aids, easy readability brochures or videotapes. Several tests of health literacy have been developed to validate research studies, but a practical, three-minute assessment can be completed in a doctor's office. A recent review on health literacy in the Journal of the American Medical Association's "Rational Clinical Examination Series" showed that single-item questions can be useful. The simple inquiry, "How confident are you in filling out medical forms by yourself?" gives a likelihood ratio (LR) for limited literacy of 5.0 (95% confidence interval [CI], 3.8-6.4) for an answer of "a little confident" or "not at all confident"; an LR of 2.2 (95% CI, 1.5-3.3) for "somewhat confident"; and an LR of 0.44 (95% CI, 0.24-0.82) for "quite a bit" or "extremely confident."

Intervention

Once identified, low health literacy patients benefit from providing limited but clear information at each visit, avoidance of medical jargon, using illustrations of important concepts and confirming information by a "teach back" method. A program called "Ask Me 3" is designed to bring public and physician attention to this issue, by letting patients know that they should ask three questions each time they talk to a doctor, nurse, or pharmacist:

- What is my main problem?
- What do I need to do?
- Why is it important for me to do this?

A public information program by the US Department of Health and Human Services encourages patients to improve healthcare quality and avoid errors by asking questions about health conditions and treatment.

The book *Decoding Medical Gobbleddygook - Health Literacy Puts Patients First* offers many resources on improving health literacy and is available free online.

The IROHLA (Intervention Research on Health Literacy of the Ageing population) project, funded by the EU, seeks to develop evidence based guidelines for policy and practice for approaches to improve health literacy of the ageing population in EU member states. The project has developed a framework, identified and validated interventions which together constitute a comprehensive approach of addressing health literacy needs of the older people. In November 2015 the IROHLA project will present its findings in an interactive web-portal informing professionals and local, regional and national policy makers.

Health Illiterate-related Diabetes Prevalence in Vietnamese-American Populations

Diabetes is a rapidly growing health problem among immigrants—affecting approximately 10 percent of Asian-Americans. It is the fifth-leading cause of death in Asian-Americans between the ages of 45 and 64. In addition, type 2 diabetes is the most common form of the disease. Those who are diagnosed with type 2 diabetes have high levels of blood glucose because the body does not effectively respond to insulin. It is a lifelong disease with no known cure. Diabetes is a chronic, debilitating, and costly social burden—costing healthcare systems about $100 billion annually.

Diabetes disproportionately affects underserved and ethnically diverse populations, such as Vietnamese-American communities. The relationship between the disease and health literacy level is in part because of an individual's ability to read English, evaluate blood glucose levels, and communicate with medical professionals. Other studies also suggest lack in knowledge of diabetes symptoms and complications. According to an observational cross-sectional study conducted, many Vietnamese-American diabetic patients show signs of poor blood glucose control and adherence due to inadequate self-management knowledge and experience. Diabetes health literacy research is needed to fully understand the burden of the chronic disease in Vietnamese-American communities, with respect to language and culture, health literacy, and immigrant status. Ethnic minority groups and immigrant communities have less knowledge of health promoting behavior, face considerable obstacles to health services, and experience poor communication with medical professionals. According to a recent review, studies has supported an independent relationship between literacy and knowledge of diabetes management and glucose control, but its impact on patients has not been sufficiently described. With the demand of chronic disease self-management (e.g., diabetic diet, glucose monitoring, etc.), a call for cultural-specific patient education is needed to achieve the control of diabetes and its adverse health outcomes in low- to middle-income Vietnamese-American immigrant communities.

eHealth Literacy

eHealth literacy is a term that describes the relatively modern concept of an individual's ability to search for, successfully access, comprehend, and appraise desired health information from electronic sources and to then use such information to attempt to address a particular health problem. Due to the increasing influence of the internet for information-seeking and health information distribution purposes, eHealth literacy has become an important topic of research in recent years. Stellefson (2011) states, "8 out of 10 Internet users report that they have at least once looked online for health information, making it the third most popular Web activity next to checking email and using search engines in terms of activities that almost everybody has done." Though in recent years, individuals may have gained access to a multitude of health information via the Internet, access alone does not ensure that proper search skills and techniques are being used to find the most relevant online and electronic resources. The lines between a reputable medical source and an amateur opinion from a so-called expert can often be blurred; however the ability to differentiate between the two is becoming increasing important.

Health literacy requires a combination of several different literacy skills in order to facilitate eHealth promotion and care. Six core skills are delineated by an eHealth literacy model referred to as the Lily model. The Lily Model's six literacies are organized into two central types: analytic and context-specific. Analytic type literacies are those skills that can be applied to a broad range of sources, regardless of topic or content (i.e., skills that can also be applied to shopping or researching a term paper in addition to health) whereas context-specific skills are those that are contextualized within a specific problem domain (can solely be applied to health). The six literacies are listed below, the first three of the analytic type and the latter three of the context-specific:

- Traditional literacy
- Media literacy
- Information literacy
- Computer literacy
- Scientific literacy
- Health literacy

According to Norman (2006), both analytical and context-specific literacy skills are "required to fully engage with electronic health resources." As the World Wide Web and technological innovations are more and more becoming a part of the health care environment, it is important for information technology to be properly utilized to promote health and deliver health care effectively.

It has been suggested that the move towards patient-centred care and the greater use of technology for self-care and self-management requires higher health literacy on the part of the patient.

Improvement

Incorporate Information Through the University Level

The United States Department of Health and Human Services created a National Action Plan to

Improve Health Literacy. One of its goals is to incorporate health and science information in child-care and education through the university level. The target is to educate people at an early stage; that way individuals are raised with health literacy and will have a better quality of life. The earlier an individual is exposed to health literacy skills the better for the person and the community.

Programs such as Head Start and Women, Infants, and Children (WIC) have impacted our society and the low income population. Head Start provides low-income children and their families early childhood education, nutrition, and health. Health literacy is integrated in the program for both children and parents through the education they give the individuals. WIC serves low-income pregnant and after pregnancy mothers by supplementing them food, health care referrals, and nutrition education. Programs like these help both, the parent and the child with health literacy creating a more knowledgeable community with health education.

Although programs like Head Start and WIC have been working with the health literacy of a specific population, much more can be done with the education of children and young adults. Now, more and more adolescents are getting involved with their health care. Due to this, it is crucial to educate these individuals in order for them to make informed decisions.

Many schools in the country incorporate a health class in their curriculum. These classes provided an excellent opportunity to facilitate and develop health literacy in today's children and adolescents. The skills of how to read food labels, the meaning of common medical terms, the structure of the human body, and education on the most prevalent disease in the United States should be taught in both private and public schools. This way new generations will grow with health literacy and would hopefully make knowledgeable health decisions.

Framework and Potential Intervention Points

The National Library of Medicine defines health literacy as:

"The degree to which individuals have the capacity to obtain, process, and understand basic health literacy

information and services needed to make appropriate health decisions."

Based on this clinical definition, health literacy gives individuals the skills that they need to both understand and effectively communicate information and concerns. Bridging that gap between literacy skills and the ability of the individual in health contexts, the *Health Literacy Framework* highlights the health outcomes and costs associated with health contexts including cognitive abilities, social skills, emotional state, and physical conditions such as visual and auditory contributions.

Potential Intervention Points are illustrated in reflection of the *Health Literacy Framework*. Outlining interactions such as those of individuals and the education systems that they are engaged with, their health systems, and societal factors as they relate to health literacy, these potential intervention points are not however, components of a casual model. The three potential intervention points are culture and society, the health system, and the education system. Health outcomes and costs are the products of the health literacy developed during diversity of exposure to these three potential intervention points.

Referring to shared ideas, meanings, and values that influence an individual's beliefs and attitudes, cultural and societal influences are a significant intervention point for health literacy development. As interactions with healthcare systems often first occur at the family level, deeply rooted beliefs and values can shape the significance of the experience. Included components that reflect the development of health literacy both culturally and societally are native language, socioeconomic status, gender, race, and ethnicity, as well as mass media exposure. These are pathways to understanding American life paralleling conquests for a health literate America.

The health system is an intervention point in the *Health Literary Framework*. For the purposes of this framework, health literacy refers to an individual's interaction with people performing health-related activities in settings such as hospitals, clinics, physician's offices, home health care, public health agencies, and insurers.

In the United States, the education system consists of K-12 curricula. In addition to this standard educational setting, adult education programs are also environments in which individuals can develop traditional literacy skills founded in comprehension and real-world application of knowledge via reading and writing. Tools for educational development provided by these systems impact an individual's capacity to obtain specific knowledge regarding health. Reflecting components of traditional literacy such as cultural and conceptual knowledge, oral literacy (listening and speaking,) print literacy (reading and writing,) and numeracy, education systems are also potential intervention points for health literacy development.

Skills Needed for Development

Health Related Goals

- Promoting and protect health and prevent disease
- Understand, interpret, and analyze health information
- Apply health information over a variety of life events and situations
- Navigate the health-care system
- Actively participate in encounters with health-care professionals and workers
- Understand and give consent
- Understand and advocate for rights

Libraries

Libraries have increasingly recognised that they can play a role in health literacy since the 2000s, influenced by the Medical Library Association. Library initiatives have included running education programs, fostering partnerships with health organisations, and using outreach efforts.

References

- Prochaska, James; Velicer, Wayne (1997). "The Transtheoretical Model of Health Behavior Change". American Journal of Health Promotion. 12 (1): 38–48. doi:10.4278/0890-1171-12.1.38

- "Behaviour Change Communication (BCC)for HIV/AIDS a Strategic Framework" (PDF). HIVPolicy.org. September 2002. Retrieved 2 August 2016
- Walkters, S (2000). "Drinking on campus: What do we know about reducing alcohol use among college students?". Journal of Substance Abuse Treatment. 19 (3): 223–228
- Glanz, Karen; Barbara K. Rimer; K. Viswanath (2008). Health behavior and health education: theory, research, and practice. (PDF) (4th ed.). San Francisco, CA: Jossey-Bass. pp. 45–51. ISBN 978-0787996147
- Sharma, M (2007). "Theory of reasoned action & theory of planned behavior in alcohol and drug education". Journal of Alcohol and Drug Education. 51 (1): 3–7
- Burnett, J. J. (1981). "Internal–external locus of control as a moderator of fear appeals". Journal of Applied Psychology. 66 (3): 390–393. doi:10.1037/0021-9010.66.3.390
- "Brazil: Behavior Change Communication for More Effective Tuberculosis Control". John Snow Inc. 2010–2011. Retrieved 2 August 2016
- Sternthal, B.; Craig, C.S. (1974). "Fear Appeals: Revisited and Revised". Journal of Consumer Research. 1 (3): 22–32. doi:10.1086/208597
- Stretcher, Victor J.; Irwin M. Rosenstock (1997). "The health belief model". In Andrew Baum. Cambridge handbook of psychology, health and medicine. Cambridge, UK: Cambridge University Press. pp. 113–117. ISBN 0521430739
- "The Power of Prevention" (PDF). www.cdc.gov. cdc. 2009. Retrieved 7 December 2016. This article incorporates text from this source, which is in the public domain
- Joint Committee on Terminology (2001). "Report of the 2000 Joint Committee on Health Education and Promotion Terminology". American Journal of Health Education. 32 (2): 89–103
- Jamison DT, Breman JG, Measham AR, et al., (eds) (2006) Disease Control Priorities in Developing Countries. 2nd edition Chapter 2: Intervention Cost-Effectiveness Retrieved February 2015
- "Health Education Code of Ethics -Health Education Credentialing: Health Education Code of Ethics". NCHEC. Retrieved 2012-10-27

4

An Overview of Occupational Health Psychology

Health issues related to employment and the working place falls under occupational health. As a person spends a significant amount of her/his time at his work place, it can have a great impact on their health. Even many researchers believe job satisfaction to be a factor in a person's well-being. It can have three aspects, social, physical and psychological. This chapter discusses in detail the theories and concepts related to occupational health.

Occupational Health Psychology

Occupational health psychology (OHP) is an interdisciplinary area of psychology that is concerned with the health and safety of workers. OHP addresses a number of major topic areas including the impact of occupational stressors on physical and mental health, the impact of involuntary unemployment on physical and mental health, work-family balance, workplace violence and other forms of mistreatment, accidents and safety, and interventions designed to improve/protect worker health. OHP emerged from two distinct disciplines within applied psychology, namely, health psychology and industrial and organizational psychology, as well as occupational medicine. OHP has also been informed by other disciplines including industrial sociology, industrial engineering, and economics, as well as preventive medicine and public health. OHP is concerned with the relationship of psychosocial workplace factors to the development, maintenance, and promotion of workers' health and that of their families. Thus the field's focus is work-related factors that can lead to injury, disease, and distress.

Historical Overview

Origins

The Industrial Revolution prompted thinkers, such as Karl Marx with his theory of alienation, to concern themselves with the nature of work and its impact on workers. Taylor's (1911) *Principles of Scientific Management* as well as Mayo's research in the late 1920s and early 1930s on workers at the Hawthorne Western Electric plant helped to inject the impact of work on workers into the subject matter psychology addresses. The creation in 1948 of the Institute for Social Research (ISR) at the University of Michigan was important because of its research on occupational stress and employee health.

Research in the U.K. by Trist and Bamforth (1951) suggested the reduction in autonomy that accompanied organizational changes in English coal mining operations adversely affected worker morale. Arthur Kornhauser's work in the early 1960s on the mental health of automobile workers in Michigan also contributed to the development of the field. A 1971 study by Gardell examined the impact of work organization on mental health in Swedish pulp and paper mill workers and engineers. Research on the impact of unemployment on mental health was conducted at the University of Sheffield's Institute of Work Psychology. In 1970 Kasl and Cobb documented the impact of unemployment on blood pressure in U.S. factory workers.

Recognition as a Field of Study

The term "occupational health psychology" first appeared in print in 1986 when Everly advocated for psychologists' role in workplace health promotion. In 1988, in response to a dramatic increase in the number of stress-related worker compensation claims in the U.S., the National Institute for Occupational Safety and Health (NIOSH) added psychological factors to its list of factors "leading occupational health risk". When this change was coupled with an increased recognition of the impact of stress on a range of problems in the workplace, NIOSH found that their stress-related programs were significantly increasing in prominence. In 1990, Raymond et al. argued that the time has come for doctoral-level psychologists to get interdisciplinary OHP training, integrating health psychology with public health, because creating healthy workplaces should be a goal for the field.

Emergence as a Discipline

Established in 1987, *Work & Stress* is the first and "longest established journal in the fast developing discipline that is occupational health psychology". Three years later, the American Psychological Association (APA) and NIOSH jointly organized the first international Work, Stress, and Health conference in Washington, DC. The conference has since become a biannual OHP meeting. In 1996, the *Journal of Occupational Health Psychology* was published by APA. That same year, the International Commission on Occupational Health created the Work Organisation and Psychosocial Factors (ICOH-WOPS) scientific committee, which focused primarily on OHP. In 1999, the European Academy of Occupational Health Psychology (EA-OHP) was established at the first European Workshop on Occupational Health Psychology in Lund, Sweden. That workshop is considered to be the first EA-OHP conference, the first of a continuing series of conferences EA-OHP organizes and devotes to OHP research and practice.

In 2000 the informal International Coordinating Group for Occupational Health Psychology (ICG-OHP) was founded for the purpose of facilitating OHP-related research, education, and practice as well as coordinating international conference scheduling. Also in 2000, *Work & Stress* became associated with the EA-OHP. In 2005, the Society for Occupational Health Psychology (SOHP) was established in the United States. In 2008, SOHP joined with APA and NIOSH in co-sponsoring the Work, Stress, and Health conferences. In 2017, SOHP began to publish an OHP-related journal *Occupational Health Science.*

Research Methods

The main purpose of OHP research is to understand how working conditions affect worker health, use that knowledge to design interventions to protect and improve worker health, and evaluate the effectiveness of such interventions. The research methods used in OHP are similar to those used in other branches of psychology.

Standard Research Designs

Self-report survey methodology is the most used approach in OHP research. Cross-sectional designs are commonly used; case-control designs have been employed much less frequently. Longitudinal designs including prospective cohort studies and experience sampling studies can examine relationships over time. OHP-related research devoted to evaluating health-promoting workplace interventions has relied on quasi-experimental designs and, less commonly, experimental approaches.

Quantitative Methods

Statistical methods commonly used in other areas of psychology are also used in OHP-related research. Statistical methods used include structural equation modeling and hierarchical linear modeling (HLM; also known as multilevel modeling). HLM can better adjust for similarities between employees and is especially well suited to evaluating the lagged impact of work stressors on health outcomes; in this research context HLM can help minimize censoring and is well-suited to experience sampling studies. Meta-analyses have been used to aggregate data (modern approaches to meta-analyses rely on HLM), and draw conclusions across multiple studies.

Qualitative Research Methods

Qualitative research methods include interviews, focus groups, and self-reported, written descriptions of stressful incidents at work. First-hand observation of workers on the job has also been used, as has participant observation.

Research Topics

Important Theoretical Models in OHP Research

Three influential theoretical models in OHP research are the demand-control-support, demand-resources, and effort-reward imbalance models.

Demand-control-support Model

The most influential model in OHP research has been the original demand-control model. According to the model, the combination of low levels of work-related decision latitude (i.e., autonomy and control over the job) combined with high workloads (high levels of work demands) can be particularly harmful to workers (they can lead to "job strain," a term representing the combination of low decision latitude and high workload leading to poorer mental or physical health). The model suggests not only that these two job factors are related to poorer health but that high levels of decision latitude on the job will buffer or reduce the adverse health impact of high levels of demands. Research has clearly supported the idea that decision latitude and demands relate to strains, but research findings about buffering have been mixed with only some studies providing support. The demand-control model asserts that job control can come in two broad forms: 'skill discretion' and 'decision authority'. Skill discretion refers to the level of skill and creativity required on the job and the flexibility an employee is permitted in deciding what skills to use (e.g. opportunity to use skills, similar to job variety). Decision authority refers to employees being able to make decisions about their work (e.g., having autonomy). These two forms of job control are traditionally assessed together in a composite measure of decision latitude; there is, however, some evidence that the two types of job control may not be similarly related to health outcomes.

About a decade after Karasek first introduced the demand-control model, Johnson, Hall, and Theorell (1989), in the context of research on heart disease, extended the model to include social isolation. Johnson et al. labeled the combination of high levels of demands, low levels of control, and low levels of coworker support "iso-strain." The resulting expanded model has been labeled the demand–control–support (DCS) model. Research that followed the development of this model has suggested that one or more of the components of the DCS model (high psychological workload, low control, and lack of social support), if not the exact combination represented by iso-strain, have adverse effects of physical and mental health.

Job Demands-resources Model

An alternative model, the job demands-resources (JD-R) model, grew out of the DCS model. In the JD-R model, the category of demands (workload) remains more or less the same as in the DCS model although the JD-R model more specifically includes physical demands. Resources, however, are defined as job-relevant features that help workers achieve work-related goals, lessen job demands, or stimulate personal growth. Control and support as per the DCS model are subsumed under resources. Resources can be external (provided by the organization) or internal (part of a worker's personal make-up). In addition to control and support, resources encompassed by the model can also include physical equipment, software, performance feedback from supervisors, the worker's own coping strategies, etc. There has not, however, been as much research on the JD-R model as there has been on the constituents of the DC or DCS model.

Effort-reward Imbalance Model

After the DCS model, the, perhaps, second most influential model in OHP research has been the effort-reward imbalance (ERI) model. It links job demands to the rewards employees receive for the job. That model holds that high work-related effort coupled with low control over job-related intrinsic (e.g., recognition) and extrinsic (e.g., pay) rewards triggers high levels of activation in neurohormonal pathways that, cumulatively, are thought to exert adverse effects on mental and physical health.

Occupational Stress and Cardiovascular Disease

A number of work-related, psychosocial factors have been linked to cardiovascular disease (CVD).

Cardiovascular Disease

Research has identified health-behavioral and biological factors that are related to increased risk for CVD. These risk factors include smoking, obesity, low density lipoprotein (the "bad" cholesterol), lack of exercise, and blood pressure. Psychosocial working conditions are also risk factors for CVD. In a case-control study involving two large U.S. data sets, Murphy (1991) found that hazardous work situations, jobs that required vigilance and responsibility for others, and work that required attention to devices were related to increased risk for cardiovascular disability. These included jobs in transportation (e.g., air traffic controllers, airline pilots, bus drivers, locomotive engineers, truck drivers), preschool teachers, and craftsmen. Among 30 studies involving men and women, most have found an association between workplace stressors and CVD.

Fredikson, Sundin, and Frankenhaeuser (1985) found that reactions to psychological stressors include increased activity in the brain axes which play an important role in the regulation of blood pressure, particularly ambulatory blood pressure. A meta-analysis and systematic review involving 29 samples linked job strain to elevated ambulatory blood pressure. Belkić et al. (2000) found that many of the 30 studies covered in their review revealed that decision latitude and psychological workload exerted independent effects on CVD; two studies found synergistic effects, consistent with the strictest version of the demand-control model. A review of 17 longitudinal studies having reasonably high internal validity found that 8 showed a significant relation between the combination of low latitude and high workload (the job strain condition) and CVD and 3 more showed a nonsignificant relation. The findings, however, were clearer for men than for women, on whom data were more sparse. In a massive ($n > 197{,}000$) longitudinal study that combined data from 13 independent studies, Kivimäki et al. (2012) found that, controlling for other risk factors, the combination of high levels of demands and low control at baseline increased the risk of CVD in initially healthy workers by between 20 and 30% over a follow-up period that averaged 7.5 years. In this study the effects were similar for men and women.

There is evidence that, consistent with the ERI model, high work-related effort coupled with low control over job-related rewards adversely affects cardiovascular health. At least five studies of men have linked effort-reward imbalance with CVD.

Job loss and Cardiovascular Health

Research has suggested that job loss adversely affects cardiovascular health as well as health in general.

Job-related Burnout and Cardiovascular Health

There is evidence from a prospective study that job-related burnout, controlling for traditional risk factors, such as smoking and hypertension, increases the risk of coronary heart disease over the course of the next three and a half years in workers who were initially disease-free.

Musculoskeletal Disorders

Musculoskeletal disorders (MSDs) involve injury and pain to the joints and muscles of the body. Approximately 2.5 million workers in the US suffer from MSDs, which is the third most common cause of disability and early retirement for American workers. In Europe MSDs are the most often reported workplace health problem. The development of musculoskelelatal problems cannot be solely explained in the basis of biomechanical factors (e.g., repetitive motion) although such factors are important contributors. There has been evidence that psychosocial workplace factors (e.g., job strain) also contribute to the development of musculoskeletal problems.

Workplace Mistreatment

There are many forms of workplace mistreatment ranging from relatively minor incivility to serious cases of bullying and violence.

Workplace Incivility

Workplace incivility has been defined as "low-intensity deviant behavior with ambiguous intent to harm the target....Uncivil behaviors are characteristically rude and discourteous, displaying a lack of regard for others" (p. 457). Incivility is distinct from violence. Examples of workplace incivility include insulting comments, denigration of the target's work, spreading false rumors, social isolation, etc. A summary of research conducted in Europe suggests that workplace incivility is common there. In research on more than 1000 U.S. civil service workers, more than 70% of the sample experienced workplace incivility in the past five years. Compared to men, women were more exposed to incivility; incivility was associated with psychological distress and reduced job satisfaction.

Abusive Supervision

Abusive supervision is the extent to which a supervisor engages in a pattern of behavior that harms subordinates.

Workplace Bullying

Although definitions of workplace bullying vary, it involves a repeated pattern of harmful behaviors directed towards an individual by one or more others who have more power than the target. Workplace bullying is sometimes termed *mobbing*.

Sexual Harassment

Sexual harassment is behavior that denigrates or mistreats an individual due to his or her gender, creates an offensive workplace, and interferes with an individual being able to do the job.

Workplace Violence

Workplace violence is a significant health hazard for employees.

-Nonfatal assault

Most workplace assaults are nonfatal, with an annual physical assault rate of 6% in the U.S. Assaultive behavior in the workplace often produces injury, psychological distress, and economic loss. One study of California workers found a rate of 72.9 non-fatal, officially documented assaults per 100,000 workers per year, with workers in the education, retail, and health care sectors subject to excess risk. A Minnesota workers' compensation study found that women workers had a twofold higher risk of being injured in an assault than men, and health and social service workers, transit workers, and members of the education sector were at high risk for injury compared to workers in other economic sectors. A West Virginia workers' compensation study found that workers in the health care sector and, to a lesser extent, the education sector were at elevated risk for assault-related injury. Another workers' compensation study found that excessively high rates of assault-related injury in schools, healthcare, and, to a lesser extent, banking. In addition to the physical injury that results from being a victim of workplace violence, individuals who witness such violence without being directly victimized are at increased risk for experiencing adverse effects, as found in a study of Los Angeles teachers.

-Homicide

In 1996 there were 927 work-associated homicides in the United States, in a labor force that numbered approximately 132,616,000. The rate works out to be about 7 homicides per million workers for the one year. Men are more likely to be victims of workplace homicide than women.

Mental Disorder

Research has found that psychosocial workplace factors are among the risk factors for a number of categories of mental disorder.

Alcohol Abuse

Workplace factors can contribute to alcohol abuse and dependence of employees. Rates of abuse can vary by occupation, with high rates in the construction and transportation industries as well as among waiters and waitresses. Within the transportation sector, heavy truck drivers and material movers were at especially high risk. A prospective study of ECA subjects who were followed one year after the initial interviews provided data on newly incident cases of alcohol abuse and dependence. The study found that workers in jobs that combined low control with high physical demands were at increased risk of developing alcohol problems although the findings were confined to men.

Depression

Using data from the ECA study, Eaton, Anthony, Mandel, and Garrison (1990) concluded that members of three occupational groups, lawyers, secretaries, and special education teachers (but not other types of teachers) showed elevated rates of *DSM-III* major depression, adjusting for social demographic factors. The ECA study involved representative samples of American adults from five U.S. geographical areas, providing relatively unbiased estimates of the risk of mental disorder by occupation; however, because the data were cross-sectional, no conclusions bearing on cause-and-effect relations are warranted. Evidence from a Canadian prospective study indicated that individuals in the highest quartile of occupational stress (high-strain jobs as per the demand-control model) are at increased risk of experiencing an episode of major depression. A meta-analysis that pooled the results of 11 well-designed longitudinal studies indicated that a number of facets of the psychosocial work environment (e.g., low decision latitude, high psychological workload, lack of social support at work, effort-reward imbalance, and job insecurity) increase the risk of common mental disorders such as depression.

Personality Disorders

Depending on the diagnosis, severity and individual, and the job itself, personality disorders can be associated with difficulty coping with work or the workplace, potentially leading to problems with others by interfering with interpersonal relationships. Indirect effects also play a role; for example, impaired educational progress or complications outside of work, such as substance abuse and co-morbid mental disorders, can plague sufferers. However, personality disorders can also bring about above-average work abilities by increasing competitive drive or causing the sufferer to exploit his or her co-workers.

Schizophrenia

In a case-control study, Link, Dohrenwend, and Skodol found that, compared to depressed and well control subjects, schizophrenic patients were more likely to have had jobs, prior to their first episode of the disorder, that exposed them to "noisesome" work characteristics (e.g., noise, humidity, heat, cold, etc.). The jobs tended to be of higher status than other blue collar jobs, suggesting that downward drift in already-affected individuals does not account for the finding. One explanation involving a diathesis-stress model suggests that the job-related stressors helped precipitate the first episode in already-vulnerable individuals. There is some supporting evidence from the Epidemiologic Catchment Area (ECA) study.

Psychological Distress

Longitudinal studies have suggested adverse working conditions can contribute to the development of psychological distress. Psychological distress refers to negative affect, without the individuals necessarily meeting criteria for a psychiatric disorder. Psychological distress is often expressed in affective (depressive), psychophysical or psychosomatic (e.g., headaches, stomach aches, etc.), and anxiety symptoms. The relation of adverse working conditions to psychological distress is thus an important avenue of research. Job satisfaction is also related to negative health outcomes.

Psychosocial Working Conditions

Parkes (1982) studied the relation of working conditions to psychological distress in British student nurses. She found that in this "natural experiment," student nurses experienced higher levels of distress and lower levels of job satisfaction in medical wards than in surgical wards; compared to surgical wards, medical wards make greater affective demands on the nurses. In another study, Frese (1985) concluded that objective working conditions give rise to subjective stress and psychosomatic symptoms in blue collar German workers. In addition to the above studies, a number of other well-controlled longitudinal studies have implicated work stressors in the development of psychological distress and reduced job satisfaction.

Unemployment

A comprehensive meta-analysis involving 86 studies indicated that involuntary job loss is linked to increased psychological distress. The impact of involuntary unemployment was comparatively weaker in countries that had greater income equality and better social safety nets. The research evidence also indicates that poorer mental health slightly, but significantly, increases the risk of later job loss.

Economic Insecurity

Some OHP research is concerned with (a) understanding the impact of economic crises on individuals' physical and mental health and well-being and (b) calling attention to personal and organizational means for ameliorating the impact of the crisis. Economic insecurity contributes, at least partly, to psychological distress and work-family conflict. Ongoing job insecurity, even in the absence of job loss, is related to higher levels of depressive symptoms, psychological distress, and worse overall health.

Work-family

Employees must balance their working lives with their home lives. Work–family conflict is a situation in which the demands of work conflict with the demands of family, making it difficult to adequately do both, giving rise to distress.

Workplace Interventions

A number of stress management interventions have emerged that have shown demonstrable effects in reducing job stress. Cognitive behavioral interventions have tended to have greatest impact on stress reduction.

Industrial Organizations

OHP interventions often concern both the health of the individual and the health of the organization. Adkins (1999) described the development of one such intervention, an organizational health center (OHC) at a California industrial complex. The OHC helped to improve both organizational and individual health as well as help workers manage job stress. Innovations included labor-management partnerships, suicide risk reduction, conflict mediation, and occupational mental health support. OHC practitioners also coordinated their services with previously underutilized local community services in the same city, thus reducing redundancy in service delivery.

Hugentobler, Israel, and Schurman (1992) detailed a different, multi-layered intervention in a mid-sized Michigan manufacturing plant. The hub of the intervention was the Stress and Wellness Committee (SWC) which solicited ideas from workers on ways to improve both their well-being and productivity. Innovations the SWC developed included improvements that ensured two-way communication between workers and management and reduction in stress resulting from diminished conflict over issues of quantity versus quality. Both the interventions described by Adkins and Hugentobler et al. had a positive impact on productivity.

OHP Research at the National Institute for Occupational Safety and Health

Currently there are efforts under way at NIOSH to help reduce the incidence of preventable disorders (e.g., sleep apnea) among heavy-truck and tractor-trailer drivers and, concomitantly, the life-threatening accidents to which the disorders lead, improve the health and safety of workers who are assigned to shift work or who work long hours, and reduce the incidence of falls among iron workers.

Military and First Responders

The Mental Health Advisory Teams of the United States Army employ OHP-related interventions with combat troops. OHP also has a role to play in interventions aimed at helping first responders.

Modestly Scaled Interventions

Schmitt (2007) described three different modestly scaled OHP-related interventions that helped workers abstain from smoking, exercise more frequently, and shed weight. Other OHP interventions include a campaign to improve the rates of hand washing, an effort to get workers to walk more often, and a drive to get employees to be more compliant with regard to taking prescribed medicines. The interventions tended reduce organization health-care costs.

Health Promotion

Organizations can play a role in the health behavior of employees by providing resources to encourage healthy behavior in areas of exercise, nutrition, and smoking cessation.

Prevention

Although the dimensions of the problem of workplace violence vary by economic sector, one sector, education, has had some limited success in introducing programmatic, psychologically-based efforts to reduce the level of violence. Research suggests that there continue to be difficulties in successfully "screening out applicants [for jobs] who may be prone to engaging in aggressive behavior," suggesting that aggression-prevention training of existing employees may be an alternative to screening. Only a small number of studies evaluating the effectiveness of training programs to reduce workplace violence currently exist.

Accidents and Safety

Psychological factors are an important factor in occupational accidents that can lead to injury and death of employees. An important influence on the incidence of accidents is the organization's safety climate that is employees' shared beliefs about how supervisors reward and support safety behavior.

Occupational Safety and Health

Occupational safety and health (OSH), also commonly referred to as occupational health and safety (OHS), occupational health, or workplace health and safety (WHS), is a multidisciplinary field concerned with the safety, health, and welfare of people at work. These terms of course also refer to the goals of this field, so their use in the sense of this article was originally an abbreviation of *occupational safety and health program/department* etc.

This painting depicts a woman examining her work on a lathe at a factory in Britain during World War II. Her eyes are not protected. Today, such practice would not be permitted in most industrialized countries that adhere to occupational health and safety standards for workers. In many countries however, such standards are still either weak or nonexistent.

The goals of occupational safety and health programs include to foster a safe and healthy work environment. OSH may also protect co-workers, family members, employers, customers, and many others who might be affected by the workplace environment. In the United States, the term occupational health and safety is referred to as occupational health and occupational and non-occupational safety and includes safety for activities outside of work.

In common-law jurisdictions, employers have a common law duty to take reasonable care of the safety of their employees. Statute law may in addition impose other general duties, introduce specific duties, and create government bodies with powers to regulate workplace safety issues: details of this vary from jurisdiction to jurisdiction.

Definition

Workers cutting marble without any protective gear, Indore, India

As defined by the World Health Organization (WHO) "occupational health deals with all aspects of health and safety in the workplace and has a strong focus on primary prevention of hazards." Health has been defined as "a state of complete physical, mental and social well-being and not merely the absence of disease or infirmity." Occupational health is a multidisciplinary field of healthcare concerned with enabling an individual to undertake their occupation, in the way that causes least harm to their health. Health has been defined as It contrasts, for example, with the promotion of health and safety at work, which is concerned with preventing harm from any incidental hazards, arising in the workplace.

Since 1950, the International Labour Organization (ILO) and the World Health Organization (WHO) have shared a common definition of occupational health. It was adopted by the Joint ILO/WHO Committee on Occupational Health at its first session in 1950 and revised at its twelfth session in 1995. The definition reads:

"The main focus in occupational health is on three different objectives: (i) the maintenance and promotion of workers' health and working capacity; (ii) the improvement of working environment and work to become conducive to safety and health and (iii) development of work organizations and working cultures in a direction which supports health and safety at work and in doing so also promotes a positive social climate and smooth operation and may enhance productivity of the undertakings. The concept of working culture is intended in this context to mean a reflection of the essential value systems adopted by the undertaking concerned. Such a culture is reflected in practice in the managerial systems, personnel policy, principles for participation, training policies and quality management of the undertaking."

—Joint ILO/WHO Committee on Occupational Health

Those in the field of occupational health come from a wide range of disciplines and professions including medicine, psychology, epidemiology, physiotherapy and rehabilitation, occupational therapy, occupational medicine, human factors and ergonomics, and many others. Professionals advise on a broad range of occupational health matters. These include how to avoid particular pre-existing conditions causing a problem in the occupation, correct posture for the work, frequency of rest breaks, preventative action that can be undertaken, and so forth.

"Occupational health should aim at: the promotion and maintenance of the highest degree of physical, mental and social well-being of workers in all occupations; the prevention amongst workers of departures from health caused by their working conditions; the protection of workers in their employment from risks resulting from factors adverse to health; the placing and maintenance of the worker in an occupational environment adapted to his physiological and psychological capabilities; and, to summarize, the adaptation of work to man and of each man to his job.

History

Harry McShane, age 16, 1908. Pulled into machinery in a factory in Cincinnati and had his arm ripped off at the shoulder and his leg broken without any compensation.

The research and regulation of occupational safety and health are a relatively recent phenomenon. As labor movements arose in response to worker concerns in the wake of the industrial revolution, worker's health entered consideration as a labor-related issue.

In the United Kingdom, the Factory Acts of the early nineteenth century (from 1802 onwards) arose out of concerns about the poor health of children working in cotton mills: the Act of 1833 created a dedicated professional Factory Inspectorate. The initial remit of the Inspectorate was to police restrictions on the working hours in the textile industry of children and young persons (introduced to prevent chronic overwork, identified as leading directly to ill-health and deformation, and indirectly to a high accident rate). However, on the urging of the Factory Inspectorate, a further Act in 1844 giving similar restrictions on working hours for women in the textile industry introduced a requirement for machinery guarding (but only in the textile industry, and only in areas that might be accessed by women or children).

In 1840 a Royal Commission published its findings on the state of conditions for the workers of the mining industry that documented the appallingly dangerous environment that they had to work in and the high frequency of accidents. The commission sparked public outrage which resulted in the Mines Act of 1842. The act set up an inspectorate for mines and collieries which resulted in many prosecutions and safety improvements, and by 1850, inspectors were able to enter and inspect premises at their discretion.

Otto von Bismarck inaugurated the first social insurance legislation in 1883 and the first worker's compensation law in 1884 – the first of their kind in the Western world. Similar acts followed in other countries, partly in response to labor unrest.

Workplace Hazards

Although work provides many economic and other benefits, a wide array of workplace hazards also present risks to the health and safety of people at work. These include but are not limited to, "chemicals, biological agents, physical factors, adverse ergonomic conditions, allergens, a complex network of safety risks," and a broad range of psychosocial risk factors. Personal protective equipment can help protect against many of these hazards.

Physical hazards affect many people in the workplace. Occupational hearing loss is the most common work-related injury in the United States, with 22 million workers exposed to hazardous noise levels at work and an estimated $242 million spent annually on worker's compensation for hearing loss disability. Falls are also a common cause of occupational injuries and fatalities, especially in construction, extraction, transportation, healthcare, and building cleaning and maintenance. Machines have moving parts, sharp edges, hot surfaces and other hazards with the potential to crush, burn, cut, shear, stab or otherwise strike or wound workers if used unsafely.

Biological hazards (biohazards) include infectious microorganisms such as viruses and toxins produced by those organisms such as anthrax. Biohazards affect workers in many industries; influenza, for example, affects a broad population of workers. Outdoor workers, including farmers, landscapers, and construction workers, risk exposure to numerous biohazards, including animal bites and stings, urushiol from poisonous plants, and diseases transmitted through animals such as the West Nile virus and Lyme disease. Health care workers, including veterinary health workers, risk exposure to blood-borne pathogens and various infectious diseases, especially those that are emerging.

Dangerous chemicals can pose a chemical hazard in the workplace. There are many classifications of hazardous chemicals, including neurotoxins, immune agents, dermatologic agents, carcinogens, reproductive toxins, systemic toxins, asthmagens, pneumoconiotic agents, and sensitizers. Authorities such as regulatory agencies set occupational exposure limits to mitigate the risk of chemical hazards. An international effort is investigating the health effects of mixtures of chemicals.

There is some evidence that certain chemicals are harmful at lower levels when mixed with one or more other chemicals. This may be particularly important in causing cancer.

Psychosocial hazards include risks to the mental and emotional well-being of workers, such as feelings of job insecurity, long work hours, and poor work-life balance. A recent Cochrane review - using moderate quality evidence - related that the addition of work-directed interventions for depressed workers receiving clinical interventions reduces the number of lost work days as compared to clinical interventions alone. This review also demonstrated that the addition of cognitive behavioral therapy to primary or occupational care and the addition of a "structured telephone outreach and care management program" to usual care are both effective at reducing sick leave days.

By Industry

Specific occupational safety and health risk factors vary depending on the specific sector and industry. Construction workers might be particularly at risk of falls, for instance, whereas fishermen might be particularly at risk of drowning. The United States Bureau of Labor Statistics identifies the fishing, aviation, lumber, metalworking, agriculture, mining and transportation industries as among some of the more dangerous for workers. Similarly psychosocial risks such as workplace violence are more pronounced for certain occupational groups such as health care employees, police, correctional officers and teachers.

Construction

Workplace safety notices at the entrance of a Chinese construction site.

Construction is one of the most dangerous occupations in the world, incurring more occupational fatalities than any other sector in both the United States and in the European Union. In 2009, the fatal occupational injury rate among construction workers in the United States was nearly three times that for all workers. Falls are one of the most common causes of fatal and non-fatal injuries among construction workers. Proper safety equipment such as harnesses and guardrails and procedures such as securing ladders and inspecting scaffolding can curtail the risk of occupational injuries in the construction industry. Due to the fact that accidents may have disastrous consequences for employees as well as organizations, it is of utmost importance to ensure health and safety of workers and compliance with HSE construction requirements. Health and safety legislation in the construction industry involves many rules and regulations. For example, the role of the Construction Design Management (CDM) Coordinator as a requirement has been aimed at improving health and safety on-site.

The 2010 National Health Interview Survey Occupational Health Supplement (NHIS-OHS) identified work organization factors and occupational psychosocial and chemical/physical exposures which may increase some health risks. Among all U.S. workers in the construction sector, 44% had non-standard work arrangements (were not regular permanent employees) compared to 19% of all U.S. workers, 15% had temporary employment compared to 7% of all U.S. workers, and 55% experienced job insecurity compared to 32% of all U.S. workers. Prevalence rates for exposure to physical/chemical hazards were especially high for the construction sector. Among nonsmoking workers, 24% of construction workers were exposed to secondhand smoke while only 10% of all U.S. workers were exposed. Other physical/chemical hazards with high prevalence rates in the construction industry were frequently working outdoors (73%) and frequent exposure to vapors, gas, dust, or fumes (51%).

Agriculture

Rollover protection bar on a Fordson tractor.

Agriculture workers are often at risk of work-related injuries, lung disease, noise-induced hearing loss, skin disease, as well as certain cancers related to chemical use or prolonged sun exposure. On industrialized farms, injuries frequently involve the use of agricultural machinery. The most common cause of fatal agricultural injuries in the United States is tractor rollovers, which can be prevented by the use of roll over protection structures which limit the risk of injury in case a tractor rolls over. Pesticides and other chemicals used in farming can also be hazardous to worker health, and workers exposed to pesticides may experience illnesses or birth defects. As an industry in which families, including children, commonly work alongside their families, agriculture is a common source of occupational injuries and illnesses among younger workers. Common causes of fatal injuries among young farm worker include drowning, machinery and motor vehicle-related accidents.

The 2010 NHIS-OHS found elevated prevalence rates of several occupational exposures in the agriculture, forestry, and fishing sector which may negatively impact health. These workers often worked long hours. The prevalence rate of working more than 48 hours a week among workers employed in these industries was 37%, and 24% worked more than 60 hours a week. Of all workers in these industries, 85% frequently worked outdoors compared to 25% of all U.S. workers. Additionally, 53% were frequently exposed to vapors, gas, dust, or fumes, compared to 25% of all U.S. workers.

Service Sector

As the number of service sector jobs has risen in developed countries, more and more jobs have become sedentary, presenting a different array of health problems than those associated with manufacturing and the primary sector. Contemporary problems such as the growing rate of obesity and issues relating to occupational stress, workplace bullying, and overwork in many countries have further complicated the interaction between work and health.

According to data from the 2010 NHIS-OHS, hazardous physical/chemical exposures in the service sector were lower than national averages. On the other hand, potentially harmful work organization characteristics and psychosocial workplace exposures were relatively common in this sector. Among all workers in the service industry, 30% experienced job insecurity in 2010, 27% worked non-standard shifts (not a regular day shift), 21% had non-standard work arrangements (were not regular permanent employees).

Mining and Oil & Gas Extraction

According to data from the 2010 NHIS-OHS, workers employed in mining and oil and gas extraction industries had high prevalence rates of exposure to potentially harmful work organization characteristics and hazardous chemicals. Many of these workers worked long hours: 50% worked more than 48 hours a week and 25% worked more than 60 hours a week in 2010. Additionally, 42% worked non-standard shifts (not a regular day shift). These workers also had high prevalence of exposure to physical/chemical hazards. In 2010, 39% had frequent skin contact with chemicals. Among nonsmoking workers, 28% of those in mining and oil and gas extraction industries had frequent exposure to secondhand smoke at work. About two-thirds were frequently exposed to vapors, gas, dust, or fumes at work.

Healthcare and Social Assistance

Beekeepers often wear protective clothing, for OHS reasons

Healthcare workers are exposed to many hazards that can adversely affect their health and well-being. Long hours, changing shifts, physically demanding tasks, violence, and exposures to infectious diseases and harmful chemicals are examples of hazards that put these workers at risk for illness and injury.

According to the Bureau of Labor statistics, U.S. hospitals recorded 253,700 work-related injuries and illnesses in 2011, which is 6.8 work-related injuries and illnesses for every 100 full-time employees. The injury and illness rate in hospitals is higher than the rates in construction and manufacturing – two industries that are traditionally thought to be relatively hazardous.

The Occupational Health Safety Network (OHSN) is a secure electronic surveillance system developed by the National Institute for Occupational Safety and Health (NIOSH) to address health and safety risks among health care personnel. OHSN uses existing data to characterize risk of injury and illness among health care workers. Hospitals and other healthcare facilities can upload the occupational injury data they already collect to the secure database for analysis and benchmarking with other de-identified facilities. NIOSH works with OHSN participants in identifying and implementing timely and targeted interventions. OHSN modules currently focus on three high risk and preventable events that can lead to injuries or musculoskeletal disorders among healthcare personnel: musculoskeletal injuries from patient handling activities; slips, trips, and falls; and workplace violence. OHSN enrollment is open to all healthcare facilities.

Workplace Fatality and Injury Statistics

United States

The Bureau of Labor Statistics of the United States Department of Labor compiles information about workplace fatalities and non-fatal injuries in the United States. In 1970, an estimated 14,000 workers were killed on the job – by 2010, the workforce had doubled, but workplace deaths were down to about 4,500. Between 1913 and 2013, workplace fatalities dropped by approximately 80%.

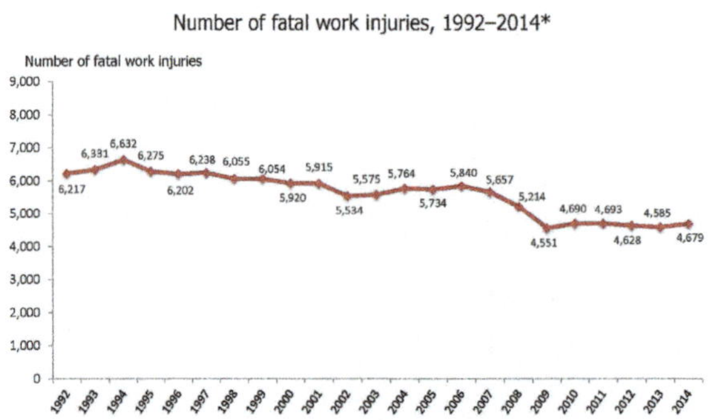

Number of occupational fatal work injuries in the U.S. from 1992 until 2014. Note, 2001 statistics do not include death related to the September 11 terrorist attacks.

The Bureau also compiles information about the most dangerous jobs. According to the census of occupational injuries 4,679 people died on the job in 2014.

Job	Fatalities	Fatalities per 100,000 employees
Fishermen	22	80.8
Pilots	81	63.2

Job	Fatalities	Fatalities per 100,000 employees
Timber cutter	77	109.5
Structural metal workers	15	25.2
Waste collectors	27	35.8
Farmers and ranchers	263	26.0
Power-line workers	25	19.2
Construction workers and miners	130	17.9
Roofers	81	46.2
Truck drivers and other drivers	835	23.4
All occupations	**4,679**	**3.3**

2014 employer-reported injuries and illnesses		
Industry	**Rate per 100 full-time employees**	**Number**
Agriculture, forestry, fishing and hunting	5.5	52,400
Mining, quarrying, and oil and gas extraction	2.0	17,900
Construction (private)	3.6	200,900
Manufacturing	4.0	483,300
Wholesale trade	2.9	163,100
Retail trade	3.6	416,100
Transportation and warehousing (private)	4.8	201,500
Utilities (private)	2.4	13,400
Information	1.4	35,300
Finance and insurance	0.7	34,800
Real estate, rental, and leasing	2.9	51,100
Professional, scientific, and technical services	0.9	69,900
Management of companies and enterprises	1.0	21,100
Administrative and support services	2.4	109,300
Waste management and remediation services (private)	5.1	19,900
Educational services (private)	2.1	38,500
Health care and social assistance (private)	4.5	612,500
Leisure and hospitality	3.6	337,500
State government: Education	4.1	31,100
State government: Health care and social assistance	8.1	43,800
State government: Justice, public order, and safety activities	6.1	43,200
Local government: Construction	8.6	8,700
Local government: Transportation and warehousing	7.5	17,900
Local government: Utilities	5.4	12,200
Local government: Education	4.1	225,100
Local government: Health care and social assistance	5.6	41,000
Local government: Justice, public order, and safety activities	9.5	84,200
All industries including state and local government	**3.4**	**3,675,800**

Cause of injury and illness	2014 rate per 10,000 full-time employees
Contact with objects	23.8
Fall to lower level	5.4
Fall on same level	18.8
Slips or trips without fall	4.4
Over-exertion in lifting/lowering	11.0
Repetitive motion	2.7
Exposure to harmful substances or environments	4.3
Transportation incidents	5.8
Fires and explosions	0.2
Violence and other injuries by person or animal	6.8
Total	**107.1**

Musculoskeletal injuries accounted for 32% of all employer-reported injuries and illnesses in 2014.

European Union

In most countries males comprise the vast majority of workplace fatalities. In the EU as a whole, 94% of death were of males. In the UK the disparity was even greater with males comprising 97.4% of workplace deaths. In the UK there were 171 fatal injuries at work in financial year 2011–2012, compared with 651 in calendar year 1974; the fatal injury rate declined over that period from 2.9 fatalities per 100,000 workers to 0.6 per 100,000 workers.

Management Systems

International

In 2001, the International Labour Organization (ILO) published ILO-OSH 2001, also titled "Guidelines a on occupational safety and health management systems" to assist organizations with introducing OSH management systems. These guidelines encourage continual improvement in employee health and safety, achieved via a constant process of policy, organization, planning & implementation, evaluation, and action for improvement, all supported by constant auditing to determine the success of OSH actions.

The ILO management system was created to assist employers to keep pace with rapidly shifting and competitive industrial environments. The ILO recognizes that national legislation is essential, but sometimes insufficient on its own to address the challenges faced by industry, and therefore elected to ensure free and open distribution of administrative tools in the form of occupational health and safety management system guidance for everyone. This open access forum is intended to provide the tools for industry to create safe and healthy working environments and foster positive safety cultures within the organizations.

OHSAS 18000 is an international occupational health and safety management system specification developed by the London-based BSI Group, a multinational business chiefly concerned with the production and distribution of standards related services. OHSAS 18000 comprises two parts,

OHSAS 18001 and 18002 and embraces a number of other publications. OHSAS 18000 is the internationally recognized assessment specification for occupational health and safety management systems. It was developed by a selection of leading trade bodies, international standards and certification bodies to address a gap where no third-party certifiable international standard exists. This internationally recognized specification for occupational health and safety management system operates on the basis of policy, planning, implementation and operation, checking and corrective action, management review, and continual improvement.

The British Standards – Occupational Health and Safety management Systems Requirements Standard BS OHSAS 18001 was developed within the framework of the ISO standards series. Allowing it to integrate better into the larger system of ISO certifications. ISO 9001 Quality Management Systems and ISO 14001 Environmental Management System can work in tandem with BS OHSAS 18001/18002 to complement each other and form a better overall system. Each component of the system is specific, auditable, and accreditable by a third party after review.

Also Standards Australia and the Association Française de Normalisation (AFNOR) in France have developed occupational safety and health management standards.

United Kingdom

Guidance note HSG65: Successful Health and Safety Management, published by the British non-departmental public body Health and Safety Executive, was substantially re-written 2013. It now promotes the Plan Do Check Act approach to health and safety management, sharing similarities with BS OHSAS 18001. This achieved a balance between the original systems-based approach, and the more modern behavioural approach to safety management.

National legislation and public organizations

Occupational safety and health practice vary among nations with different approaches to legislation, regulation, enforcement, and incentives for compliance. In the EU, for example, some member states promote OSH by providing public monies as subsidies, grants or financing, while others have created tax system incentives for OSH investments. A third group of EU member states has experimented with using workplace accident insurance premium discounts for companies or organisations with strong OSH records.

Australia

In Australia, the Commonwealth, four of the six states and both territories have enacted and administer harmonised Work Health and Safety Legislation in accordance with the *Intergovernmental Agreement for Regulatory and Operational Reform in Occupational Health and Safety*. Each of these jurisdictions has enacted Work Health & Safety legislation and regulations based on the Commonwealth Work Health and Safety Act 2011 and common Codes of Practice developed by Safe Work Australia. Some jurisdictions have also included mine safety under the model approach, however, most have retained separate legislation for the time being. Western Australia intends to adopt a moderated version of the model approach and Victoria has retained its own regime, although the Model WHS laws themselves drew heavily on the Victoria approach.

Canada

In Canada, workers are covered by provincial or federal labour codes depending on the sector in which they work. Workers covered by federal legislation (including those in mining, transportation, and federal employment) are covered by the Canada Labour Code; all other workers are covered by the health and safety legislation of the province in which they work. The Canadian Centre for Occupational Health and Safety (CCOHS), an agency of the Government of Canada, was created in 1966 by an Act of Parliament. The act was based on the belief that all Canadians had "...a fundamental right to a healthy and safe working environment." CCOHS is mandated to promote safe and healthy workplaces to help prevent work-related injuries and illnesses. The CCOHS maintains a useful (partial) list of OSH regulations for Canada and its provinces.

European Union

Number of full-time OSH inspectors per 100,000 full-time employees	
Italy	17.7
Finland	17.5
Denmark	11.9
United Kingdom	11.1
Norway	10.6
Sweden	10
Belgium	5.3
Netherlands	4.8
Ireland	4.5
Greece	4.1
France	3.5
Spain	2.1

In the European Union, member states have enforcing authorities to ensure that the basic legal requirements relating to occupational health and safety are met. In many EU countries, there is strong cooperation between employer and worker organisations (e.g. unions) to ensure good OSH performance as it is recognized this has benefits for both the worker (through maintenance of health) and the enterprise (through improved productivity and quality). In 1996, the European Agency for Safety and Health at Work was founded.

Member states of the European Union have all transposed into their national legislation a series of directives that establish minimum standards on occupational health and safety. These directives (of which there are about 20 on a variety of topics) follow a similar structure requiring the employer to assess the workplace risks and put in place preventive measures based on a hierarchy of control. This hierarchy starts with elimination of the hazard and ends with personal protective equipment.

However, certain EU member states admit to having lacking quality control in occupational safety services, to situations in which risk analysis takes place without any on-site workplace visits and to insufficient implementation of certain EU OSH directives. Based on this, it is hardly surprising that the total societal costs of work-related health problems and accidents vary from 2.6% to 3.8% of GNP between the EU member states.

Denmark

In Denmark, occupational safety and health is regulated by the Danish Act on Working Environment and cooperation at the workplace. The Danish Working Environment Authority carries out inspections of companies, draws up more detailed rules on health and safety at work and provides information on health and safety at work. The result of each inspection is made public on the web pages of the Danish Working Environment Authority so that the general public, current and prospective employees, customers and other stakeholders can inform themselves about whether a given organization has passed the inspection, should they wish to do so.

Spain

In Spain, occupational safety and health is regulated by the Spanish Act on Prevention of Labour Risks. The Ministry of Employment and Social Security is the authority responsible for issues relating to labour environment. The National Institute for Labour Safety and Hygiene is the technical public Organization specialized in occupational safety and health.

Sweden

In Sweden, occupational safety and health is regulated by the Work Environment Act. The Swedish Work Environment Authority is the government agency responsible for issues relating to the working environment. The agency should work to disseminate information and furnish advice on OSH, has a mandate to carry out inspections, and a right to issue stipulations and injunctions to any non-compliant employer.

United Kingdom

In the UK, health and safety legislation is drawn up and enforced by the Health and Safety Executive and local authorities (the local council) under the Health and Safety at Work etc. Act 1974 (HASAWA). HASAWA introduced a general duty on an employer to ensure, so far as is reasonably practicable, the health, safety and welfare at work of all his employees; with the intention of giving a legal framework supporting 'codes of practice' not in themselves having legal force but establishing a strong presumption as to what was reasonably practicable (deviations from them could be justified by appropriate risk assessment). The previous reliance on detailed prescriptive rule-setting was seen as having failed to respond rapidly enough to technological change, leaving new technologies potentially un-regulated or inappropriately regulated. HSE has continued to make some regulations giving absolute duties (where something must be done with no 'reasonable practicability' test) but in the UK the regulatory trend is away from prescriptive rules, and towards 'goal setting' and risk assessment. Recent major changes to the laws governing asbestos and fire safety management embrace the concept of risk assessment. The other key aspect of the UK legislation is a statutory mechanism for worker involvement through elected health and safety representatives and health and safety committees. This followed a similar approach in Scandinavia, and that approach has since been adopted in Australia, Canada, New Zealand and Malaysia, for example.

For the UK, the government organisation dealing with occupational health has been the Employment Medical Advisory Service but in 2014 a new occupational health organisation - the Health and Work Service - was created to provide advice and assistance to employers in order to get back to work employees on long-term sick-leave. The service, funded by government, will offer medical assessments and treatment plans, on a voluntary basis, to people on long-term absence from their employer; in return, the government will no longer foot the bill for Statutory Sick Pay provided by the employer to the individual.

India

In India, the Labour Ministry formulates national policies on occupational safety and health in factories and docks with advice and assistance from Directorate General of Factory Advice Service and Labour Institutes (DGFASLI), and enforces its Policies through inspectorates of factories and inspectorates of dock safety. DGFASLI is the technical arm of the Ministry of Labour & Employment, Government of India and advises the factories on various problems concerning safety, health, efficiency and well - being of the persons at work places. The DGFASLI provides technical support in formulating rules, conducting occupational safety surveys and also for conducting occupational safety training programs.

Malaysia

In Malaysia, the Department of Occupational Safety and Health (DOSH) under the Ministry of Human Resource is responsible to ensure that the safety, health and welfare of workers in both the public and private sector is upheld. DOSH is responsible to enforce the Factories and Machinery Act 1967 and the Occupational Safety and Health Act 1994.

People's Republic of China

Hardware stores in China specializing in safety equipment

In the People's Republic of China, the Ministry of Health is responsible for occupational disease prevention and the State Administration of Work Safety for safety issues at work. On the provincial and municipal level, there are Health Supervisions for occupational health and local bureaus of Work Safety for safety. The "Occupational Disease Control Act of PRC" came into force on May 1, 2002. and Work safety Act of PRC on November 1, 2002. The Occupational Disease Control Act is under revision. The prevention of occupational disease is still in its initial stage compared with industrialised countries such as the US or UK.

Singapore

In Singapore, the Ministry of Manpower operates various checks and campaigns against unsafe work practices, such as when working at height, operating cranes and in traffic management. Examples include Operation Cormorant and the Falls Prevention Campaign.

South Africa

In South Africa the Department of Labour is responsible for occupational health and safety inspection and enforcement in commerce and industry apart from mining and energy production, where the Department of Mineral Resources is responsible.

The main statutory legislation on Health and Safety in the jurisdiction of the Department of Labour is *Act No. 85 of 1993: Occupational Health and Safety Act as amended by Occupational Health and Safety Amendment Act, No. 181 Of 1993.*

Regulations to the OHS Act include:

- *General Administrative Regulations, 2003*
- *Certificate of Competency Regulations, 1990*
- *Construction Regulations, 2003*
- *Diving Regulations 2009*
- *Driven Machinery Regulations, 1988*
- *Environmental Regulations for Workplaces, 1987*
- *General Machinery regulations, 1988*
- *General Safety Regulations, 1986*
- *Noise induced hearing loss regulations, 2003*
- *Pressure Equipment Regulations, 2004*

Taiwan

In Taiwan, the Occupational Safety and Health Administration of the Ministry of Labor is in charge of occupational safety and health. The matter is governed under the Occupational Safety and Health Act.

2007, official release the document TOSHMS (Taiwan Occupational Safety and Health Management System),which defined the basic rule about occupational safety standard.

United States

In the United States, President Richard Nixon signed the Occupational Safety and Health Act into law on December 29, 1970. The act created the three agencies that administer it. They include the Occupational Safety and Health Administration, National Institute for Occupational Safety and Health, and the Occupational Safety and Health Review Commission. The act authorized the Occupational Safety and Health Administration (OSHA) to regulate private employers in the 50 states, the District of Columbia, and territories. The Act establishing it includes a general duty clause (29 U.S.C. § 654, 5(a)) requiring an employer to comply with the Act and regulations derived from it, and to provide employees with "employment and a place of employment which are free from recognized hazards that are causing or are likely to cause death or serious physical harm to his employees."

OSHA was established in 1971 under the Department of Labor. It has headquarters in Washington, DC and ten regional offices, further broken down into districts, each organized into three sections; compliance, training, and assistance. Its stated mission is *to assure safe and healthful working conditions for working men and women by setting and enforcing standards and by providing training, outreach, education and assistance.* The original plan was for OSHA to oversee 50 state plans with OSHA funding 50% of each plan. Unfortunately it has not worked out that way. There are currently 26 approved state plans (4 cover only public employees) and no other states want to participate. OSHA manages the plan in the states not participating.

OSHA develops safety standards in the Code of Federal Regulation and enforces those safety standards through compliance inspections conducted by Compliance Officers; enforcement resources are focussed on high-hazard industries. Worksites may apply to enter OSHA's Voluntary Protection Program (VPP); a successful application leads to an on-site inspection ; if this is passed the site gains VPP status and OSHA no longer inspect it annually nor (normally) visit it unless there is a fatal accident or an employee complaint until VPP revalidation (after 3–5 years)(VPP sites have injury and illness rates less than half the average for their industry).

It has 73 specialists in local offices to provide tailored information and training to employers and employees at little or no cost Similarly OSHA produces a range of publications, provides advice to employers and funds consultation services available for small businesses.

OSHA's Alliance Program enables groups committed to worker safety and health to work with it to develop compliance assistance tools and resources, share information with workers and employers, and educate them about their rights and responsibilities. OSHA also has a Strategic Partnership Program that zeros in on specific hazards or specific geographic areas. OSHA manages Susan B. Harwood grants to nonprofit companies to train workers and employers to recognize, avoid, and prevent safety and health hazards in the workplace. Grants focus on small business, hard-to-reach workers and high-hazard industries.

The National Institute for Occupational Safety and Health, created under the same act, works closely with OSHA and provides the research behind many of OSHA's regulations and standards.

Professional Roles and Responsibilities

The roles and responsibilities of OSH professionals vary regionally, but may include evaluating working environments, developing, endorsing and encouraging measures that might prevent injuries and illnesses, providing OSH information to employers, employees, and the public, providing medical examinations, and assessing the success of worker health programs.

Europe

In Norway, the main required tasks of an occupational health and safety practitioner include the following:

- Systematic evaluations of the working environment
- Endorsing preventative measures which eliminate causes of illnesses in the workplace
- Providing information on the subject of employees' health
- Providing information on occupational hygiene, ergonomics, and environmental and safety risks in the workplace

In the Netherlands, the required tasks for health and safety staff are only summarily defined and include the following:

- Providing voluntary medical examinations
- Providing a consulting room on the work environment to the workers
- Providing health assessments (if needed for the job concerned)

'The main influence of the Dutch law on the job of the safety professional is through the requirement on each employer to use the services of a certified working conditions service to advise them on health and safety'. A 'certified service' must employ sufficient numbers of four types of certified experts to cover the risks in the organisations which use the service:

- A safety professional
- An occupational hygienist
- An occupational physician
- A work and organisation specialist.

In 2004, 37% of health and safety practitioners in Norway and 14% in the Netherlands had an MSc; 44% had a BSc in Norway and 63% in the Netherlands; and 19% had training as an OSH technician in Norway and 23% in the Netherlands.

US

The main tasks undertaken by the OHS practitioner in the US include:

- Develop processes, procedures, criteria, requirements, and methods to attain the best possible management of the hazards and exposures that can cause injury to people, and damage property, or the environment;
- Apply good business practices and economic principles for efficient use of resources to add to the importance of the safety processes;

- Promote other members of the company to contribute by exchanging ideas and other different approaches to make sure that every one in the corporation possess OHS knowledge and have functional roles in the development and execution of safety procedures;
- Assess services, outcomes, methods, equipment, workstations, and procedures by using qualitative and quantitative methods to recognise the hazards and measure the related risks;
- Examine all possibilities, effectiveness, reliability, and expenditure to attain the best results for the company concerned

Leather craftsman gloves, safety goggles, and a properly fitted hardhat are crucial for proper safety in a construction environment.

Knowledge required by the OHS professional in the US include:

- Constitutional and case law controlling safety, health, and the environment
- Operational procedures to plan/develop safe work practices
- Safety, health and environmental sciences
- Design of hazard control systems (i.e. fall protection, scaffoldings)
- Design of recordkeeping systems that take collection into account, as well as storage, interpretation, and dissemination
- Mathematics and statistics
- Processes and systems for attaining safety through design

Some skills required by the OHS professional in the US include (but are not limited to):

- Understanding and relating to systems, policies and rules
- Holding checks and having control methods for possible hazardous exposures
- Mathematical and statistical analysis

- Examining manufacturing hazards
- Planning safe work practices for systems, facilities, and equipment
- Understanding and using safety, health, and environmental science information for the improvement of procedures
- Interpersonal communication skills

Differences between Countries and Regions

Because different countries take different approaches to ensuring occupational safety and health, areas of OSH need and focus also vary between countries and regions. Similar to the findings of the ENHSPO survey conducted in Australia, the Institute of Occupational Medicine in the UK found that there is a need to put greater emphasis on work-related illness in the UK. In contrast, in Australia and the US, a major responsibility of the OHS professional is to keep company directors and managers aware of the issues that they face in regards to occupational health and safety principles and legislation. However, in some other areas of Europe, it is precisely this which has been lacking: "Nearly half of senior managers and company directors do not have an up-to-date understanding of their health and safety-related duties and responsibilities."

Identifying Safety and Health Hazards

Hazards, Risks, Outcomes

The terminology used in OSH varies between countries, but generally speaking:

- A hazard is something that can cause harm if not controlled.
- The outcome is the harm that results from an uncontrolled hazard.
- A risk is a combination of the probability that a particular outcome will occur and the severity of the harm involved.

"Hazard", "risk", and "outcome" are used in other fields to describe e.g. environmental damage, or damage to equipment. However, in the context of OSH, "harm" generally describes the direct or indirect degradation, temporary or permanent, of the physical, mental, or social well-being of workers. For example, repetitively carrying out manual handling of heavy objects is a hazard. The outcome could be a musculoskeletal disorder (MSD) or an acute back or joint injury. The risk can be expressed numerically (e.g. a 0.5 or 50/50 chance of the outcome occurring during a year), in relative terms (e.g. "high/medium/low"), or with a multi-dimensional classification scheme (e.g. situation-specific risks).

Hazard Identification

Hazard identification or assessment is an important step in the overall risk assessment and risk management process. It is where individual work hazards are identified, assessed and controlled/ eliminated as close to source (location of the hazard) as reasonably as possible. As technology, resources, social expectation or regulatory requirements change, hazard analysis focuses controls more closely toward the source of the hazard. Thus hazard control is a dynamic program of prevention. Hazard-based programs also have the advantage of not assigning or implying there are "acceptable risks" in the workplace. A hazard-based program may not be able to eliminate all risks, but neither does it accept "satisfactory" – but still risky – outcomes. And as those who calculate and manage the risk are usually managers while those exposed to the risks are a different group, workers, a hazard-based approach can by-pass conflict inherent in a risk-based approach.

The information that needs to be gathered from sources should apply to the specific type of work from which the hazards can come from. As mentioned previously, examples of these sources include interviews with people who have worked in the field of the hazard, history and analysis of past incidents, and official reports of work and the hazards encountered. Of these, the personnel interviews may be the most critical in identifying undocumented practices, events, releases, hazards and other relevant information. Once the information is gathered from a collection of sources, it is recommended for these to be digitally archived (to allow for quick searching) and to have a physical set of the same information in order for it to be more accessible. One innovative way to display the complex historical hazard information is with a historical hazards identification map, which distills the hazard information into an easy to use graphical format.

Risk Assessment

Modern occupational safety and health legislation usually demands that a risk assessment be carried out prior to making an intervention. It should be kept in mind that risk management requires risk to be managed to a level which is as low as is reasonably practical.

This assessment should:

- Identify the hazards
- Identify all affected by the hazard and how
- Evaluate the risk
- Identify and prioritize appropriate control measures

The calculation of risk is based on the likelihood or probability of the harm being realized and the severity of the consequences. This can be expressed mathematically as a quantitative assessment (by assigning low, medium and high likelihood and severity with integers and multiplying them to obtain a risk factor), or qualitatively as a description of the circumstances by which the harm could arise.

The assessment should be recorded and reviewed periodically and whenever there is a significant change to work practices. The assessment should include practical recommendations to control the risk. Once recommended controls are implemented, the risk should be re-calculated to determine if it has been lowered to an acceptable level. Generally speaking, newly introduced controls should lower risk by one level, i.e., from high to medium or from medium to low.

Contemporary Developments

On an international scale, the World Health Organization (WHO) and the International Labour

Organization (ILO) have begun focusing on labour environments in developing nations with projects such as Healthy Cities. Many of these developing countries are stuck in a situation in which their relative lack of resources to invest in OSH leads to increased costs due to work-related illnesses and accidents. As a 2007 Factsheet from the European Agency for Safety and Health at Work states: "Countries with less developed OSH systems spend a far higher percentage of GDP on work-related injury and illness – taking resources away from more productive activities ... The ILO estimates that work-related illness and accidents cost up to 10% of GDP in Latin America, compared with just 2.6% to 3.8% in the EU." There is continued use of asbestos, a notorious hazard, in some developing countries. So asbestos-related disease is, sadly, expected to continue to be a significant problem well into the future.

Nanotechnology

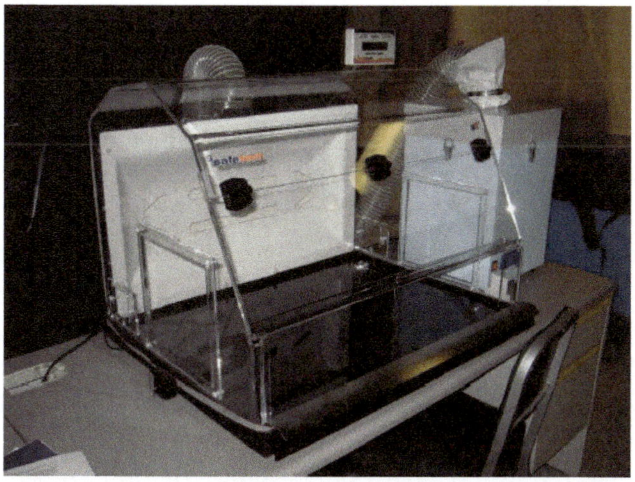

A nanomaterial containment hood, an example of an engineering control used to protect workers handling them on a regular basis.

Nanotechnology is an example of a new, relatively unstudied technology. A Swiss survey of one hundred thirty eight companies using or producing nanoparticulate matter in 2006 resulted in forty completed questionnaires. Sixty five per cent of respondent companies stated they did not have a formal risk assessment process for dealing with nanoparticulate matter. Nanotechnology already presents new issues for OSH professionals that will only become more difficult as nanostructures become more complex. The size of the particles renders most containment and personal protective equipment ineffective. The toxicology values for macro sized industrial substances are rendered inaccurate due to the unique nature of nanoparticulate matter. As nanoparticulate matter decreases in size its relative surface area increases dramatically, increasing any catalytic effect or chemical reactivity substantially versus the known value for the macro substance. This presents a new set of challenges in the near future to rethink contemporary measures to safeguard the health and welfare of employees against a nanoparticulate substance that most conventional controls have not been designed to manage.

Occupational Health Disparities

Occupational health disparities refer to differences in occupational injuries and illnesses that are closely linked with demographic, social, cultural, economic, and/or political factors.

Education

There are multiple levels of training applicable to the field of occupational safety and health (OSH). Programs range from individual non-credit certificates, focusing on specific areas of concern, to full doctoral programs. The University of Southern California was one of the first schools in the US to offer a Ph.D. program focusing on the field. Further, multiple master's degree programs exist, such as that of the Indiana State University who offer a master of science (MS) and a master of arts (MA) in OSH. Graduate programs are designed to train educators, as well as, high-level practitioners. Many OSH generalists focus on undergraduate studies; programs within schools, such as that of the University of North Carolina's online Bachelor of Science in Environmental Health and Safety, fill a large majority of hygienist needs. However, smaller companies often don't have full-time safety specialists on staff, thus, they appoint a current employee to the responsibility. Individuals finding themselves in positions such as these, or for those enhancing marketability in the job-search and promotion arena, may seek out a credit certificate program. For example, the University of Connecticut's online OSH Certificate, provides students familiarity with overarching concepts through a 15-credit (5-course) program. Programs such as these are often adequate tools in building a strong educational platform for new safety managers with a minimal outlay of time and money. Further, most hygienists seek certification by organizations which train in specific areas of concentration, focusing on isolated workplace hazards. The American Society for Safety Engineers (ASSE), American Board of Industrial Hygiene (ABIH), and American Industrial Hygiene Association (AIHA) offer individual certificates on many different subjects from forklift operation to waste disposal and are the chief facilitators of continuing education in the OSH sector. In the U.S. the training of safety professionals is supported by National Institute for Occupational Safety and Health through their NIOSH Education and Research Centers. In Australia, training in OSH is available at the vocational education and training level, and at university undergraduate and postgraduate level. Such university courses may be accredited by an Accreditation Board of the Safety Institute of Australia. The Institute has produced a Body of Knowledge which it considers is required by a generalist safety and health professional, and offers a professional qualification based on a four-step assessment.

World Day for Safety and Health at Work

On April 28 The International Labour Organisation celebrates "World Day for Safety and Health" to raise awareness of safety in the workplace. Occurring annually since 2003, each year it focuses on a specific area and bases a campaign around the theme.

Aspects of Occupational Health

Physical Aspects

Physical aspects of the environment concern exposure to toxins, hazardous conditions and other risks that the employee is exposed to as part of his/her job. Repeated exposure increases the chances of disease, injury and mortality. In India, with gross under reporting the annual estimated occupational fatalities are 36,700, occupational injuries are 18,300 and occupational diseases are 1,850,000 (Brecker, 2010). Only 10% of approximately 500 million workers have health coverage. Poor access to health care compounded by poor base levels of health due to poverty increase the vulnerability of workers to hazards at the work place.

In a review of occupational health in India, Agnihotram (2005) has reviewed the incidence of morbidity in various industries, which are briefly reviewed in this section.

In Agriculture which is a major occupational category in India, hazards include exposure to extreme weather, working in water in the paddy fields, crouching posture for women in the fields, organic dust during threshing, exposure to fertilizer and pesticide and injuries from machines. Some of the effects of these conditions result in dermatitis on the arms and legs, chronic backache, chronic respiratory ailments from inhaling dust from threshing, neurological damage from exposure to toxins in fertilizer and pesticide and injuries from machinery that result from lack of training.

There are a very high number of child agricultural labourers in India estimated at more than 10 million who suffer from chemical exposure, heat induced ailments, insect bites and mechanical injuries.

Carpet Weaving is another industry that employs children who indicate acute respiratory problems as compared with other children, from the fibre dust inhaled and the kneeling posture and long hours of work . Adults in this industry also report chronic respiratory ailments.

The Textile Industry which employs 20 million workers in India, has a high incidence of bysinosis – an asthma like chronic condition characterized by coughing and wheezing and tightening of the chest. The incidence of bysinosis was officially recorded for the first time in 1995 in India in the 150 year history of the industry. Bysinosis is aggravated by smoking.

Fireworks and Incense Making also employ child labour. The hazards of inhaling chlorate dust result in asthma, respiratory problems, eye infections, dizziness.

In Beedi making and the Tobacco industry, workers were found to have elevated levels of nicotine in the urine.

Most industrial units have poor industrial hygiene and safety standards and the workers health and safety are not a priority for the employers. Many workers have chronic respiratory problems and some have asbestosis and silicosis and these conditions are exacerbated by smoking and tobacco use. Industrial hygiene refers to improving working conditions such as reducing airborne particulate matter (dust) that can be inhaled by using filters, regular cleaning and maintenance of machines, changing filters regularly and maintaining general hygiene at the shop floor or factory or foundry. Other stressors are noise, odors, lack of ventilation, poorly maintained bathrooms, lack of a place to eat and in some cases even access to drinking water. The feeling that the white collar workers are shielded from these inconveniences whereas the blue collar workers needs go unnoticed causes resentment. Employees should be provided with masks and other appropriate protective equipment and safety standards must be followed strictly and enforced by the management. The general attitude in India and in some developing countries is that these precautions are unnecessary and what is to happen will happen and that workers lives are not so valuable.

Other hazardous jobs are in mines, ship breaking yards and waste processing including e waste.

Health care workers are also exposed to infection and are especially at risk in government hospitals where they are overworked and see a large number of patients. Hygiene protocols are not standardized and strictly adhered to.

Two readings will discuss the exposure to toxins that workers face as part of their jobs.

Sociological Aspects

The high level of income inequality translates into inadequate pay for workers and labourers that is often not enough to meet the basic needs of their family. This results in a situation of chronic poverty for the mass of laborers and workers.Pervasive poverty renders people powerless and ensures a continuous supply of labour at very low wages and submission to any conditions and hazards.

Social status of jobs and perceived status of jobs contributes to satisfaction and well being. Certain jobs are considered inferior and people in those positions consider themselves powerless and at the mercy of the employers. In India this situation is exacerbated due to the caste system which had hereditary occupations. In India in some parts there are people who still carry human waste and dry latrines still exist. Dry latrines exist because there are people to carry the waste and they are always of a certain caste.

India ranks very low in terms of women's participation in economic activity. Gender disparity in income is universal but in India it is wider. The intersection of caste and gender results in the most oppressed groups (women who carry human waste, women who are forced into the sex trade as a religious ritual).

A situation characterized by a vast informal sector (casual labour who have no bargaining power) weak trade unions and poor industrial regulations results in the oppression and exploitation of workers.

In most developing countries such as India the strong profit motive of the industrial sector leads them to turn a blind eye to many safety regulations and standards that merely exist on paper but not in actuality. Many polluting and high risk industries are relocating to developing countries such as India from developed countries because of environmental concerns and pressure from their unions.

The current law on workers compensation stipulates a minimum payment of Rs 50, 000 to Rs 3 lacs in the case of loss of life and Rs 60,000 for disability. The compensation amount depends on the pay grade of the workman and the time period for which he has worked (Kanhere, 2005). This is rather a paltry sum and places at a disadvantage younger, newer and lower level workers whose families paradoxically would need more support

Poor Training in skills and low education levels for workers increases the risk of accidents and injuries. Poor surveillance data - regarding accidents and fatalities and morbidities at the work place is available. For private firms and in the informal sector minimal data is available.When surveillance data is not available, then the pattern of injuries and its correspondence to high risk jobs and companies cannot be identified.

Psychological Aspects

The psychological aspects that have been researched are job demands and perceived control of the employee. Job roles, stress and relationships at the work place compose another section of study.

Karasek's (1979) demand – control model highlight these two elements as crucial for job satisfaction. Role demand had to do with working at a fast pace or intensively or having conflicting demands. Control or decision latitude is concerned with decision authority and skill discretion. Decision authority is the extent to which the employee can decide the pace, the methods, order of the work, when to take breaks and have control over other more meaningful aspects of the work. Skill discretion is concerned with the scope to learn new skills, have a wide variety of tasks and opportunity to improve oneself. The interaction of high role demand and low control impacts on mental health (Mausner-Dorsch and Eaton, 2000) immune functioning (Meijman et al, 1995) and physical health (Sacker et al, 2001, as cited in Kenyon, 2008).

- Warr (1994) proposed a list of environmental foundations for health at work.
- Decision latitude – optimal level of control is necessary for well being and helps to moderate strain.
- Skill use – the extent to which the employee perceives that skills are being used appropriately is related to job satisfaction. Job strain may lead to depression and anxiety may hamper the development of new skills. Depression is related with lowered motivation to deal with challenges and avoidance of challenges (Freese & Stewart, 1984) and reduced self efficacy (Bandura, 1997). Anxiety inhibits understanding and experimentation with new ideas (Warr & Downing, 2000) and skill acquisition (Colquitt et al, 2000). Thus employees are not motivated to learn new skills and stay abreast of changes that are continually taking place in the industry.

Role

Role refers to the employee's primary responsibilities in the organization. A lot of research has been done in the area of role strain, role ambiguity and role conflict primarily in industrial organizations. Role Ambiguity refers to the lack of available information necessary to conduct the role. Effective communication on role boundaries, working procedures and practice, expected time frame and outcome can contribute to role clarity(Kenyon, 2008).

Role Conflict refers to incompatible demands on the individual. Role conflict impedes achievement and organizational strategies that minimize role conflict need to be utilized. Role Stability is related to control and security at the workplace – such as being in a contract position versus a permanent position. Unstable positions are related to poor well being (Kenyon, 2008).

Stress at the Workplace

Stress is experienced when the environmental demands exceed the individual's ability to deal with it. The individual's perception and assessment of the situation determines their response. Research in the area of job stress has revealed outcomes such as decreased job satisfaction (Fox et al, 1993), poor mental health (Mausner-Dorsch & Eaton, 2000) and compromised immune function (Meijman et al, 1995).People, however adapt to stressors and develop coping strategies and personal resources.

Social Support

High levels of social support at the workplace contribute to enhanced physical health and job satisfaction. Social support also moderates the negative impact of stress.

Studies by Unden et al., (1991) and Evans & Steptoe (2001) showed that low support at work correlated with elevated heart rate. A study by Greenglass & Burke (1988) found that social support was negatively associated with burnout in women but not men. However evidence from studies have been mixed regarding the role of social support.

Career Growth

Most people aspire to having positions with increased responsibility and challenges at their workplace. A higher position is also associated with greater control and autonomy and increased financial reward and valued social position. The lack of opportunities for career growth is a primary source of job dissatisfaction. Organizations and employers that encourage skill acquisition and career growth at all levels will have better morale and productivity than organizations that are rigid(Kenyon, 2008).

Unemployment

Work contributes to psychological well-being through the opportunity to utilize skills, financial rewards, interpersonal contact, time structure, status and identity.

Unemployment thus is a state that has many ramifications such as loss of purpose and meaning in life, identity, financial resources, relationships, status and time structure. These effects result in lowered self esteem and a higher incidence of depression (Evans & Haworth, 1991).

These consequences are more apparent among the middle aged, men, single women and the long term unemployed. Morris et al., (1994) found a strong causal relationship between unemployment and mortality (even when tobacco and alcohol use was controlled for). Job insecurity has similar consequences. However the presence of social support and perceived control moderate the negative impact of job insecurity (Kenyon, 2008).

Antisocial Behavior in the Workplace

Antisocial behavior refers to incidents such as assaults, fights, harassment, aggression and other negative behaviors. This behavior comes at a cost both for employers as well as employees. For the employer it results in lost productivity due to absenteeism and high turnover. For employees it results in reduced job satisfaction and well being (Kenyon, 2008).

Health Promotion

Employers can make a concerted effort to improve safety standards and industrial hygiene conditions. Stricter regulations would aid in ushering in these changes. Employees can be trained in safety and made aware of their rights by unions. Given that employers make an effort to make the workplace more healthy and safe, attention can be focused on improving employee health behaviors.

People spend a major part of their lives at the work place and hence this is an ideal setting for initiating behavior change for better health. High stress jobs are associated with increased tobacco and alcohol consumption(Cohen & Williamson, 1988 as cited in Kenyon, 2008)) . Tobacco and alcohol consumption exacerbate existing occupational ailments over and above their harmful effects on health. Behaviour change initiatives to overcome tobacco and alcohol addiction would improve employee health and morale as well as productivity. However focusing on employee health behaviors without improving the working conditions is not an effective or fair strategy.

It would be necessary to improve surveillance data (records of morbidities, fatalities and accidents) to see the pattern of occupational morbidity and changes that occur. Only when data is available are trends revealed which in turn influences the development of policies and legislations that are effective and appropriate.

Safety and Health Training

Voluntary Protection Programs (VPP is an Occupational Safety and Health Administration (OSHA) initiative that encourages private industry and federal agencies to prevent workplace injuries and illnesses through hazard prevention and control, worksite analysis, training; and cooperation between management and workers. VPP enlists worker involvement to achieve injury and illness rates that are below national Bureau of Labor Statistics averages for their respective industries.

Levels/Types of Certification

VPP offers two levels of certification :

Star

Star is the highest level. It recognizes employers and employees for developing and implementing continuous improvement workplace safety and health management programs that result in injury/illness rates that are below the national averages for their industries.

Merit

Merit is for employers and employees that have implemented good safety and health programs but require additional improvements. They must also commit to seeking to advance to Star level within three years.

VPP offers three types of certification:

Site-based

Site-based Star and Merit certifications are offered for permanent work sites and long-term construction sites. It may also be used to certify resident contractors at participating VPP sites or under a corporate program.

Mobile Workforce

This type of certification is for companies whose employees work on location at various sites.

Corporate

Large organizations that implement organization-wide health and safety management programs that extend to it individual sites are able to seek corporate VPP certification.

As of 10/31/2012 2,370 entities were registered as VPP certified with the vast majority achieving the Star level. All organizations are re-evaluated every three to five years to remain in the programs.

References

- Caplan, R.D., Cobb, S., & French, J.R.P., Jr. (1975). Relationships of cessation of smoking with job stress, personality, and social support. Journal of Applied Psychology, 60, 211-219. doi:10.1037/h0076471
- "Milestones in the history of occupational health psychology", (February 2002). Monitor on Psychology, American Psychological Association. 33(2). [3] Retrieved July 28, 2014
- Zickar, M.J. (2003). Remembering Arthur Kornhauser: Industrial psychology's advocate for worker well-being. Journal of Applied Psychology, 88, 363–369. doi: 10.1037/0021-9010.88.2.363
- "Guidance note: General duty of care in Western Australian workplaces 2005" (PDF). Government of Western Australia. Retrieved 15 July 2014
- Stephan, Constantin (2012), Industrial Health, Safety and Environmental Management, epubli, Berlin, 3rd edition 2012, ISBN 978-3-7418-7478-9, pp. 70-71
- Stansfeld, S., & Candy, B. (2006). Psychosocial work environment and mental health--a meta-analytic review. Scandinavian Journal of Work, Environment & Health, 32(6), 443-462
- ^Hutchins, B L; Harrison, A (1911). A history of factory legislation by ; Published 1911 (2nd ed.). Westminster: P S King & Son. Retrieved 30 June 2015
- Chaturvedi, Pradeep (2006-01-01). Challenges of Occupational Safety and Health: Thrust : Safety in Transportation. Concept Publishing Company. ISBN 9788180692840
- Bond, F.W., & Bunce, D. (2001). Job control mediates change in a work reorganization intervention for stress reduction. Journal of Occupational Health Psychology, 6, 290-302. doi:10.1037/1076-8998.6.4.290
- Abrams, Herbert K. (2001). "A Short History of Occupational Health" (PDF). Journal of Public Health Policy. 22 (1): 34–80. doi:10.2307/3343553. PMID 11382089. Retrieved 9 August 2012
- Health and Safety Executive (2009): A Guide to Safety and Health Regulation in Great Britain. 4th edition. ISBN 978-0-7176-6319-4
- Flaxman, P. E., & Bond, F. W. (2010). Worksite stress management training: Moderated effects and clinical significance. Journal of Occupational Health Psychology, 15, 347-358. doi:10.1037/a0020522
- "Noise and Hearing Loss Prevention". Workplace Safety & Health Topics. National Institute for Occupational Safety and Health. Retrieved 3 August 2012
- Keenan, A., & Newton, T.J. (1985). Stressful events, stressors and psychological strains in young professional engineers. Journal of Occupational Behaviour, 6(2), 151-156. doi:10.1002/job.4030060206

5

Health Care: Statistics and Systems

A health care system is an organization that provides people with health care facilities. Although health care systems' structure varies from nation to nation, every country usually shares common elements such as public health measures and primary health care. All the diverse aspects of health statistics and health care systems have been carefully analyzed in this section.

Health Statistics

A system to collect data and maintain accurate records regarding diseases and their incidence in various areas is an urgent need that is recognized for its value in planning and addressing disease outbreaks and dealing with prevention.

National Disease Surveillance Network

The need for an integrated system that provides disease information in real time from the lowest level upward that would allow effective intervention is recognized and the policy aims to develop such a system.

Women's Health

Women's lack of access to existing facilities is acknowledged and the role of women in improving family health is also mentioned.

Environmental and Occupational Health:

Issues of sanitation and pollution are mentioned in the Environmental Section and in the Occupational section the risks of the vulnerable section from chronic morbidity and child labour are mentioned.

Providing Medical Facilities to Users from Overseas:

The quality and cost effectiveness of medical facilities attracts users from overseas. Apart from the allopathic system there are takers for the Ayurvedic system and the government mentions encouraging development of packages for this purpose.

Impact of Globalization on the Health Sector:

Concern over the cost of medication in the post TRIPS (Trade Related Intellectual Property Rights) era is expressed and the policy aims to maintain the low price of drugs and the availability of generic drugs.

Alternative Systems of Medicine:

AYUSH – Ayurvedic, Unani, Sidha and Homeopathic systems are perceived as having a significant role in health care delivery in the rural areas. Evidence based research regarding their efficacy is proposed.

Delivery of Health Services:

The poor state of infrastructure is discussed – the dilapidated buildings, the obsolete equipment, unavailability of drugs and other consumables are acknowledged.

Personnel/ Training

The lack of personnel (doctors, nurses & technicians) especially in the rural areas is mentioned. The government has no schemes to offer incentives to move to the rural areas. The role of alternative systems of medicine to fill this gap is discussed. The training of personnel is also discussed – the quality and relevance of the curriculum, the lack of colleges, the uneven distribution of colleges and the uneven quality of education are all mentioned.

Public Private Partnerships:

A government based insurance scheme that covers the cost of consulting a private doctor (currently in use in some states) could be scaled up.

Government Programs :

That cover health care and other allied matters such as solid waste management, sanitation, education, housing are interrelated and impact on health.

National Rural Health Mission (NRHM) (2005-2012)

The stated goals of NRHM are

- Reduction in Infant Mortality Rate and Maternal Mortality Rate
- Universal access to public health services
- Prevention and control of communicable and non-communicable diseases (locally endemic diseases)
- Population stabilization, gender and demographic balance
- Revitalize local health traditions and mainstream AYUSH (Ayurveda, Yoga, Unani, Sidha and Homeopathic –there are university programs in these areas)
- Promotion of healthy life styles

Some Strategies espoused by them are

- Train and enhance capacity of Panchayati Raj Institutions (PRIs) to own, control and manage public health services

- Promote access to improved healthcare at household level through the female health activist (ASHA – accredited social health activist).
- Strengthening PHCs and CHCs, provision of a 30-50 bedded CHC per lakh population

Health Care

New York-Presbyterian Hospital in New York City is one of the world's busiest hospitals. Pictured is the Weill-Cornell facility (white complex at centre).

Health care or healthcare is the maintenance or improvement of health via the diagnosis, treatment, and prevention of disease, illness, injury, and other physical and mental impairments in human beings. Healthcare is delivered by health professionals (providers or practitioners) in allied health professions, chiropractic, physicians, physician associates, dentistry, midwifery, nursing, medicine, optometry, pharmacy, psychology, and other health professions. It includes the work done in providing primary care, secondary care, and tertiary care, as well as in public health.

Access to healthcare varies across countries, groups, and individuals, largely influenced by social and economic conditions as well as the health policies in place. Countries and jurisdictions have different policies and plans in relation to the personal and population-based health care goals within their societies. Healthcare systems are organizations established to meet the health needs of target populations. Their exact configuration varies between national and subnational entities. In some countries and jurisdictions, healthcare planning is distributed among market participants, whereas in others, planning occurs more centrally among governments or other coordinating bodies. In all cases, according to the World Health Organization (WHO), a well-functioning healthcare system requires a robust financing mechanism; a well-trained and adequately-paid workforce; reliable information on which to base decisions and policies; and well maintained health facilities and logistics to deliver quality medicines and technologies.

Healthcare can contribute to a significant part of a country's economy. In 2011, the healthcare industry consumed an average of 9.3 percent of the GDP or US$ 3,322 (PPP-adjusted) per capita across the 34 members of OECD countries. The USA (17.7%, or US$ PPP 8,508), the Netherlands

(11.9%, 5,099), France (11.6%, 4,118), Germany (11.3%, 4,495), Canada (11.2%, 5669), and Switzerland (11%, 5,634) were the top spenders, however life expectancy in total population at birth was highest in Switzerland (82.8 years), Japan and Italy (82.7), Spain and Iceland (82.4), France (82.2) and Australia (82.0), while OECD's average exceeds 80 years for the first time ever in 2011: 80.1 years, a gain of 10 years since 1970. The USA (78.7 years) ranges only on place 26 among the 34 OECD member countries, but has the highest costs by far. All OECD countries have achieved universal (or almost universal) health coverage, except Mexico and the USA.

Healthcare is conventionally regarded as an important determinant in promoting the general physical and mental health and well-being of people around the world. An example of this was the worldwide eradication of smallpox in 1980, declared by the WHO as the first disease in human history to be completely eliminated by deliberate health care interventions.

Delivery

Primary care may be provided in community health centres.

The delivery of modern health care depends on groups of trained professionals and paraprofessionals coming together as interdisciplinary teams. This includes professionals in medicine, psychology, physiotherapy, nursing, dentistry, midwifery and allied health, plus many others such as public health practitioners, community health workers and assistive personnel, who systematically provide personal and population-based preventive, curative and rehabilitative care services.

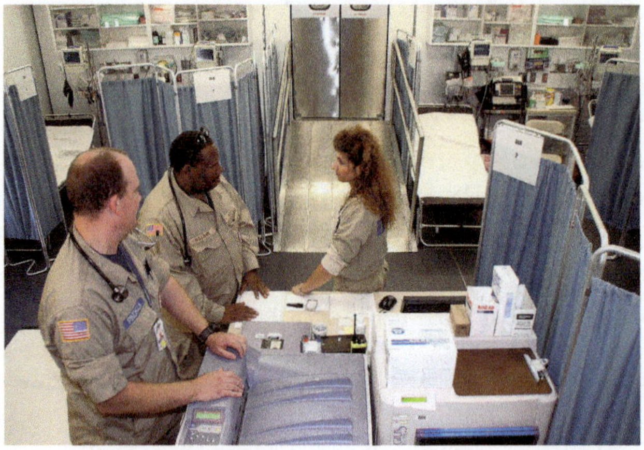
The emergency room is often a frontline venue for the delivery of primary medical care.

While the definitions of the various types of health care vary depending on the different cultural, political, organizational and disciplinary perspectives, there appears to be some consensus that primary care constitutes the first element of a continuing health care process, that may also include the provision of secondary and tertiary levels of care. Healthcare can be defined as either public or private.

Primary Care

Medical train "Therapist Matvei Mudrov" in Khabarovsk, Russia

Primary care refers to the work of health professionals who act as a first point of consultation for all patients within the health care system. Such a professional would usually be a primary care physician, such as a general practitioner or family physician, a licensed independent practitioner such as a physiotherapist, or a non-physician primary care provider (mid-level provider) such as a physician assistant or nurse practitioner. Depending on the locality, health system organization, and sometimes at the patient's discretion, they may see another health care professional first, such as a pharmacist, a nurse (such as in the United Kingdom), a clinical officer (such as in parts of Africa), or an Ayurvedic or other traditional medicine professional (such as in parts of Asia). Depending on the nature of the health condition, patients may then be referred for secondary or tertiary care.

Primary care is often used as the term for the health care services which play a role in the local community. It can be provided in different settings, such as Urgent care centres which provide services to patients same day with appointment or walk-in bases.

Primary care involves the widest scope of health care, including all ages of patients, patients of all socioeconomic and geographic origins, patients seeking to maintain optimal health, and patients with all manner of acute and chronic physical, mental and social health issues, including multiple chronic diseases. Consequently, a primary care practitioner must possess a wide breadth of knowledge in many areas. Continuity is a key characteristic of primary care, as patients usually prefer to consult the same practitioner for routine check-ups and preventive care, health education, and every time they require an initial consultation about a new health problem. The International Classification of Primary Care (ICPC) is a standardized tool for understanding and analyzing information on interventions in primary care by the reason for the patient visit.

Common chronic illnesses usually treated in primary care may include, for example: hypertension, diabetes, asthma, COPD, depression and anxiety, back pain, arthritis or thyroid dysfunction. Primary care also includes many basic maternal and child health care services, such as family planning services and vaccinations. In the United States, the 2013 National Health Interview Survey found that skin disorders (42.7%), osteoarthritis and joint disorders (33.6%), back problems (23.9%), disorders of lipid metabolism (22.4%), and upper respiratory tract disease (22.1%, excluding asthma) were the most common reasons for accessing a physician.

In the United States, primary care physicians have begun to deliver primary care outside of the managed care (insurance-billing) system through direct primary care which is a subset of the more familiar concierge medicine. Physicians in this model bill patients directly for services, either on a pre-paid monthly, quarterly, or annual basis, or bill for each service in the office. Examples of direct primary care practices include Foundation Health in Colorado and Qliance in Washington.

In context of global population aging, with increasing numbers of older adults at greater risk of chronic non-communicable diseases, rapidly increasing demand for primary care services is expected in both developed and developing countries. The World Health Organization attributes the provision of essential primary care as an integral component of an inclusive primary health care strategy.

Secondary Care

Secondary care includes acute care: necessary treatment for a short period of time for a brief but serious illness, injury or other health condition, such as in a hospital emergency department. It also includes skilled attendance during childbirth, intensive care, and medical imaging services.

The term "secondary care" is sometimes used synonymously with "hospital care". However, many secondary care providers do not necessarily work in hospitals, such as psychiatrists, clinical psychologists, occupational therapists, most dental specialties or physiotherapists (physiotherapists are also primary care providers, and a referral is not required to see a physiotherapist), and some primary care services are delivered within hospitals. Depending on the organization and policies of the national health system, patients may be required to see a primary care provider for a referral before they can access secondary care.

For example, in the United States, which operates under a mixed market health care system, some physicians might voluntarily limit their practice to secondary care by requiring patients to see a primary care provider first, or this restriction may be imposed under the terms of the payment agreements in private or group health insurance plans. In other cases medical specialists may see patients without a referral, and patients may decide whether self-referral is preferred.

In the United Kingdom and Canada, patient self-referral to a medical specialist for secondary care is rare as prior referral from another physician (either a primary care physician or another specialist) is considered necessary, regardless of whether the funding is from private insurance schemes or national health insurance.

Allied health professionals, such as physical therapists, respiratory therapists, occupational therapists, speech therapists, and dietitians, also generally work in secondary care, accessed through either patient self-referral or through physician referral.

Tertiary Care

The National Hospital for Neurology and Neurosurgery in London, United Kingdom is a specialist neurological hospital.

Tertiary care is specialized consultative health care, usually for inpatients and on referral from a primary or secondary health professional, in a facility that has personnel and facilities for advanced medical investigation and treatment, such as a tertiary referral hospital.

Examples of tertiary care services are cancer management, neurosurgery, cardiac surgery, plastic surgery, treatment for severe burns, advanced neonatology services, palliative, and other complex medical and surgical interventions.

Quaternary Care

The term quaternary care is sometimes used as an extension of tertiary care in reference to advanced levels of medicine which are highly specialized and not widely accessed. Experimental medicine and some types of uncommon diagnostic or surgical procedures are considered quaternary care. These services are usually only offered in a limited number of regional or national health care centres. This term is more prevalent in the United Kingdom, but just as applicable in the United States. A quaternary care hospital may have virtually any procedure available, whereas a tertiary care facility may not offer a sub-specialist with that training.

Home and Community Care

Many types of health care interventions are delivered outside of health facilities. They include many interventions of public health interest, such as food safety surveillance, distribution of condoms and needle-exchange programmes for the prevention of transmissible diseases.

They also include the services of professionals in residential and community settings in support of self care, home care, long-term care, assisted living, treatment for substance use disorders and other types of health and social care services.

Community rehabilitation services can assist with mobility and independence after loss of limbs or loss of function. This can include prosthesis, orthotics or wheelchairs.

Many countries, especially in the west are dealing with aging populations, and one of the priorities of the health care system is to help seniors live full, independent lives in the comfort of their own homes. There is an entire section of health care geared to providing seniors with help in day-to-day activities at home, transporting them to doctor's appointments, and many other activities that are so essential for their health and well-being. Although they provide home care for older adults in cooperation, family members and care workers may harbor diverging attitudes and values towards their joint efforts. This state of affairs presents a challenge for the design of ICT for home care.

With obesity in children rapidly becoming a major concern, health services often set up programs in schools aimed at educating children in good eating habits; making physical education compulsory in school; and teaching young adolescents to have positive self-image.

Ratings

Health care ratings are ratings or evaluations of health care used to evaluate process of care, healthcare structures and/or outcomes of a healthcare services. This information is translated into report cards that are generated by quality organizations, nonprofit, consumer groups and media. This evaluation of quality can be based on:

- Measures of Hospital quality
- Measures of Health Plan Quality
- Measures of Physician Quality
- Measures of Quality for Other Health Professionals
- Measures of Patient Experience

Related Sectors

Health care extends beyond the delivery of services to patients, encompassing many related sectors, and set within a bigger picture of financing and governance structures.

Health System

A health system, also sometimes referred to as health care system or healthcare system is the organization of people, institutions, and resources to deliver health care services to meet the health needs of target populations.

Health Care Industry

The health care industry incorporates several sectors that are dedicated to providing health care services and products. As a basic framework for defining the sector, the United Nations' International Standard Industrial Classification categorizes health care as generally consisting of hospital activities, medical and dental practice activities, and "other human health activities". The last class involves activities of, or under the supervision of, nurses, midwives, physiotherapists, scientific or diagnostic laboratories, pathology clinics, residential health facilities, patient advocates, or other allied health professions, e.g. in the field of optometry, hydrotherapy, medical massage, yoga therapy, music therapy, occupational therapy, speech therapy, chiropody, homeopathy, chiropractics, acupuncture, etc.

A group of Chilean 'Damas de Rojo' volunteering at their local hospital

In addition, according to industry and market classifications, such as the Global Industry Classification Standard and the Industry Classification Benchmark, health care includes many categories of medical equipment, instruments and services as well as biotechnology, diagnostic laboratories and substances, and drug manufacturing and delivery.

For example, pharmaceuticals and other medical devices are the leading high technology exports of Europe and the United States. The United States dominates the biopharmaceutical field, accounting for three-quarters of the world's biotechnology revenues.

Health Care Research

The quantity and quality of many health care interventions are improved through the results of science, such as advanced through the medical model of health which focuses on the eradication of illness through diagnosis and effective treatment. Many important advances have been made through health research, including biomedical research and pharmaceutical research, which form the basis for evidence-based medicine and evidence-based practice in health care delivery.

For example, in terms of pharmaceutical research and development spending, Europe spends a little less than the United States (€22.50bn compared to €27.05bn in 2006). The United States accounts for 80% of the world's research and development spending in biotechnology.

In addition, the results of health services research can lead to greater efficiency and equitable delivery of health care interventions, as advanced through the social model of health and disability, which emphasizes the societal changes that can be made to make population healthier. Results from health services research often form the basis of evidence-based policy in health care systems. Health services research is also aided by initiatives in the field of AI for the development of systems of health assessment that are clinically useful, timely, sensitive to change, culturally sensitive, low burden, low cost, involving for the patient and built into standard procedures.

Health Care Financing

There are generally five primary methods of funding health care systems:

1. general taxation to the state, county or municipality
2. social health insurance
3. voluntary or private health insurance
4. out-of-pocket payments
5. donations to health charities

In most countries, the financing of health care services features a mix of all five models, but the exact distribution varies across countries and over time within countries. In all countries and jurisdictions, there are many topics in the politics and evidence that can influence the decision of a government, private sector business or other group to adopt a specific health policy regarding the financing structure.

For example, social health insurance is where a nation's entire population is eligible for health care coverage, and this coverage and the services provided are regulated. In almost every jurisdiction with a government-funded health care system, a parallel private, and usually for-profit, system is allowed to operate. This is sometimes referred to as two-tier health care or universal health care.

For example, in Poland, the costs of health services borne by the National Health Fund (financed by all citizens that pay health insurance contributions) in 2012 amounted to 60.8 billion PLN (approximately 20 billion USD). The right to health services in Poland is granted to 99.9% of the population (also registered unemployed persons and their spouses).

Health Care Administration and Regulation

The management and administration of health care is another sector vital to the delivery of health care services. In particular, the practice of health professionals and operation of health care institutions is typically regulated by national or state/provincial authorities through appropriate regulatory bodies for purposes of quality assurance. Most countries have credentialing staff in regulatory boards or health departments who document the certification or licensing of health workers and their work history.

Health Information Technology

Health information technology (HIT) is "the application of information processing involving both computer hardware and software that deals with the storage, retrieval, sharing, and use of health care information, data, and knowledge for communication and decision making." Technology is a broad concept that deals with a species' usage and knowledge of tools and crafts, and how it affects a species' ability to control and adapt to its environment. However, a strict definition is elusive; "technology" can refer to material objects of use to humanity, such as machines, hardware or utensils, but can also encompass broader themes, including systems, methods of organization, and techniques. For HIT, technology represents computers and communications attributes that can be networked to build systems for moving health information. Informatics is yet another integral aspect of HIT.

Health information technology can be divided into further components like Electronic Health Record (EHR), Electronic Medical Record (EMR), Personal Health Record (PHR), Practice Management System (PMS), Health Information Exchange (HIE) and many more. There are multiple purposes for the use of HIT within the health care industry. Further, the use of HIT is expected to improve the quality of health care, reduce medical errors, improve the health care service efficiency and reduce health care costs.

Primary Care

Primary care is the day-to-day healthcare given by a health care provider. Typically this provider acts as the first contact and principal point of continuing care for patients within a healthcare system, and coordinates other specialist care that the patient may need. Patients commonly receive primary care from professionals such as a primary care physician (general practitioner or family physician), a nurse practitioner (adult-gerontology nurse practitioner, family nurse practitioner, or pediatric nurse practitioner), or a physician assistant. In some localities such a professional may be a registered nurse, a pharmacist, a clinical officer (as in parts of Africa), or a Ayurvedic or other traditional medicine professional (as in parts of Asia). Depending on the nature of the health condition, patients may then be referred for secondary or tertiary care.

Background

The World Health Organization attributes the provision of essential primary care as an integral component of an inclusive primary healthcare strategy. Primary care involves the widest scope of healthcare, including all ages of patients, patients of all socioeconomic and geographic origins, patients seeking to maintain optimal health, and patients with all manner of acute and chronic physical, mental and social health issues, including multiple chronic diseases. Consequently, a primary care practitioner must possess a wide breadth of knowledge in many areas. Continuity is a key characteristic of primary care, as patients usually prefer to consult the same practitioner for routine check-ups and preventive care, health education, and every time they require an initial consultation about a new health problem. Collaboration among providers is a desirable characteristic of primary care.

The International Classification of Primary Care (ICPC) is a standardized tool for understanding and analyzing information on interventions in primary care by the reason for the patient visit. Common chronic illnesses usually treated in primary care may include, for example: hypertension, angina, diabetes, asthma, COPD, depression and anxiety, back pain, arthritis or thyroid dysfunction. Primary care also includes many basic maternal and child health care services, such as family planning services and vaccinations.

In context of global population ageing, with increasing numbers of older adults at greater risk of chonic non-communicable diseases, rapidly increasing demand for primary care services is expected around the world, in both developed and developing countries.

Primary Care by Country

United Kingdom

In the United Kingdom, patients can access primary care services through their local general practice, community pharmacy, optometrist, dental surgery and community hearing care providers. Services are generally provided free-of-charge through the National Health Service. In the UK, unlike many other countries, patients do not normally have direct access to hospital consultants and the GP controls access to secondary care. This practice is referred to as "gatekeeping"; the future of this role has been questioned by researchers who conclude "*Gatekeeping policies should be revisited to accommodate the government's aim to modernise the NHS in terms of giving patients more choice and facilitate more collaborative work between GPs and specialists. At the same time, any relaxation of gatekeeping should be carefully evaluated to ensure the clinical and non-clinical benefits outweigh the costs*".

599 GP practices closed between 2010–11 and 2014–15, while 91 opened and average practice list size increased from 6,610 to 7,171.

According to the Local Government Association 57 million GP consultations in England in 2015 were for minor conditions and illnesses, 5.2 million of them for blocked noses.

Canada

In Canada, access to primary and other healthcare services are guaranteed for all citizens through the Canada Health Act.

Nigeria

In Nigeria, healthcare is a concurrent responsibility of three tiers of government. Local governments focus on the delivery of primary care (e.g. through a system of dispensaries), state governments manage the various general hospitals (secondary care), while the federal government's role is mostly limited to coordinating the affairs of the Federal Medical Centres and university teaching hospitals (tertiary care).

United States

A 2009 report by the New England Healthcare Institute determined that an increased demand on primary care by older, sicker patients and decreased supply of primary care practitioners has led to a crisis in primary care delivery. The research identified a set of innovations that could enhance the quality, efficiency and effectiveness of primary care in the United States.

On March 23, 2010 President Obama signed the Patient Protection and Affordable Care Act (ACA) into law. The law is expected to expand health insurance coverage by 32 million people by 2016 and 34 million people by 2021. The success of the expansion of health insurance under the ACA in large measure depends on the availability of primary care physicians. Unfortunately, The ACA has drastically exacerbated the projected deficit of primary care physicians needed to ensure care for insured Americans. According to the Association of American Medical Colleges (AAMC) without the ACA, the United States would have been short roughly 64,000 physicians by 2020; with the implementation of the ACA, it will be 91,000 physicians short. According to the AAMC's November 2009 physician work force report, nationally, the rate of physicians providing primary care is 79.4 physicians per 100,000 residents.

Primary healthcare results in better health outcomes, reduced health disparities and lower spending, including on avoidable emergency room visits and hospital care. With that being said, primary care physicians are an important component in ensuring that the healthcare system as a whole is sustainable. However, despite their importance to the healthcare system, the primary care position has suffered in terms of its prestige in part due to the differences in salary when compared to doctors that decide to specialize. In a 2010 national study of physician wages conducted by the UC Davis Health System found that specialists are paid as much as 52 percent more than primary care physicians, even though primary care physicians see far more patients.

Primary care physicians earn $60.48 per hour; specialists on average earn $88.34. A follow up study conducted by the UC Davis Health System found that earnings over the course of the careers of primary care physicians averaged as much as $2.8 million less than the earnings of their specialist colleagues. This discrepancy in pay has potentially made primary care a less attractive choice for medical school graduates. In 2011, about 17,000 doctors graduated from American medical schools and only 7 percent of graduates chose a career in primary care. The average age of a primary care physician in the United States is 47 years old, and one quarter of all primary care physicians are nearing retirement. Fifty years ago roughly half of the physicians in America practiced primary care; today, fewer than one third of them do.

US Strategies to Address the Primary Care Shortage

The Patient Protection Affordable Care Act contains a number of provisions to increase primary care capacity. These provisions are directed towards medical school graduates and include payment reform, student loan forgiveness programs and increased primary care residency positions The PPACA also provides funding and mandates to increase the role of physician extenders like nurse practitioners and physician assistants to enhance the primary care workforce. The PPCA is projected to increase patient demand for primary care services. Through the adoption of new patient care delivery models that include physicians working in tandem with nurse practitioners and physician assistants, demand for future primary care services could be met. Consumer surveys have found the American public to be open to a greater role for physician extenders in the primary care setting. Policies and laws, primarily at the state level, would need to redefine and reallocate the roles and responsibilities for non-physician licensed providers to optimize these new models of care.

Acute care

Acute care is a branch of secondary health care where a patient receives active but short-term treatment for a severe injury or episode of illness, an urgent medical condition, or during recovery from surgery. In medical terms, care for acute health conditions is the opposite from chronic care, or longer term care.

Acute care services are generally delivered by teams of health care professionals from a range of medical and surgical specialties. Acute care may require a stay in a hospital emergency department, ambulatory surgery center, urgent care centre or other short-term stay facility, along with the assistance of diagnostic services, surgery, or follow-up outpatient care in the community. Hospital-based acute inpatient care typically has the goal of discharging patients as soon as they are deemed healthy and stable. Acute care settings include but are not limited to: emergency department, intensive care, coronary care, cardiology, neonatal intensive care, and many general areas where the patient could become acutely unwell and require stabilization and transfer to another higher dependency unit for further treatment.

Current Issues in Acute Care

Australia

The 2009 "Final Report of the Special Commission of Inquiry into Acute Care Services in NSW Public Hospitals", known as The Garling Report, documented a series of high profile medical controversies in the New South Wales public hospital system, and issued over one hundred recommendations that stimulated considerable discussion and controversy.

United States

A federal law known as the Emergency Medical Treatment and Active Labor Act (EMTALA), "requires most hospitals to provide an examination and needed stabilizing treatment, without consideration of insurance coverage or ability to pay, when a patient presents to an emergency room for attention to an emergency medical condition."

Health Care Ratings

Health care ratings are ratings or evaluations of health care.

Technological advances played a key role in facilitating the data collection and number crunching needed to generate health care ratings.

Health care ratings are coming of age in a time of rising levels of consumer health literacy. Surveys consistently show that consumers rely heavily on friends and family when making healthcare decisions. With social networking and global connectivity, some of these family and friend referrals will include a wider network and will increasingly rely on quality data retrieved from multiple sources. Government, non-profit and private organizations are building public-private collaborations focused on the development of a nationwide system in the United States.

Types of Measures

Quality measures are standards that are used to assess the various aspects of the healthcare system. Using the Donabidien framework, these measures evaluate process of care, healthcare structures and/or outcomes of a healthcare services. This information is translated into report cards that are generated by quality organizations, nonprofit,consumer groups and media. This evaluation of quality is based on:

- Measures of Hospital quality
- Measures of Health Plan Quality

- Measures of Physician Quality
- Measures of Quality for Other Health Professionals
- Measures of Patient Experience

Reporting Organizations

Measures are collected and disseminated by a number of quality reporting organizations.

Consumer Assessment of Health Professionals and Systems(CAHPS)

The Joint Commission

The National Quality Forum (NQF)

National Quality Measures Clearinghouse

The Robert Wood Johnson Foundation (RWJF), the largest philanthropy in the United States dedicated to improving health and health care, provides support for multiple efforts dedicated to increasing public awareness of the performance of health professionals:

- Aligning Forces for Quality is a national initiative that is focused on improving the overall quality of care in local communities. As part of this initiative, collaborative teams in 16 targeted communities work to make information about hospital and physician performance available to the public.
- Consumer-Purchaser Disclosure Project is a collaboration of leading consumer, employer and labor organizations working to ensure that all Americans have access to publicly reported health care performance information.
- National Quality Forum is a nonprofit membership organization created to develop and implement a national strategy for health care quality measurement and reporting.

Possible Benefits

Organizations are sensitive to public reporting As the healthcare system moves from supply driven to demand driven, transparency of such quality reporting is important for informed decision making and efficiency improvements.

A 2001 retrospective cohort study found that health plans voluntarily generating public reports had higher quality ratings than those that chose not to publicly report. Another retrospective study of HMO's yielded similar results, revealing that HMOs with lower quality scores were more likely to stop public reporting while higher performing HMOs continued to publicly report. Analysis of hospital performance reporting and consumer selection found mixed results about public perception and market share. A 1997 study "reported that releasing hospital-specific mortality rates was associated with small but statistically significant effects on utilization, whereas press reports of single, unexpected deaths were associated with a relatively large effect."

More recent studies have identified the potential of public disclosure of performance in encouraging providers to focus on gaps in quality and stimulate performance improvement In addition, from a consumer perspective, health quality reports can encourage patients to preferentially choose high quality healthcare such as best health plans or assess the performance of providers

Possible Challenges

Low Use of Ratings

A 2007 survey of factors impacting individual consumer health professional selections found that only 11 percent of American adults looked for a new primary care physician. Of those 11% went online for information, 38% used doctor or healthplan information. Nearly 40% used multiple sources. 28 percent needed a new specialist physician and 16 percent underwent a medical procedure at a new facility. Few of those relied on price or quality information and relied almost exclusively on physician referrals. Only 3% of patients undergoing procedures and 7% choosing a specialist went online for information.

A 2008 survey of public awareness and use of healthcare quality reports reported that: 20% of Americans surveyed said they had seen quality information about hospitals and only 7% said they used the information to make a decision. 12% of Americans surveyed said they had seen quality information about doctors and only 6% said they used the information to make a decision.

Although public reporting has taken center stage in qualitative and health policy research, there has been a slow uptake. Barriers identified are related to consumer behaviors and challenges with the conceptual framework. Health literacy is a key component to comprehend and use performance data. However, complexity of the performance data, technicality and presentation of the quality data makes the quality reports difficult to understand. Another impediment to the development of health quality reports is the challenge associated with measuring performance at the individual physician level (due to inadequate sample sizes, difficulty adjusting for the severity of patients medical condition) . This has led to group-level reporting which makes these reports less useful for consumers.

Thus, given the changing healthcare landscape, further research to understand consumer behaviors will be important to inform the development and increased uptake of health grade reports.

Accessibility

There appears to be a breakdown in creative use of technology to get the information in the hands of those interested in using it. As pointed out by Kristen Madison, Senior Fellow at the Leonard Davis Institute of Health Economics, searching the Internet for "the term 'hospital quality' or' hospital report card' does not always turn up relevant report cards, even if they do exist". To make these reports more accessible, large philanthropies, including the Robert Wood Johnson Foundation, have funded major initiatives that are focused on performance measurement like the Aligning Forces for Quality program.

History of Health Quality Reporting

The earliest efforts to report on health professionals or facilities date to the mid-1980s when the Health Care Financing Administration (HCFA) – now the Centers for Medicare and Medicaid Services (CMS) – published nationwide hospital-specific mortality data. The information was controversial at the time and HCFA ended publication of the mortality information in the early 1990s.

The media, state governments and the employer community have also contributed to the development of public reporting. Newsday published mortality rates for heart bypass surgery for 140 New York surgeons in December, 1991. The information resulted from a Freedom of Information lawsuit seeking data from the New York State Department of Health. State agencies in California, New York and Pennsylvania also published cardiac surgery hospital and physician information in the early-mid-1990s. Some states also report on other types of hospital and physician information in their licensing and regulatory roles. Information on complaints, sanctions and other disciplinary actions has slowly become available through state licensing boards and Departments of Health. The Cleveland Health Quality Choice Coalition was an early collaborative effort between hospitals, physicians and purchasers that provided public information on hospital quality, though it is no longer in operation.

Largely at the urging of employers implementing managed care plans in the late 1980s and early 1990s, the development of health plan measures and reports began to emerge. Prompted by concerns about possible quality of care problems in managed care plans, the National Committee for Quality Assurance's (NCQA) Healthcare Effectiveness Data and Information Set (HEDIS) was developed to capture information about health plan quality of care. This measure set has been widely used by large employers, states and the Federal government as the basis for accrediting plans and for public reporting. At the same time, the Agency for Healthcare Research and Quality (AHRQ) funded the development of a survey instrument to assess patient experience with receiving care from their managed care plan. The tool, the Consumer Assessment of Healthcare Providers and Systems (CAHPS) has been widely embraced and was embedded in NCQA's health plan accreditation program. The CAHPS program has expanded over time to include a suite of survey tools to assess patient experience, including the CAHPS Hospital Survey (H-CAHPS) and the Clinician and Group CAHPS Survey.

The federal government re-entered the public reporting field in the late 1990s and the early years of the 21st century with the launch of the Compare websites , including Health Plan Compare and Nursing Home Compare, and subsequently Home Health Compare and Dialysis Compare. During the same period, AHRQ was building on its quality indicator work through the Hospital Care and Utilization Project (HCUP) (now Healthcare Cost and Utilization Project) with the development of the AHRQ Quality Indicators in 2001 and the AHRQ Patient Safety measures in 2002. Starting in 2007, AHRQ launched a learning network of community collaboratives (i.e., the Charter Value Exchanges), which were committed to measuring and publicly reporting on provider performance in their communities. Those efforts were supplemented by the regional collaborative work of the Robert Wood Johnson Foundation's Aligning Forces for Quality in 17 communities nationwide.

Other key organizations were also forming or expanding their portfolio to include measure development – particularly related to hospitals. The National Quality Forum (NQF) became operational in 2000 with the mission of standardizing health care performance measurement and strategies. Following on the release of the Institute of Medicine report To Err is Human, employers formed the Leapfrog Group, whose mission was to push hospitals to adopt safe practices. Leapfrog asked hospitals to voluntarily complete an annual survey to report on their safety practices, and these results were made public and, in some cases, became embedded in pay-for-performance programs. The Joint Commission was incorporating performance measurement into their accreditation process and multi-stakeholder groups such as the Hospital Quality Alliance (HQA) were working with Centers for Medicare and Medicaid Services on the development of Medicare's Hospital Compare.

Measure development and reporting on the physician side lagged measurement efforts at the plan and hospital level. In part due to methodological challenges involved in reporting given smaller sample sizes at the physician level, and also due to provider resistance. Recognizing increased pressure to measure performance and reduce variation, physician organizations began their own efforts to develop a set of performance measures. In 2000, the American Medical Association convened the Physician Consortium for Performance Improvement.page (PCPI) to develop, test and maintain physician performance measures. In September 2004, the American Academy of Family Physicians, the American College of Physicians, America's Health Insurance Plans and AHRQ created the Ambulatory Care Quality Alliance (AQA) to implement performance measurement at the physician level. Legislation in 2006 created the Physician Quality Reporting Initiative (PQRI), now termed as the Physician Quality Reporting System (PQRS), sponsored by Centers for Medicare and Medicaid Services. This "pay-for-reporting" program provides incentive payments to physicians who report quality data; however, to date individual physician performance results are not publicly available for use by consumers. Similar to the hospital compare website, the new Physician Compare website, provides information on physicians and other healthcare professionals who are currently enrolled in Medicare. Data on their affiliation, certification status and participation in CMS quality improvement programs is also made available to the Medicare beneficiaries.

In the last decade the eHealth world for consumers has exploded with the growth of online advocacy and support groups.

The Patient Protection and Affordable Care Act passed in 2010 also calls for more public reporting of information about health professionals. As efforts by employers and health plans to assess the performance of both the quality and efficiency of individual physicians have grown, physicians have challenged these efforts for lack of transparency on the methods used to score them. In response to a settlement by the New York Attorney General, a coalition of purchasers and consumer groups developed the Patient Charter for Physician Performance Measurement, Reporting and Tiering (The Patient Charter"), which was released in 2008. The Patient Charter provided a process for reviewing the methods used to score providers and a framework for making the methods transparent.

Today, there are hundreds of public reporting activities across many types of health facilities and professionals including hospitals, physician groups, nursing homes, home health agencies, dialysis facilities, hospices and nurses. Some of these reporting activities result from government action, some from internal health professional or facility efforts to become more transparent, some from investigative journalism, some from community collaboratives, and others from employer or consumer groups. The ability to publish and update information through the Internet has facilitated the dissemination of information about health care performance. However, the information available to any given patient or family member still varies substantially in terms of its breadth, relevance and accessibility.

Health System

A health system, also sometimes referred to as health care system or as healthcare system, is the organization of people, institutions, and resources that deliver health care services to meet the health needs of target populations.

There is a wide variety of health systems around the world, with as many histories and organizational structures as there are nations. Implicitly, nations must design and develop health systems in accordance with their needs and resources, although common elements in virtually all health systems are primary healthcare and public health measures. In some countries, health system planning is distributed among market participants. In others, there is a concerted effort among governments, trade unions, charities, religious organizations, or other co-ordinated bodies to deliver planned health care services targeted to the populations they serve. However, health care planning has been described as often evolutionary rather than revolutionary.

Goals

The World Health Organization (WHO), the directing and coordinating authority for health within the United Nations system, is promoting a goal of universal health care: to ensure that all people obtain the health services they need without suffering financial hardship when paying for them. According to WHO, healthcare systems' goals are good health for the citizens, responsiveness to the expectations of the population, and fair means of funding operations. Progress towards them depends on how systems carry out four vital functions: provision of health care services, resource generation, financing, and stewardship. Other dimensions for the evaluation of health systems include quality, efficiency, acceptability, and equity. They have also been described in the United States as "the five C's": Cost, Coverage, Consistency, Complexity, and Chronic Illness. Also, continuity of health care is a major goal.

Definitions

Often health system has been defined with a reductionist perspective, for example reducing it to healthcare system. In many publications, for example, both expressions are used interchangeably. Some authors have developed arguments to expand the concept of health systems, indicating additional dimensions that should be considered:

- Health systems should not be expressed in terms of their components only, but also of their interrelationships;
- Health systems should include not only the institutional or supply side of the health system, but also the population;
- Health systems must be seen in terms of their goals, which include not only health improvement, but also equity, responsiveness to legitimate expectations, respect of dignity, and fair financing, among others;
- Health systems must also be defined in terms of their functions, including the direct provision of services, whether they are medical or public health services, but also "other enabling functions, such as stewardship, financing, and resource generation, including what is probably the most complex of all challenges, the health workforce."

World Health Organization Definition

The World Health Organization defines health systems as follows:

A health system consists of all organizations, people and actions whose primary intent is to promote, restore or maintain health. This includes efforts to influence determinants of health as well as more direct health-improving activities. A health system is therefore more than the pyramid of publicly owned facilities that deliver personal health services. It includes, for example, a mother caring for a sick child at home; private providers; behaviour change programmes; vector-control campaigns; health insurance organizations; occupational health and safety legislation. It includes inter-sectoral action by health staff, for example, encouraging the ministry of education to promote female education, a well known determinant of better health.

Providers

Healthcare providers are institutions or individuals providing healthcare services. Individuals including health professionals and allied health professions can be self-employed or working as an employee in a hospital, clinic, or other health care institution, whether government operated, private for-profit, or private not-for-profit (e.g. non-governmental organization). They may also work outside of direct patient care such as in a government health department or other agency, medical laboratory, or health training institution. Examples of health workers are doctors, nurses, midwives, dietitians, paramedics, dentists, medical laboratory technologists, therapists, psychologists, pharmacists, chiropractors, optometrists, community health workers, traditional medicine practitioners, and others.

Financial Resources

Norfolk and Norwich University Hospital, a National Health Service hospital in the United Kingdom.

There are generally five primary methods of funding health systems:

1. general taxation to the state, county or municipality
2. national health insurance
3. voluntary or private health insurance
4. out-of-pocket payments
5. donations to charities

Most countries' systems feature a mix of all five models. One study based on data from the OECD concluded that all types of health care finance "are compatible with" an efficient health system. The study also found no relationship between financing and cost control.

The term health insurance is generally used to describe a form of insurance that pays for medical expenses. It is sometimes used more broadly to include insurance covering disability or long-term nursing or custodial care needs. It may be provided through a social insurance program, or from private insurance companies. It may be obtained on a group basis (e.g., by a firm to cover its employees) or purchased by individual consumers. In each case premiums or taxes protect the insured from high or unexpected health care expenses.

By estimating the overall cost of health care expenses, a routine finance structure (such as a monthly premium or annual tax) can be developed, ensuring that money is available to pay for the health care benefits specified in the insurance agreement. The benefit is typically administered by a government agency, a non-profit health fund or a corporation operating seeking to make a profit.

Many forms of commercial health insurance control their costs by restricting the benefits that are paid by through deductibles, co-payments, coinsurance, policy exclusions, and total coverage limits and will severely restrict or refuse coverage of pre-existing conditions. Many government schemes also have co-payment schemes but exclusions are rare because of political pressure. The larger insurance schemes may also negotiate fees with providers.

Many forms of social insurance schemes control their costs by using the bargaining power of their community they represent to control costs in the health care delivery system. For example, by negotiating drug prices directly with pharmaceutical companies negotiating standard fees with the medical profession, or reducing unnecessary health care costs. Social schemes sometimes feature contributions related to earnings as part of a scheme to deliver universal health care, which may or may not also involve the use of commercial and non-commercial insurers. Essentially the more wealthy pay proportionately more into the scheme to cover the needs of the relatively poor who therefore contribute proportionately less. There are usually caps on the contributions of the wealthy and minimum payments that must be made by the insured (often in the form of a minimum contribution, similar to a deductible in commercial insurance models).

In addition to these traditional health care financing methods, some lower income countries and development partners are also implementing non-traditional or innovative financing mechanisms for scaling up delivery and sustainability of health care, such as micro-contributions, public-private partnerships, and market-based financial transaction taxes. For example, as of June 2011, UNITAID had collected more than one billion dollars from 29 member countries, including several from Africa, through an air ticket solidarity levy to expand access to care and treatment for HIV/AIDS, tuberculosis and malaria in 94 countries.

Payment Models

In most countries, wage costs for healthcare practitioners are estimated to represent between 65% and 80% of renewable health system expenditures. There are three ways to pay medical practitioners: fee for service, capitation, and salary. There has been growing interest in blending elements of these systems.

Fee-for-service

Fee-for-service arrangements pay general practitioners (GPs) based on the service. They are even more widely used for specialists working in ambulatory care.

There are two ways to set fee levels:

- By individual practitioners.
- Central negotiations (as in Japan, Germany, Canada and in France) or hybrid model (such as in Australia, France's sector 2, and New Zealand) where GPs can charge extra fees on top of standardized patient reimbursement rates.

Capitation

In *capitation payment systems*, GPs are paid for each patient on their "list", usually with adjustments for factors such as age and gender. According to OECD, "these systems are used in Italy (with some fees), in all four countries of the United Kingdom (with some fees and allowances for specific services), Austria (with fees for specific services), Denmark (one third of income with remainder fee for service), Ireland (since 1989), the Netherlands (fee-for-service for privately insured patients and public employees) and Sweden (from 1994). Capitation payments have become more frequent in "managed care" environments in the United States."

According to OECD, "Capitation systems allow funders to control the overall level of primary health expenditures, and the allocation of funding among GPs is determined by patient registrations. However, under this approach, GPs may register too many patients and under-serve them, select the better risks and refer on patients who could have been treated by the GP directly. Freedom of consumer choice over doctors, coupled with the principle of "money following the patient" may moderate some of these risks. Aside from selection, these problems are likely to be less marked than under salary-type arrangements."

Salary Arrangements

In several OECD countries, general practitioners (GPs) are employed on *salaries* for the government. According to OECD, "Salary arrangements allow funders to control primary care costs directly; however, they may lead to under-provision of services (to ease workloads), excessive referrals to secondary providers and lack of attention to the preferences of patients." There has been movement away from this system.

Information Resources

Sound information plays an increasingly critical role in the delivery of modern health care and efficiency of health systems. Health informatics – the intersection of information science, medicine and healthcare – deals with the resources, devices, and methods required to optimize the acquisition and use of information in health and biomedicine. Necessary tools for proper health information coding and management include clinical guidelines, formal medical terminologies, and computers and other information and communication technologies. The kinds of data processed may include patients' medical records, hospital administration and clinical functions, and human resources information.

The use of health information lies at the root of evidence-based policy and evidence-based management in health care. Increasingly, information and communication technologies are being utilised to improve health systems in developing countries through: the standardisation of health information; computer-aided diagnosis and treatment monitoring; informing population groups on health and treatment.

Management

The management of any health system is typically directed through a set of policies and plans adopted by government, private sector business and other groups in areas such as personal healthcare delivery and financing, pharmaceuticals, health human resources, and public health.

Public health is concerned with threats to the overall health of a community based on population health analysis. The population in question can be as small as a handful of people, or as large as all the inhabitants of several continents (for instance, in the case of a pandemic). Public health is typically divided into epidemiology, biostatistics and health services. Environmental, social, behavioral, and occupational health are also important subfields.

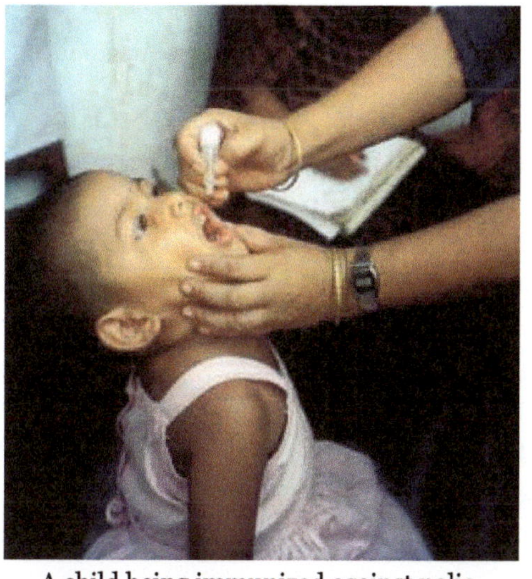

A child being immunized against polio.

Today, most governments recognize the importance of public health programs in reducing the incidence of disease, disability, the effects of ageing and health inequities, although public health generally receives significantly less government funding compared with medicine. For example, most countries have a vaccination policy, supporting public health programs in providing vaccinations to promote health. Vaccinations are voluntary in some countries and mandatory in some countries. Some governments pay all or part of the costs for vaccines in a national vaccination schedule.

The rapid emergence of many chronic diseases, which require costly long-term care and treatment, is making many health managers and policy makers re-examine their healthcare delivery practices. An important health issue facing the world currently is HIV/AIDS. Another major public health concern is diabetes. In 2006, according to the World Health Organization, at least 171 million people worldwide suffered from diabetes. Its incidence is increasing rapidly, and it is estimated that by the year 2030, this number will double. A controversial aspect of public health is the control of tobacco smoking, linked to cancer and other chronic illnesses.

Antibiotic resistance is another major concern, leading to the reemergence of diseases such as tuberculosis. The World Health Organization, for its World Health Day 2011 campaign, is calling for intensified global commitment to safeguard antibiotics and other antimicrobial medicines for future generations.

Health Systems Performance

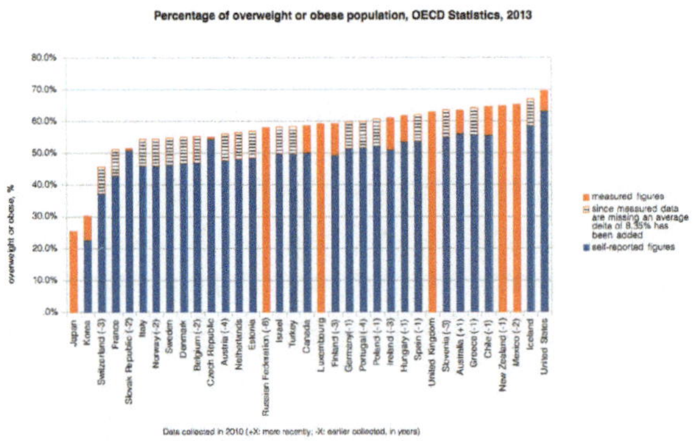

Percentage of overweight or obese population in 2010

Since 2000, more and more initiatives have been taken at the international and national levels in order to strengthen national health systems as the core components of the global health system. Having this scope in mind, it is essential to have a clear, and unrestricted, vision of national health systems that might generate further progresses in global health. The elaboration and the selection of performance indicators are indeed both highly dependent on the conceptual framework adopted for the evaluation of the health systems performances. Like most social systems, health systems are complex adaptive systems where change does not necessarily follow rigid epidemiological models. In complex systems path dependency, emergent properties and other non-linear patterns are under-explored and unmeasured, which can lead to the development of inappropriate guidelines for developing responsive health systems.

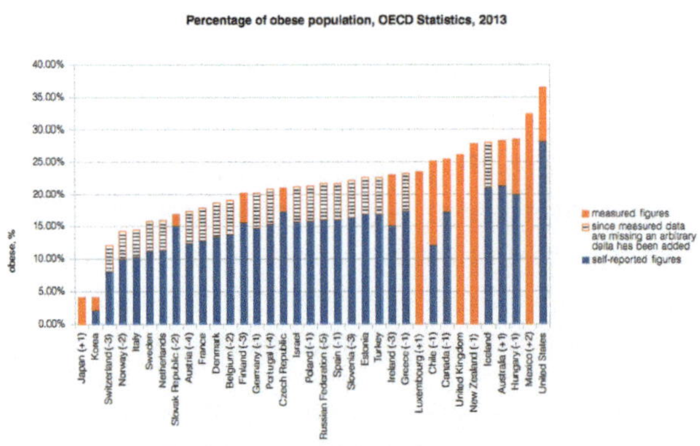

Percentage of obese population in 2010

An increasing number of tools and guidelines are being published by international agencies and development partners to assist health system decision-makers to monitor and assess health systems strengthening including human resources development using standard definitions, indicators and measures. In response to a series of papers published in 2012 by members of the World Health Organization's Task Force on Developing Health Systems Guidance, researchers from the Future Health Systems consortium argue that there is insufficient focus on the 'policy implementation gap'. Recognizing the diversity of stakeholders and complexity of health systems is crucial to ensure that evidence-based guidelines are tested with requisite humility and without a rigid adherence to models dominated by a limited number of disciplines.

Health Policy and Systems Research (HPSR) is an emerging multidisciplinary field that challenges 'disciplinary capture' by dominant health research traditions, arguing that these traditions generate premature and inappropriately narrow definitions that impede rather than enhance health systems strengthening. HPSR focuses on low- and middle-income countries and draws on the relativist social science paradigm which recognises that all phenomena are constructed through human behaviour and interpretation. In using this approach, HPSR offers insight into health systems by generating a complex understanding of context in order to enhance health policy learning. HPSR calls for greater involvement of local actors, including policy makers, civil society and researchers, in decisions that are made around funding health policy research and health systems strengthening.

International Comparisons

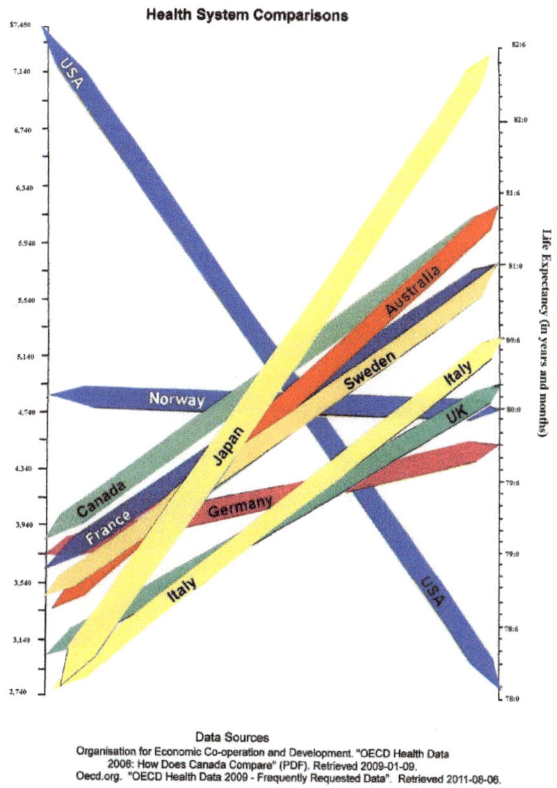

Chart comparing 2008 health care spending (left) vs. life expectancy (right) in OECD countries.

Health systems can vary substantially from country to country, and in the last few years, comparisons have been made on an international basis. The World Health Organization, in its *World Health Report 2000*, provided a ranking of health systems around the world according to criteria of the overall level and distribution of health in the populations, and the responsiveness and fair financing of health care services. The goals for health systems, according to the WHO's *World Health Report 2000 – Health systems: improving performance* (WHO, 2000), are good health, responsiveness to the expectations of the population, and fair financial contribution. There have been several debates around the results of this WHO exercise, and especially based on the country ranking linked to it, insofar as it appeared to depend mostly on the choice of the retained indicators.

Direct comparisons of health statistics across nations are complex. The Commonwealth Fund, in its annual survey, "Mirror, Mirror on the Wall", compares the performance of the health systems in Australia, New Zealand, the United Kingdom, Germany, Canada and the United States Its 2007 study found that, although the United States system is the most expensive, it consistently underperforms compared to the other countries. A major difference between the United States and the other countries in the study is that the United States is the only country without universal health care. The OECD also collects comparative statistics, and has published brief country profiles. Health Consumer Powerhouse makes comparisons between both national health care systems in the Euro health consumer index and specific areas of health care such as diabetes or hepatitis.

References

- Adamiak, E. Chojnacka, D. Walczak, Social security in Poland – cultural, historical and economical issues, Copernican Journal of Finance & Accounting, Vol 2, No 2, p. 23
- "Health at a Glance 2013 - OECD Indicators" (PDF). OECD. 2013-11-21. pp. 5, 39, 46, 48. (link). Retrieved 2013-11-24
- Handler A, Issel M, Turnock B. A conceptual framework to measure performance of the public health system. American Journal of Public Health, 2001, 91(8): 1235–39
- "The Pharmaceutical Industry in Figures" (pdf). European Federation of Pharmaceutical Industries and Associations. 2007. Retrieved February 15, 2010
- Royal Commission on the NHS Chapter 7. HMSO. July 1979. ISBN 0101761503. Retrieved 19 May 2015
- "Europe's competitiveness". European Federation of Pharmaceutical Industries and Associations. Archived from the original on 23 August 2009. Retrieved February 15, 2010
- "The effectiveness of CAHPS among women enrolling in Medicaid managed care". Journal of Ambulatory Care Management. 24 (4): 76–91. 2001. doi:10.1097/00004479-200110000-00006
- World Health Organization. "Regional Overview of Social Health Insurance in South-East Asia.' Retrieved December 02, 2014
- Risse, Guenter B (April 1999). Mending Bodies, Saving Souls: A History of Hospitals. Oxford University Press. p. 59. ISBN 0-19-505523-3
- "The Number of Practicing Primary Care Physicians in the United States". U.S. Department of Health and Human Services. Retrieved 30 May 2017

Permissions

All chapters in this book are published with permission under the Creative Commons Attribution Share Alike License or equivalent. Every chapter published in this book has been scrutinized by our experts. Their significance has been extensively debated. The topics covered herein carry significant information for a comprehensive understanding. They may even be implemented as practical applications or may be referred to as a beginning point for further studies.

We would like to thank the editorial team for lending their expertise to make the book truly unique. They have played a crucial role in the development of this book. Without their invaluable contributions this book wouldn't have been possible. They have made vital efforts to compile up to date information on the varied aspects of this subject to make this book a valuable addition to the collection of many professionals and students.

This book was conceptualized with the vision of imparting up-to-date and integrated information in this field. To ensure the same, a matchless editorial board was set up. Every individual on the board went through rigorous rounds of assessment to prove their worth. After which they invested a large part of their time researching and compiling the most relevant data for our readers.

The editorial board has been involved in producing this book since its inception. They have spent rigorous hours researching and exploring the diverse topics which have resulted in the successful publishing of this book. They have passed on their knowledge of decades through this book. To expedite this challenging task, the publisher supported the team at every step. A small team of assistant editors was also appointed to further simplify the editing procedure and attain best results for the readers.

Apart from the editorial board, the designing team has also invested a significant amount of their time in understanding the subject and creating the most relevant covers. They scrutinized every image to scout for the most suitable representation of the subject and create an appropriate cover for the book.

The publishing team has been an ardent support to the editorial, designing and production team. Their endless efforts to recruit the best for this project, has resulted in the accomplishment of this book. They are a veteran in the field of academics and their pool of knowledge is as vast as their experience in printing. Their expertise and guidance has proved useful at every step. Their uncompromising quality standards have made this book an exceptional effort. Their encouragement from time to time has been an inspiration for everyone.

The publisher and the editorial board hope that this book will prove to be a valuable piece of knowledge for students, practitioners and scholars across the globe.

Index